D0806722

# The Sociology of Religion

# The Sociology of Religion

## A Critical Agenda

### Second Edition

Grace Davie

Los Angeles | London | New Delhi
Singapore | Washington DC

Los Angeles | London | New Delhi
Singapore | Washington DC

SAGE Publications Ltd
1 Oliver's Yard
55 City Road
London EC1Y 1SP

SAGE Publications Inc.
2455 Teller Road
Thousand Oaks, California 91320

SAGE Publications India Pvt Ltd
B 1/I 1 Mohan Cooperative Industrial Area
Mathura Road
New Delhi 110 044

SAGE Publications Asia-Pacific Pte Ltd
3 Church Street
#10-04 Samsung Hub
Singapore 049483

Editor: Chris Rojek
Editorial assistant: Martine Jonsrud
Production editor: Katherine Haw
Copyeditor: Solveig Gardner Servian
Proofreader: Neil Dowden
Indexer: Anne Fencott
Marketing manager: Michael Ainsley
Cover design: Lisa Harper
Typeset by: C&M Digitals (P) Ltd, Chennai, India
Printed by CPI Group (UK) Ltd, Croydon, CR0 4YY

**Library of Congress Control Number: 2012941666**

**British Library Cataloguing in Publication data**

A catalogue record for this book is available from
the British Library

MIX
Paper from
responsible sources
FSC
www.fsc.org   FSC® C013604

ISBN 978-1-84920-586-3
ISBN 978-1-84920-587-0 (pbk)

For P, J and J
and those they love

# contents

# about the author

Grace Davie is Professor Emeritus in the Sociology of Religion in the University of Exeter, England, where she taught both general sociology and the sociology of religion for some 20 years. She is a past-president of the American Association for the Sociology of Religion (2003) and of the Research Committee 22 (Sociology of Religion) of the International Sociological Association (2002–06).

In 2000–01 she was the Kerstin-Hesselgren Professor in the University of Uppsala, Sweden, where she returned for extended visits in 2006–07, 2010 and 2012. In January 2008, she received an honorary degree from Uppsala. She has also held visiting appointments at the École Pratique des Hautes Études (1996) and at the École des Hautes Études en Sciences Sociales (1998 and 2003), both in Paris.

In addition to numerous chapters and articles, she is the author of *Religion in Britain since 1945* (Blackwell, 1994), *Religion in Modern Europe* (OUP, 2000) and *Europe: The Exceptional Case* (DLT, 2002); she is co-author of *Religious America, Secular Europe* (Ashgate, 2008), and co-editor of *Predicting Religion* (Ashgate, 2003) and *Welfare and Religion in 21st Century Europe* (2 vols) (Ashgate, 2010 and 2011).

# preface to the second edition

I was delighted when Sage Publications asked me to consider a second edition of *The Sociology of Religion*. I needed to think, however, how best to do this – a question that became all the more urgent given the sea-change in the study of religion that has taken place in the last half decade. The reasons for this change and the forms that it has taken constitute the substance of this Preface; both raise crucially important issues.

Happily, the 'how' question quickly resolved itself: it became clear almost immediately that this new material (whether empirical, methodological or theoretical) could not be inserted piecemeal into the original chapters – the sheer amount of data and thinking that this body of work provoked required a discussion in its own right. For this reason, the text of the first edition has been updated in detail only (mostly for factual accuracy). Each chapter needs, however, to be read against the background of the new Preface which takes the form of an extended essay on the recent changes in the study of religion and their implications not only for the sociology of religion as such, but for the social sciences as a whole. Where appropriate, the discussion will note the places in the original text that anticipated the debates which were to follow. It will also point to an ever increasing range of resources, indicating where these may be found. With this in mind, key references only have been added to the original Bibliography.

Before engaging these necessarily challenging questions, one or two preliminaries are important. I would like first to record my thanks for the positive feedback that the first edition provoked, not least from the four individuals and their publishing houses who chose to translate the text – into Spanish, Greek, Polish and Hungarian. I learnt something new from each encounter. The second point concerns readership. I remain convinced as I did in 2007 that the text is suitable both for teaching and for wider discussion in the discipline. As a teaching text, however, the book works best in a graduate or advanced undergraduate class in that it assumes a certain amount of sociological knowledge. My aim has been to challenge students to think sociologically about new areas of experience, not to introduce the sociological agenda as such. A third point develops from this in that the book has accompanied me as a teaching aid to many different parts of the world: all over Europe, to

New Zealand, and – most memorably – to China. I have been pleased to discover that the principal ideas resonate in a wide variety of contexts, in which students have been able to construct a sociological map of religion in their own country using the tools, concepts and methodologies set out in the first half of the book.

Most important of all, however, is the increasing urgency of the topic as such. Broadly speaking the sequence runs as follows. As the twentieth century drew to a close, religion increased in visibility in almost every part of the world – there are multiple examples in the chapters that follow. But given the secular expectations of the great majority of commentators, social scientists included, this so-called resurgence of religion is still considered a 'problem', in that it was not supposed to happen. It becomes, therefore, anomalous: something to be explained away rather than explained. Important questions follow from this which must be addressed with care. Is it really the case that religion has returned to a world from which it was absent for most of the twentieth century? Or is this primarily a question of perception? We are now sensitized to a phenomenon that previously we chose to ignore. Or is it a combination of both these things? Something has indeed changed and we need to know why, acknowledging that we have moved somewhat abruptly from a set of assumptions in which religion was nowhere to an approach in which it is everywhere – to the extent that 'post-secular' has become a fashionable term. There were hints of these questions (and indeed some answers) in the 2007 text; they are further developed here.

As ever I remain enormously grateful to all those who have contributed to my thinking in this field, both in Britain and elsewhere. The ferment of activity described above has meant new opportunities in new places – a wealth of possibilities for discovering new data and for furthering the sociological discussion. I have enjoyed them all.

## NEW INITIATIVES

What I want to describe is essentially a delayed reaction. Religion, it is clear, is increasing in significance in many parts of the world (Chapters 9 and 10). Its ramifications, moreover, are more and more present in Western societies, not least in Europe – brought there by immigration (Chapter 8). In terms of social science, these very evident trends were initially seen in terms of ethnicity rather than religion – unsurprisingly in that racial or ethnic differences fitted better into existing paradigms than their religious equivalents. Bit by bit, however, the mismatch between the perceptions of Western scholars and the preferred identities of the incoming communities had to be acknowledged, a debate in which the presence of Islam was central. However unexpected, religion and religious differences were making themselves felt in the public agendas of European societies, leading at times to protracted and difficult exchanges.

Hence the reaction: denial increasingly gave way to alarm, generating an impressive array of publically funded research programmes, a wide variety of government initiatives, and a flood of publications. A surprising number of these came into being just as the first edition of this book went to press – an interesting 'coincidence'. The following illustrations are necessarily selective but they are sufficient to indicate the kind of thing that is happening. For the most part they draw from the European case in that the shift in perspective is even more striking here than in other parts of the world. Not only is Europe regarded as a relatively secular global region, it is European (specifically French) understandings of the Enlightenment that lie behind the paradigms that are predicated on the assumption that to be modern means to be secular. How, then, are European scholars, and those who fund their research, responding to the current situation?

It is important first of all to differentiate between projects and programmes. There have always been research *projects* relating to religion, many of which have yielded significant data, not to mention new ways of thinking. These have been valuable initiatives. In the last half decade, however, something rather different has appeared: that is, a series of research *programmes*, which are designed to gather together a wide variety of projects and to ensure that the latter add up to more than the sum of their parts. It is the systematic approach to the study of religion which is new. This development, together with the strikingly generous funding that supports it, needs both documentation and explanation.

I will start with a British example. The Religion and Society Research Programme, funded jointly by the Arts and Humanities Research Council and the Economic and Social Research Council, exemplifies the trend perfectly.[1] This £12 million initiative, which ran from 2007 to 2012, was without precedent in the UK. It was designed to stimulate collaborative research across the arts, humanities and social sciences, and has done precisely that – the range of projects contained in the programme is impressive. The work, moreover, has been innovative: the researchers have been asking new things in new ways, and have discovered creative methodologies to achieve their goals. The purpose of the programme was unequivocal: it existed in order to inform public debate and to advance understanding about religion in an ever more complex world. Specifically it aimed to further both research and research capacity in the field of religion (with a strong emphasis on training), to facilitate knowledge exchange between the academic community and a wide variety of stake-holders (including the religious communities themselves), and to make links with similar ventures in different parts of the world. Two such ventures can be noted at this point: the remarkably similar Religions, the State, and Society funded by the Swiss National Science Foundation,[2] and the Religion and Diversity Project, based at the University of Ottawa, which despite the term 'project' in the title is a major collaborative research initiative (MCRI) funded by the Canadian Social Sciences and Humanities Research Council.[3] There are many other examples, both in Europe and beyond.[4]

It is worth pausing for a moment to consider the impact of these programmes, taking the British Religion and Society initiative as an example. In the spring of 2012, the programme co-organized the strikingly successful Westminster Faith Debates, which permitted a number of the lead researchers on selected projects within the programme to present their work. Two presenters took part in each debate alongside respondents from the relevant constituencies in public life: politicians, policy-makers, church leaders and so on. The media coverage was extensive.[5] Will this interest convert into policy? One theme to be followed carefully in this respect concerns the constant plea for more work on religious literacy, both inside and outside the programme. The need for this has come about for a very precise reason. Two things are happening at once in British – and indeed European – society. On one hand, the process of secularization continues, sometimes remorselessly; on the other, religion has returned to the public sphere. The combination is difficult to handle. At precisely the moment that British people need them most, they are losing the vocabulary, concepts and narratives that are necessary to take part in serious conversation about religion. The result, all too often, is a debate that is both ill-mannered and ill-informed.[6]

A parallel set of activities to those outlined above exists at the European, as opposed to national, level. Excellent examples can be found in the emphasis on religion found in the Sixth and Seventh Framework Programmes of the European Commission, both of which supported a series of projects relating to the growing diversity of Europe and its consequences for economic, political and social life.[7] It is worth noting the strong, top-down emphasis in these programmes on policy-making, revealed amongst other things in the close attention paid to social cohesion. Indeed the subtext, indicative almost certainly of anxiety, is clear: is the growing religious diversity of Europe damaging to social cohesion, and if so, what is to be done? The projects themselves interrogate these questions in a wide variety of fields (politics, democracy, law, education, welfare), in which key values (tolerance, acceptance, respect, rights, responsibilities, inclusion, exclusion) are thoroughly explored. Many of these programmes foreground the presence and aspirations of religious minorities in Europe and the reactions of host societies to these groups. Identities can no longer be taken for granted in a part of the world where movement and migration are commonplace, including the movement of significant numbers of people from one part of Europe to another.

A third way of working can be found in university-wide programmes, which draw from the range of interests, skills and training found in one institution in order to foster imaginative and above all inter-disciplinary work on a common theme. One such, Religion in the 21st Century, was located in the University of Copenhagen from 2003–07 – it was one of four Research Priority Areas established by the university. In this capacity, it 'housed' more than 70 initiatives of various kinds, including a strong emphasis on the training of doctoral students.[8] Somewhat similar is the Centre of Excellence hosted by the Faculties of Theology and Law at Uppsala University. This programme is entitled The Impact of Religion – Challenges for Society, Law and Democracy, and is jointly funded by the Swedish Research Council through their Linneaus Research Programme and the University itself. It brings together 40 plus researchers from six different faculties, including the hard sciences, and will run for 10 years (2008–18). It is organized into six wide-ranging and inter-disciplinary themes: religious and social change; integration and democracy; families, law and society; well-being and health; welfare organization and welfare values; and science and religion.[9]

The fact that so many initiatives have occurred at more or less the same time is, I contend, evidence of a step change in activity in the study of religion. The numbers of scholars involved in these programmes, their individual and joint publications, the conferences that they both host and attend, and the impact that their work will have outside as well as inside the academy will undoubtedly make a difference. New knowledge will be generated in abundance, a new generation of scholars will be trained, and new possibilities for collaboration will emerge. Quite apart from this, new fields of study are becoming apparent almost by the day.

Three of these will be taken as examples: the growing significance of religion for law and law-making, new initiatives in medical practice, and the renewed attention to religion in connection with welfare. All three require the input of very different groups of scholars and have come about at much the same time. All three, moreover, were introduced in the 2007 edition (see Chapters 6, 8 and 11) – each field, however, has developed rapidly since then. It is no coincidence, for instance, that the inaugural meeting of the International Consortium for Law and Religion Studies (ICLARS) took place in 2009. The emphasis of this meeting was on state-church, or more accurately state–religion, relations and brought together constitutional lawyers from all over the world. Clearly the presence of new forms of religion and the aspirations of very different religious actors (both individuals and groups) are straining current arrangements – tensions displayed in both the case studies and the more thematic papers presented at the meeting. A selection of these can be found in Ferrari and Cristofori (2010). A new journal *Law and Religion* was established in 2012 in which the debate continues.[10]

Human Rights lawyers are similarly engaged, recognizing that rights and freedoms often collide with each other. Freedom of expression (in the form of legitimate critique or satire), for example, is not always easy to distinguish from unwarranted criticism of religion, and legislation to outlaw discrimination on the grounds of sexual orientation is likely to conflict with the rights of those who espouse more traditional forms of belief. There are no easy answers to these clashes of interest.[11] Family lawyers are also facing new issues – not least the very definition of a family. The beginnings and ends of life are increasingly imprecise as medical technologies advance, and as the unimaginable becomes the possible: a foetus can exist outside the womb, single-sex couples procreate, living wills are more and more common and assisted suicide is legal in some parts of Europe. These, moreover, are all questions on which religious groups have strong and not always compatible views.

Reactions to the re-emergence of religion in late-modern societies are in fact markedly contradictory – a tendency well illustrated by two medical examples. It is clear, on the one hand, that religious issues are taken far more seriously that they used to be in certain branches of modern medicine. Clinical psychiatry is a case in point. John Cox, for instance, advocates an approach that takes account of the whole person, acknowledging that more and more patients (notably those who come from overseas) present with 'religious' symptoms. Such an approach draws very directly on the ideas and beliefs of Paul Tournier. Applied systematically, Tournier's 'medicine of the person' (a turning away from the bio-medical model) could have far-reaching effects in many areas of healthcare (Cox et al., 2006). Conversely, certain forms of religious display are more consciously outlawed from the medical environment than used to be the case. In the spring of 2010, an English nurse refused either to remove or to hide a cross while working, and was consequently moved to a desk job. She took her case to an industrial tribunal, which found against her.[12]

In terms of the argument presented here, the two medical examples are doubly interesting in that the first regards religion, or spirituality, as a resource in good medical practice, but the second quite clearly sees it as a 'problem' – as something that should be literally hidden from view. Such contradictions are not only commonplace in late-modern societies but are likely to continue. An important reason both for the inconsistencies themselves and for the intractability of the underlying issues lies in the fact that they hover on the edge of the public and the private. Simply deeming religion to be a private matter – the 'traditional' European answer – is no longer an adequate solution (it hides the issue that demands a solution). But what is? Serious attempts to resolve these questions drive a great deal of the current research agenda, in which many disciplines have a role to play. Reconciling both the rights and responsibilities of different groups of people requires insight from specialists in diverse bodies of knowledge.

The third field of study concerns the work on religion and welfare introduced in Chapter 11. For a whole range of reasons already explained, late-modern societies find themselves in serious difficulty regarding the provision of welfare. Demand is rising, but resources are scarce and in the present economic climate are likely to become more so – a situation in which the economic crisis of 2008 becomes an important marker. The focus of the debate varies from place to place, but the underlying themes are the same: the imbalance in the working and non-working sections of the population (especially the growth in the number of elderly people) and a growing awareness that the state can no longer provide from the cradle to the grave – a realization that leads in turn to a search for alternative providers. It is important to make a distinction at this point between the developed welfare states of many European societies and the very different ways of dealing with these issues in the United States. In the latter, faith-based welfare has always been the norm rather than the exception, but all over Europe, policymakers are looking again at faith communities as possible providers. In this sense, though sometimes grudgingly, religion is once again seen as a resource for the wider society. Early projects (for example the work recorded in Bäckström et al., 2010, 2011) have been followed by others, two of which, significantly, were funded simultaneously by the Framework 6 Programme of the European Commission (see above).[13]

One final point concludes this section. It concerns a series of print and online publications which have appeared in the last five years. Three handbooks provide the starting point. In 2007, coinciding with the first edition of this text, Sage published their *Handbook of the Sociology of Religion* (Beckford and Demerath, 2007); one year later, Oxford University Press followed suit with an even larger *Handbook of the Sociology of Religion* (Clarke, 2008); in 2010 Blackwell completed the trio with a *New Blackwell Companion to the Sociology of Religion*

(Turner, 2010a). The previous *Companion* (Fenn, 2000) was barely a decade old. Three moderately expensive hardback publications in as many years is hardly a coincidence – there is surely a shift in the market, which has also brought forth a series of encyclopedias (see Chapter 11 for two examples). Also worth noting are new opportunities for online debate. Outstanding here is The Immanent Frame,[14] which was founded in 2007 in conjunction with the American Science Research Council's programme on Religion and the Public Sphere – an important initiative in its own right. The latter was established 'to foster engagement and cooperation among social scientists and others working on religion, secularism, and related topics, to support new and innovative scholarship in this critical area of study, and to elevate the quality of both academic and public discussion'.[15] The Immanent Frame is similar and 'serves as a forum for ongoing exchanges among leading thinkers across the social sciences and humanities, featuring invited contributions and original essays that have not been previously published in print or online'. Particularly pertinent to the argument here is the conversation thread entitled 'Towards a new sociology of religion', which turns on the notion of religion as an independent variable with causal impact. Equally important are the informed discussions of key (almost iconic) publications in the field: notably Charles Taylor's *A Secular Age* (Taylor 2007) and the subsequent *Varieties of Secularism in a Secular Age* (Warner et al., 2010). Without doubt, these books have opened the discussion about religion and secularism to new audiences. It is important to note, moreover, that the thrust in this respect is coming from the mainstream of sociology, not from the sociology of religion. The debate about religion and modernity introduced in Chapter 5 is developing fast.

The publications listed in the previous paragraph can be found in the Bibliography. The flood of writing that is continuing to emerge from the research initiatives introduced in this section will continue for some time. For the most part this is referenced on their respective websites. Also useful are the various handbooks and bulletins that gather this material together. A good example of the latter can be found in the publications of the Equality and Human Rights Commission relating to 'Religion and Belief' – itself an important initiative (see note 11). Much of the material on Islam in Europe is summarized in Nielsen et al. (2009 and following).

## NEW QUESTIONS

It is quite clear from even a brief summary that religion is rising in the public agenda, prompting renewed attention to the topic – this is expressed in a vigorous research sector and a stream of publications. Much of this activity is policy oriented and driven by the changing nature of society. It provokes, however, new questions for the discipline. Two of these will be addressed as a conclusion to this Preface: the notion of the post-secular and the need to engage the mainstreams of social science in the study of religion. The discussion is necessarily brief but it reflects the key question posed in the original edition of this book: that of a 'critical agenda' understanding this term in two ways. I was critical of the agenda in the sociology of religion in that I called into question, at times quite sharply, its adequacy to deal with the current situation regarding religion in the modern world. The agenda is critical in a different sense given the paramount importance of religion in global affairs at the start of the new millennium.

The term 'post-secular' is widely used, but to mean very different things (Beckford 2012). For a start, it raises once again the possibility that perception may be more important than reality: the world is *deemed* post-secular because we have chosen to take notice of religion rather than to ignore it. The religious situation itself has not changed that much. Post-secular, moreover, is rarely a neutral term. The increasing visibility of religion is welcome or less welcome depending on who you are, what you do and where you are situated in society. It may please you, it may not. Religion, finally, 'returns' in different ways – some of these are easier to accommodate than others, as indeed are the reactions they provoke. What has become known as 'new atheism', for example, is largely a response – a vehement one at that – to the re-emergence of religion in the *public* sphere. Indeed new atheism can in many ways be seen as an interesting example of secular fundamentalism, applying the approach set out in Chapter 9. The argument runs as follows. Secularism (rightly or wrongly) had become the assumed ideology of modern Europe: both scholars and activists expected a future that was more rather than less secular, even if belief endured in the private sphere. In these terms the return of religion to public discussion is anomalous in that it undermines the taken-for-grantedness of the secular. One reaction (among others) to this unexpected recurrence has been a regrouping amongst secularists to re-state and re-affirm, at times stridently, what they consider to be the essential (fundamental) truths of their position. Such an approach is helpful in that it demonstrates very clearly why the advent of new atheism coincides with renewed attention to religion. This is not a zero–sum game: each encourages the other.

Regarding the post-secular as such, my own view is the following. I welcome the current debate concerning this concept and the growing body of literature that surrounds it (see, for example, Molendijk et al.,

2010; Baker and Beaumont, 2011). Both are signs that religion is taken seriously in academic discussion – that is a good thing. The notion of the post-secular needs, however, considerable refinement. Here we can find an interesting extension of the work of David Martin (see Chapter 3), notably his insistence that the secularization is a process that takes place differently in different parts of the world. The point to grasp is that exactly the same is true of the post-secular. The latter, if it exists at all, is unlikely to be a single or unitary thing. It will be as patterned as its predecessor. Indeed for precisely this reason, Martin (2011) is highly suspicious of the term. The interactions of the religious and secular should rather be seen in the long-term. 'Religious thrusts' and 'secular recoils' have happened for centuries rather than decades and – crucially for Martin – they work themselves out differently in different places. The shorthand of 'God is back' (Micklethwait and Wooldridge, 2009) cannot do justice to this necessarily complex agenda. Such complexities must be squarely faced; it is in working through them that a better understanding of late-modern society will emerge, not in an exaggerated contrast between unitary, and thus distorting, understandings of both secular and post-secular.

All that said, and appreciating that views on these issues will continue to differ sharply, it is my firm belief that the sociology of religion, indeed the study of religion in general, is now in better shape than it was a decade ago. I welcome this shift unreservedly even if I remain sceptical about the motivations for much of the work being done. By and large, religion is still perceived negatively, and in order to be better managed, it must be thoroughly researched: it is this sentiment that lies behind the initiatives outlined above. In a nutshell, the right thing (the careful and systematic study of religion across a wide variety of disciplines) has been done for the wrong reason (the assumption that religion leads necessarily to division rather than cohesion).

Such a statement requires immediate qualification. It is more applicable in some places than in others, to some disciplines than to others, and to some researchers than to others. Broadly speaking the potential of religion to become a positive resource is most easily appreciated by those who know it best. Specifically, American scholars find it easier that their European equivalents, and those who work in the developing world find it easier still – notably anthropologists and at least some development workers (see Chapter 10). Right from the start, the former were less affected by the secular turn than their sociological cousins. The latter are practical people driven by the circumstances in which they find themselves – very often they work in places where religious networks are both more intact and more reliable than their secular equivalents. It seems, moreover, that researchers who 'live' in the field (in whatever capacity and in whatever kind of society) are more likely to display a respect for their subjects and the lifestyles they embrace. Respect includes, of course, a critical perspective.

What next? As we have seen, large numbers of researchers from many different disciplines are currently engaged in the study of religion – much of their work is innovative and insightful. In itself, however, this success suggests further steps: the need to penetrate the philosophical core of the associated disciplines and to enquire what difference the serious study of religion might make to their ways of working. The size of the task should not be underestimated. Most of the disciplines in question have emerged more or less directly from the European Enlightenment, implying that they are underpinned by a markedly secular philosophy of social science. Interestingly it is precisely this point that Jürgen Habermas appreciates so clearly and addresses in his recent writing (Habermas, 2006). This was noted, but barely developed, in Chapter 5. Habermas has become increasingly aware that the political philosophies associated with modern liberal democracies have to take religion into account – to ignore this is not a sensible policy. He insists, moreover, that others disciplines have a similar responsibility: that is, to rethink the foundations of their respective fields of study in order to accommodate fully the implications of religion and religious issues in their analyses of modern societies. This, moreover, means accepting religion as it is, not as we would like it to be. Above all, it must be driven by the data, not by the assumptions of overly secular social science.

*xix*

If this were to happen systematically, it would go a long way to meet the deficiencies that I noted in 2007: that is, the mismatch between the preoccupations in both the sociology of religion and in its parent discipline(s) and the realities of religion of the modern world. At the same time it would overcome once and for all what Beckford (2003) terms the 'insulation and isolation of religion' from the mainstreams of social science. There is, however, an interesting sting in the tail. Is it possible for a set of disciplines which take very seriously the secular philosophies of science that underpin their work to engage with an area of human living that, by definition, challenges these ways of thinking? In this respect the debate has barely begun.

## NOTES

1 See www.religionandsociety.org.uk/ (accessed 16 May 2012) for more details about the Religion and Society Programme itself and the very varied projects that contribute to this.

2 See www.nfp58.ch/e_index.cfm (accessed 16 May 2012) for further details about the Swiss programme and the special reports that are emerging from this.

3 See www.religionanddiversity.ca/ (accessed 16 May 2012). The aim of this project is to address the following question: What are the contours of religious diversity in Canada and how can we best respond to the opportunities and challenges presented by religious diversity in ways that promote a just and peaceful society?

4 There is an interesting Dutch equivalent, The Future of the Religious Past, which ran from 2002–05: www.nwo.nl/nwohome.nsf/pages/NWOP_68YGPN_Eng?opendocument&nav=FRP_02_NL (accessed 16 May 2012). Outside Europe and particularly noteworthy are the systematic attempts to document the religious situation in China. See the work of the Center on Religion and Chinese Society at Purdue University: www.purdue.edu/crcs/ (accessed 16 May 2012).

5 Full coverage of the debates and the ensuing media coverage can be found on www.religionandsociety.org.uk/faith_debates (accessed 16 May 2012).

6 This is one reason why the Religion and Society Programme has paid careful attention to religious education in schools. Also important in this respect is the work of the Religious Literacy Leadership Programme, which concentrates more on higher education. See http://religiousliteracyhe.org/ for more details (accessed 16 May 2012).

7 See http://cordis.europa.eu/home_en.html (accessed 16 May 2012) for information about the European Commission's Framework Programmes, both past and present.

8 See www.ku.dk/priority/Religion/index.asp (accessed 16 May 2012) for information about the Religion in the 21st century Research Priority Area and the publications emerging from this.

9 See www.crs.uu.se/Impact_of_religion/ (accessed 16 May 2012) for the content and structure of this programme.

10 See http://ojlr.oxfordjournals.org/ (accessed 16 May 2012).

11 In the UK context, the Equalities and Human Rights Commission is an important source of information regarding these issues. See www.equalityhumanrights.com/advice-and-guidance/your-rights/religion-and-belief/ and www.equalityhumanrights.com/about-us/vision-and-mission/our-business-plan/religion-belief-equality/ (both accessed 16 May 2012). The latter lists a growing series of reports regarding religion and equality matters.

12 This controversial case was widely reported in the press. See, for example, www.telegraph.co.uk/news/uknews/8709828/Equality-watchdog-drops-plan-to-protect-religious-rights.html (accessed 16 May 2012). The case is one of several concerning the rights (or otherwise) of employees to wear religious symbols in the workplace. At the time of writing, the case had been referred to the European Court of Human Rights in Strasbourg.

13 The two projects are Welfare and Values in Europe (WaVE) and Faith Based Organisations and Welfare in European Cities (FACIT). See www.crs.uu.se/Research/Former_projects/WaVE/?languageId=1 and http://ec.europa.eu/research/social sciences/projects/387_en.html respectively (both accessed 16 May 2012).

14 See http://blogs.ssrc.org/tif/about/ (accessed 16 May 2012). The Immanent Frame contains a wealth of information relevant to this Preface.

15 See www.ssrc.org/programs/religion-and-the-public-sphere/ (accessed 16 May 2012) for more information about this programme.

# preface to the first edition

This book could be placed in the hands of two very different groups of people. On the one hand, it could be given to a class of students embarking for the first time on a course in the sociology of religion. They would gain from it a clear idea of both the agenda itself and the principal debates of the sub-discipline. They would learn, moreover, where to find the associated data sets and how these have been interpreted by different scholars in different parts of the world. On the other hand, the book could – and I hope will – be used to initiate a debate within the sub-discipline itself regarding the adequacy of the current agenda in the sociology of religion. The backdrop to this discussion can be found in the realities of the modern world in which religion is becoming an ever more dominant feature.

The deliberately ambiguous subtitle has been chosen with this in mind. The agenda is 'critical' in the sense that we need to get it right; religion is a crucially important issue in the modern world order about which students need to be properly informed. But I am 'critical' in the sense that I am not always sure that we perform this task as well as we should. I do not want to sound negative: a great deal of excellent work is being done in this field. There remains, however, a deep-seated resistance to the notion that it is entirely normal in most parts of the world to be both fully modern and fully religious. To overturn this resistance, both in the sociology of religion and in the social sciences more generally, is the principal aim of this book.

The text has been a long time in the making and draws together a number of different strands. It reflects two decades of research, writing and teaching in the sociology of religion, and in a wide variety of contexts. In addition to Exeter, I have worked and taught in many parts of Europe and in the United States. I am deeply grateful to all those colleagues who have made this possible, most recently at Hartford Seminary in Hartford, Connecticut where the text was finally completed. Early chapters were written in Paris during a visit to the École des Hautes Études en Sciences Sociales in 2003; others were drafted in the course of my many visits to 'DVI' (the Institute for Diaconal and Social Studies) in Uppsala.[1] A good deal of editing was achieved during a short visit to the Institute on Culture, Religion and World Affairs in Boston, in June 2005. In every case, I have benefited not only from colleagues, but also from students – highly perceptive ones who have helped me to know their own countries better. The same is true of the students who have come to the Centre for European Studies in Exeter. It was they, for example, who first encouraged my interest in Turkey.

The financial support has been equally diverse, coming both from inside and outside the University of Exeter: from the University's Research Fund, allowing me a light teaching load in the 2004–05 academic year, from the École des Hautes Études in Paris as *professeur invité* and from the Leverhulme Trust. In the autumn of 2005 I held a Leverhulme Study Abroad Fellowship, which permitted not only the last stages of writing but sustained contact with American colleagues.

I am grateful for institutional support. I am even more grateful to particular individuals and groups of individuals: notably to my colleagues in Exeter in the then School of Humanities and Social Sciences, in the Department of Sociology and Philosophy, and in the Centre for European Studies. In the latter Jacquie Fox and Chris Longman kept the show on the road during my frequent absences. Maddy Morgan, a doctoral student from the Department of History, helped me extensively with the Bibliography. A special place goes to my own doctoral students in the sociology of religion who are often the first to hear about my thinking in this field.

I have discovered similar, very supportive, colleagues and students all over Europe and America, not least in the many organizations that exist within the sociology of religion: the British Sociological Association's Sociology of Religion Study Group, the International Society for the Sociology of Religion, the American Association for the Sociology of Religion (of which I was President in 2003) and the Research Committee 22 of the International Sociological Association (of which I was President for the 2002–06 period). Many of the ideas in this book were 'tried out' in the meetings of these various groups, most notably the 2003 Conference of ASR in Atlanta, Georgia, where the conference theme concerned the agenda of the sociology of religion and how this is constructed. These organizations are full of friends as well as colleagues. Such is most definitely the case with my most critical reader – David Voas – who dispensed with the niceties of anonymous reviewing for the publisher and gave me 8,000 words of invaluable comment on the first version of the typescript. He does not always agree with me, nor I with him, but I value his input enormously. Long may the debate continue.

The largest debts of all are, as ever, personal: to my husband who bears with extraordinary patience both my repeated absence from home and my preoccupation with my work, and to my children who keep me from excess at least in terms of the latter. It is to my children and those they love that this book is dedicated.

Earlier versions of some chapters or sections of chapters have already appeared. All have been extensively rewritten, but the following debts should be noted:

Versions of the material in Chapters 1 and 2 formed part of my Presidential Address to the 2003 meeting of the Association for the Sociology of Religion in Atlanta, Georgia. This was subsequently published as 'Creating an agenda in the sociology of religion: common sources/different pathways', *Sociology of Religion*, 65, 2004: 323–40.

Earlier versions of the material in Chapter 5 appeared as 'New approaches in the sociology of religion: a Western perspective', *Social Compass*, 51, 2004: 73–84.

The material on mainstream religions in Europe found its first expressions in the following journal articles: 'From obligation to consumption: patterns of religion in Northern Europe at the start of the twenty-first century', *Studia Religiosa Helvetica*, 8/9, 2004: 95–114 and 'From obligation to consumption: a framework for reflection in Northern Europe', in *Political Theology*, 6, 2005: 281–301.

Parts of the material on religious minorities in Chapter 8 were presented at a conference on 'The New Religious Pluralism and Democracy' held at Georgetown University in March 2005. This material appeared in T. Banchoff (ed.) *The New Religious Pluralism and Democracy*, New York, Oxford: OUP, 2007.

The argument in Chapter 9 was first worked out some 20 years ago in 'Competing fundamentalisms', published in *Sociology Review*, 4, 1995: 2–7.

*xxiii*

---

## NOTE

1 On 1 January 2007, the Institute for Diaconal and Social Studies in Uppsala became the Centre for the Study of Religion and Society (Centrum för studier av religion och samhälle). That in turn is now linked to a major programme of research on the Impact of Religion – Challenges for Law, Society and Democracy. See www.crs.uu.se/Impact_of_religion/ for more details (accessed 3 April 2012).

# *one*

# introduction: a critical agenda

Putting together a book about the sociology of religion at the start of the twenty-first century is a daunting task, given the increasing importance of religion as a factor in world affairs and as a powerful influence in the lives of countless individuals – the great majority of the world's citizens. It is bound to raise controversial as well as strategic issues. My task, however, is to produce a book about the sociology of religion and the debates within this particular sub-discipline, not to write a book about religion in the modern world per se – a significantly different enterprise. The difference, moreover, is crucial; it will have implications not only for our understanding of the subject matter, but for the argument of this book as a whole. The tension between global realities and sociological understanding is continually changing and will surface in almost every chapter.

The essential point can be put quite simply: why is it that the debates about religion in the modern world are so different from those that, until very recently, have predominated in the sub-discipline? What has caused this mismatch and how will it be overcome? For overcome it must be if we are to appreciate fully the significance of religion in the modern world order. Hence the subtitle of this book and the title of this chapter – the agenda is critical in that it calls into question, at times quite sharply, dominant ways of thinking. It is critical in a different sense given the paramount importance of religion in global affairs at the start of the new millennium.

The task, moreover, is urgent: we need to understand the ways in which religion, or more accurately religions, not only influence but are influenced by the behaviour of both individuals and collectivities (of all sizes), working on the principle that this will be the case in late modernity just as it has been in previous generations. Assuming the centrality of religion to late-modern societies is the key to what follows. More precisely this book is premised on the fact that, in global terms, it is as modern to draw on the resources of religion to critique the secular as it is to draw on the resources of the secular to critique the religious. Religion is not something that can be safely or sensibly relegated either to the past or to the edge.

The phrase 'in global terms' offers an important clue in this respect. Sociology, and within this the sociology of religion, has developed from a particular historical context – a set of circumstances which coloured not only the subject matter of the discipline but the tools and concepts which emerged in order to understand that context better. Hence, in the early days of sociology, a preoccupation with the upheavals taking place in Europe at the time of the industrial revolution and, as part and parcel of this, a sensitivity to the impact that these were having on the nature and forms of religious life in this part of the world. A pervasive, but ultimately false assumption gradually began to assert itself: namely that the process of modernization was *necessarily* damaging to religion. Exactly what form the damage might take and its possible consequences for individual and social life were major topics of debate, but its inevitability was increasingly taken for granted – unsurprisingly given the evidence surrounding the early sociologists. The traditional structures of religious life, deeply embedded in the economic and political order of pre-modern Europe, were crumbling visibly under the mutually reinforcing pressures of industrialization and urbanization.

The process itself is significant for the development of sociology. Even more far-reaching, however, were the conceptual implications that came with it, as sociology looked for ways not only to describe but to explain the 'damage' being done. An overwhelming preoccupation with secularization as the dominant paradigm in the sociology of religion should be seen in this light; it emerged from the specificities of the European case in which it worked relatively well – an understanding of secularization was clearly important to late-nineteenth- and early-twentieth-century Europeans. The next stage in the argument is, however, more difficult. The empirical connections present in Europe gradually – but inexorably – turned into theoretical assumptions, with the strong implication that secularization would necessarily accompany modernization whenever and wherever the latter occurred. More than this, Europe became the case against which all other cases were measured and, it is often implied, found wanting. The connections between modern and secular became normative. With this in mind, it becomes easier to understand why European sociologists, just as much as European journalists, have considerable difficulty accepting the fact that religion is, and remains, a profoundly normal part of the lives of the huge majority of people in the late-modern world.

The following anecdote illustrates this process perfectly. From 1998–2003, I took part in a working group associated with the World Council of Churches. The group was charged with understanding better the nature and forms of religion in the modern world, paying careful attention to the implications of these changes for the future of the ecumenical movement.[1] About 10 of us met regularly over the five-year period, each individual representing a different part of the Christian world. The Europeans were in a minority. Two of our number (one from the Philippines and one from West Africa) each told the same story regarding the secularization paradigm. Both of them, educated in the late 1960s and 1970s, had been obliged to learn the 'secularization thesis' as part of their professional formation. Both of them knew from their own experience that the thesis was at best inappropriate, at worst simply wrong, a point of view overwhelmingly vindicated by subsequent events. But learn the thesis they had to – it was part of 'proper' education, necessary if they were to receive the qualifications essential for their respective careers. The empirical situation which they knew so well was simply put on one side: theory took precedence over data.

The anecdote raises many questions. Exactly what is meant by the secularization thesis is far from straightforward. Its various ramifications will form the substance of a key chapter in this book. So, too, the alternative perspectives that have emerged to replace this in different parts of the world. But the essence is clear enough: the sociology of religion has been dominated by a frame of reference which has its roots in a global region with a *particular*, as opposed to typical, experience of religion and religious change. A crucial part of the evolution of the sub-discipline lies (and will continue to lie) in its capacity to discern the implications of these beginnings for the formation of sociological thinking and to escape from them where necessary.

The last phrase is important. Not everything in or about the secularization thesis needs to be discarded. Important insights have emerged not only from the thesis itself, but also from the European context which need to be carried forward into the twenty-first century. One of these, paradoxically, is the aspect of secularization that the Europeans resisted for longest – the gradual separating out of different and more and more specialized institutions (political or educational, for example) as part of the modernizing process. Societal functions that were previously dominated by the church (education, healthcare, etc.) became increasingly autonomous. Once again, the detail of this discussion will be left until a later chapter. The key point to grasp at this stage is that institutional separation – a normal and 'healthy' part of modernization – need not bring with it either the marginalization of religion to the private sphere or the decline in religious activity (Casanova, 1994). Neither have occurred in most parts of the modern or modernizing world; nor are they likely to in the foreseeable future.

So much for the European context and its somewhat negative influence on the long-term development of the sociology of religion. Much more positive from this point of view was the centrality of religion to the work of the early sociologists, not least the founding fathers. All of them (Marx, Weber, Durkheim and Simmel) took religion seriously in their attempts to account for the changes taking place in the societies of which they were part. The different ways in which they did this form the substance of the following chapter. The close attention to religion on the part of social scientists was not, however, to last. In this respect, an essentially promising start gave way to what Beckford has termed a growing 'insulation and isolation' of the sociology of religion from its parent discipline (Beckford, 1989, 2003), a move which has been damaging in two respects. On the one hand, mainstream sociology has been rather too inclined to ignore both religion itself and the sociological debate that surrounds this. And on the other, sociologists of religion have withdrawn from mainstream sociological discussion, concentrating instead on the specificities of their own subject matter, whether empirically or theoretically.

The over-preoccupation with secularization is part and parcel of this process. Why should mainstream sociology, or indeed any other discipline, take seriously a phenomenon which is reputedly disappearing as the modernization process takes its inevitable course? The residues and reactions to modernization that take a religious form may be of interest to the specialists in the field, but given their inevitably short-term nature they need not trouble the mainstream. Conversely a withdrawal by sociologists of religion from the central debates of sociology has meant a lack of engagement with the assumptions that accompany these discussions, not least the assumption that modernization necessarily implies secularization. The vicious circle intensifies – a chain of reactions that must be broken if progress is to be made.

The case for breaking the chain is, moreover, overwhelming if we are to respond adequately to the empirical realities of the modern world which, following Berger (1992), is 'as furiously religious as ever'. The facts are undeniable – they cover the world's press on a daily basis and will form the subject matter of the later chapters of this book. There is an equally urgent need to devise tools and concepts appropriate to the task. Both (facts and tools) will be easier to handle if contact with the parent discipline is encouraged. Much is to be gained, for example, from a better understanding of the modernization process in all its fullness, of which the complex and continuing relationships with religion are but one part. The same goes for globalization (see Chapter 10). A rather more domestic illustration can be found in the parallels between the religious field and other areas of society – a point that can be exemplified many times over in Britain. Institutional religion, at least in its traditional forms, is in trouble (a fact that is rarely disputed), but so are the corresponding institutions of political and economic life. That is the crucial

4

point. Both political parties and trade unions are struggling to maintain members (and therefore income) in exactly the same way as the mainstream churches. The reasons for these shifts lie primarily in the changing nature of economic and social life, the subject matter of mainstream sociology. Religious indifference is less important; it is, in fact, more likely to be the result than the cause of the institutional changes that are so clearly occurring.[2]

How then can we understand the changing nature of religion in the modern world in ways that build on what has gone before, but avoid the pitfalls of generalizing from a particular, but not necessarily typical, case? Will we all do this in the same way? Bearing this challenge in mind, the following paragraphs set out both a central theme and a set of variations. The theme is concerned with sociological approaches to religion, as opposed to those of other disciplines. The variations relate to the very different ways that the sociological task can be achieved. Specifically they pay careful attention to the situation in which the work takes place, a point already exemplified (albeit negatively) in the limitations that have emerged from the European context.

Rather more creative understandings will emerge as we try to determine how the agenda of the sociology of religion has been shaped by a wide variety of factors. The political/religious context in which the debate occurs is indeed important, but it is not the only influence. Others include the language restrictions (or opportunities) of the sociologists in question, their access to data, the requirements of the institutions in which they work (including political constraints), and crucially the subtle and ongoing relationships between observer and observed: that is, between the sociological community and the constituencies that form the primary object of their study. The agenda is not simply given; it becomes in itself something to be scrutinized – not least its capacity to be proactive as well as reactive. The ambiguous relationship between the nature and development of religiousness in the modern world and the interests of those who study it will become, in fact, a *fil conducteur* for this book as a whole. It is a vitally important issue if the sociology of religion is to flourish in the twenty-first century.

5

## A THEME AND VARIATIONS: SOCIOLOGICAL APPROACHES TO RELIGION

### the theme

The discipline of sociology is about pattern; it is concerned both with the non-random ways that individuals, communities and societies order their lives and with finding explanations for these ways of behaving. It follows that the sociology of religion aims to discover the patterns of social living associated with religion in all its diverse forms, and to find explanations for the data that emerge. It is not, in contrast, concerned with the competing truth claims of the great variety of belief systems that are and always have been present in human societies. That is the sphere of theology, with the relatively modern discipline of religious studies hovering, at times uneasily, in between.

It is hardly surprising that sociological distancing from 'truth' causes difficulties for some adherents of religion. Truth for the believer is absolute rather than relative, and any attempt to explain that some individuals or groups are, or appear to be, closer to the truth because of their socioeconomic backgrounds (social class, age and gender, for example) is bound to provoke unease. The point is well taken, but it is important to grasp that the difficulty does not pertain only to the study of religion. Interestingly, it is equally problematic with respect to science – and the higher the view of 'science' or scientific knowledge, the worse the problem is likely to be. Or to put the same point in a different way, advocates of the superiority of science over religion have exactly the same problem as religious believers when it comes to sociology. Both resist a discipline which is concerned more with the context and institutional attachments of adherents than with the status of the knowledge or belief system as such. No one makes this point more forcefully than Mary Douglas:

> When the scientist has a very serious message to convey he faces a problem of disbelief. How to be credible? This perennial problem of religious creed is now a worry for ecology. Roughly the same conditions that affect belief in a denominational God affect belief in any particular environment. Therefore in a series of lectures on ecology, it is right for the social anthropologist to address this particular question. We should be concerned to know how beliefs arise and how they gain support. (Douglas, 1982: 260)

A further point follows from this. To indicate that the many and varied aspects of religious life form patterns does not imply that they are *caused* by the different variables that appear to correlate with them. For example, to observe that in large parts of the Christian West women appear to be more religious than men implies neither that all women are necessarily religious, nor that no men are. Women, just like men, are free to choose their degree of religiousness. Even a limited scrutiny of the data reveals, however, that the choices of women with respect to religion in the Western world (whether in terms of belief or of practice) are markedly different from those of men. This is an obvious and pervasive example of pattern in Western societies. *Why* this should be so moves us inevitably to the level of explanation, and in more ways than one. We have indeed to consider why it is that women appear to be more religious than men; we also have to consider why the difference was ignored for so long in the sociological literature. Both points will be dealt with in Chapter 11.

An additional danger needs firm underlining before going further. Sociologists must resist the temptation to subsume the study of religion into alternative, and for some at least more congenial, areas of interest. This has happened in the past (all too often) and has impeded understanding. It is in fact a further, if indirect, consequence of a tendency to think primarily in terms of secularization. So doing implies that the presence, rather than the absence, of religion in the modern world requires an explanation. Why is it still there? One way round this 'problem' lies in arguing that what appears to be religion is 'really something else', the principal suspects being ethnicity and nationalism. These are the real issues to be tackled; religion is simply an epiphenomenon masking the realities of a world necessarily dominated, if the protagonists of secularization are correct, by forces other than religion.

The global situation is changing, however. It is becoming more and more difficult to ignore the presence of religion in the modern world or to claim that this is really something else. Two defining moments in this respect occurred towards the end of the twentieth century. The first, in 1979, brought religion centre stage in a particularly dramatic way. The date that the British remember as the beginning of the Thatcher era coincided, give or take a month of two, with the year in which Karol Wojtyla became Pope and the Shah of Iran fled before the Ayatollah. Across the globe, there was a conservative reaction in more ways than one (economic, political and religious), a change associated with the decline in secular confidence so dominant in the 1960s. The implications for the sociology of religion are immense and will be spelled out in detail in the chapters that follow. The second, precisely 10 years later, engendered a further shift in perspective. An understanding of global politics based on ideology, the essence of the Cold War, has given way to a politics centred on identity (or identities) within which religion finds a natural place (Sacks, 2002). Samuel Huntington's celebrated 'clash of civilizations' (Huntington, 1993, 1997) articulates this shift, offering ample space for religion in the ensuing debate. The controversial nature of this work lies in Huntington's conceptualization of civilizational (and within this religious) relationships as a 'clash' rather than a dialogue. Unsurprisingly, the potential for conflict – and especially that between Islam and its neighbours – has caught the attention of public as well as professional commentators; it has become, rightly or wrongly, a pervasive frame of reference.

Scholars of many disciplines must come to terms with these changes, the more so since the shock of 9/11 ensured that they remained central to the world's agenda. Rather more modestly there is an urgent need for sociologists of religion to take responsibility in this field and, where necessary, to challenge 'the clash'. They are, or should be, motivated by a common task: the better understanding of the place of religion in the ordering (patterning) of human societies and on a global scale. How then do sociologists, including sociologists of religion, go about their work in practice? Runciman (1983) offers a helpful, and in essence very simple, response to this question, elaborating four separate but overlapping dimensions to the sociological role. He uses the following terms to introduce these: reportage, explanation, description and evaluation or policymaking.

Runciman begins with reportage: that is, the gathering of as much information as possible and in a wide variety of ways. Chapter 6 on the different methodologies available to the sociologist of religion will expand these opportunities further, demonstrating the range of data on which it is possible to draw and how these sources can be used to maximum advantage. But sociologists do more than this: they seek to explain as well as to report their data, explanations that take many different forms. What, for example, are the connections between religious vitality and religious pluralism? Is it the case that the latter undermines the former, or is religious life stimulated by diversity? Chapters 3 and 4 offer alternative understandings of this important issue. At the same time, such understandings raise questions about causality and correlation; patterns that appear to coincide are not necessarily related to each other by causal links.

Runciman uses his third term 'description' in a somewhat specialized sense. By this he means an attempt to describe what it is like for the individuals and groups involved in religious or indeed other activities; in other words, seeing what is happening through the eyes of the religious actor. A major challenge in this respect lies in the capacity to 'understand' a world view which challenges, sometimes very profoundly, the values of the observer. Is it possible, for instance, to empathize with views that appear to run counter to principles of Western democracy? The answer must be 'yes', but requires at times both effort and imagination, a point underlined in Chapter 6. The fourth and final aspect of the sociological task concerns its more practical applications. Sociologists are invited to suggest policies which might boost the membership of an ailing institution or, alternatively, reduce the possibility of religious conflict. The likelihood of differing views, and therefore different policies, is however almost unavoidable. Policy after all will relate very closely to explanation; disagreements about the latter (why the conflict takes place) very quickly turn into disagreements about the former (how it might be resolved).

All four of these elements will emerge in the chapters that follow. Not all of them will be followed through in each case, but the framework set out here provides a useful guide to the territory.

## variations on the theme

Before embarking definitively, however, a rather different point requires attention; it lies in the diversity of resources available to the sociologist as he or she sets about the task or tasks already outlined. The question can be asked in a variety of ways. At one end of the scale are the intellectual (including linguistic) constraints; at the other lie a range of institutional issues – bearing in mind the inevitable overlap between them. Intellectual constraints find expression in distinctive institutional settings; institutions epitomize 'schools of thought', which in turn become self-perpetuating.

There is no need to go far in the sociology of religion – an international conference will suffice – without becoming aware of the very different intellectual *formations* (to use a French term) encountered in the sub-discipline. Scholars of religion are exposed not only to different theoretical frameworks but to different academic traditions which relate, in their turn, both to linguistic boundaries (who can access what?) and even more profoundly to the philosophies that underpin the discipline. The bodies of knowledge that build up in different places embody significantly different approaches to the subject matter, quite apart from divergent interests and skills. The implications for academic exchange are considerable. It is unreasonable, for instance, to expect a natural convergence between a French sociologist of religion – influenced from an early age by Cartesian philosophy, schooled in the classics of French sociology of religion (see Chapter 2) and preoccupied with essentially French debates about *laïcité* – and his or her American equivalent, who draws from Anglo-Saxon literature and Anglo-Saxon empiricism in order to understand better the implications of American voluntarism in the religious field. Both will have to work hard if an effective dialogue is to take place – the whole point of the international conference.

Add to this the fact that each of these scholars may be working in a very different institutional environment and the possibilities for misunderstanding multiply. This is true even within Europe, let alone between old world and new. In the Nordic countries, for example, the sociology of religion is almost always found in faculties of theology (now broadened to include religious studies in addition to philosophy, anthropology and sociology of religion). In France, in contrast, the teaching of religion as such is proscribed from state-funded universities just as it is from public schools. The sociology of religion has grown from a very different environment; hence the need to distance itself from its Catholic roots in pastoral sociology. The Catholic universities of continental Europe are different again – offering their own combination of restriction and opportunity, as indeed do the pastoral institutes of the relatively wealthy German churches which produce data sets unheard of in Britain, but not always in ways that assist the sociologist. All of these, moreover, contrast sharply with their counterparts in North America, where the implications of the First Amendment sit alongside the opportunities for financial support that come from private as well as public foundations – remembering, of course, that private funding bodies have institutional requirements of their own. The grass on the other side of the fence is not always greener, though in funding terms it sometimes appears so.

The examples multiply the further afield one goes. Particularly interesting are the venues for scholarship establishing themselves in the postcommunist world, as the lifting of restrictions in the religious field itself are accompanied by attempts to understand this better and to track the debates specific to the region – not least careful attention to religious freedom and how this should be interpreted in countries that have emerged from Soviet control. The answers are far from straightforward. Constructing an appropriate body of theory becomes an essential part of the task in an environment dominated for several generations by a philosophy that, officially at least, proscribed religion altogether. Attempts to emerge from this past are moderately well advanced in much of central and East Europe (though more so in some places than in others);[3] the Chinese case will be the one to watch in the early decades of the twenty-first century.[4]

Intellectual traditions and their associated institutions offer one route into this debate. Another lies in the religious organizations themselves: first, in their capacity to employ professionally trained sociologists, but second, in their willingness to contribute – in other words, to lay themselves open to sociological enquiry. How do they regard the social scientist: as potential friend or probable foe? Voyé and Billiet (1999) offer an interesting range of case studies in this respect. Most of these are European, but not quite all: they include some tentative remarks on the possibilities for the sociological study of Islam and on the study of new religious movements in Japan. The title and sub-title of this volume – *Sociology and Religions: An Ambiguous Relationship* – catch something of the complexities involved. The relationships are multiple; so too are the associated ambiguities as different faith communities react differently to the social-scientific observer and to the findings that emerge from the latter's enquiries – a point that will be discussed in more detail at the end of Chapter 6.

## THE STRUCTURE OF THE BOOK

Bearing such considerations in mind, this book will be structured as follows. It is divided into two halves: the first half will deal primarily with theory and method within the sub-discipline, and the second with a range of substantive issues. Quite clearly the two overlap; they should be thought of as different approaches to a single body of material rather than discrete or free-standing enterprises.

### part I

Chapter 2 begins, predictably enough, with some discussion of the founding fathers and the importance of religion to their thinking. Following the approaches already set out, careful attention will be paid to the European context and the manner in which this influenced their work, albeit in different ways. The second section takes a rather different turn and illustrates the distinctive paths that sociology, and within this the sociology of religion took in the next generation as American influences began to dominate in the English-speaking world. A markedly different sociological 'canon' emerges on each side of the Atlantic, the more so given the dominance of the French (and French speakers) in European developments. The rather special place of the British contribution forms a central section within this chapter. As English speakers, the British draw extensively on the American sources. The context in which they work is, however, closer to their relatively secular continental neighbours than their Anglo-Saxon counterparts across the Atlantic. Debates centred on American voluntarism do not translate easily into European terms. Britain turns out, in fact, to be a hybrid case: institutionally it is pulled in one direction, linguistically in another.

The core of the theoretical discussion lies, however, in three longish chapters each with a different theme. The first of these (Chapter 3) is devoted to secularization and begins with the essentially European genesis of the concept and its inherent ambiguities. Secularization is (and always has been) a term with multiple meanings, each of which needs separating out if we are to avoid unnecessary confusions. That is the first task. The second lies in outlining the positions of the different contributors to the debate, paying particular attention to the comparative aspects of their work. By and large the scholars who have paid more attention to the ways in which the process of secularization has occurred in different parts of the world are less likely to commit themselves to the inevitability of what is happening.

The third section of this chapter reflects a more radical change. The whole notion of secularization has come under attack in recent years as the empirical data began to suggest that the assumption of secularization as the most likely outcome of modernization might be incorrect. Not everyone has been persuaded by this argument. Indeed it is important to think carefully about what can and what cannot be sustained in terms of secularization given the unexpected (at least for some) resurgence of religion in the modern world. This is not an all-or-nothing situation. Particular attention will be paid to the work of Peter Berger, which spans three to four decades. In the 1960s Berger was a major contributor to the idea of secularization, paying careful attention to the ways in which modern people believe. Some 40 years later his views are markedly different. In many ways Berger's earlier intuitions (especially those in *The Heretical Imperative*, 1980) were correct; the consequences, however, were not those that he initially anticipated.

Rational choice theory (RCT) is to America what secularization theory is to Europe. It offers an alternative approach to religion in the modern world and leads in a very different direction. Once again the stress will lie on the 'fit' between context and theory, exemplifying on one hand the 'gloriously American' nature of RCT but on the other its necessary limitations if used indiscriminately. With this in mind, an important section of Chapter 4 will emphasize the differences between Europe and America, looking carefully at religious mentalities as well as religious institutions. Suggesting changes at the level of institutions is one thing, changing mentalities, religious or secular, is quite another. It is at this level that we find the real resistance to RCT in the European context. Europeans do not, for the most part, regard their religious institutions as competing firms in a religious market from which they can choose the product that offers the best deal (the economic language is deliberate); they regard them as 'public utilities' – there at the point of need for a population that delegates to someone else, historically the state, the responsibility for maintaining that institution until the need arises.

The last section of this chapter turns briefly to Latin America, suggesting that an essentially European (Latin) pattern, established here in the sixteenth century, may be gradually mutating into something closer to the American model. These paragraphs pay particular attention to a more special-ized application of RCT; they are concerned with the choices open to the Catholic Church (rather than to the religious believer) in two very dif-ferent Latin American countries, as church leaders devise policies which aim to retain or recapture the loyalties of the mass of the population – itself seduced by religious as well as secular alternatives. The exponen-tial growth of Pentecostalism in this part of the world becomes a crucial factor in the somewhat delicate equations that surround these attempts to make policy.

The third theoretical chapter (Chapter 5) scrutinizes the concept of modernity and its application to the understanding of religion. This is done in two ways. The first section draws from the concluding chapter of my own *Religion in Britain since 1945* (Davie, 1994), which devel-oped in some detail the shifts from pre-modern, through modern, to postmodern, explaining how each of these approaches offers different opportunities and/or difficulties for religion. The material is approached first in terms of the structural opportunities and constraints; the cultural equivalents follow. The later sections of the chapter draw from a book published almost a decade later, *Europe: the Exceptional Case* (Davie, 2002a), in which the concept of 'multiple modernities' provides the theo-retical frame. Here the emphasis lies on the very different natures of modernity in different parts of the world. The key theorist in this respect is Shmuel Eisenstadt from the Hebrew University in Jerusalem. The period between the two books (1994–2002) has seen a transformation in the religious agenda. No longer is the necessarily secular and Western nature of modernity, in the singular, so readily assumed: modernities are multiple and only some of these, the minority in fact, embody the notion of secularization.

Chapter 6 on methodology completes the first half of the book. The emphasis here lies on diversity. There are many ways to collect socio-logical data, the great majority of which are complementary. The chap-ter acknowledges the difference between quantitative and qualitative methods but indicates how they can be brought together to build a more complete picture. It is important to grasp from the outset what a par-ticular way of working is likely to produce in the way of data and what it is unreasonable to expect. Large-scale surveys of the population, for example, will yield little material about minorities apart from their existence. In order to investigate the minority in more detail, it will be necessary to effect a rather different kind of enquiry, frequently combining

*13*

a more focused survey with qualitative methodology. The increasing range of possibilities in terms of qualitative work forms an important part of this discussion.

The chapter ends with a short note on cognate disciplines, bringing together a number of ideas already introduced, not least the need to explain as well as establish sociological data. Different disciplines contribute different insights in this respect. Within this broadly interdisciplinary framework, the tension between theological and social scientific approaches to religious life is developed in some detail, given the controversial nature of some recent exchanges in this field.

## part II

The second half of the book concentrates on a number of substantive themes. Selecting and prioritizing these has not been easy, the more so given the evident mismatch between the realities of the modern world and the nature of the sociological agenda. Which of these should dictate the subject matter and what exactly should be included? The following choices require some explanation. They are restricted, first of all, to post-war debates, noting that many of these necessarily reflect earlier concerns. Bearing this in mind, the selected topics should be viewed as points of entry into a complex agenda. Their presentation is chronological, broadly speaking, taking as a guideline the order in which the issues concerned became significant in sociological debate.

This is not meant to imply that one debate stops and another begins as the decades pass – the issues run concurrently as the agenda gradually gathers steam. They also overlap. What is mainstream in one context may not be so in another; 'Western' positions are reversed in many parts of the world. Fashions, moreover, come and go – certain issues lie dormant for a bit before reviving, sometimes in new forms. They also move about. The debate about new religious movements provides an excellent illustration of the latter. It first emerges in the 1960s within the relative pluralism of the Anglo-Saxon world; its recent impact, in contrast, is most noticeable in France and in the former communist countries. The agenda has altered accordingly and will be examined from several points of view. If there is an underlying thread to the chapters as a whole, it lies in the gradual, if somewhat belated, escape from the preoccupations of the West to a more global perspective; the demands on the practitioner are correspondingly increased.

In the immediate post-war period, both European and American scholars were primarily concerned with what, for them, were mainstream churches, but for different reasons (Chapter 7). Europeans (and notably the French) were aware of decline, whereas Americans were trying to account not only for the diversity of their religious institutions but also for their continuing vitality. In Europe, moreover, there is a certain nostalgia about this period – it embodied in many places (and notably in Britain) an attempt to reconstruct the patterns of pre-war life and the place of the churches within this. Such nostalgia came to an abrupt end in the 1960s, a decade that turned almost everything (institutional and cultural) on its head, including the churches. It is at this point, moreover, that the mainstream churches of Europe begin to haemorrhage at a truly alarming rate, particularly in the North. The degree to which the Catholic churches of Latin Europe were likely to follow suit, and when, became an important topic of discussion. Hence all over the continent, a renewed and justifiable preoccupation with secularization.

American sociologists were undoubtedly influenced by these ideas, not least a taken-for-granted incompatibility between religion and urbanization. Cox (1968), for example, in an influential text simply assumes the secularity of the modern city. Bit by bit, however, the American data assert themselves: the statistics of church attendance were not falling in the same way that they were in Europe and the phenomenon of the New Christian Right (conspicuous by its absence in Europe) was beginning to make an impact on political life. In terms of institutional church life, the gap between the United States and Europe was, if anything, getting wider. It is at this point that we rejoin the theoretical debate, as rational choice theory gradually, and entirely understandably, replaces secularization as the dominant paradigm in the United States. In recent decades, it has been supported by key studies on American voluntarism such as Ammerman (1997, 2005) or Livezey (2000).

Turn of the twenty-first century work in Europe reveals a complex picture. A series of large-scale empirical studies[5] yielded useful comparative data on the place of religion, including the historic churches, in European societies. On the one hand, these data affirm the decline of the mainstream; on the other, they reveal *both* the relative tenacity of certain forms of religious activity *and* the gradual emergence of new forms of religious belonging. The pattern is changing: European populations are beginning to opt in rather than out of their churches – a shift which introduces noticeably different attitudes and approaches. Membership is increasingly chosen; it is no longer assumed or ascribed. The comparisons with the United States are important in this respect: is Europe becoming more like America in its religious life, or is this an authentic and distinctively European mutation?

We need, however, to return to the 1960s and to appreciate the change that the associated upheaval brought to the sociological agenda. It was at this point that the interest in alternative forms of religion began to assert itself, a tendency that came almost to dominate the sub-discipline. Its implications for the sociology of religion are discussed in Chapter 8. There are those, for example, who see in the study of new religions a tendency to marginalization (i.e. self-marginalization) taken to an extreme. There are others who discover in new religious movements the potential for new connections with the sociological mainstream – through, for instance, the work on new social movements of which religious movements are but one example. Whatever the position taken one point is abundantly clear: the amount of work on new religious movements is disproportionate to the numbers involved in the movements themselves, which for the most part remain very small.

Why then has the debate provoked so much interest, and in public as well as sociological life? One reason for this lies in the issues raised by new forms of religious life – not least the question of religious liberty. Beckford (1985) is entirely correct to indicate that new religious movements act as 'barometers' of more general social change. We learn as much about ourselves as about the religious movements as such as we examine their position in society. The essential question is straightforward enough: which forms of religion are acceptable and which are not? And in which societies in particular? The latter point becomes central to the whole debate: not all societies (even within Western Europe) react in the same way. Why not? The discussion concludes with a detailed examination of the French case, drawing largely on the work of Hervieu-Léger (2001a). Her study is seminal: it reveals the essence of Frenchness just as much as it informs the reader about the sects (the French prefer this term) that exist in France and the difficulties that they face.

The later sections of this chapter indicate a step change. They are concerned with the growing presence of other faith communities in Europe, revealing an obvious possibility for convergence with mainstream sociology. Debates about race, ethnicity and racism have been prominent in sociological discourse, but have failed very frequently to take the religious factor into account. The situation is changing, however – a shift brought about by the transformations in the global context already described. Ignoring either the presence of religion in the modern world or its penetrations into Western societies is becoming increasingly difficult to do. In the 1990s critically important debates concerning both took place in Britain and France: in Britain, the Rushdie controversy raised crucial issues for the understanding of modern forms of religion;

in France the *affaire du foulard* provided the catalyst. In the new millennium, the Dutch, Danish, Swiss and Swedish cases have moved centre stage; equally important and rather more alarming is the question of religious terrorism.

None of these cases can be separated from what is happening worldwide. Once again 1979 turns out to be a key date, as much for the sociology of religion as for the transformation in world politics. It is at this point, moreover, that the study of fundamentalism (or more accurately fundamentalisms) begins to gather momentum (Chapter 9). In some respects, such initiatives mark a step forward for the sociological agenda: no longer are the religious forms under review those of the West (at least not exclusively). But in others, they are almost a step back: the study of religion in the modern world becomes essentially the study of something negative – fundamentalism is seen primarily as an anti-modern reaction. The basic incompatibility between being religious and being modern is still very largely assumed.

An immense amount of work was done in the field, however, epitomized in the Fundamentalism Project centred in the University of Chicago. It is impossible to ignore the five enormous volumes emanating from this enterprise, if only to take issue with some (by no means all) of the findings. The genesis and content of the project will be described in some detail. Equally interesting, however, are the gradual shifts in perspective, as it becomes clear that fundamentalisms are as much an expression *of* modernity as they are a reaction *to* this. For the second time, the work of Eisenstadt (1999) will be central to the argument. For Eisenstadt, fundamentalist movements are not eruptions of traditional or pre-modern forces; they constitute distinctive, modern, political movements – a type, moreover, with strong Jacobin tendencies. The content of their ideologies may be anti-modern, or more specifically anti-enlightenment, but the manner and means through which they are constructed are quintessentially modern. A range of empirical examples will illustrate the point.

Similar questions will be engaged in Chapter 10 on globalization, a discussion which deals both with the theoretical dimensions of the debate and the place of religion within these. Markedly different perspectives immediately become clear. A great deal depends, in fact, on how globalization itself is conceptualized. Is this a powerful, unstoppable, economic force, sweeping everything – including religion – before it? Or is it something far more complex embodying all kinds of economic and social movements some of which go with the economic flows and some of which resist them? If the latter view is taken religion becomes inseparable from it and can be found on both sides of the equation. Religion, for example, is intimately linked with transnational migrations (the movement of labour), new social

**17**

movements (transnational NGOs), new understandings of gender and the struggles for economic justice, all of which are part and parcel of the globalization process. Religion, however, can also act as a resistor, providing fresh understandings of identity – whether national, ethnic, gendered, generational or simply religious – for those who feel threatened by the pace of global change.

The chapter includes a wide variety of illustrations, both Christian and other, using as its take-off point the undeniably global reaction to the death of John Paul II. More generally this discussion is concerned with the very marked shifts that are taking place in historic forms of Christianity, taking the Catholic Church and the Anglican Communion as examples. In terms of membership the weight of both these churches now lies in the Southern hemisphere, a fact with considerable importance for the religious agendas that will be pursued in the twenty-first century. The numbers moreover are huge, dwarfing the constituencies 'back home'. A parallel illustration can be found in Pentecostalism, the form of Christianity which is growing fastest in the modern world. So far this too is a religion of the global South, growing exponentially in Latin America in the 1960s, spreading to Africa a decade or so later, and by the 1990s to the Pacific Rim. The potential for expansion in the last of these, not least in China, is immense.

The discussion ends with two studies of Islam (Turkey and Indonesia), chosen specifically to balance the more conservative (fundamentalist) illustrations found in the previous chapter. They concentrate on the possibility that there might be an authentic Muslim modernity – or indeed more than one; in other words, on forms of Islam that fit relatively easily into the modern world but which remain distinct from their Western counterparts. The resonance with the idea of *multiple* modernities is immediately clear.

Chapter 11 is rather different. It takes up a number of themes not so far engaged, many of which resonate with the preoccupations of anthropology rather than sociology. Such topics include the manifest differences between men and women, the continuing importance of religion to the life-cycle, and the increasing overlap between religion and health (encapsulated in the idea of well-being). The last of these is interesting in many ways. Theoretically it challenges even the dimension of the secularization thesis which is easiest to accept (see p. 3) – that of institutional separation. Whilst it is clear that healthcare in the modern West is primarily the responsibility of the state, the emergence of alternative forms of medicine have begun to erode this autonomy. The evolution of childbirth from pre-modern, through modern (a highly medicalized model) to postmodern (a reaction to excessive medicalization) exemplifies this process perfectly. The space for religion, or in this case spirituality, shifts accordingly.

Recent work on death and dying has become almost a sub-discipline in its own right. After decades of silence, comparable to the Victorian distaste for talking about sex, both society and sociologists have become increasingly preoccupied with the greatest mystery of all: what happens to us when we die? The work of Walter (1990, 1994, 1995) has been seminal in this area, describing the evolution in death and death practices from traditional, through modern to neo-modern societies. Beneath his analysis, however, lies a powerful sub-text: both the dying and the grieving individual must be considered as a person, not simply a bundle of symptoms or sorrows. The argument is driven to a provocative conclusion, challenging yet again both the institutional arrangements of modern societies and the theoretical assumptions that go with these. Increasing specialization is obliged to give way as 'holy' and 'whole' reacquire their common root. The set-apart, or the sacred, becomes integral to the well-being of both individual and collective life. Religion is rediscovered at the turning points of life.

The concluding chapter (Chapter 12) returns to a theme set out at the outset: namely the noticeably imperfect relationship between the debates of the sub-discipline and the realities of the modern world. A central question emerges in these discussions: who precisely sets the agenda, and for whom? And, more searchingly, is the sub-discipline of the sociology of religion adequately prepared for the tasks that will confront it in the twenty-first century? If not, how is it possible to 'do better'? The changing nature of sociology as well as the sociology of religion itself will be central to this crucially important discussion.

**19**

## A NOTE ON DEFINITIONS

It is customary to begin a textbook in the sociology of religion with a chapter, or at least a section of a chapter, on definitions of religion and the debate that ensues from the difficulties in this area. Excellent accounts of these issues exist in a number of places and need not be repeated here.[6] The following paragraphs aim simply to make one or two essential points – essential, that is, for the arguments that follow.

There are two ways of defining religion in terms of its relationship to society. The first is *substantive*: it is concerned with what religion *is*. Religion involves beliefs and practices which assume the existence of supernatural beings. The second approach is *functional*: it is concerned with what religion *does* and how it affects the society of which it is part.

For example, religion offers solutions to otherwise unanswerable questions (what happens when we die?), or religion binds people together in distinctive forms of collective action. The tension between the two types of definition has existed from the first days of sociology. Max Weber worked from a substantive point of view; Emile Durkheim developed a functionalist perspective.

Each standpoint has advantages and disadvantages. Substantive definitions limit the field to beliefs or activities which involve supernatural entities or beings. Such a limitation is helpful in that the boundaries are easier to discern, but even a preliminary survey will reveal the amazing diversity of forms that the supernatural can take in human society. More particularly, non-Western forms of the supernatural often sit uneasily within frames of reference which derive from Western culture. These are practical difficulties. The sharpest critique of substantive definitions comes, however, from those sociologists who maintain that the presence of the supernatural (however described) should not be the defining feature of religion. Such an emphasis is likely to exclude a whole range of activities or behaviour which – to the participants at least – take on the character of 'sacred' even if the supernatural as such is not involved. Any ideology, for instance, which addresses the ultimate problems of existence could be thought of as a religion, whether or not it makes reference to the supernatural. Ecological or green movements provide topical examples at the start of the twenty-first century. Also included are certain forms of nationalism which undoubtedly provide collective frames of meaning and powerful inspiration for the populations involved, even if the goals remain firmly of this world rather than the next.

Where, though, can the line be drawn once the need for a supernatural element within the definition of religion has been discarded? This is the crucial problem with functional definitions and it remains for the most part unresolved. Once the gold standard, in the form of the supernatural, has been abandoned, it is very difficult to draw any precise or undisputed boundary about what should or should not be included in the sociological study of religion.

There have been various attempts to square the circle and to synthesize the two types of definition. Hervieu-Léger (2000) offers one of these; it solves some problems but undoubtedly creates others (Davie, 2000a: 31). Much more penetrating in this respect is Hervieu-Léger's more recent work on sects in France, where she demonstrates how the definition of 'religion' as a concept colours the whole understanding of the question. Herein lies the clue to the French problem: both the Catholic Church and its alter ego, the secular state, have immense difficulty comprehending forms of religion which do not correspond with the French understanding of the term. Paradoxically the Catholic model of religion is exerting itself strongly in one of the most secular societies of the world. It is this, moreover, that goes to the heart of the matter. It is possible to talk ad infinitum about the nature/definitions of religion and the pros and cons of different approaches without once engaging reality. We need, though, to be sharply aware of the tools and concepts that we are using (including definitions) and the baggage that they carry. Only then can effective debate begin. In bringing this essentially constructivist argument to our attention, Beckford (2003) offers an excellent starting point for this book as well as for his own.

## NOTES

1 The findings of this working party can be found in De Santa Ana (2005); see also the discussion of the World Council of Churches in Chapter 10.

2 The similarity between religious and secular behaviour can be seen in other ways as well. In the Nordic countries, for example, nominal membership remains high in both the churches and the trade unions. In Britain both have fallen. Putnam (1995, 2000) deals with the American case. See Chapter 5 for a fuller discussion of these questions.

3 The work and publications of the International Study of Religion in Central and Eastern Europe Association (ISORECEA) are important in this respect. See www.isorecea.net for more information (accessed 3 April 2012).

4 See in this context the special issue of *Social Compass* on 'Religions in contemporary China' (50/4, 2003) and Yang (2005, 2011).

5 These studies, notably the European Values Surveys, will be discussed in Chapter 6.

6 One of the best of these expositions can be found in Blasi (1998).

# *Part I*

Theoretical perspectives

# *two*

# common sources/different pathways

The following discussion is as much about the sociology of knowledge as it is about the sociology of religion. It is concerned with the early developments of the sub-discipline and the ways in which this has evolved in different parts of the world and in different academic communities. It is divided into three sections. The first deals with the founding fathers, notably Karl Marx, Max Weber, Emile Durkheim and (more briefly) Georg Simmel. Certain points need firm underlining if the work of these pioneers is to be properly understood, not least the association between the early development of sociology and the European context from which it emerged. It is the same factor, moreover (or rather its absence), that accounts for the very different directions that the sociology of religion has taken in other parts of the world and in different academic environments.

The second section will outline these contrasting trajectories in more detail, notably those discovered in Europe (itself diverse) and in the United States. In accordance with the dominant theme of this book, both sections will pay particular attention to the complex relationships that exist between the different ways of being religious, the various theoretical perspectives that emerge to explain what is happening, and the markedly different topics that dominate the agenda as a result. The geographically contingent nature of the material will form a crucial thread in the argument; so too will linguistic influences. It follows that the generalization of any such approaches to other parts of the world cannot simply be assumed, a point that will resonate repeatedly.

The third section closes the loop. It does so by interrogating the relevance of the founding fathers at the start of the twenty-first as opposed to the twentieth century. To what extent do the frames of reference set out at the onset of industrialization in Europe help us to understand the transformations in religious life taking place almost 100 years later? The question will be posed first in general terms. The argument is continued with reference to selected texts that work within the themes laid out by the founding fathers, but using these in innovative ways to understand the realities of late as opposed to early modernity.

## THE FOUNDING FATHERS

The beginnings of sociology are firmly rooted in the transformations of European society as the constituent nations of the continent embarked, each in its own way, on the industrialization process. Marx, Weber, Durkheim and Simmel were participant observers of this massive upheaval, sharing a common aim: to comprehend more fully the processes that were taking place, and to establish a discipline that could enhance this understanding. What was happening? Why was it happening in some places rather than others? And what were the likely consequences for different groups of people? All four concluded that the religious factor was a central feature at every level of this process – in terms, that is, of the changes taking place, the reasons for these transformations and their implications for human living.

It is important to remember that Karl Marx (1818–1883) predates the others by at least a generation. There are two essential elements in the Marxist perspective on religion: the first is descriptive, the second evaluative. Marx conceptualized religion as a dependent variable; in other words, its form and nature are dependent on social and above all economic relations, which constitute the bedrock of social analysis. Nothing can be understood apart from the economic order and the relationship of the capitalist/worker to the means of production. The second aspect follows from this but contains an important evaluative element. Religion is a form of alienation; it is a symptom of social malformation which disguises the exploitative relationships of capitalist society. Religion persuades people that such relationships are natural and, therefore, acceptable. It follows that the real causes of social distress cannot be tackled until the religious element in society is stripped away to reveal the injustices of the capitalist system; everything else is a distraction. Both ideas are brought together in one of the most famous quotations of the sociological literature:

> Religious distress is at the same time the expression of real distress and also the protest against real distress. Religion is the sigh of the oppressed creature, the heart of the heartless world, just as it is the spirit of a spiritless condition. It is the opium of the people.
>
> To abolish religion as the illusory happiness of the people is to demand their real happiness. The demand to give up illusions about the existing state of affairs is the demand to give up a state of affairs which needs illusions. The criticism of religion is therefore in embryo the criticism of the vale of tears, the halo of which is religion. (Marx and Engels, 1975: 38)

Subsequent debates concerning Marx's approach to religion have, however, to be approached with care. It has become increasingly difficult to distinguish between (a) Marx's own analysis of religious phenomena, (b) a subsequent school of Marxism as a form of sociological thinking and (c) what has occurred in the twentieth century in the name of Marxism as a political ideology. The essential and enduring point to grasp from Marx himself is that religion cannot be understood apart from the world of which it is part; this is a crucial sociological insight and central to the evolution of the sub-discipline. It needs, however, to be distinguished from an over-deterministic interpretation of Marx which postulates the dependence of religion on economic forces in mechanical terms. This is unhelpful. An additional point is more political: it may indeed be the case that one function of religion is to mitigate the very evident hardships of this world and so disguise them. Marx was correct to point this out. Nowhere, however, does Marx legitimate the destructive doctrines of those Marxist regimes which maintained that the only way to reveal the true injustices of society was to destroy – sometimes with hideous consequences – the religious element of society. Marx himself took a longer-term view, claiming that religion would disappear of its own accord given the advent of the classless society: quite simply it would no longer be necessary. The inevitable confusions between Marx, Marxism and Marxist regimes have, however, had a profound effect on the reception of Marx's ideas in the twentieth century. The total, dramatic and unforeseen collapse of Marxism as an effective political creed in 1989 is but the latest twist in a considerably longer tale.

A significant breakthrough in Marxist thinking about religion can be found in the work of Antonio Gramsci (1891–1937), a founder of the Italian Communist Party, who died in prison under the fascist regime in Italy. Gramsci gives far more weight than earlier Marxists to the autonomous nature of the superstructure (i.e. the world of ideologies, culture, religion and politics) affirming its capacities to exert influence independently of economic forces. More precisely, the concept of 'hegemony' is central to Gramsci's thinking, by which he means the process through which a dominant class, or elite, strives to maintain their hold on political life, by exploiting public opinion or the popular consensus. The process is so total that the status quo is considered 'normal' – it is beyond question.

Religion, however, can be used to attack as well as to affirm the dominant world view. Disaffected religious groups become critical of the dominant elite in the name of new ideas and new theologies. Or to use Gramsci's own terminology, organic (as opposed to traditional) intellectuals can assist an oppressed group in awakening a revolutionary consciousness. One example of this way of thinking can be seen in the Christian–Marxist dialogue, which became an important conversation for significant groups of post-war intellectuals.[1] Liberation theologians exemplified this trend. The factors that encouraged such exchanges were, however, symptomatic of a particular period. Bit by bit, the atmosphere changed again: on the one hand, Catholic authorities became increasingly opposed to communism; on the other, Marxism was rapidly losing its credibility. Each of these shifts has encouraged the other to produce very different formulations, notably in Latin America (see Chapter 10).

Max Weber's (1864–1920) contribution to the sociology of religion is in many respects part of the same debate: Weberian formulae have prospered as Marxist ideas become more problematic. The similarities between Marx and Weber are, however, as important as the differences. More precisely, Weber's theorizing about the place of religion in human society vindicates much of what Marx himself suggested, as opposed to the vulgarizations of later Marxists (those who insisted on a somewhat simplistic economic determinism). Above all, Weber stresses the multi-causality of social phenomena, including religion; in so doing he conclusively refutes the standpoint of what he calls 'reflective materialism' whereby the religious dimensions of social living simply reflect the material (Giddens, 1971: 211). The causal sequence is not, however, simply reversed. Indeed the emergence of what Weber calls 'elective affinities' between material and religious interests are entirely compatible with Marx's own understanding of ideology. The connections between particular ways of thinking (including religious ones) and the material interests of particular groups of people are not random: they are mutually reinforcing and mutually advantageous.

Weber's influence spread into every corner of sociology, including the sociology of religion, generating a huge secondary literature – the remarks that follow are inevitably skeletal. Absolutely central to Weber's understanding of religion is the conviction that this aspect of human living can be constituted as something other than, or separate from, society or 'the world'. Three points follow from this. First, the relationship between religion and the world is contingent and variable; how a particular religion relates to the surrounding context will vary over time and in different places. Second, this relationship can only be examined in its historical and cultural specificity. Documenting the details of these relationships (of which elective affinities are but one example) becomes, therefore, the central and very demanding task of the sociologist of religion. Third, the relationship between the two spheres, religion and society, is being steadily eroded in modern societies. This erosion, to the point where the religious factor ceases to be an effective force, lies at the heart of the process known as secularization – through which the world becomes progressively 'disenchanted'. The latter point quite clearly reflects Weber's own, and essentially European, experience of the modernization process.

These three assumptions underpin Weber's magnum opus in the field, *The Sociology of Religion* (1963): that is, his comparative study of the major world faiths and their impact on everyday behaviour in different parts of the world. It is at this point, moreover, that the question of definition outlined at the end of the previous chapter begins to resonate, for it is clear that, de facto at least, Weber is working with a substantive definition of religion, despite his well-known unwillingness to provide a definition as such (Weber, 1963: 1). He is concerned with the ways in which the *content* (or substance) of a particular religion, or more precisely religious ethic, influence the ways in which people behave, both individually and collectively. In other words, different types of belief have different outcomes. Weber goes on to elaborate this theme: the relationship between ethic and behaviour not only exists, it is socially patterned and contextually varied. Central to Max Weber's understanding in this respect is the complex relationship between a set of religious beliefs and the particular social stratum which becomes the principal carrier of such beliefs in any given society, the elective affinities already referred to. The sociologist's task is to identify the crucial social stratum and the ethic that they choose to adopt at the key moments in history; it requires careful comparative analysis.

Weber's celebrated work on the Protestant ethic should be seen in this light. It is but one example of a more general theme – one, however, which has become seminal to the sociology of religion. The case study became known in the English-speaking world largely through the translation of Talcott Parsons (published in 1930), since when it has generated a seemingly endless debate both within and beyond the sociology of religion (Swatos et al., 1998). Bearing such controversies in mind, it is important to appreciate what the Protestant ethic thesis does and doesn't say. It does *not* argue that Protestantism (or more precisely Calvinism) in itself caused modern capitalism to develop; it does suggest that certain types of action, themselves the result of deeply held religious beliefs, were a crucial part of a complex causal process that resulted in the emergence of new forms of economic life in early modern Europe which were to transform, in the fullness of time, the global economy. The *principle* embedded in the Protestant ethic thesis is even more important than the content: that is, the possibility that any system of religious belief can, in theory, engender forms of action that have an important impact in everyday life, including the economic sphere. Whether they do or not has to be determined empirically.

Emile Durkheim (1858–1917), the exact contemporary of Weber, began from a very different position. Working outwards from his study of totemic religion among Australian Aborigines, he became convinced above all of the binding qualities of religion, through which people form societies. In other words, his perspective is a functional one. Durkheim is concerned with what religion does; it binds people together. What then will happen when time-honoured forms of society begin to mutate so fast that traditional patterns of religion inevitably collapse? How will the essential functions of religion be fulfilled? This was the situation confronting France in the early part of the twentieth century – as a supporter of the Third Republic Durkheim was looking for a coherent moral base for the new, essentially secular, regime in the difficult conditions of the First World War. Hence the significance of his work in public (educational) as well as sociological debate.

Durkheim responded to his own question as follows: the religious aspects of society should be allowed to evolve alongside everything else, in order that the symbols of solidarity appropriate to the developing social order (in this case incipient industrial society and a secular state) may emerge.[2] The theoretical position follows from this: religion as such will always be present for it performs a necessary *function*. The precise nature of that religion will, however, differ between one society and another and between different periods of time in order to achieve an appropriate 'fit' between religion and the prevailing social order. The systemic model, so dear to functionalists, is immediately apparent.

Of the early sociologists, Durkheim was the only one to provide his own definition of religion. It has two elements: '[A] religion is a unified system of beliefs and practices relative to sacred things, that is to say, things which are set apart and forbidden – beliefs and practices which unite into one single moral community called a Church, all those who adhere to them' (Durkheim, 1976: 47). On the one hand, there is the celebrated distinction between the sacred (the set-apart) and the profane (everything else); there is an element of substantive definition at this point. On the other the sacred enjoys a *functional* quality not possessed by the profane; by its very nature it has the capacity to bind, for it unites the collectivity in a set of beliefs and practices which are centred

30

on the sacred object. Acting collectively in a moral community, following Durkheim, is of greater sociological importance than the object of such actions. The uncompromisingly 'social' aspects of Durkheim's thinking are both an advantage and disadvantage. The focus is clearly distinguishable from the psychological (a good thing), but the repeated emphasis on society as a reality *sui generis* brings with it the risk of a different sort of reductionism – taken to its logical conclusion religion is nothing more than the symbolic expression of social experience. Such a conclusion disturbed many of Durkheim's contemporaries; it is still to some extent problematic, and for sociologists as well as theologians.

Less attention has been paid to Georg Simmel's (1858–1918) work on religion until relatively recently. There were good reasons, however, for a revival in interest towards the end of the twentieth century, given that Simmel's approach encapsulates the ambiguities both of modernity itself and of the place of religion within this. At one and the same time, he is concerned with the permanence and the fluidity of religious life. The dialectical distinctions between content and form (religiosity and religion), between individual and group, between self and other, and between reason and emotions are central to this analysis. Simmel argues that religion as such emerges through the structuration of the underlying spiritual aspirations of individuals; religiosity and the state of mind that it refers to precede the institutional forms that are associated with religion.

It follows that modern people are not necessarily less religious than their forebears, but differently so as the forms of religion mutate together with the society of which they are part. Changes in religious forms are part and parcel of the shifts taking place in modern societies as life becomes increasingly segmentalized. Specifically religious concerns are differentiated from other aspects of life and become more and more individualized; no longer are they determined by kinship or neighbourhood ties. Whether these changes free or enslave the individual becomes a central theme in Simmel's work: at one level the individual escapes the stultifying restriction of the pre-modern community, including its religious forms; at another this very freedom leads to a world of objects that by their very nature constrain and dominate both needs and desires. Much of Simmel's sociology is concerned with these dilemmas, which become most acute in urban life – hence his preoccupation with the city. It is here that 'objective' culture is most likely to acquire a life of its own and to dominate or alienate the subjective spirit. Half optimistic and half pessimistic about what he saw, Simmel's prescience about the ambiguities of urban living and the place of religion within this anticipates very accurately the debates of late modernity.

*31*

## a note on translation

It is already clear that the evolution of the sociology of religion cannot be understood without extensive knowledge of the founding fathers and an appreciation of their continuing influence (see below). The availability of their writing should not, however, be taken for granted; it depended on competent translations. A good and very positive example can be found in Talcott Parsons's role in introducing Weber to the English-speaking world. An effective précis of this story can be found in Swatos et al. (1998) – an analysis that explores the relationship between translations of Weber and their reception in a primarily American context, an environment in which the religious actor has always been given a central role. Hence not only the appeal of Weber's sociological thinking but the increasing availability of his work, or to be more accurate parts of his work, at a relatively early stage in the development of the sub-discipline.[3]

Willaime (1999, 2004) and Hervieu-Léger and Willaime (2001) tell a very different story – this time underlining the relatively slow and at times painful reception of Weber by French sociologists, including those interested in religion. The lack of available translations until the late 1950s was, moreover, a symptom of something more profound: a visible incompatibility between Weber's ways of working and the preoccupations of French sociologists, a question that can be approached from several points of view – philosophical, political, academic, methodological and religious (Hervieu-Léger and Willaime, 2001: 64; Willaime, 2004). In short, what Weber proposed did not fit well in the intellectual climate of France, a milieu preoccupied by the opposition between religion (Catholicism) and modernity (the secular state) – the framework for Durkheim's sociological thinking. Weber, in contrast, was primarily concerned with the influence of a religious ethos on the habits and actions of individuals (religious actors). In the end it was the French sociologists interested in religious minorities, including Protestantism, who made greatest use of the Weberian perspective, not those working in the mainstream (Séguy, 1972).

It follows that a careful mapping of the dates of translations of key texts between German, French and English would reveal interesting combinations of theoretical resource in different European societies, as indeed in the United States. What was available to whom in the development of sociological thinking is not something that should be taken for granted; it could and should be subject to empirical investigation. Such studies are crucial to our understanding of the sociology of religion as a sub-discipline and become in themselves a significant element in the sociology of knowledge. The point is already important in connection with the classics; it is even more the case with respect to later developments.

## SUBSEQUENT DEVELOPMENTS: OLD WORLD AND NEW

Whatever their differences, Marx, Weber, Durkheim and Simmel were all aware of the importance of religion to the functioning of human societies and paid careful attention to this factor in their different analyses. Such commitment cannot, however, simply be assumed – by no means all of the subsequent generation shared this interest or recognized the importance of religion to sociological thinking. Indeed almost half a century passed before a second wave of activity took place. It came, moreover, from a very different quarter – from within the churches themselves. A second point is immediately apparent: the churches were in a very different position on each side of the Atlantic, leading to very different preoccupations for American scholars on the one hand and for Europeans on the other.

### American developments

In the United States, for example, where religious institutions remained relatively buoyant and where religious practice continued to grow, sociologists of religion in the early twentieth century were both motivated by and concerned with the social gospel. A second, less positive theme ran parallel – one in which religion became increasingly associated with the social divisions of American society. *The Social Sources of Denominationalism* (Niebuhr, 1929) and rather later *Social Class in American Protestantism* (Demerath, 1965) are titles that represent this trend. Demerath, a second-generation sociologist in the United States, was one of the first to use survey research in the understanding of religion in order to establish the social correlates of religious activity.

By the 1950s and 1960s, however, the principal focus of American sociology lay in the normative functionalism of Talcott Parsons, who stressed above everything the integrative role of religion. Religion, a functional prerequisite, was central to the complex models of social systems and social action elaborated by Parsons. In bringing together these two elements (i.e. social systems and social action), Parsons is drawing on both Durkheim and Weber. Or, as Lechner puts this, 'Durkheim came to provide the analytical tools for Parsons's ambivalent struggle with Weber' (1998: 353). Ambivalent this struggle may have been, but Parsons's influence was lasting; it can be seen in subsequent generations of scholars, notably Robert Bellah (in America) and Niklaus Luhmann (in Germany). The relationship with American society is particularly important. The functionalism of Parsons emerged from a social order entirely different from either the turbulence of rapid modernization that motivated the founding fathers or the long-term confrontations between church and state in the Catholic nations of Europe, most notably in France; post-war America symbolized a relatively settled period of industrialism in which consensus appeared not only desirable but possible. The assumption that the social order should be underpinned by religious values was widespread and to a large extent convincing.

Such optimism did not last. As the 1960s gave way to a far less confident decade, the sociology of religion shifted once again – this time to the social construction of meaning systems epitomized by the work of Berger and Luckmann. The Parsonian model is inverted; social order exists but it is constructed from below. So constructed, religion offers believers crucial explanations and meanings which they use to make sense of their lives, especially during times of personal or social crisis. Hence the idea of religion as a form of 'sacred canopy' that shields both individual and society from 'the ultimately destructive consequences of a seemingly chaotic, purposeless existence' (Karlenzig, 1998: 52). The mood of the later 1970s, profoundly shaken by the oil crisis and its effects on economic growth, reflects this need for meaning or purpose – no longer could these simply be assumed. The 1970s merged, moreover, into the modern period, a world in which conflict, including religious conflict, rather than consensus dominates the agenda. Religion has not only become increasingly prominent but increasingly contentious, both within societies and between them. Models that assumed a religious consensus, one that could be handed on intact from one generation to the next, are less and less able to resonate.

Berger's contribution to the debate on secularization and his subsequent change of mind will be considered in more detail in the following chapters. One point, however, requires immediate attention, namely the assumed connections between pluralization and secularization. Berger, like many others, maintained in his early work that the two ideas were mutually reinforcing. An increase in religious choice necessarily undermined the taken-for-grantedness of religion. It followed that an increase in religious pluralism would lead to greater secularization – to the extent that the protective canopy became both less sacred (i.e. less able to protect either individuals or societies from the threat of chaos or societal disintegration) and less able to discipline the beliefs and behaviour of individuals (hence a tendency to look elsewhere, itself a stimulus to pluralism). A downward spiral was inevitable. This assumption and its later critique have become a touchstone in the evolution of the sub-discipline – the argument will form a central theme in the theoretical sections of this book.

One point, however, remains clear: compared with most Europeans, Americans not only enjoy almost limitless choice but remain active in their religious lives. Just how active is not always easy to say and reflects important methodological issues (see Chapters 5 and 7), but in the modern United States the notion that pluralism necessarily generates religious decline becomes increasingly difficult to sustain. Quite simply, it hasn't happened.

## European assumptions

Unsurprisingly, the assumptions of European sociologists of religion are radically different. So too the point of departure, which can be found in the titles published in France in the early years of the war. The most celebrated of these, *La France, Pays de Mission* (Godin and Daniel, 1943), illustrates the mood of a growing group within French Catholicism who were increasingly worried by the weakening position of the Catholic Church in French society. Anxiety proved, however, a powerful motivator. In order that the situation might be remedied, accurate information was essential; hence a whole series of enquiries under the direction of Gabriel Le Bras with the intention of discovering what exactly characterized the religion of the people, or lived religion (*la religion vécue*) as it became known.

The importance of Le Bras's work is recognized by Hervieu-Léger and Willaime (2001), though even for these authors his inclusion among the sociological 'classics' requires some justification. This they find in his threefold contribution: his meticulous enumeration and mapping of Catholicism in France, his institutionalization and encouragement of the sociology of religion; and the historical dimensions of his work. The energy devoted to the gathering of accurate information acquired, however, a momentum of its own, which led to certain tensions. There were those, in France and elsewhere, whose work remained motivated by pastoral concern; there were others who felt that knowledge was valuable for its own sake and resented the ties to the Catholic Church. What emerged in due course was an independent section within the Centre National de la Recherche Scientifique (CNRS), the Groupe de Sociologie *des Religions*. The change in title was significant: 'religious sociology' became 'the sociology of religions' in the plural. There was, however, continuity as well as change. The initial enthusiasm for mapping, for example, which began with Boulard and Le Bras on rural Catholicism (see, for example, Boulard, 1945), and continued through the work of Boulard and Rémy on urban France (1968), culminated in the magnificent *Atlas de la pratique religieuse des catholiques en France* (Isambert, 1980). Alongside such cartographical successes developed explanations for the geographical differences which emerged. These explanations were primarily historical, their sources lying deep within regional cultures. There was nothing superficial about this analysis which could, quite clearly, be applied to religions other than Catholicism.

Willaime (1995: 37–57, 1999), Voyé and Billiet (1999) and Hervieu-Léger and Willaime (2001) tell this primarily French (or more accurately francophone) story in more detail: that is, the emergence of accurate and careful documentation motivated primarily by pastoral concerns; the establishment of the Groupe de Sociologie des Religions in Paris in 1954; the gradual extension of the subject matter beyond Catholicism; the development of a distinctive sociology of Protestantism; the methodological problems encountered along the way; and finally the emergence of an international organization and the 'déconfessionalisation' of the sociology of religion. The evolution of the Conférence International de Sociologie Religieuse, founded in Leuven in 1948, through the Conférence Internationale de Sociologie des Religions (1981) to the present Société Internationale de Sociologie des Religions (1989) epitomizes this story. It marks a shift from a group primarily motivated by religion to one that is motivated by science, an entirely positive feature. It is, however, a story that emerges – and could only emerge – from a particular intellectual context: Catholic Europe. Such initiatives have been crucial to the development of the sociology of religion; they lead, however, to preoccupations that are not always shared by scholars from other parts of the world.

**36**

## hybrid cases

The discussion so far has contrasted francophone Europe with the United States – two very different modernities as far as religion is concerned, engendering different ways of thinking about the subject. British sociologists of religion have a particular place within these parameters. It is clear, first of all, that they draw considerably on American

(English-speaking) literature, but they operate necessarily in a European context (i.e. one of low levels of religious activity). In many respects, therefore, they face in two directions (see Davie, 2000b). They have been more influenced by pluralism than most of their continental colleagues, prompting a long-term preoccupation with new religious movements rather than popular religion; this fits well with the American literature. The levels of religious activity in Britain are, however, quite different from those in the United States and here the work of American scholars has proved less helpful. What is evident, however, is the inability of most (if not quite all) British – and indeed American – scholars to access the sociological literature in any language other than their own. The question of translation continues to resonate. Most European scholars can do better, leading to a noticeable imbalance in sociological writing. Many of the latter, for example, make reference to the English-speaking literature in their work; the reverse is seldom the case until the pressure to provide an English-language edition becomes overwhelming.

Britain is not the only 'hybrid' case. A second very obvious example can be found in Canada where the linguistic divide within the nation has led effectively to two academic establishments, each of which draws on a distinctive literature and each of which reflects the parameters of faith found in different parts of the country (Beyer, 1998). Interestingly, Beyer himself is trilingual in English, French and German, enabling him to cut right across both linguistic and cultural divisions. In Canada as a whole, however, each group of scholars has developed links with the appropriate language community outside the country – amongst which the links between the French-speaking universities of Québec and the French-speaking scholars in France, Belgium and Switzerland stand out. It was not by chance that the 1995 meeting of the Société Internationale de Sociologie des Religions took place at the Université Laval in Québec City.

More generally Canada, like Australia and New Zealand, represents a mid-point in a continuum of state or elite control versus voluntarism. In the mid-nineteenth century, the Protestant communities of English-speaking Canada were not so very different from their counterparts in the United States – the possibilities for voluntarism were, and in some senses still are, real. Such tendencies were, however, counterbalanced by the hegemonic Catholic identity of French-speaking Québec, a subculture which persisted until the 1960s when it collapsed dramatically – secularization may have come late, but it came fast to French-speaking Canada. The closest parallel in Europe can be found in the Netherlands. Indeed Catholicism in general has played a far larger part in

Canadian history that in her markedly more Protestant neighbour, an important reason for very different understandings of church and state and, without exaggeration, markedly different sociologies of religion (O'Toole, 1996).

Two further scholarly communities are interesting. First, the German speakers who bring to the debate not only their unique experience of European life but a distinctive body of theorizing. In terms of empirical data, Germany is a particularly interesting case, given the very different patterns of religious life that have emerged in the West and the former East. East Germany is without doubt the most secular country in Europe – Berlin has become the capital of both secularity and secularism. It is tempting, but incorrect, to say that this is simply the consequence of aggressive secularization policies under communism, an argument that is difficult to sustain given the entirely different outcome in neighbouring Poland. East German secularism is more likely to be the result of a specific combination of factors: a Protestant rather than Catholic tradition, a long rather than short history of secularization (McLeod, 1997, 2000; Froese and Pfaff, 2005) and the effects of communism itself.

Quite apart from the German data, two German-speaking sociologists have contributed massively to the sociology of religion in the late twentieth century. Both, moreover, are equally respected in general sociology. Thomas Luckmann, for example, both in his work with Berger and alone has had a seminal influence on the development of sociology as a theorist, philosopher and methodologist.[4] Within the sociology of religion as such, he is best known for a slim but immensely influential volume published in English under the title *The Invisible Religion* (Luckmann, 1967). The text forms part of Luckmann's concerted effort to understand the locus of the individual in the modern world. Using approaches to religion which derive from the classics, Luckmann argues that the problem of individual existence in society is essentially a 'religious' one:

> It is in keeping with an elementary sense of the concept of religion to call the transcendence of biological nature by the human organism a religious phenomenon. ... We may, therefore, regard the social processes that lead to the formation of Self as fundamentally religious. (1967: 48)

In making these claims, Luckmann aimed to re-establish the role of theory within the sociology of religion at a time when the dominant trend in the field lay in the empirical study of ever smaller (at least in the European case) religious organizations.

Niklaus Luhmann was born in the same year as Thomas Luckmann (1927). The influence of Talcott Parsons is clearly present in his writings – unsurprisingly given that Luhmann was Parsons's student in the 1960s. Luhmann went on, however, to develop a distinct and independent version of systems theory. Within this framework, he analyses religion in terms of its systemic functions, but conceptualizing systems not as groups of people but as the lines of communication between them. The specific character of religion as communication lies in the fact that it is both immanent and transcendent: i.e. that it operates between people (immanence), but that its subject lies beyond the world, concerned with managing and giving meaning to life (transcendence). The emphasis on meaning is crucially important in this highly abstract and at times very difficult body of theory.[5]

An interesting meeting between English- (primarily American) and German-speaking sociologists took place in New York in the spring of 2004.[6] This was both similar to and different from the encounters with the French speakers already described. As ever, the contrasts between patterns of religious life in Europe and America formed a dominant theme, a debate which found its inspiration in the paradigms developed in Chapters 3 and 4 of this book. The discussion, however, was enriched by innovative theoretical contributions, many of which drew very specifically on German-speaking sociology. As a result, German as opposed to French issues came to the fore – in not only a continued awareness of the impact of contrasting religious traditions on the political and policy making spheres of European societies,[7] but also of the ongoing contribution made to German society by academic theologians, a 'species' that barely exists in France.

The second group of scholars, whose work in many ways draws the threads of this section together, can be found in those parts of Europe which until 1989 were under communist domination – a point already mentioned in connection with the German case. Their task is twofold: first, to document the nature and forms of religion that are emerging in this part of the world, bearing in mind the volatility of these indicators and their considerable diversity across the region; and second, to establish theoretical frames of reference which enable a fuller understanding of what is happening in those parts of Europe where the study of religion had been proscribed from the academic agenda. This point reflects the remarks already made in Chapter 1 (p. 10). Here, however, the emphasis is different in so far as it lies primarily in the linguistic evolution that has accompanied these shifts.

Central European intellectuals born before the Second World War were part of a German-speaking community; they were socialized at a time when German was the lingua franca in this part of the world, permitting easy access to German scholarship – the driving force of European science, social science and philosophy. The Nazi regime, both before and during the war, definitively destroyed this hegemony with a twofold consequence. The scholars of central Europe who remained at home became imprisoned in the Soviet Empire (thereby becoming Russian speakers); those who escaped to the United States contributed, consciously or not, to the dominance of English as the language of academic enquiry.

For Central and East Europeans the implications are clear. The new generation of scholars emerging since 1989 are rapidly turning into highly proficient English speakers and, as a result, draw increasingly on the associated literature. The possibilities for academic exchange with the West are growing all the time, despite considerable financial difficulties. The parameters of the debate shift accordingly, but introduce some interesting dilemmas, exemplified in the following question. Is it necessarily the case that the debates of the English-speaking world, dominated for the most part by American sociology, furnish the best resources to understand the complex evolutions of religion in the post-communist world? An obvious illustration can be found in discussions of religious liberty that derive from the American literature, but resonate in entirely different ways in the Orthodox world. More precisely, American protagonists have difficulty appreciating the presence of an historic religious tradition, be this Orthodox, Catholic or Reformed. Herein lies perhaps an opportunity for the British contribution – one that is conversant with the English-speaking literature, but more aware than many American scholars of the nature and forms of European religious life.

## CLOSING THE LOOP

The final section of this chapter brings the argument full circle. It is concerned with the current use of the classics in the sociology of religion and addresses a very specific question: to what extent are the ideas of Marx, Weber, Durkheim and Simmel still relevant for sociologists of religion in a world which continues to transform itself, though in different ways in different places? Given the wealth of material available, the following examples are necessarily selective. They have been chosen to illustrate the role of the classics in creative thinking about the place of religion in late as opposed to early modernity.

The writings of Karl Marx present the greatest ambiguity for modern scholars. This, in many respects, was always so, a point underlined by O'Toole: 'A presence in the subdiscipline only since the decline of functionalism and the rise of "conflict sociology" in the discipline as a whole, he [Marx] remains a somewhat marginal figure in the pantheon' (2000: 147). This was even more the case given the Durkheimian assumption that religion should bind rather than divide; an emphasis on Durkheim (i.e. on the recurrent theme of social order) necessarily diminishes the influence of Marx. The remarks about Central and East Europe at the end of the previous section, and the search for alternative frames of reference from those that dominated prior to 1989, provide a further clue with respect to the present period. The following extract from one of the most distinguished social scientists in modern Europe is, for example, instructive. It refers to the radical change in perspective in East German scholarship following the fall of the Berlin Wall in 1989:

> Marxism is dead. Whereas in the old times when Europe was still divided, no one could obtain a job in an East German University without knowing half of *Das Kapital* by heart, today no one can remain in his job who is not able to prove that he was forced to buy the blue volumes of MEW (Marx-Engels Werke) without actually reading them. (Lepenies, 1991)

More worryingly, a new orthodoxy (drawing primarily on Weber instead of Marx) is emerging to replace the old; both are dangerous when taken to extreme. This is not the place to develop in detail the various ideologies that have emerged since the collapse of Marxism as a political system. Nor should it be assumed that the thinking associated with free markets and the 'end of history' will remain dominant indefinitely; both were called sharply into question during the banking collapse of 2008. But whatever the case, all of us need to recall the central insight of Marxist thinking – i.e. that religion cannot be understood apart from the world of which it is part, even if we reject any kind of mechanical causality. In the meantime, those who went a little too far down the Marxist track in the mid-post-war decades (the liberation theologians in Latin America or the purveyors of a Christian–Marxist dialogue in Europe), or whose policies were very much coloured by the Cold War perspective and the need to maintain a dialogue with the East (not least the World Council of Churches), have had to rethink their priorities. Both, in their different ways, have been overtaken by events.

Max Weber is, of course, the gainer in these particular exchanges, but quite apart from the see-saw effect, his influence on the sociology of religion was and remains immense. The following are simply two among hundreds of possible examples. Taken together, however, they

**41**

demonstrate not only the range and scope of Weber's thinking but its continuing capacity to generate new work and new ideas. The first, Stephen Sharot's *A Comparative Sociology of World Religions* (2001), offers a book-length demonstration of Weberian inspiration. The second is taken from an essay by David Martin which draws very directly on Weber's classic presentation of 'Politics as a Vocation', but is written with contemporary figures in mind (Martin, 2004).

Sharot articulates the goal of his book as follows: a comparative analysis of 'what are variously called the popular, common, folk, unofficial religious forms, or little traditions, and their relationships with the elite, official forms, or great traditions, of the world religions' (2001: 3). In order to do this Sharot draws on an extensive body of interdisciplinary literature concerned with popular religion and organizes this 'within an analytic scheme of religious action that builds principally on the writings of Max Weber' (2001: 4). The Weberian influence is pervasive: the brilliance of the analysis lies, however, in linking Weber's thinking about religious action with popular rather than elite forms of religious life.

Sharot's book is divided into two parts. The first, the theoretical frame, pays particular attention to the concept of religious action. Employing two intersecting dimensions – one which contrasts the transformative with the thaumaturgical, and one which contrasts this-worldly action with other-worldly action – Sharot suggests four types of religious goals (2001: 36). These are the nomic (the maintenance of existing order anchored in the supramundane), the transformative (with an emphasis on change in nature, society and individual being), the thaumaturgical (where release rather than change is expected), and the extrinsic (where mundane goals are the object of actions purported to be supramundane). Goals, however, are only one aspect of religious action. We need also to look at means, which, like goals, are infinitely varied in the different world faiths and in different types (elite and popular) of believers. The framework of means as well as goals is used to organize the material on elite and popular religion in the chapters that follow, which cover all the major world faiths.

Martin's work on secularization is similarly inspired by Weber and will be discussed in the following chapter. Here reference is made to a particular essay: one which draws on Weberian thinking to understand more fully the tensions between different professional groups – the politician, the Christian and the academic/journalist. A perceptive reader, acquainted with the British political scene post 9/11, could very easily give names to these protagonists, but the real point lies elsewhere: that is, in appreciating the different parameters within which the politician, the Christian and the journalist work and the near impossibility of crossing the associated boundaries. Politicians, for example, must be pragmatic; they must know when and how to compromise and how to effect the 'best possible' within the present situation. The Christian, on the other hand, deals in absolutes (the Sermon on the Mount, the Prince of Peace) – ideas which do not, indeed cannot, translate into political realities, either in secular life or in ecclesiastical policymaking. The latter in many ways can be even more deadly than the former. The journalist, finally, is free in three respects: he or she is *free to* subject both the politician and the Christian to merciless scrutiny, whilst remaining *free from* the obligations of office. Third, the journalist is free to move on to the next debate at will, leaving others to sweep up the broken china. A failure to grasp these essential differences of role leads not only to serious misunderstandings but to policy disasters, a point fully grasped by Max Weber but equally relevant today.

Durkheim was concerned with social as well as individual constraints. Like Weber, his work has been continually influential in the sociology of religion and in many parts of the world. The concept of civil religion, for example, has crossed and re-crossed the Atlantic. Rousseau's original formulation was taken up by Robert Bellah (under the influence of Durkheim and Parsons) in order to understand key aspects of American life, within which certain forms of religion played a crucial part, a debate with widespread and continuing resonance. The same concept can be deployed to understand aspects of religion in Europe, not least the complexities of the United Kingdom and its constituent nations.[8] In the 1990s the presence of a European civil religion, without which, it could be argued, Europe does not really exist, formed an important element in European debate (Bastian and Collange, 1999; Davie, 2000a). It is this issue, surely, that lay behind the heated discussion concerning references to religion in the Preamble to the European Constitution, a statement that tried, and maybe failed, to capture what it means to be European at the beginning of the twenty-first century.

A striking and even more direct application of Durkheimian ideas to modern sociological thinking about religion can be found in the work of Philip Mellor and Chris Shilling, who (like their role model) are as much social theorists as sociologists of religion. In a series of book-length analyses, Mellor and Shilling rework the Durkheimian themes in innovative ways. In *Re-forming the Body* (1997) religion becomes central to the theoretical account. Different forms of community (medieval, early modern, baroque and postmodern) are analysed in relation to different forms of embodiment and different religious cultures, in an approach which throws light on modern as well as historical forms of society – in terms not only of human embodiment itself but also the manner in which communities are constructed. Their argument is developed in *The Sociological Ambition* (2001). In this the recurrent theme concerns the 'elementary forms of social and moral life', meaning the conditions under which individuals acquire a sense of responsibility, obligation or duty towards others, and are able to develop normative ideals, mediated through different types of social order or grouping. More specifically, the manner in which human beings and human societies deal with death is as central to sociological discussion as it is to human living itself.

Working alone, Mellor (2004a, 2004b) has completed the 'trilogy' in a robust defence of the study of society. In many respects this approach counters the more extreme versions of the 'cultural turn', insisting that we pay attention to the continuing importance of society, not least in terms of religion. It is simply not the case that 'real' human beings live in a free-floating global culture driven by information technology. A nice example can be found in post-war patterns of immigration to be discussed in Part II of this book. Significant immigrant populations have arrived in Europe in the latter half of the twentieth century, undoubtedly influenced by economic, technological and cultural factors. They arrive, however, in different European societies in which their experiences will be correspondingly varied – for specific historical reasons. The Muslim headscarf is an acceptable part of public life in Britain, but not in France. Understanding why requires careful attention to detail of each of the societies in question.

Rather more briefly, the revival of interest in Georg Simmel's contribution in recent decades quite clearly reflects the very evident 'fit' not only between his writing and emergent forms of religious life, but in the debates about modernity itself, bearing in mind that the latter goes well beyond the limits of this chapter. Regarding the former, at least in the West, increasing attention is being paid to the forms of religiousness that exist outside the institutional churches. An obvious example can be found in the tendency to 'believe without belonging' (Davie, 1994). The rapidity with which this phrase was picked up by those working in the field, both scholars and practitioners alike, remains striking (see pp. 140–3 for a fuller discussion of this point). Clearly it resonates for a wide range of people. The distinction between religion and spirituality offers a similar formulation, an observation that reflects very directly the Simmelian contrast between form and content – an increasingly important distinction in the religious field. Chapters 7 and 8 will explore these ideas in some detail.

The dominant themes of *this* chapter can now be drawn together. They lie in the very varied discourses that have emerged in the sociology of religion in different parts of the world, paying particular attention to the debt that the global community of scholars still owes to the classics. Within these parameters, Europeans (including the founding fathers) remain more concerned than most with religious decline – in other words, with the process of secularization. Such preoccupations are hardly surprising given the profiles of religious life in Europe, where no one disputes that the indices of active religiosity (notably regular practice and assent to the historic formulae of the Christian churches) point downwards. It is this situation that provides the starting point for Chapter 3.

## NOTES

1 In Europe, Henri Desroche offers an excellent example. Desroche was for many years a Dominican priest. Having left the order, he engaged with Marxism in some depth, though never became a Marxist as such (Cipriani, 1998).

2 The quintessentially French ideology that emerged to fill this gap is known as *laïcité*, a word which is difficult to translate into English. It means the absence of religion in the public sphere – notably the state and the school system. It will be discussed in Chapter 8.

3 The *General Economic History* was translated into English in 1927 and *The Protestant Ethic and the Spirit of Capitalism* in 1930.

4 See the special issue of *Social Compass* dedicated to Thomas Luckmann's work (*Social Compass*, 50, 2003).

5 Peter Beyer has been of central importance in making Niklaus Luhmann's work known to English-speaking scholars in the sociology of religion (Beyer, 1993). See also Pace (2011).

6 The papers from this conference can be found in Pollack and Olson (2008).

7 See in particular Manow (2004), a paper also presented in New York.

8 Bocock and Thompson (1985) and Davie (1994) offer several examples of civil religion in Britain, many of which revolve around liminal moments in national life within which royal occasions remain surprisingly prominent.

# *three*

## secularization: process and theory

This chapter is concerned with two things: the process of secularization itself and the theoretical frameworks that have emerged to explain as well as to describe what is happening. The following paragraphs aim, first of all, to examine the genesis of secularization as a sociological concept and the circumstances in which it first emerged, bearing in mind that some of this story has already been told. In so doing, the multiple meanings within the idea of secularization become immediately clear, each of which needs separating out. Disentangling the threads is therefore the second task. The third lies in plotting the positions of a whole range of authors on a continuum best described as running from 'hard' to 'soft' concerning attitudes to secularization. There have always been differences in this respect which need careful articulation. A crucial aspect of these differences relates to the context in which the process of secularization takes place. By and large the scholars who have paid more attention to place are less likely to commit themselves to the inevitability of the process. The section ends with a short summary of the factors that must be taken into account in an informed discussion of both the process and theory of secularization.

The final part of the chapter reflects a step change in the debate. In the last decades of the twentieth century, the concept of secularization has been subject to ever closer scrutiny as the empirical data begin to suggest, at least for some scholars, that the whole idea of secularization as a necessary part of modernization might be mistaken. Once again the positions vary – from those who wish to discard the concept altogether to those who want to draw from it certain elements but abandon what might be called the 'package deal'. Particular attention will be paid first to David Martin's recent work, but also to Peter Berger's contributions. Berger's later writings illustrate more clearly than anything else the dramatic changes in perspective that have come about in the sub-discipline in the later decades of the twentieth century. Quite simply, the default positions have altered (Berger 1999a).

It is important that the primarily theoretical discussions in this chapter and the following two are read alongside the empirical material set out in the second part of this book; each approach to the topic of religion in the modern world complements the other.

## GENESIS AND DEVELOPMENT

The notion of secularization as an identifiable social process is inextricably bound up with the discipline of sociology as such. It starts with the precursors of the discipline, among them Auguste Comte (1798–1857), who not only coined the term 'sociology' but worked on the assumption of a three-stage historical model. Society evolved from a theological to a metaphysical stage, before moving into the current scientific – with the strong implication of better – stage. Two points are immediately clear. The first is ideological: the notion that modern societies leave both God and the supernatural behind, turning increasingly to the natural and the scientific as the primary modes of explanation. Understanding society (the essential task of sociology) requires the application of 'scientific' ideas to social as well as physical phenomena. Sociologists become therefore *part of* the secularization process. The second concerns the intellectual climate in which such ideas find their roots. The pioneers of sociological thinking drew directly from the European Enlightenment. The philosophical shifts associated with this movement both inspired and informed their thinking. A distinctive epistemology emerged which embodied above everything else a notion of the future that was realizable through human agency.[1]

The founding fathers of sociology, Karl Marx, Max Weber, Emile Durkheim and Georg Simmel, have already been introduced. All four must have a central place in a chapter concerned with secularization, given their common preoccupation with the influence of rapid industrialization in the European context and the effect that these changes were having on the institutional forms of religion found in this part of the world. They differed, of course, in their attitudes to what was happening. Marx actively desired the removal of religion, seeing this primarily as a symbol of malfunction within human societies – a fully socialist society would have no need of the panaceas offered by the supernatural. Weber was considerably more apprehensive, anticipating with some anxiety the consequences of 'disenchantment'; much of his writing about modern societies is concerned with the dehumanizing consequences of increasing bureaucratization. Durkheim's central preoccupation was the need for social order and the place of religion within this. And if the traditional forms of religion were no longer able to fulfil their binding role, how then was this essential function to be achieved in a

47

modern industrial society? Simmel, finally, separated form from content in religion as in so much else.

These seminal figures in the evolution of sociology were entirely correct to underline the significance of the modernization process for the historic forms of European religion. For centuries, Europe's religious life had been associated not only with political power but with the application, indeed legitimation, of such power at local as well as national or supranational level, not least in the parish. European religion was, and to some extent still is, rooted in localities (i.e. in territory); herein lies both its strength and weakness. It can still evoke powerful instincts, clearly illustrated in local celebrations and feast days – the Spanish examples come immediately to mind. The local parish as both a geographical and sociological entity was, however, profoundly disturbed at the time of the industrial revolution, a shock from which the mainstream religions of Europe have never fully recovered. Both civil and ecclesiastical parishes fitted easily into the dominant patterns of pre-modern rural life, much less so into rapidly growing industrial cities.

The shift, however, should not be exaggerated. In many parts of Europe, the traditional model endured well into the post-war period, not least in France where it sustained an effective Catholic culture until the early 1960s. The collapse came relatively late in France, but was all the more cataclysmic when it happened (Hervieu-Léger, 2003). Something rather similar happened in Spain some 30 to 40 years later. Elsewhere, the rural model had been seriously eroded for nearly a century, notably in Britain, where a rather different process occurred. Here, new forms of religious life emerged alongside the historic model, some of which grew as rapidly as the cities of which they were part. Both nonconformists and Catholics mushroomed in the nineteenth-century city, albeit for different reasons. The first filled the spaces left by the historic church; the latter catered for new sources of labour coming in from Ireland. Either way, an incipient market was beginning to develop. The complexities of the secularization process are already apparent.

The transformations of a pre-industrial and primarily rural society remain, however, pivotal. They indicate a critical disjunction in the evolution of religious life in Europe – one that is central not only to secularization as a process and to the theories that emerged to explain this, but to the discipline of sociology as such. Something very significant was happening which the founders of sociology took it upon themselves to explain. Too quickly, however, the wrong inference was drawn: that is, a *necessary* incompatibility between religion per se and modern, primarily urban life. This is simply not the case. Something quite different happened in the United States, for example, where territorial embedding had never taken place and where pluralism appears to have stimulated rather than inhibited religious activity, not least in urban areas. Equally distinctive are the global regions of the developing world, where some of the largest cities house some of the largest churches, not to mention tens of thousands of smaller ones. These differences and the theoretical frameworks that have emerged to explain them will form the subject matter both of this chapter and of the two that follow from it.

## ONE WORD, MANY MEANINGS

What though does the term 'secularization' mean? Answers vary considerably depending on the discipline in which the debate is taking place. Theologians, philosophers, historians, lawyers and social scientists approach the issue differently – that is hardly surprising.[2] It is equally clear, however, that the debate continues within social science itself.

The essential point to grasp is that a wide variety of ideas are embedded within a single concept, not all of which are compatible with each other – hence the need to disentangle the threads. Two scholars in particular have helped in this task. The first, Karel Dobbelaere, produced in 1981 an issue of *Current Sociology* entitled 'Secularization: a multidimensional concept', a volume which rapidly became required reading for teachers and students alike (Dobbelaere, 1981). The text has since been republished in book form, which includes as a postscript some reflections on more recent work (Dobbelaere, 2002). The second contribution comes from José Casanova (by training a political scientist), whose work on *Public Religions in the Modern World* (1994) had an immediate impact in the sociological community as much for the theoretical insights as for the case studies that followed.

Dobbelaere (1981, 2002) distinguishes three dimensions of secularization, which operate at different levels of society: the societal, the organizational and the individual. At the societal level, the emphasis lies on functional differentiation: sectors of society which historically were controlled by the church begin gradually to emerge as separate and autonomous spheres. No longer do people look to the church as the primary provider of healthcare, education or social services – this responsibility now belongs to the state which grows in stature as the churches diminish. Few scholars dispute either the principle or the process of functional differentiation in most modern societies, at least

*49*

in their Western forms.[3] The Muslim world is, of course, very different; so too those parts of the world where the state has manifestly failed in its obligations. But even in the West, not everything happens in the same way. A great deal depends, for example, on the starting point. Does the process of separation of church and state mean the breaking apart of entities that were once fused (the European case) or was that fusion, or more modestly a partnership of some kind, never allowed in the first place (the American model)? The outcomes will be correspondingly different.

Nor is the process of differentiation necessarily complete. All over Europe the traces of collusion between religion and power leave their mark. Religious authorities continue to fill the gaps in state provision, commanding in some places considerable resources. The German churches, for example, are major providers of both healthcare and welfare for large numbers of German citizens. Educational structures offer a further illustration. In many parts of Europe, the churches remain the owners and managers of significant numbers of schools. Church–state relationships are an important factor in these arrangements. These vary from the definitive break where almost no collaboration is possible, to various forms of state–church or concordat arrangements where the overlaps in provision are much larger.

50

Paradoxically, in the part of the world (the United States) where the separation of powers, and therefore of institutional responsibilities, has been rigorously enshrined in the constitution from the beginning, religious activity (measured over a wider range of indicators) remains far stronger than in Europe. Such a statement brings us immediately to the second and third levels of Dobbelaere's analysis – those of organizational activity (encompassing a huge variety of religious associations) and individual religiousness (expressed in belief as well as activity). Both are just as much an indicator of secularization as structural differentiation, but do not necessarily move in the same direction. Indeed, in a comparative perspective, the absence of a *direct* relationship between differentiation and levels of activity is particularly striking. So much so that the reverse is, or seems to be, the most likely outcome. In those parts of the modern world where the separation of powers has been most resisted – for the most part Western Europe – the indicators of religious activity (both organizational and individual) have dropped furthest, unless there is a specific reason for these to remain high.[4] Conversely in modern America, where institutional separation is a way of life, religious activity remains strong (how strong raises important methodological issues, to be discussed in Chapter 4). The possibility of a causal connection between these statements has become a major preoccupation of sociologists of religion (see below). For the time being it is sufficient to endorse Dobbelaere's insistence on the multidimensional nature of secularization.

In many respects, José Casanova's discussion (1994, 2001a) complements that of Dobbelaere.[5] Both authors affirm that the paradigm of secularization has been the main theoretical frame through which the social sciences have viewed the relationship of religion and modernity, and both acknowledge that the very real confusion about this relationship lies within the concept of secularization itself. It follows that a clearer articulation of what is meant by secularization is essential before the debate can be taken any further. An attempt at conceptual clarification provides, therefore, the starting point for Casanova's approach to religion in the modern world, as it did for Dobbelaere, a sentiment nicely caught in the following extract from the concluding sections of *Public Religions in the Modern World*:

> A central thesis and main theoretical premise of this work has been that what usually passes for a single theory of secularization is actually made up of three very different, uneven and unintegrated propositions: secularization as differentiation of the secular spheres from religious institutions and norms, secularization as decline of religious beliefs and practices, and secularization as marginalization of religion to a privatized sphere. If the premise is correct, it should follow from the analytical distinction that the fruitless secularization debate can end only when sociologists of religion begin to examine and test the validity of each of the three propositions independently of each other. (Casanova, 1994: 211)

**51**

Secularization as a concept should not be abandoned but refined, enabling a more accurate analysis of religion in different parts of the world – one which takes into account the different 'propositions' within the concept itself. If we are to understand properly the place of religion within the modern world, we need to work out the connections between these factors, case by case and country by country. Such connections cannot be assumed a priori.

For Casanova, it is clear that secularization as differentiation constitutes the essential core of the secularization thesis: '[T]he differentiation and emancipation of the secular spheres from religious institutions and norms remains a modern structural trend' (1994: 212). It is not the case, however, that modernity necessarily implies either a reduction in the level of religious belief or practice or that religion is necessarily relegated to the private sphere. Indeed the intention of Casanova's book is not only to discover, but also to affirm a legitimate *public* role for religion in the modern world. A second, and by now familiar point follows from this: it is precisely those churches that have resisted the structural differentiation of church and state which have had the greatest difficulty in coming to terms with the pressures of modern lifestyles. Hence the decline, relatively speaking, of religious vitality in much of modern Europe where state churches are more likely to persist, relatively speaking. This is not an inevitable outcome of modernity, but the consequence of the particular arrangements of church and state that predominate in European history. It is a European phenomenon with a European explanation; it is not an axiomatic connection between religion and the modern world taken as a whole.[6]

The two European case studies selected by Casanova provide contrasting illustrations of this approach. The first, Spain, exemplifies the argument. Here the long, protracted – and indeed tragic – resistance of the Catholic Church to modern forms of economic and political life has had inevitable and profoundly negative consequences for religious life in Spain; only now can the Spanish Church begin to shake off the associations of its past and come to terms with a modern democratic regime. The Spanish case is particularly instructive sociologically in that it constitutes an artificially delayed and therefore speeded-up version of modernity, in which the competing tensions display themselves with unusual clarity. What has taken a century in most parts of Europe has happened within a generation in Spain and can be analysed accordingly. The statistics tell the same story – the drop in religious practice between the 1981 and the 1990 European Values surveys was larger in Spain than anywhere else, as indeed was the fall in vocations to the priesthood (Pérez Vilariño, 1997). A very significant generation gap has emerged.

In Casanova's second case study, there has been a different juxtaposition altogether: in Poland a powerful and increasingly monolithic church became the focus of opposition to, rather than the ally of, a state which itself lacked legitimacy. Here resistance to secularization became associated with resistance to an illegitimate power: a combination which strengthened rather than diminished the position of the church in question and resulted in unusually high figures of religious practice throughout the communist period. But what of the future? Post-1989 the Polish Church, like its Spanish counterpart, has had to find its place in a modern democracy where a monolithic, semi-political presence (even one that could take pride in its resistance to communism) is, quite clearly, no longer sustainable. Paradoxically the most powerful church in central Europe is, it seems, the one least able to trust itself to the democratic process.

## FROM 'HARD' TO 'SOFT': DIFFERENT APPROACHES TO SECULARIZATION

Peter Berger's work has already been mentioned; in the 1960s and 1970s, he – both alone and in partnership with Thomas Luckmann – contributed extensively to the discussion of secularization as part of their work within the discipline of sociology as such. Inspired by Alfred Schutz and a growing number of phenomenologists, Berger and Luckmann were concerned above all with the meaning that individuals give to their lives and the resources they require to establish the necessary frameworks. Religion is part of this process; it is a social construction, built from below as individuals struggle to come to terms with the vicissitudes of human existence. The 'sacred canopy' (Berger, 1967) that emerges from these constructions protects the individual believer (and by implication the groups of believers that form societies) from the possibility that life has neither meaning nor purpose – thoughts that are a permanent part of the human condition but which are more likely to break the surface in times of crisis. Death, whether individual or collective, is the most obvious, and inescapable, trigger.

How then is the sacred canopy sustained? How, in other words, do the meaning systems set in place over centuries maintain their plausibility (i.e. their essential taken-for-grantedness)? What, conversely, happens when their plausibility is undermined and how might this happen? In the 1960s, competition, for Berger, spelt danger. If there is more than one sacred canopy present in society, or more than one claim to ultimate explanations of the human condition, they cannot both (or indeed all) be true. The next question is unavoidable: could it be that there is no ultimate truth at all? Hence, following Berger, the need to pay particular attention to religious pluralism and its effects on religious belief. The relationship is dialectic: pluralism erodes the plausibility structures generated by monopolistic religious institutions insofar as it offers alternatives. The alternatives then compete with the older traditions, further contributing to the undermining of their plausibility – in other words, to secularization. Pluralism, moreover, is part and parcel of modernization given the increasing mobilities (of both people and ideas) of the modern world. Pluralism becomes, therefore, the key variable in understanding the relationship between modernization and secularization. It is the pluralizing tendencies of modernity that are corrosive of religion.

But is this true of all forms of religion, or only of some? It is at this point that we rejoin an earlier argument, namely that the secularization process takes place in different ways in different places. It may indeed be the case that pluralism erodes forms of religion that historically have found their strength in a religious monopoly (herein lies their plausibility), but something rather different is likely to occur where pluralism has been present from the outset – here the outcome may be very different. Once again the contrast between old and new world becomes a central feature of the argument; it becomes, in fact, a constant refrain. It is not, however, the whole story, for there are common as well as distinctive features in the two cases. The *common* features find expression in a conceptual rather than empirical argument, which is central to Berger's understanding of religion in modern societies. It is this. In so far as pluralism necessarily undermines the taken-for-grantedness of religious thinking, it changes *the way in which we believe*. No longer can we simply assume the sacred canopies of those who went before us; we have instead to decide for ourselves. This is true even if such changes stimulate rather than erode belief systems as such. Beliefs that are chosen are not necessarily weaker than those that are assumed, but they are noticeably different. That difference – the 'how' of believing in modern and plural societies – has crucial significance for our understanding of modern forms of religious life. Berger's firm underlining of this point receives book-length treatment in *The Heretical Imperative* (1980).

54

We will return to Berger's more recent work on religion in the final section of this chapter. In the meantime, it is important to introduce two other exponents of the 'classic' versions of secularization theory, both of whom are British – Bryan Wilson and Steve Bruce. Until his death in 2004, Wilson retained his position as the senior defender of the 'old secularization theory' – i.e. that secularization is a 'fundamental social process occurring in the organization of society, in the culture and in the collective *mentalité*' (Wilson, 1998: 49). It becomes therefore an integral part of modernization. Wilson's definition of secularization frames the argument as a whole: secularization does not imply the disappearance of religion as such but is the process whereby religious thinking, practices and institutions lose their significance for the operation of the social system. The notion of declining social significance was established early on and continues as a leitmotiv in Wilson's writing about secularization over several decades and through numerous publications (1969, 1976 and 1982). A particularly clear statement of his position can be found in a chapter contributed to the collection brought together by Laermans et al. in honour of Karel Dobbelaere (1998), in which Wilson not only lays out his own point of view but answers a number of criticisms. This is an excellent summary to place in the hands of students:

it is measured in tone and meticulous in detail, a fitting tribute to a friend and colleague.

The secularization thesis, following Wilson, involves change in three areas of social organization: changes in the locus of authority in the social system (political power is freed from religious sanction and acquires its own legitimacy); changes in the character of knowledge as empirical enquiry and ethically neutral investigation lead to the development of scientific discovery; and a growing demand that those engaged in the workplaces of modern societies should conduct their lives in accordance with rational principles (rationality becomes, in fact, the *sine qua non* of the system). It is these transformations in behaviour and belief that characterize modern societies; they are, moreover, mutually reinforcing. Exactly how they occur will vary from place to place, but the underlying trend is clear, leading Wilson to an unequivocal conclusion: despite some differences in detail, 'secularization in the West has been a phenomenon concomitant with modernization' (Wilson, 1998: 51).

So much for the theory itself. Wilson then articulates six propositions about the secularization thesis, each of which calls into question some aspect of his thinking. First, that the process of secularization necessarily implies that there was once an age of faith. And if this is the case, when exactly was this age? The second proposition concerns the American exception: why is it that the experience of the United States is so different from Europe? The third involves the emergence of new forms or styles of religiosity to replace the old, notably the proliferation of new religious movements. The fourth looks at fundamentalism as a global religious movement. The fifth considers the re-emergence of religion in the parts of the world that were dominated by communism until 1989, paying particular attention to Poland and East Germany. And the sixth looks at the so-called privatization of religions – that religion as such continues, but in private rather than public forms. That in turn has already been challenged by scholars such as Casanova, who have reopened the debate concerning the *public* role of religion in late modernity.

There follows a patient and careful rebuttal of each of these arguments, an analysis which concludes once again with reference to his definition, the *fil conducteur* of Wilson's approach to secularization. With this in mind, he reiterates his core theme: that the 'secularization thesis focuses not on the decline of religious practice and belief *per se*, but on their diminishing *significance* for the social system' (1998: 63). In other words, claims about secularization rest on three interrelated facts. First, they rest on the recognition, or not, of religious authorities by those who are responsible for the management of our societies (i.e. the secular state). Second, we need to look at the impact that religion can or cannot make on the normative framework of the society in question and what proportion of that society's resources are devoted to religious goals. The third measure lies in the way in which a society's institutions are ordered: are they concerned primarily with religious or secular goals, and how might these be achieved? These are the grounds on which Wilson makes a prima facie claim that large parts of the modern world, including the United States, are not only relatively secularized but likely to become more so. The structural changes associated with the modernization process lie behind these claims.

Steve Bruce's approach to religion is in many respects similar to Wilson's. His style, however, is noticeably different. Both prolific and outspoken, Bruce demands that we pay attention to his thinking on this and other subjects. His writing is direct, clear and punchy; not everyone agrees with what Bruce says, but there can be no doubt at all about his position.

Bruce (1996) offers a classic statement of his view. Claiming as his starting point the work of the founding fathers, Talcott Parsons, Peter Berger, David Martin and Bryan Wilson, Bruce sets out what he claims to be the necessary connections between modernity and the demise of traditional forms of religious life. The key for Bruce lies in the Reformation, which hastened the rise both of individualism and of rationality, currents which were to change fundamentally the nature of religion and its place in the modern world. Bruce expresses these essential connections, the basis of his argument, as follows: '[I]ndividualism threatened the communal basis of religious belief and behaviour, while rationality removed many of the purposes of religion and rendered many of its beliefs implausible' (1996: 230). The two, individualism and rationality, epitomize the nature of modern cultural understanding – each, moreover, encourages the other.

The process should not be oversimplified; it is both complex and long term. An underlying pattern can nonetheless be discerned, which took four centuries to complete. For at least three of these, religious controversy dominated much of Europe's political, military and cultural life; it took the form of competing convictions about the nature of God and his (sic) relationship to the individual believer, notably Catholic and Protestant understandings about the right (and only) way to salvation. These centuries were, moreover, typified by the emergence of the nation-state as the effective form of political organization in Europe, a process inseparable from the break-up of Christendom. Only very gradually did a *modus vivendi* emerge as greater toleration of difference became the norm both within and between the states of Europe. But toleration is itself two-edged; it implies, following the argument already put forward by Berger, a lack of conviction, a capacity to live and let live which becomes not only dominant but pervasive. A further epistemological shift is, it seems, inevitable. In the late-modern period the concept of God, *him-* or *herself*, becomes increasingly subjective; individuals simply pick and mix from the diversity on offer. Religion, like so many other things, has entered the world of options, lifestyles and preferences. For the great majority, serious convictions are not only rejected from a personal point of view, they become difficult to comprehend altogether. Religious institutions evolve accordingly: church and sect give way in Bruce's terminology to denomination and cult – forms of religious organization that reflect the increasing individualism of religious life. Notably absent is the overarching sacred canopy, the all-encompassing religious frame expressed organizationally as the universal church. This is no longer able to resonate in the modern world.

Bruce returns to these themes in *God is Dead* (2002a), in which he sets out the evidence for and against the secularization thesis found within the British case in particular. Bruce is sanguine about this limitation, claiming that much 'of what matters here can be found elsewhere' (2002a: xii). Britain becomes, therefore, an exemplar of Western democracy, which, following Bruce, contains within itself inevitably secularizing tendencies. Embedded in this approach, therefore, is the notion of a lead society: that which British or Northern European societies do today, others will do tomorrow, all other things being equal. This assumption is crucial to Bruce's understanding of the secularization process. Precisely this idea, however, is increasingly challenged by recent trends in sociological thinking.

Interestingly, Bruce himself examines the place of Western democracies within the modern world in a subsequent publication (2003). Here the argument is somewhat different: *against* the current consensus of social scientific opinion, or so Bruce claims, 'religious cultures have, one way or another, contributed a great deal to modern politics' in different parts of the world (2003: 254). There are, in addition, important and observable differences in the ways that these influences occur. It is the job of the social scientist both to discern these connections and to explain them – the substance of the following chapters. This, at first glance, is paradoxical. Bruce, as we have seen, is primarily known as a defender of the secularization thesis, executing this task with considerable vigour. So, given the argument of *Politics and Religion*, has he changed his mind? It seems not. Broad themes emerge within the comparative frame, not least the difference between Islam and Christianity and between the communal nature of Catholicism and a much more individualistic Protestantism – at which point the traditional Brucean themes emerge: the influence of the Protestant Reformation in Western Europe and the gradual emergence of liberal democracy which, by its very nature, is inimical to religion. Liberal democracy, strongly linked to modernization at least in the West (including the United States), implies religious diversity which necessarily undermines plausibility, all of which is reassuringly familiar. The leopard has not changed his spots and in the final pages of this text re-establishes his place as a committed defender of the 'traditional' secularization thesis.[7]

A certain amount of support for this position can be found in the interesting work of David Voas. Voas is trained as a demographer rather than sociologist, and – with the possible exception of Robin Gill – is more than any other British scholar[8] entirely at home in the large data sets that are increasingly available to those working in the field – including the material emerging from the 2001 and 2011 British Censuses. He is a quantitative sociologist par excellence. In his interpretations of these data, Voas follows Wilson's definition of secularization, emphasizing the declining social significance of religion. With this in mind, Voas argues that on most conventional indicators – activity, belief, formal affiliation, self-ascribed affiliation, the nature of the state – Britain is ceasing to be a Christian country in anything but a residual sense. The trends (i.e. those that can be measured quantitatively) indicate decline, not growth (Voas, 2003a, 2003b; Voas and Crockett, 2005). Voas is markedly less responsive to the more qualitative assessments addressed in Chapter 6 and the arguments that emerge if they are taken into account. It is important to note in parenthesis that Voas has also worked on the impressive data sets emerging from the United States, enabling an important comparative dimension. His perceptive contributions to the rational choice debate will be dealt with in the following chapter.

No discussion of secularization would be complete without extensive reference to David Martin's unique and hugely significant contribution to the debate. Right from the start, Martin has been less convinced than others about the inevitability of secularization. As early as the 1960s, for example, he expressed serious misgivings about the concept itself; these were voiced in a much quoted article, published in the *Penguin Survey of the Social Sciences*, under a provocative title 'Towards eliminating the concept of secularisation' (Martin, 1965). Such were the confusions surrounding the concept that it might be better, following Martin, to abandon it altogether. It is, however, Martin's classic text *A General Theory of Secularization* (1978) that offers the key to his thinking in this area. The initial chapter takes the form of a five-finger exercise in which Martin sets out the different trajectories that the secularization process takes in different parts of the world and the key reasons for these contrasts. Not only does he underline the marked difference between old world and new, he also points out the different patterns in different parts of Europe. The analyses that follow, many of which have become classics in the literature, work through the detail of the different cases.

Crucial to the distinction between Europe and America, for example, are the different modes of insertion of religion into the host society. In Europe, religion embeds itself horizontally, a process which reflects the patterns of power that have been present in West Europe for centuries. In the United States, in contrast, the insertion has been more vertical than horizontal. As each new group of settlers brought with them their own version of (mostly) Christianity, they formed identities which sink deep into American life – interestingly these both cut across and embody social and economic difference. Religion, for instance, can both override and signify economic status. One of the most significant sectors in this respect is the black community, with its many varieties of churches and the close connections between political and religious movements.

Both Europe and America are, however, internally diverse. In the United States there is a marked difference between the South and the North: as a rule of thumb, religion declines in vitality as you move North and towards the coast. In each case, a mountain range turns out to be a significant marker. In Europe, the variety is even more marked – between, for example, the Protestant North (noting both the similarities and differences between Anglo-Saxon Britain and Lutheran Scandinavia), the religiously mixed countries exemplified by the Netherlands and (then) West Germany, and finally the Latin countries of the South where Catholicism remains the dominant, and more or less monopoly tradition. Martin explains as well as describes these differences, establishing a series of patterns and connections which, to some extent, can become predictive. Not always, however. In 1978, much of Central and East Europe was still under communist control, a part of Europe where secularism, as well as secularization, formed part of the dominant ideology. The fall of the Berlin Wall remained a dream. Since 1989, however, Martin (1996a) has led from the front in both observing and explaining post-communist developments – once again paying attention to difference as well as similarity. One point becomes increasingly clear: in those parts of Europe where religion was officially proscribed – where it became the carrier of an alternative, rather than mainstream ideology – a quite different set of relationships has emerged and quite different futures can be envisaged.

Martin's growing interest in the Latin American case can be seen in this light (Martin, 1990, 2002a); in many ways it has become the missing chapter in *A General Theory of Secularization*. Martin has pioneered the study of the unexpected but enormously significant rise of Pentecostalism in this part of the world, bringing this to the attention of a sociological community that was not always willing to see what was happening. Martin's input into this field will form a crucial element in the final section of this chapter, not to mention a more developed discussion in Part II. More immediately, an additional and rather different feature of his work requires attention: that is, the importance of cognate disciplines in understanding the secularization process. Martin's approach demonstrates, perhaps more than anyone else, first the significance of an informed historical perspective and second, the close connections between religion and the political process. Serious misunderstandings are likely to occur if either of these is ignored; the study of religion is necessarily a multi-disciplinary enterprise.[9]

So far this chapter has concentrated on the English-speaking debate, bearing in mind that a number of the contributors are working with English as a second language. That is not the whole story, however. Hence the need to introduce at least one of the distinguished group of French scholars who are concerned with the place of religion in the modern world. Danièle Hervieu-Léger (1986, 2000, 2003) has generated a rather different approach to secularization in her ongoing writing in this field – unsurprisingly in that she draws not only on the French case as an empirical example, but also on a distinctive sociological discourse. It is true, following Hervieu-Léger (1986), that modern societies are destructive of certain forms of religious life (regular attendance at Mass, for example, or the unquestioning acceptance of Christian teaching), but it is equally evident that modern societies create their own need for religion. Twentieth-century individuals are encouraged to seek answers, to find solutions, to make progress and to move forwards, and as modern societies evolve, such aspirations become an increasingly normal part of the human experience. Their realization, however, is – and must remain – problematic, for the goal will always recede. There is a permanent gap between the realities of everyday life and the expectations that lie on or beyond the horizon. It is this utopian space that generates the need for the religious in Hervieu-Léger's analysis, but in forms compatible with modernity. The process of secularization becomes, therefore, not so much the disappearance of religion altogether, but an ongoing reorganization of the nature and forms of religion into configurations which are compatible with modern living. The two examples cited by Hervieu-Léger are the supportive emotional communities that can be discovered both inside and outside the mainline churches of Western society (these are frequently charismatic in nature) and the types of religion which provide firm indicators of identity (both ethnic and doctrinal) in the flux of modern life.

*Religion as a Chain of Memory* ([1993]2000) takes these ideas further, examining in some detail both the definitional questions unavoidable in the study of religion (see Chapter 1) and the process of religious transmission. It is the latter point that is important here. If the chain of memory breaks and the process of religious transmission becomes deficient, it is hard not to conclude that some form of secularization has taken place. My own *Religion in Modern Europe* (2000a) is to a considerable extent an application of these ideas to the European case. It looks in detail at the institutional frameworks, paying attention to secular as well as religious examples, by which the religious memory (or more accurately memories) of Europe are or are not maintained. The results are complex: in some respects the chain of memory is hanging by a thread, if not broken altogether;[10] but in others, it is remarkably resilient, finding new ways of existing in late modernity. Both old and new forms of religious life in Europe will be examined in Part II.

One further point is important. It concerns the implications of both Hervieu-Léger's and Davie's arguments. Both agree that there has been some sort of ending in Europe – that the taken-for-grantedness of a shared religious memory, held in place by the historic churches, can no longer be assumed, echoing Berger's essential point. The process is more advanced in some places than in others; why this is so reflects the different trajectories set out by Martin. The breaking of the chain (whether actual or potential) is, however, only half the story. We need to look forwards as well as back, asking the inevitable question: what emerges once this collapse has taken place? In so far as the analyses of Hervieu-Léger and Davie open new debates in addition to closing old ones, their contributions are significantly different from Wilson or Bruce who envisage little in the way of a future for religion apart from a continuing decline in social significance. We will return to Berger and Martin in the final section.

61

## gathering up the threads

How then can the material presented so far be brought together? What are the central features of secularization and how can they be explained? And how does the academic debate reflect these features?

Secularization is a multi-dimensional concept; its dimensions, moreover, frequently operate independently of each other. Hence the need for conceptual clarity in order to ensure that like is being compared with like and that accurate inferences are drawn from the argument, a point repeatedly underlined by Dobbelaere and Casanova. Pluralism emerges as a very significant theme: both Berger and Bruce agree that an increase in the range of religious choices necessarily undermines the taken-for-granted nature of religious assumptions. Whether this necessarily leads to secularization is a more difficult question – the point at which Bruce and Berger (see below) go in different directions. Wilson's definition of the secularization process – that religion declines in social significance in modern societies – provides an important reference point for many scholars. Such decline, however, has occurred more in some places than others – hence the need to pay very careful attention to the specificities of history. The present is shaped by the past; the future, moreover, remains open. At this stage, even in Europe, it seems more likely that religion will transform rather than disappear. The nature of these transformations will require close and careful scrutiny, the task envisaged by both Hervieu-Léger and Davie.

**62**

## TOWARDS THE MILLENNIUM: A STEP CHANGE IN THE DEBATE

Towards the end of the twentieth century, a step change occurred in the debate. Until the early 1990s, the links between modernization and secularization were still generally assumed. Exceptional cases existed, but for particular reasons. It was possible, for example, to explain the religiousness of Ireland or Poland with reference to the links between religion and national identity. The American case was treated in similar ways, though here the challenge was somewhat greater: how was it possible to explain the continuing religiousness of the technologically most advanced country in the world? It is with reference to America, moreover, that the whole argument begins to shift. Instead of arguing that there are particular reasons for the religious vitality of modern America which require careful analysis – a subject that preoccupied scholars for much of the post-war period – Europe begins to emerge as the exceptional case. The parameters of the debate alter accordingly. European forms of religion are no longer seen as the global prototype; they become instead one strand among many which make up what it means to be European. Or to put the same point in a different way, the relative secularity of Europe is not a model for export; it is something distinct, peculiar to the European corner of the world. What then has been the nature of this strand in the latter part of the twentieth century and what will it be like in subsequent decades? It is precisely these issues that have underpinned my recent writing in the sociology of religion (Davie, 2002a, 2006b).

Two scholars in particular exemplify the wider change in perspective; their work has already been introduced. The first is David Martin, who in 1991 published a second key article, this time in the *British Journal of Sociology*. Once again the title was significant. The initial pages of 'The secularization issue: prospect and retrospect' recall Martin's earlier analysis – that theories of secularization were essentially one-directional in so far as they embodied 'covert philosophical assumptions, selective epiphenomenalism, conceptual incoherence, and indifference to historical complexity' (1991: abstract). The second section articulates a by now familiar theme: the connections between stronger versions of the secularization thesis and the European context from which they emerged. The essential point is firmly underlined: that there are particular circumstances or conditions in West Europe that account for the relatively strong indicators of secularization that can be discerned in this part of the world (and even here, more in some places than in others). Exactly how the process occurred varies: in the Protestant North, the churches were incorporated into the state; in the Latin South (most notably in France) they were excluded from it. Either way the significance of religion as an independent force is inevitably diminished. But outside Europe (and even in the parts of Europe that experienced communism at first hand), very different combinations have occurred. The key elements have aligned in different ways, leading to entirely different futures. The active religiosity of the United States, the massive shift to the South of global Christianity, and the emergence of Islam as a major factor in the modern world order are some of these; all are ill-served by theories that emerge from a European context. The question, moreover, is urgent: it becomes abundantly clear that we need new and different paradigms in the sociology of religion if we are to understand the nature of religion in the modern world.

Martin himself has worked in two areas in particular: on the post-communist situation in Central and East Europe and on the exponential rise of Pentecostalism in the Southern hemisphere. It is these empirically driven cases that have led him to articulate even more forcefully than before his initial misgivings about the secularization thesis. The penultimate paragraph of the 1991 article contains a final sting in the tail (see also Martin, 1996c). The very factors that across Europe accounted for the decline in historical forms of religion (the negative associations with power in the North and the rationalist alternative associated above all with the French Republic) are themselves in decline, liberating spaces hitherto occupied by opponents of certain forms of religion. At precisely the same time, new forms of religion (both Christian and non-Christian) are flooding into Europe, not least a significant Muslim population. The outcome of this entirely new combination is far from clear: predictions vary from total fragmentation to significant revival. My own interpretation of these events lies somewhere between the two; it is developed in Chapter 7. Using a kind of shorthand, it can be summarized as follows: as a shift from 'opting out' (from the historic churches) to 'opting in' (to many different kinds of religious groups, *including* the historic churches), but in ways that are specific to the European context.[11]

Berger's change in direction is even more dramatic; in many respects, he has moved full circle, from an advocacy of secularization as a central feature of modern, necessarily plural societies, to a trenchant critique of this position (bearing in mind that the misgivings begin to show as early as the 1970s). Berger has altered his theoretical position in light of the data that are emerging all over the world. Once again it is the continued religious activity of many Americans and the increasing salience of religion in almost all parts of the developing world that fly in the face of secularization theory. It is worth quoting from Berger himself to appreciate the volte-face that has occurred in his thinking:

> My point is that the assumption that we live in a secularized world is false. The world today, with some exceptions, to which I will come presently, is as furiously religious as ever. This means that a whole body of literature by historians and social scientists loosely labeled 'secularization theory' is essentially mistaken. In my early work I contributed to this literature. I was in good company – most sociologists of religion had similar views, and we had good reasons for upholding them. Some of the writings we produced still stand up. ...
>
> Although the term 'secularization theory' refers to works from the 1950s and 1960s, the key idea of the theory can indeed be traced to the Enlightenment. The idea is simple: Modernization necessarily leads to a decline of religion, both in society and in the minds of individuals. And it is precisely this key idea that turned out to be wrong. (1999b: 2–3)

Following this line of argument, secularization should no longer be the assumed position for theorists in the sociology of religion; it becomes instead a theory with relatively limited application, particularly suited to the European case, but very much less helpful elsewhere. The task of the sociologist shifts accordingly: he or she is required to explain the absence rather than the presence of religion in the modern world. This amounts to nothing less than a paradigm shift in the sociology of religion.

By no means everyone is in favour of the new perspective. Bruce, for example, describes Berger's change in view as an 'unnecessary recantation' (Bruce, 2001). Voas would agree. In a chapter devoted to precisely this aspect of Berger's work, Bruce argues that 'his original contributions to the secularization approach remain valid, that he is confessing to sins that he did not commit, and that his arguments against his own case are unpersuasive' (2001: 87). Bruce takes each of Berger's arguments – the growth of conservative and evangelical churches in the United States, the decline of liberal churches, the persistence of religion (if not church-going) in other Western societies, and the vitality of religion in other parts of the world – offering in each case an alternative view in line with his own perceptions of secularization. In so doing he raises a crucial question: will the societies of the developing world in all its diversity follow the model that Bruce claims to be irrefutable in modern liberal democracies? Is there, in other words, a necessary connection between increasing prosperity and a decline in commitment to religious orthodoxies? The answer can only lie in painstaking empirical enquiry. The work of Norris and Inglehart (2004) constitutes an important contribution in this respect; interestingly they find in favour of the secularization thesis. Their argument will be dealt with in more detail in Chapter 5.

In the meantime, Berger, Martin, and indeed myself, are less and less convinced that the connection between modernization and secularization holds in significant parts of the prosperous West, let alone the developing world – a shift in perspective that is clearly gathering steam.[12] And if this is the case, the implications for policy as well as for sociological theory are immense. It is crucially important, therefore, that we – academics, journalists, politicians, policymakers and practitioners – get it 'right'.

65

## NOTES

1 It is important to remember that the Enlightenment took different forms in different places, even in Europe. It was, moreover, the French form of the Enlightenment (that most familiar to Comte) that contained the strongest opposition

to religion. This was much less the case elsewhere – a point that will resonate more than once in the chapters that follow.

2 An initial summary of these different discourses can be found in Lübbe (1975). See also Tschannen (1991, 1992).

3 Functional separation is reconsidered in Chapter 11 in a discussion that centres on de-differentiation at both societal and individual levels.

4 In, for example, Poland – the case outlined on p. 52.

5 There are obvious similarities between Karel Dobbelaere and José Casanova. In his writing, however, Casanova acknowledges a particular debt to David Martin.

6 The argument is strongly reminiscent of de Tocqueville, who made a similar observation following his encounter with North America in the nineteenth century.

7 In 2011, Steve Bruce published *Secularization: In Defence of an Unfashionable Theory*. The title itself is revealing. As a theory, secularization has become unfashionable; Bruce remains, however, a staunch defender, using this text to say why and to clarify the arguments on both sides of the debate.

8 David Voas is in fact an American who currently works in Britain. He is increasingly well known as a contributor to the debate about religion on both sides of the Atlantic.

9 Quite apart from his writing in the social sciences, David Martin is an accomplished theologian. Increasingly his work is best described as a form of socio-theology.

10 The breaking of the chain in the French case is underlined by Hervieu-Léger in a more recent book, *Catholicisme, la fin d'un monde* (2003). The title itself is significant: Hervieu-Léger argues that French Catholicism has indeed collapsed, in so far as this implies a shared culture, drawing in turn on a shared body of knowledge and accepted norms of behaviour.

11 See also David Martin (2005a, 2011). Both these volumes collect together a series of essays, many of which are relevant to the themes of this book. A shorter account, summarizing a position arrived at over some 40 years ago with respect to secularization, can be found in Martin, 2005b.

12 See, for example, the important collection of articles in 'After secularization', a double issue of *The Hedgehog Review*, 8/1&2, 2006.

# *four*

## rational choice theory

This chapter follows from the last in that it is concerned with a theoretical framework whose protagonists claim that it is able to explain the complex relations between religion and the modern world, with very little qualification. The approach, a product of American sociological thinking, has become known as rational choice theory (RCT) and there can be no doubt of its impact on the sociological study of religion. The contrasts with secularization theory are immediately apparent in so far as RCT is a mode of theorizing which recognizes the positive rather than negative connections between religious pluralism and religious activity, seeing the absence of a religious market as the principal reason for the relative lack of religious vitality in Western Europe. Indeed in many respects RCT is to America what secularization theory is to Europe, leading some commentators to describe the theory as 'gloriously American' (Simpson, 1990). Rather more modestly, there is an obvious fit between the context from which the thinking emerges and the nature of the theory itself, a fact which raises inevitable questions about the application of a rational choice approach in other parts of the world. The following discussion is structured with this in mind.

The first section will introduce the notion of a paradigm shift in the sociology of religion taking as its starting point an article published by R. Stephen Warner in the early 1990s. The second sets out the principles of RCT itself, introducing the major scholars involved in this enterprise and outlining their principal ideas. The third section indicates – albeit selectively given their number – the kind of applications that are possible within the RCT framework, paying particular attention to both European and Latin American examples. The fourth takes a more critical stance, outlining a range of reservations concerning the theory and dividing these into different groups: those which are concerned primarily with conceptual or methodological questions, those which express doubts about certain parts of the analysis but accept others, and those which reject the RCT approach lock, stock and barrel. Careful attention will be paid, finally, to the use of RCT outside the American context, asking in particular how far the theory is able to resonate in Europe. Is this a zero–sum game?

## TOWARDS A PARADIGM SHIFT

As in the case of secularization theory, key stages in the emergence of RCT can be linked to particular publications. Warner's article on 'Work in progress towards a new paradigm for the sociological study of religion in the United States', published in the *American Journal of Sociology* in 1993, is one such, keeping in mind Warner's insistence that the new paradigm that he is working towards is close, but not coterminous with RCT (1997: 196). From 1993 on, however, the secularization thesis, already critiqued by increasing numbers of scholars on both sides of the Atlantic, has had to justify its applicability to the American situation; no longer can its assumptions be taken for granted. The shift was a gradual one, and as Warner himself makes clear, his own article was part of the process that he was trying to describe. In retrospect, however, no scholar can afford to ignore this contribution to the literature, whether they agree with it or not. Decisions have to be made regarding the appropriateness of secularization theory to the American case (or indeed to any other), where once they were simply assumed.

Even more relevant to the argument of both the last chapter and this, however, is the point underlined by Warner in the 1993 article, but considerably expanded in 1997 (Warner, 1997: 194–6): that is, the European origins of the secularization thesis as opposed to the American genesis of the new paradigm. The beginnings of the two models go back centuries rather than decades. The secularization thesis, following Warner, finds its roots in medieval Europe some 800 years ago. The key element is the existence of a monopoly church with authority over the whole society; both church and authority are kept in place by a series of formal and informal sanctions. It is, moreover, the monopoly itself which provides the plausibility structure – the authority is not only unquestioned, but unquestionable. Given the inseparability of monopoly and plausibility, the latter will inevitably be undermined by increasing ideological and cultural pluralism, a relentless process with multiple causes. Documenting this process, the gradual undermining of the monopoly, is a central task of sociologists, who quite correctly describe their subject matter (a metanarrative) as the process of secularization.

**68**

The alternative paradigm, or metanarrative, begins rather later – say 200 rather than 800 years ago and in the new world not the old, to be more precise in the early years of the United States as an independent nation. Here there was no monopoly embodied in a state church, simply a quasi-public social space that no single group could dominate. All kinds of different groups or denominations emerged to fill this space, each of them utilizing particular religious markers as badges of identity (religion was much more important in this respect than social class). Simply surviving required considerable investment of time, talent and money, not least to attract sufficient others to one's cause in face of strong competition. The possibilities of choice were endless, and choice implies rejection as well as acceptance. The affinities with modern-day America are immediately apparent.

Interestingly, as Warner himself makes clear, the classics can be drawn upon in both situations, though in rather different ways. Identities, for example, can be constructed in Durkheimian terms in relation to the whole society (in Europe) or to a particular community within this (in the United States). Likewise, Protestant sects can be seen as undermining a European monopoly or as competitors in an American market – either way Weber's insights are helpful. Conversely, attempts to impose either the secularization or the RCT paradigm wholesale on to the alternative context are likely to cause trouble. Such attempts arise from a conviction that one paradigm, and only one, must be right in all circumstances. That, it will be strongly argued, is not a sensible policy. Which is not to say that elements of each approach cannot be used to enlighten certain aspects of the alternative situation – clearly that can be done and to considerable effect. In order to develop the argument, however, it is important to grasp both the core elements of RCT and the theoretical background from which this springs.

**69**

## THE THEORY AND THE THEORISTS

The theory itself is relatively simple: it postulates that individuals are naturally religious (to be so is part of the human condition) and will activate their religious choices, just like any other choices, in order to maximize gain (however conceptualized) and to minimize loss. The phrase 'just like any other choices' is crucial; it reminds us that RCT is a theory deployed by different branches of social science to account for many different aspects of human behaviour. The result is a significantly greater theoretical unity among disciplines as diverse as economics, sociology, certain kinds of psychology, political science, moral philosophy and law (Young, 1996: xi). Quite apart from religious decisions, RCT can be used to explain economic activity, cultural consumption, political choices (including voting behaviour), moral choices and voluntary commitments of all kinds. The links between religious activity and other forms of individual and social living become immediately clear, an entirely positive feature of the RCT approach.

More specifically, RCT draws on two forms of social-scientific theorizing: first, on the economic ways of thinking epitomized by Gary Becker in *The Economic Approach to Human Behavior* (1976), which in turn derive from the utilitarian individualism espoused by Adam Smith; and second, on elements of exchange theory taken from psychology, an approach initiated by George Homans and Peter Blau in the 1960s in which the actor is central to sociological thinking. In bringing these two strands together, rational choice theorists work on the principle of 'a purposive rational actor who tries to avoid costs to maximize gains' (Hak, 1998: 403). For some theorists of religion, even the starting point is controversial: those, for instance, who see the maximization of gain as necessarily inimical to religion. This need not be the case; it all depends on how gain is conceptualized (gain, for example, might include spiritual enlightenment). Nor need it be the case that maximization of gain necessarily implies selfishness. If an individual aspires to altruism as one of his or her goals, it follows that purposive action for that individual will be directed to an increase in altruistic, as opposed to egoistic, activity.

Put very simply, the application of RCT to religion develops along two lines. It assumes on the one hand a rational actor who is looking, amongst many other things, for religious satisfaction and, on the other, the existence of a religious market from which the actor makes his or her selections. It follows that for many exponents of RCT, if not for all, the theory works in terms of supply rather than demand: religious activity will increase where there is an abundant supply of religious choices, offered by a wide range of 'firms' (religious organizations of various kinds); it will diminish where such supplies are limited. RCT's strongest advocates are Stark and Bainbridge, Roger Finke and Laurence Iannaccone, bearing in mind that many of the articles and books in this field are jointly authored. The following paragraphs are but a summary of a large and growing corpus of theoretical work by this group (and indeed others). In reading this account, it is important to bear in mind that the application of RCT to the religious field is relatively new; in many respects the thinking is still evolving.

## Rodney Stark and William Sims Bainbridge

Two books appeared in the 1980s, the first *The Future of Religion* (Stark and Bainbridge, 1985), the second *A Theory of Religion* (Stark and Bainbridge, 1987). Both volumes brought together ideas that had appeared in earlier articles (for example, Stark and Bainbridge, 1980) and both became ground-breaking texts in the sociology of religion. *The Future of Religion* is an attempt to come to terms with the persistence of religion, not least in American society, at a time when the demise of religion was confidently (even joyously) predicted by most social scientists. Secularization exists, to be sure, but is found in all religious economies, not only, or necessarily, in modern ones. Secularization, moreover, is part of an ongoing cycle; as secularization takes hold in any given society, it necessarily stimulates two counter-veiling processes: revival and religious innovation. It follows that religion is not something that disappears in modern societies, but something which ebbs and flows in all societies over the long term:

> [S]ocial scientists have misread the future of religion, not only because they so fervently desire religion to disappear, but also because they have failed to recognize the dynamic character of religious economies. To focus only on secularization is to fail to see how this process is part of a much larger and reciprocal structure ... We argue that the sources of religion are shifting constantly in societies but that the amount of religion remains constant. (1985: 2–3)

71

Hence the bold statement at the end of the introductory chapter: '[A]ll our work shows religion to be the direct expression of universal human needs, and thus the future is bright for both religion and the social-scientific study of it' (1985: 18).

A great deal depends, of course, on how religion is defined. A consideration of this topic leads Stark and Bainbridge straight into a set of logical propositions which build themselves into a deductive theory of religion. These building blocks form the core of RCT as it is applied to religion. Using Homans as a starting point, Stark and Bainbridge show how human beings seek out what they perceive to be rewards and try to avoid what they perceive to be costs. Central to the argument at this stage in their work is the idea of compensators. Some rewards (e.g. the assurance of life after death) are simply not attainable however much an individual desires this; instead he or she opts for a compensator – a kind of IOU that the reward will be obtained provided certain actions or commitments are fulfilled in the meantime. Religious organizations of all kinds become the source of particular kinds of compensators;

through their mediation of the supernatural, they offer answers to the existential questions that face us all. Hence for Stark and Bainbridge, religions are defined as 'human organizations primarily engaged in providing general compensators based on supernatural assumptions' (1985: 8).

Some two years later, *A Theory of Religion* (1987) offers just what the title implies: a deductive theory of religion based on 344 interlinked propositions, which in turn are built on axioms. Axioms are concerned with human nature and the conditions of human existence, from which can be deduced both the emergence and the persistence of religion in all human societies. The aim of the theory was not only to accommodate the continuing vitality of religion in modern America, but also to explain the various forms of religious life that emerge amongst different groups of people and in different places. Why, for example, are some people attracted to the relative exclusivity of sects and others to the more inclusive model found in churches? Do these patterns vary between different societies and for what reasons? Are they stable or liable to change? And if the latter is the case, how do such changes come about?

The theory builds from the bottom up. Individual choices about religion are made 'rationally' in the sense that they are purposive rather than random. It is the job of the social scientist to track these changes and to understand them better. Such choices, moreover, are cumulative, allowing the social scientist not only to understand collective as well as individual behaviour – notably the forms of religious organization that are likely to do well and those that, for one reason or another, appear less attractive, bearing in mind that the results may be counter-intuitive (see below). None of this is understandable, however, without due attention to the religious regime of the society as a whole. Is there an effective choice of religious activity and if not, why not? Can something be done about this and if so by whom? And even if the regime or constitution is modified, does this necessarily imply a shift in the way that people think about their religious lives and the choices available to them? The questions flow freely once the RCT framework is in place. Not everyone agrees with the deductive theorizing of Stark and Bainbridge. No one, however, can deny the fruitfulness of the theory in terms of the hypotheses that have emerged from it, many of which lend themselves to empirical testing. That is not to say that the process of testing is necessarily free from pitfalls, some of which were not foreseen at the outset – a point to be covered in some detail.

## Roger Finke

Stark's contribution to Young's very useful edited volume on *Rational Choice Theory and Religion* (1996) takes the form of an autobiographical account of his work in the sociology of religion, including his major contributions to the rational choice debate. Central to this account are the individuals who at one stage or another became part of the RCT team. Roger Finke was one of these, a collaboration that produced two major volumes: *The Churching of America* (Finke and Stark, 1992) and, some years later, *Acts of Faith* (Stark and Finke, 2000). In the first, the link between religious pluralism and religious vitality not only becomes explicit, but is situated within an historical account. As a general rule, religious pluralism invigorates the life of religious organizations, which in turn attract religious participation. In historical terms, America is 'churched' as the colonies become more interdependent from an economic point of view, a trend that led in turn to a greater tolerance of religious diversity. A growing religious marketplace enabled new religious groups to flourish, reflecting a central tenet of Roger Finke's work: namely that an increase in religious supply generates an increase in demand, not the other way round (Finke, 1996).

*Acts of Faith* is interesting for a number of reasons, including the fact that the always slippery notion of 'compensators' has largely disappeared from the account. In other respects, however, *Acts of Faith* builds very directly on the earlier work of the RCT theorists – still taking time to refute the old (secularization) paradigm before constructing the new one. In terms of the former, the book includes the by now celebrated chapter on 'Secularization: R.I.P.' which first appeared in *Sociology of Religion* (Stark, 1999). In terms of the latter, RCT builds once more from the bottom up, starting with the religious individual (Part 2), before moving to the religious groups (Part 3).

It is at this point that the link between high levels of religious commitment and high levels of success becomes clear: that more 'costly' faiths do better in the religious market than those which demand less (a persistent problem for secularization theorists whose thinking leads in the opposite direction). What initially seems paradoxical becomes logical within the RCT framework: the fact 'that costly churches are strong churches *because* they are costly – that rational actors will prefer more demanding churches because they offer a more favourable cost/benefit ratio' (Stark and Finke, 2000: 22). In other words, religious organizations which demand a lot also give a lot; assurance becomes

**73**

real, but at a price. Part 4, finally, moves to the societal level and is concerned once again with the religious economy taken as a whole. A substantial part of this analysis centres on the relative lack of religious vitality in Europe and the reasons for this. Finke and Stark argue – predictably enough – that this is due to a restricted supply rather than a fall off in demand. Once again the protagonists of RCT come into direct conflict with the advocates of secularization.

## Laurence Iannaccone

Before working through this controversy in a number of case studies, it is important to make reference to the work of Laurence Iannaccone, whose writing is the most explicitly economic of the RCT group. An instructive example of the application of economic thinking to the problems of religious organizations can be found in Iannaccone's consideration of the 'free rider problem', not least its relationship to the point already mentioned: that is, the relative success of costly as opposed to undemanding churches (Iannaccone, 1992, 1994, 1996). Once again, the logic is compelling. Successful churches require commitment from their members; it follows that those who 'free-ride' on religious organizations are a problem in that they absorb the benefits without making a corresponding contribution to the group, whether this be financial or otherwise. The next step is clear enough: the free-rider problem is far more likely to occur in liberal or less demanding churches than it is in their stricter, more demanding equivalents. Iannaccone summarizes the argument succinctly:

74

> Costly demands mitigate the free-rider problems that otherwise undermine a religious group. They do so for two reasons. First, they create a social barrier that tends to screen out half-hearted members. No longer is it possible simply to drop by and reap the benefits of attendance or membership. To take part, one must pay a price, bearing the stigma and sacrifice demanded of all members. Second, they increase the relative value of group activities, thereby stimulating participation among those who do join the group. ... To put the matter crudely: a comprehensive ban on dances, movies, gambling, drinking, and 'worldly' friendships will turn Friday church socials into the highlight of one's week. (1996: 36)

The stricter the codes (in terms of belief and behaviour), the less easy it is to have your cake and eat it. The believer is forced one way or the other, resulting in a more committed membership. The half-hearted simply drop away.

## MULTIPLE APPLICATIONS

On one point there can be no doubt: RCT has generated an enormous number of empirical applications, and in many different parts of the world. One focus of the ensuing debate can be found in the *Journal for the Scientific Study of Religion*, which became in the 1990s an important source of information regarding both the theoretical and empirical aspects of RCT. Particularly useful are the discussion groups, symposia and 'conversations' that permit article, response and rejoinder in consecutive issues. Quite apart from anything else, these clusters furnish admirable teaching tools for a class or series of classes on RCT, given the diversity of opinion represented. The sheer volume of this work is, however, daunting. With this in mind, it is necessary to be selective in what follows. The criteria for selection reflect the argument of this book as a whole: that is, the relationship between the context from which a theory emerges and the theory itself, which in turn has bearing on the applicability of that theory outside the original field. Hence the following examples, which include first a series of European cases followed by an interesting, if somewhat unusual, application of RCT in Latin America.

### RCT and Europe

Stark and Iannaccone (1994) are responsible for the first and crucial illustration. The article 'A supply-side reinterpretation of the "Secularization of Europe"' is much quoted in the literature. Its structure reflects a by now familiar pattern: a rejection of the 'conventional' theorizing (i.e. the assumption that secularization is the dominant trend) followed by the RCT alternative, which is based, as ever, on a set of interlinked definitions and seven further propositions (some of which involve additional definitions). The European material is presented within these parameters: the stress lies on the two different kinds of monopolies found in West Europe – one Catholic and one Protestant (among the latter, particular attention is paid to the Swedish case). A short section (a couple of paragraphs) quantifies 'religious regulation' drawing on a six-item scale established by Chaves and Cann (1992).[1] So much for the theory. The later sections of the article are concerned with multiple testings of the central tenets of RCT using a range of data sources. One set of tests looks at comparative data between societies; a second considers the impact of pluralism within societies. The hypothesis is simple enough: it concerns 'the impact of religious pluralism and regulation on the overall levels of religious participation in societies' (Stark and Iannaccone, 1994: 239). The anticipated conclusion (at least anticipated for RCT theorists) is repeatedly discovered: namely that religious activity will remain diminished in those countries, most of West Europe, where regulation stifles supply.

Stark and Iannaccone turn next to a long-term historical perspective, arguing that the assumption of an 'age of faith' in Europe's past is essentially false. It is true that many people believed in medieval Europe – indeed *potential* demand was very high. But the potential remained unfulfilled given the lack of aggressive suppliers. The same was true in their second, somewhat different example: nineteenth-century Ireland, where, the authors claim, less than one-third of the population went to mass in 1840. Mass attendance rose in Ireland, not in this case as a result of pluralization, but as a result of the growing link between Catholicism and Irish nationalism, a factor which overrides the market. In the Irish case, religion becomes a form of cultural defence – an explanation maintained by secularization theorists as well. A third historical example is taken from New England, where, as we have seen already, religious activity rose only when successive waves of deregulation permitted the development of a more varied religious economy.

The last step of the argument is the most provocative: are things so very different in *modern* Europe given that belief in some sort of God remains relatively high but commitment (measured in terms of regular practice or assent to strong statements of credal belief) continues to drop? Understandably I find myself implicated in these suggestions given my own work on 'believing without belonging'. My first response is clear: modern Europe is so entirely different from medieval Europe that comparisons are hardly possible. Having said this, the religious life of modern Europe is clearly shifting and in ways that require our attention. In the short term the emphasis lies on the persistent disjunction between belief and belonging – a topic to be discussed in Part II. In the longer term, it is much harder to say what will happen: will the secularization process continue (as argued by Wilson and Bruce) or will a genuine religious market not only emerge in the vacuum which is left but, as a result, drive up the religious indicators? Not for the foreseeable future in my opinion. In the medium term, I find two ideas increasingly persuasive. The first, 'vicarious religion',[2] will be developed at some length in later chapters, including the discussion of methodology. The second involves the shift from obligation to consumption in the European context, a theme that will repeat itself in the theoretical and substantive discussions that lie ahead. Together they illustrate a genuine mutation in the religious life of Europe towards a greater emphasis on choice, but within the parameters of the European past. In this respect my thinking draws on both secularization theory and RCT.

Stark and Iannaccone refer repeatedly to the Swedish example, which forms a case study in its own right within the same issue of the *Journal for the Scientific Study of Religion*.[3] In this, Hamberg and Pettersson (1994) test the principal hypotheses generated by the RCT approach, using the truly excellent data that are available in Sweden as in the other Nordic countries. Using these statistics, the authors are able to establish that religious provision varies from one municipality to another, depending considerably on the relative presence of free churches in the area. They then examine the relationship between even the modest forms of competition that exist in the Swedish case and levels of religious activity. Their results confirm the RCT hypothesis: 'In those municipalities where the level of religious pluralism was higher than the average, religious participation was also higher. Moreover, where the free churches were stronger, the Church of Sweden tended to offer a more varied supply of divine services and the average level of church attendance was higher' (1994: 213). In other words, the state church and the free churches benefit from each other's presence, both directly and indirectly, bearing in mind that the overall levels of religious activity remain low – once again a finding entirely in line with RCT expectations.

The final section of Hamberg and Pettersson's article illustrates the free-riding 'problem'. The Church of Sweden is full of free riders. Given a relatively well-funded quasi-monopoly, the mass of the Swedish population are able to use the church on special occasions without committing themselves on a regular basis. There is plenty of evidence that Swedish people do precisely this – for individual or family events, or for national celebrations or tragedies (most notably after the sinking of the *Estonia* in the Baltic in 1994).[4] And why not? The situation is, in fact, entirely 'rational'. What, after all, is the point of going regularly to a church that is well provided for by church tax (or its more recent equivalent), full of professionals who do the necessary work efficiently and effectively, and who offer services (in every sense of the word) to and for the population as a whole? This, in fact, is an excellent case of vicarious religion (see note 2). Exactly what it tells us about the religious sentiments of the Swedish populations poses an interesting methodological question (see Chapter 6). The question of value judgements follows from this: is vicarious religion (an institutionalized form of free-riding) necessarily a bad thing? American rational choice theorists would probably say 'yes'; I, a European, am not so sure.

Two further illustrations should be noted. The first compares the religiousness of Germans and German Americans, revealing – according to the author – a particularly sharp contrast between Europe and America (Stark, 1997). Interestingly the study is semi-autobiographical in that Stark's mother came from a German Lutheran background (*her* father figures in the story). The argument proceeds as follows:

> A crucial experiment would assess these competing claims by selecting a random sample of Europeans and transporting them to America. Does their religious behavior (and that of their children) become 'Americanized' as they are exposed to a vigorous supply-side? In this paper I approximate such an experiment by comparing the religiousness of first-, second-, and third-generation German Americans with their German 'cousins.' The results very strongly support the supply-side explanation. (1997: 182)

In other words, the relative lack of active religiousness manifested in the West German population in the later decades of the twentieth century is explained by the lack of religious competition in a country dominated by two, heavily subsidized, religious firms – one Catholic and one Protestant. The same is not true of Germans who moved to America. Here levels of religiousness increase in each generation as immigrant Germans respond to the much more vibrant and relatively free American market. Interestingly the proportion of Catholics in the sample maintains itself; conversely the proportion of Protestants not only increases markedly, but becomes more and more diverse. A constituency that was overwhelmingly Lutheran on arrival begins to frequent a wide variety of Protestant denominations. Thus, for Stark, the supply-side argument is supported in terms of denominational identification, religious attendance and selected indices of religious belief.

The second illustration draws on the writing of the unbelievably prolific Andrew Greeley, whose recent work, among many other things, examines current trends in European religion (Greeley, 2003). The book covers a wide range of cases drawn both from West and East Europe. Greeley is entirely correct to emphasize the considerable diversity found across the continent and the complexity of the evidence – not all the indicators move in the same direction. This is even more the case if the post-communist countries are taken into account. In some cases I concur with Greeley's analysis. On the whole, for example, his analysis of Norway recognizes the latent religiosity found in that country and the marked lack of animosity towards the churches that is common to the Nordic countries. In many ways Norway replicates the Swedish situation already described. I also agree with Greeley when he suggests that the Norwegian model may be more stable than many may suggest (including the supply-side analysts) given that Norwegians, like Swedes, are on the whole happy with the way that their religious lives have evolved.[5]

Greeley is also correct in insisting that the concept of religious membership (even if latent) found in the Nordic countries is very different from the patterns of religion found in other parts of Northern Europe – notably the Dutch, French and even British cases – where the number of people within the population who are choosing to detach themselves from the institutional churches (whether Protestant or Catholic) is increasing fast. Hence the notably more secular nature of these three countries. I am less happy, however, about the arguments presented to explain this situation. One reason for this lies in Greeley's apparent ignorance of the extensive corpus of work now available in this field. To analyse the religious life of Europe without reference to David Martin's *General Theory of Secularization* (1978) is not sensible. The failure to understand the English case and the unwise inclusion of France under the heading 'Orange Exceptionalism' follows from this. Such groupings make no sense at all. Greeley recognizes the distinctive nature of the secular core of Europe, but fails to appreciate that these countries are as different from each other as they are from the rest of Europe: residual establishment in England, collapsing pillars in the Netherlands and the secular state in France lead in different directions, a fact with important implication for minorities as well as majorities (see Chapter 8).

Unsurprisingly, Steve Bruce's contribution to the RCT debate is rather different and will be dealt with in stages. His book-length onslaught on the theory itself will be covered in the following section; at this point it is important to pay attention to two case studies. In the first, 'The truth about religion in Britain' (1995b), Bruce draws both on the long-term historical data and on more recent statistics to explode both RCT itself and its usefulness in the British case. Following the pattern established by Stark and Iannaccone, Bruce covers the Middle Ages, the modern period (i.e. the nineteenth and twentieth centuries) and the present (considering both practice and belief). The data are necessarily selective, but they are used to refute as strongly as possible the assumptions on which RCT rests and its capacities to explain what is happening in Britain. Following Bruce, the British data, both historical and contemporary, powerfully endorse the secularization thesis, not RCT. It is simply not the case that the growing diversity of religious supply in Britain results in an increase in demand; precisely the reverse has happened. A second contribution from Bruce elaborates the argument. In 'The pervasive world-view: religion in pre-modern Britain' (1997) Bruce dwells in more detail on the nature of religion in pre-Reformation Britain. He rejects with customary vehemence the 'revisionist' view of history which maintains that the past was considerably less religious than we had assumed and the present rather more so. The evidence from Britain leads him to conclude with Peter Laslett (1983) that 'the world we have lost' was a religious world. The article becomes, in fact, an endorsement of the position that was taken for granted some 30 years ago – and in two respects. On the one hand, Bruce affirms the essential religiousness of pre-Reformation Britain, and on the other, he reiterates the continuing persuasiveness of the secularization thesis in its conventional forms.

### the Latin American case

If the application of RCT to Europe encounters difficulties, are there other parts of the world where the theory might work better? Latin America offers a suggestive example. There is, first of all, constant reference in the literature to the increasing evidence of religious 'competition' in Latin America, a point to be discussed in Part II. Such competition is more apparent in the cities than in rural areas, but exists in most, if not all, parts of the continent. Pentecostal congregations are not only springing up in their thousands, but are recruiting actively, not to say aggressively for members. This, surely, is evidence of a religious market – a term that is used with increasing frequency in Latin America – with all the implications that follow.

Given this situation it is surprising that the rational choice theorists came somewhat late, if at all, to the Latin American field.[6] A notable exception can be found, however, in the work of Anthony Gill, who draws on RCT in his studies of Catholic policymaking (Gill, 1998, 1999). Specifically, Gill uses RCT to explain the decisions of the Catholic churches in the region which favour an 'option for the poor', despite their 'traditional' stance as the ally of economic and political elites. The argument can be summarized as follows. RCT concentrates on the balance between incentives and costs. Using this framework, Gill sets out the combination of factors that in his view will provide sufficient incentives for the Church to opt in favour of the poor, thus overcoming the costs of abandoning an alternative, and familiar, policy. To be precise, in those places where the Catholic Church faces competition in the recruitment of believers – and especially from socialist and Protestant alternatives – the Catholic authorities will oppose authoritarian regimes in order to maintain credibility with the poor. It is clear that the presence of emergent Pentecostal movements becomes a crucial, if by no means the only, variable in this process. Gill exemplifies his theory with reference to the very different stances of the Catholic Church in Chile and Argentina. In the former where there is a noticeable presence of both socialist and evangelical movements, the Pinochet regime was heavily criticized by the Church. In the latter, where the alternatives are far less developed, the traditional accommodation between church and state to a large extent continues.

The approach offers an unusual (in the sense that it is concerned with the choices made by churches rather than the choices made by believers) application of RCT to the understanding of Latin American religion. Interestingly, in a subsequent article, Finke and Stark (2003) draw on Gill's analyses as they review the possible applications of RCT outside the United States. The question of time-lag is crucial to their argument: in Latin America (as indeed was the case in the United States) religious growth follows deregulation but *not* immediately, a point with obvious resonance to the European case.

## CLARIFICATIONS, CRITICS AND CRITICISMS

Rational choice theorists constitute a relatively small group of scholars, most of whom are American, whose impact has been considerable. RCT remains, however, controversial – indeed, more than most theories, it has a tendency to polarize opinion. The following paragraphs examine a range of responses to the rational choice approach. They begin with questions about theory and data. These are followed by a series of hesitations or refinements. The section ends with a more radical critique of the theory, notably Bruce's full-scale attack on RCT and its 'malign' influence in the sociology of religion.

### conceptual clarifications

Two small clarifications must be raised at this point. The first takes the form of a question: is RCT simply a circular argument? Religious actors (just like any other actors) are assumed to act 'rationally': that is, they will choose the forms of religion that, for them, maximize gain and minimize loss. It follows that the choices that are made – whatever their precise content – are the result of 'rational' decision making; they cannot be otherwise. But this runs the risk, surely, of taking us round in circles, and fails to explain *why* what appears to be rational for one person is not so for another and *why* what is considered rational in one place is not so in another.

The second point reveals different emphases within the theory itself. An acceptance of rationality (i.e. a theory based on rational action) need not mean commitment to the supply-side model. The two ideas are distinct and may become more so. Larry Iannaccone's Association for the Study of Religion, Economics and Society, for example, seeks to promote the use of economics in the understanding of religion.[7] Much of this work is unrelated to the theories of Stark and Finke. In short, those who have difficulty with the supply-side aspects of RCT need not discard the baby with the bathwater.

## questions about data

In terms of data, two somewhat different issues have been brought to the fore by the RCT debate. The first questions the degree of religiousness claimed by many modern Americans; the second relates to the supposed relationship between religious pluralism and religious involvement.

In 1993, Hadaway and colleagues published their findings on American church-going in the *American Sociological Review*. Generally speaking, the American evidence about church attendance is (or has been) supportive of RCT; it is indicative of a vibrant religious market which in turn has generated high levels of religious activity. It is correspondingly awkward for advocates of secularization theory. But is the evidence correct? Hadaway et al. painstakingly examined the evident disparity between the data gathered from opinion polls (what Americans say they do) and the evidence assembled by counting the people who are in church (or an equivalent) on any given Sunday. Around 40 per cent of the American population declare that they attend church on a regular basis – that figure is surprisingly stable and frequently quoted. If, however, the methodology shifts to headcounting of various kinds (as opposed to reported behaviour) something rather different emerges. Using the figures assembled by these authors, it seems that '[C]hurch attendance rates for Protestant and Catholics are approximately *one-half* the generally accepted levels' (1993: 742). Such a finding makes quite a difference to how we think about religion in modern America.

Some five years later, the same journal ran a symposium on church attendance in the United States, gathering a number of responses to

Hadaway et al. A wide range of issues are raised in these papers, some methodological and some interpretative. By and large the methodological issues are concerned with the data sets themselves (whether actual or reported) and their reliability. The interpretative issues are more interesting. Assuming that Americans do indeed inflate their reported levels of church attendance, what are their reasons for this? Why, in other words, do Americans wish to portray themselves as church-goers and what does this tell us about modern America? And how does this compare with other populations, not least most Europeans?[8] The implications are fascinating and go to the heart of the matter. A whole series of questions unfolds. Is consistent over-reporting evidence for or evidence against secularization? It is evidence for in the sense that church-going levels are lower than most commentators had assumed. It is evidence against in that large numbers of Americans wish – for whatever reason – to be known as church-goers. How then do we interpret the data? Two examples will illustrate the point. 'I will say that I was in church last Sunday even if I was not' is, surely, indicative of a culture in which church-going is viewed positively. 'I would be ashamed to admit that I was in church last week so I will say that I didn't go' reveals a very different peer group. In focusing their attention on the gap between reported and actual behaviour, Hadaway et al. have opened up a crucial area of sociological enquiry – one, moreover, which reveals the qualitative difference in religious life between the United States and much of Europe.

The second methodological issue is both similar and different. Once again it raises queries about what exactly is being measured and what inferences can be drawn, but the questioning comes from a different angle. Voas et al. (2002) examine the ever multiplying tests of a central RCT hypothesis: the connection between religious diversity (the extent of supply) and religious activity. A review of the literature discovered 193 tests of this question in 26 published articles (including some of those mentioned above) – an indication in itself of research activity in this area. Voas et al. are not, however, concerned with the findings of these articles as such (i.e. with the evidence for or against the RCT hypothesis), though they agree that this is an important question. Their argument works at a deeper level. They are increasingly convinced that the studies under review do not measure the relationship that they have in mind. More precisely, a close examination of the data reveals that the 'observed relationships between diversity and involvement are predictable on the basis of wholly nonsubstantive factors' (2002: 231). They depend on the nature of the size distributions of the religious groups across geographical areas in a particular data set. In other

83

words, pluralism as such is not the key variable; it is replaced by size distribution: '[T]he general principle is that when the larger denominations have the greatest size variation, correlations tend to be negative, but when the smaller denominations are more variable, correlations tend to be positive' (2002: 215). It follows that almost all of those 193 studies will have to be re-evaluated before their results can be taken as evidence for or against the pluralism hypothesis – a daunting task. No doubt the controversy will continue.

## hesitations

The second half of Young's very useful collection of material on RCT is concerned with more substantive reservations. Two of these will be taken as illustrative: the work of Neitz and Mueser and the work of Ammerman. Neitz and Muser (1996) examine the evident difference between men and women, arguing that male rather than female experience is embedded in the rational choice model. At one level, it is easy enough to incorporate gender differences into the RCT approach, noting that women make different religious choices from those of men. Miller and Stark (2002) do precisely this in their work on the significance of gender as a variable in religious decision making, concluding that men are less risk averse than women – hence their lower uptake of religion. Neitz and Mueser's unease, however, goes deeper than this; it operates at a conceptual level. They remind us that a whole set of questions which relate to the religious lives of women – those which reflect relationality, connectedness, reproduction, negotiation, interpretation, narrative and so on – do not fit easily into the RCT frame. Not only do men and women make different religious choices, they conduct their religious lives in entirely different ways.

Ammerman (1996) is equally insistent that we need to take into account emotion and affect as well as reason – a purely cognitive theory does not do this. She takes, however, a both/and rather than an either/ or approach to the question, seeing in RCT a welcome acceptance that modern people, including women, make rational choices about their religious lives. It is not the case that religion is necessarily a sign of a pre-modern, irrational way of living, as at least some versions of the secularization thesis seem to imply. The theory needs, however, to be refined, not least the assumed link between pluralism and activity. We need to ask *under what conditions* is it likely that an increase in religious pluralism will stimulate the market; and – conversely – in what circumstances will the outcome be negative rather than positive? In order to answer this question, Ammerman draws on her own empirical work on congregations and communities in the United States. The attention to detail is paramount: that is, to the local context and its particular history (these factors are not generalizable). It is even more important to listen to the voices of the people themselves – to those (the religious actors) who are making the choices. The methodological implications of both these requirements are considerable; both demand small-scale, qualitative research alongside the analysis of large-scale data sets.

## condemnations

Condemnation, perhaps, is too strong a word for Robin Gill's contribution to the debate in that it has evolved as a separate framework of understanding rather than an attack on RCT as such. Indeed Gill (1993, 1999) conceives of his work as a critique of one of the central 'myths' of secularization theory (the notion that a decline in church-going results primarily from a gradual loss of belief), not of RCT. His conclusions, however, are so diametrically opposed to the RCT claim that an increase in religious supply generates an increase in religious demand that they merit inclusion in this section.

Gill draws on an impressive range of longitudinal data to argue that a major problem in the religious life of Britain lies in the long-term oversupply of church buildings. The competitive building between different Protestant denominations that took place in the nineteenth century offers an excellent example. No lazy monopoly here! Using detailed local evidence, Gill demonstrates that in some areas the churches could never be full even if substantial sections of the populations went regularly to worship: quite simply there were too many buildings and too many seats. The problem intensified as populations moved from the country to the city and from the city centre to the suburbs – not only were there too many churches, they were in the wrong places. Overprovision, moreover, leads to expensive plant which is difficult to maintain. Small congregations struggle to continue but become increasingly disillusioned. Disillusionment leads to decline and decline to disillusionment: a downward spiral is set in motion and becomes more and more difficult to reverse. Occasional success stories, moreover, are likely to exacerbate the problem as a diminishing body of church-goers moves from one church to another. Paul Chambers's work on the dock area of Swansea offers an excellent example of Gill's thesis. Here in parts of the city, cavernous non-conformist chapels can be found on every street corner, all built at about the same time and now nearly all in a state of decay (Chambers, 2004); quite clearly the local economy was oversupplied. And in those parts of the city where church-going has picked up – due largely to the policies of particular churches – this has been at the expense of others. There is little or no increase in the overall numbers.

Steve Bruce's attack is altogether more focused. In the introduction to *Choice and Religion*, Bruce explains its genesis:

> A brief account of why this book was written might also explain its tone. If there are occasional hints of exasperation, it is because the whole project was born out of frustration with the malign influence of a small clique of US sociologists of religion. (1999: 1)

This statement is followed by a whole set of sentences that begin 'I know', each of which indicates the profound changes in Scottish society since, say, the seventeenth century, all of which add up to overwhelming evidence for a deep-seated process of secularization. Nor can it be argued that the gaps that are emerging from the decline in historic forms of religion are currently being filled by innovative alternatives. In other words, the evidence for religious decline in Scotland – as indeed in the whole of Britain – is comprehensive and no amount of 'revision' will alter this basic fact. Following Bruce, RCT flies in the face of all available evidence.

The first two chapters of Bruce's book set out the two paradigms: secularization and RCT. The two that follow look at a range of different cases before returning to the central theme: that is, the fundamental flaws in an approach to religion based on rational choice. These lie in the impossibility of applying rational choice to the religious field – it simply doesn't work. Religious actors have histories and identities that impinge upon their choices; they live in contexts where different religious organizations are more or less available. Neither demand nor supply follow the rules of the market; both are skewed by all sorts of influences. Most social environments are not yet conducive to choosing a religion, which in most societies remains too important to be simply a matter of preference (Bruce, 1999: 129).

I find the latter poir t somewhat difficult in view of Bruce's insistence in earlier volumes (notably *Religion in the Modern World*, 1996) that religious choices, at least in the West, are made in an increasingly 'individualistic and idiosyncratic manner' (1996: 233). Among the minority who are still interested in religion, there is a growing tendency to adopt in their religious lives, as in everything else, the dominant ethos of late capitalism: that is, a 'world of options, lifestyles and preferences'

(1996: 233). The point, as we saw in the previous chapter, is that the increase in religious diversity and the choices that follow from this necessarily undermine plausibility – not that the religious arena is a domain where choice does not operate. In 1999, the argument appears to have shifted to oppose the notion of choice altogether. The only way to reconcile these views is, it seems, to make an exception of the modern West – where choice is evident but necessarily corrosive of religious vitality. Either way Bruce firmly rejects both the theory and the advocates of RCT and their pernicious influence in the sub-discipline. For Bruce the secularization process is part and parcel of modern liberal democracy, unless there are structural reasons (such as cultural defence) to oppose or retard the dominant trend. A society in which religious choice is possible will, necessarily, be secular.

## CONCLUSION

Who then is right and who is wrong – the advocates of secularization or the protagonists of RCT? Neither probably. The crucial point lies deeper – well beneath the surface – and illustrates, once again, the essential difference between Europe and the United States in terms of religious understandings. More specifically, it lies in the fact that Europeans, as a consequence of the state church system (an historical fact whether you like it or not) regard their churches as public utilities rather than competing firms. That is the real legacy of the European past. With this in mind, it is hardly surprising that Europeans bring to their religious organizations an entirely different repertoire of responses from their American counterparts. Most Europeans, it is clear, look at their churches with benign benevolence – they are useful social institutions, which the great majority in the population are likely to need at one time or another in their lives (particularly at the time of a death). It simply does not occur to most people that the churches will or might cease to exist but for their active participation. It is this attitude of mind which is both central to the understanding of European religion and extremely difficult to eradicate. It, rather than the presence or absence of a market, accounts for a great deal of the data on the European side of the Atlantic. It is not that the market isn't there (it quite obviously is in most parts of Europe, if not quite in all); it is simply that the market doesn't work given the prevailing attitudes of large numbers in the population.

But that is not to say that patterns of religion in Europe can never change. Indeed a close analysis of what is happening in Europe reflects at least some of the connections between choice and religion suggested by RCT. It is quite clear, for example, that the historic churches have lost their capacity to discipline either the belief systems or the behaviour of most Europeans. They remain, however, an important marker of identity and allegiance for many European people, and continue to function as significant public utilities. At the same time a culture of choice is beginning to emerge which is distinctive to the European case. This shift from obligation to consumption will emerge as a leitmotiv in subsequent chapters (both theoretical and empirical). As an idea it embodies elements of both the secularization and the RCT approaches to religion. The process of secularization has undoubtedly taken its toll. Hence the failure of the historic churches to maintain their capacities to 'oblige' people to go to church, to believe in certain things and to behave in certain ways. But a minority in the population continues to attend a religious institution – for a wide variety of reasons. Who these people are, what choices they make and why they make them will constitute an important part of the material presented in the second half of this book.

All too easily, however, the debate turns into a sociological fight to the death in which one paradigm has to emerge the winner. One form of this 'fight' can be found in repeated attempts to identify the real 'exceptionalism'. Is this the United States: that is, a vibrant religious market in a highly developed country, but clearly without parallel in the modern (developed) world? Or is this Europe, the only part of the world where secularization can be convincingly linked to modernization, but no longer – as was assumed for so long – a global prototype with universal applicability? Casanova (2001b, 2003) is one author anxious to escape from this repetitious and circular argument; we need, he argues, to think increasingly in global terms. The following chapter offers a theoretical perspective in which this is increasingly possible.

## NOTES

1 The scale suggested by Chaves and Cann produces some strange results – for example, placing Ireland and the Netherlands on a par with the United States in terms of religious regulation. Stark and Iannaccone are entirely right to say the elimination of legal ties between church and state are not the whole story and that de facto regulation lingers when de jure separation has already occurred. I would go much further and say that a scale such as this is not measuring like with like. As Warner correctly said, the links between church and state in Europe go back some 800 years; relatively recent legal changes need to be seen in this context.

2 By vicarious religion, I mean the notion of religion performed by an active minority but on behalf of a much larger number, who (implicitly at least) not only understand but, quite clearly, approve of what the minority is doing. For a more detailed discussion, see pp. 128–30 and pp. 143–6.

3 Comparatively speaking, Sweden is about as near as it is possible to get to religious monopoly within a political system that recognizes religious freedom. It is important, however, to bear in mind the constitutional changes that took place in 2000 (Bäckström et al., 2004). In the longer term these are likely to have an effect on membership.

4 An interesting parallel can be found in the tragedy that befell Norway in the summer of 2011 when a right-wing extremist killed almost 80 people, many of them teenagers. Norwegians turned naturally to the state church for the appropriate rituals and to find comfort in adversity.

5 Debates about disestablishment continue in Norway. Norway is almost certain to follow the Swedish example in this respect (see note 3).

6 Note, however, Chesnut (1997, 2003) and Smith and Prokopy (1999).

7 See www.thearda.com/asrec/ (accessed 4 April 2012).

8 Hadaway et al. (1998: 129) claim that a similar tendency can be found in Britain, though the indices are lower overall. Many European social scientists would, I think, challenge this statement.

# *five*

## modernity: a single or plural construct?

The following discussion offers an alternative path into the material already introduced. It is concerned above all with the conceptual tools that are necessary for a proper understanding of modernity and of the place of religion within this. In order to gain a purchase on a necessarily complex debate, I have taken the evolution in my own thinking as a starting point. The first section draws directly, but not exclusively, on *Religion in Britain since 1945* (Davie, 1994), particularly the discussion in the final chapter, which reflects on the notion of modernity with respect to the British case. The second section updates this material, making use of more recent work relating primarily to the patterns of religion in Northern Europe (Davie, 2004a, 2005, 2006a, 2006b). The third, relatively short, section introduces a much more diverse range of sources, thus providing a broader context for reflection.

The fourth and final section of the chapter returns to my own thinking, drawing in particular on the theoretical aspects of *Europe: The Exceptional Case* (Davie, 2002a). The reason for doing this is clear. The questions addressed in this section reflect a primary theme of the later book: that is, the tools and concepts of sociology of religion and their adequacy for understanding the many different forms of religion that are emerging in the modern world. And if their adequacy is found wanting, what is to be done?

### MODERNITY AND MODERNISM IN A BRITISH CONTEXT

The point of departure for the final chapter of Davie (1994) lies in a developed discussion of two sets of ideas: modernity and postmodernity on the one hand, modernism and postmodernism on the other – understanding the former primarily in terms of economic and social structures and the latter in terms of cultural forms, bearing in mind that the distinction between them is necessarily fluid. The aim of the discussion is to appreciate more fully the implications for religion of both social structures and cultural forms, taking into account that each of these, like the societies of which they were part, was changing as the century drew to a close.

The essentials of the argument are set out in Figure 5.1. Its contents must, however, be approached with caution: the diagram neither postulates nor establishes a set of necessary relationships – indeed such links will be firmly denied. The information, moreover, is schematic; the intention is to indicate in outline form what in reality are profound, complex and confusing changes experienced in different ways by different groups of individuals, communities and societies as the pressures of late modernity, or post-industrialization, assert themselves.

A further question is immediately apparent: that is, the form of society (in both structural and cultural terms) that preceded modernity. Or to put the same point in diagrammatic terms, should the scheme outlined in Figure 5.1 have three rather than two columns, the left-hand one

| Modernity | Postmodernity |
|---|---|
| Industrialization | Post-industrialization/information technology |
| Urbanization | De-urbanization |
| Production | Consumption |

Both modernity and postmodernity are problematic for religion but in different ways

| Modernism | Postmodernism |
|---|---|
| The grand narrative: religious or anti-religious | Fragmentation/decentring of the religious narrative, but also of the secular; i.e. of the scientific, rational or anti-religious narrative e.g. rationalism/communism |
| Progress | |
| Secularization/secularism | A space for the sacred but often in forms different from those which have gone before |
| God the Son | The Holy Spirit |
| The institutional churches | Varied forms of the sacred |
| Medical science | Healing/alternative medicine |
| Agribusiness | Ecology/organic food |
| *Obligation* | *Consumption* |

Figure adapted from Davie (1994: 192)

Figure 5.1 Religion and modernity: a schematic representation

referring to pre-industrial and pre-urban society: in other words, a society which was primarily rural and in which certain forms of traditional religion were, without doubt, more secure that they have ever been since? The shifts from pre-modern to modern have, quite rightly, caught the attention of sociologists interested in the secularization process – a point already discussed; so, too, have the differences between different European societies, including very marked contrasts in timing. In some parts of Europe, the modernization process began a full century ahead of even a neighbouring state (Britain and France exemplify this point); in others (e.g. Spain and Portugal) the process was artificially retarded for political reasons, but then happened very fast indeed.

Such differences indicate a more general problem. Exactly when does one form of society give way to another, and when (if ever) do such shifts have discernible and corresponding effects on particular cultural forms? Clearly it is difficult to put dates on these metamorphoses. Some observers, for example, date the beginnings of modernity long before others – it is associated with the global expansion of Europe in the fifteenth and sixteenth centuries, well before any part of Europe became an industrial or production-based society. The establishment of the nation-state as the dominant form of political organization (normally considered a prerequisite of modernity) is equally difficult to pin down; both the nature of the state itself and the moment of its appearance vary widely even within the European context, never mind in different parts of the world (see below). Hence the problems with the left-hand column. Happily, the crucial point lies elsewhere: namely that the forms and processes of religious life in any given place can only be fully understood within a long-term and relatively specific historical perspective. The fact that the dates cannot be generalized from one case to another does not detract from the general principle.

What then does the approach set out in Figure 5.1 bring to our attention? Taking the shifts in economic and social structure first, it is increasingly clear that both modern and postmodern societies make heavy demands on most forms of organized religion, but in different ways. The movement, for example, of large sections of the population into the large conurbations associated with certain kinds of industry was, as we have seen, profoundly disruptive of patterns of life that had existed for centuries all over Europe – a process that stimulated not only the development of sociology itself but the place of religion within this. Getting on for a century later, however, religious organizations – much reduced though not always in ways that the founding fathers anticipated – find themselves in a different situation. The larger industrial cities, so

**92**

often the focus of apprehension on the part of more traditional forms of religion, are declining all over the West alongside the industries that brought them into place. So, proportionally, are the social class or classes traditionally most reluctant to attend their churches.

The corollary, however, is far from straightforward, a point that can be nicely illustrated from the findings of the 2001 British Census.[1] Those parts of England and Wales that revealed the largest number of people with 'no religion' were *not* the large conurbations of the industrial North of Britain, but a markedly different group of cities in the South; very often those where a university and its employees form a sizeable section of the population. The industrial North, in contrast, established itself as relatively traditional (i.e. more rather than less attached to Christianity than the South) but with a marked presence of other faith communities in some, if not all, of these cities. Such patterns were not expected; nor were the relatively large percentages of the population that declared themselves Christian wherever they lived – the figures for nominal attachment were unexpectedly high.[2]

The more you look, in fact, the more complex the data become, remembering that the structural changes just described (i.e. the shift from industrial to post-industrial society) have equally important consequences for the institutions of economic and political life. Shifts in the economy, for example, put considerable pressure on the trade union movement, the membership of which has declined steadily since the 1970s. Only part of this decline can be attributed to the punitive legislation introduced by the Thatcher government (to take the British case); far more radical in their effects have been the transformations in the work environment. Specifically, those segments of the economy that are growing are those where union influence is weak, a situation exacerbated by the presence of women in the service sector (women are more resistant to unionism than men). Male manual work (the core of the trade union movement) is a diminishing feature of the late-modern labour market and not only in Britain, necessarily transforming the situation in which wage bargaining takes place. As a result trade unions find themselves in an increasingly difficult position: their numbers decrease, together with their traditional sources of income.

Political parties are similarly discomfited as the traditional divisions between capital and labour, right and left, conservative and socialist, no longer resonate. Political divisions now run through the major parties rather than between them, and the parties themselves are losing members in proportions similar to the churches with similar consequences for their financial health. Even more serious is a pervasive disillusionment with the political process itself, reflected in low

93

turnouts and a barely concealed contempt for politicians of all parties. Electorates display their feelings by withholding their votes from the major parties, sometimes with disastrous consequences.[3] Single-issue or one-off campaigns, however, attract considerable attention, bringing together diverse groups of people, frequently with very different motivations.[4] Interestingly, exactly the same is true with respect to religious activities – the expressions of religious sentiment following a prominent or unexpected death offer an obvious example. The growth in pilgrimage, of all kinds, reflects a similar tendency.

How then should these changes be interpreted? Or, more specifically, do the similarities between different sectors of society prompt us to think again about the reasons for the evident decline in religious activity? Personally, I am more persuaded by arguments that take into account economic and social change in these explanations rather than those which see the decline first and foremost as a sign of religious indifference. An interesting exchange in this respect can be found in the *Journal of Contemporary Religion* (2002/3). Not for the first time, I find myself taking a rather different view from that espoused by Steve Bruce, arguing that the shifts and changes in the religious life of West Europe can only be understood if they are placed alongside parallel changes in the secular sphere (Davie, 2001). Bruce (2002b) constitutes a reply to this position, in which he explains the decline in religious activity in Britain purely in terms of the secularization thesis – parallel changes in society are simply a side issue, a distraction from the main argument.

It is unwise, in my view, to dichotomize these choices. There is strong evidence to support some, if not all, aspects of the secularization process in the European case, following Bruce and many others (the point has already been made in Chapter 3). But the causal sequence needs careful attention. The shifts in the nature of belief, for example, are as much the *consequence* of the decline in religious activity as its *cause*. Religious institutions, just like their secular counterparts, are undermined by the features of late modernity which erode the willingness of European populations to gather anywhere on a regular and committed basis. Fewer people attend churches, political parties and trade unions, or indeed many other voluntary organizations – no one argues about this. As a result the beliefs and sympathies of these people begin to drift. In terms of the religious life of modern Britain beliefs as such maintain themselves, but in forms that have little to do with the historic formularies of the Christian tradition. They become increasingly detached, individualized and heterogeneous. This situation, the direct consequence of 'believing without belonging', will be explained in more detail in Part II.

94

The work of Helen Cameron (2001, 2003, 2004) on the voluntary sector is not only interesting but very helpful in this respect. Cameron (2001) discerns four very different models of voluntary membership which should not be confused: these are activity-based groups (which often involve practical service); fun, friends and fundraising groups (with the emphasis on joining in and fundraising); affinity groups (largely based on subscription membership with only a small core actively involved); and groups which are based primarily on the requirement of membership in order to obtain specialized insurance (often associated with sporting or outdoor activities). No sensible conclusions can be drawn if the four groups are simply aggregated for they display very different trends. Cameron concludes that it is the groups most closely associated with the generation of social capital (whether secular or religious) that are currently in decline in modern societies; conversely groups which demand relatively little from their members are the ones which are growing. There is little evidence of a switch from religious to secular membership *within* any of the categories above.

So much for the structural changes in modern Britain, and elsewhere, and their effects on both believing and belonging. It is now time to turn to the lower half of the diagram in Figure 5.1 (i.e. to the cultural rather than the structural sphere, remembering that the links between these are speculative rather than proven). The changing nature of modern thinking, from the certainties that prevailed in the 1960s (probably the peak of modernism) to the very different mood that set in barely a decade later, form the core of this discussion – a shift that has provoked a huge and contentious sociological literature, markedly larger now than it was in 1994. Some indications of this literature, in so far as it applies to religion, will be given in the third section of this chapter.

The central point made in 1994 still stands, however. Underlying all of these commentaries lies a basic philosophical shift, arguably as significant as the movement that occurred some two centuries earlier and became known as the Enlightenment. These changes in thinking are brought together in the catch-all phrase of 'postmodernism' – an outlook that subjects the Enlightenment Project to penetrating scrutiny, calling into question the essentially optimistic foundations on which the project is built. Faced with this onslaught and with the unpredicted and unpredictable swings in the global economy following the oil crisis of the early 1970s, neither the Western form of the Enlightenment (rationalism) nor its Eastern counterpart (communism) were able to sustain the certainties which until the 1970s seemed unassailable. Even more radical

95

was the collapse in certainty itself. No longer was it a question of find-ing one grand narrative to replace another; the whole idea of a grand narrative, of whatever type, becomes deeply suspect, a mood which infected religious thinking as well as secular. Postmodern approaches to theology, for example, undermine the traditional formulae, both sub-stantive or methodological. What you do in theology and how you do it can no longer be taken for granted.

The situation that emerges becomes, therefore, not only complex but qualitatively different from that which preceded it. The competition between a variety of creeds, both secular and religious, gives way to a pervasive self-questioning on each side of the classic divide. The locus of the debate alters as each profession or 'ideology' struggles with the dis-turbing ideas introduced under the banner of postmodernism. For our purposes the essential point lies in the following: the secular certainties (science, rationalism, progress, etc.), the erstwhile competitors of reli-gious truth, are themselves seen in a different light. Science does not simply provide answers: on the contrary, the development of science poses new and ever more difficult questions, which in turn make heavy demands on resources other than scientific if answers are to be found. Hence an entirely different situation from that which was taken for granted in the early post-war decades. No longer is it assumed that a secular discourse will gradually overcome a recognizable and unified religious alternative. Instead both secular and religious thinking will evolve as multiple groups of people look for new ways forward, and new creeds (both secular and religious) to live by in the early years of the twenty-first century.

The next question follows naturally enough. What then are these creeds in modern British or European society: that is, in a part of the world caught up in a changing global economy, but which has a deeply rooted Christian past experienced in a particular and historically defin-able way? Some of these possibilities are set out in the lower half of Figure 5.1. They were developed in some detail in Davie (1994: 199–200), in which – in terms of the sacred – I underlined two possible alternatives or two clusters of belief. The first were the forms of religious life that adapted most easily to the flux of late modernity, not least the ways of thinking and being that are associated with the term 'new age'. The second alternative offers a very different way of coming to terms with flux: the tightly bound groups, both inside and outside the mainstream churches, that provide havens for those people who find it difficult to live with change and uncertainty, the hallmarks of postmodernism. Taken to an extreme, this tendency has been associated with various forms of fundamentalism. Both these tendencies remain important to the

96

understanding of religion in the modern world and will be described in the later chapters of this book.

## FROM OBLIGATION TO CONSUMPTION: A EUROPEAN MUTATION

Some 10 years later, I was still thinking about the same issues, building on to the framework already outlined, but formulating the question in a rather different way and with greater attention to the European, as opposed to British, context (Davie, 2004a, 2005). In some respects little had changed. Almost all commentators agreed, for example, that the historic churches of Europe – despite their continuing presence – were systematically losing their capacity to discipline the religious thinking of large sections of the population, especially amongst the young. At the same time, the range of choice was becoming wider as innovative forms of religion came into Europe from outside, largely as the result of the movement of people. Populations that have arrived in Europe primarily for economic reasons brought with them different ways of being religious, some Christian and some not. And quite apart from the incoming movements, European people increasingly travelled the world, experiencing amongst other things considerable religious diversity. In this sense a genuine religious market was emerging in most parts of the continent.

The crucial question lies, however, not in the existence of the market in itself but in the capacities of Europeans to make use of this, a major point of contrast with the United States, which has already been discussed. There are, however, similarities as well as differences. In Europe as well as America, a new pattern is gradually emerging: that is, a shift away from an understanding of religion as a form of obligation and towards an increasing emphasis on consumption or choice. What until moderately recently was simply imposed (with all the negative connotations of this word) or inherited (a rather more positive spin) becomes instead a matter of personal inclination. I go to church (or to another religious organization) because I want to, maybe for a short period or maybe for longer, to fulfil a particular rather than a general need in my life and where I will continue my attachment so long as it provides what I want, but I have no *obligation* either to attend in the first place or to continue if I don't want to.

If such a shift is indeed taking place, what might be the implications for the patterns of religion in modern Europe? The first point to grasp, paradoxically, is that the emergent pattern is not only compatible with

**97**

the historic model of Europe's churches, but to a large extent depends upon it: the churches, including the state churches, need to be there in order that individuals may attend them if they so choose. The 'chemistry', however, gradually alters – a change which is discernible in both practice and belief, not to mention the connections between them. An obvious illustration of this process can be found in the patterns of confirmation in the Church of England. It is true that the overall numbers of confirmations have dropped dramatically in the post-war period, evidence once again of institutional decline. In England, though not yet in the Nordic countries, confirmation is no longer a teenage rite of passage imposed by the institution, but a relatively rare event undertaken as a matter of personal choice by people of all ages. Hence the marked rise in the proportion of adult confirmations amongst the candidates overall – by no means enough, however, to offset the fall among teenagers.

Confirmation becomes, therefore, a very significant event for those individuals who choose this option – an attitude that is bound to affect the rite itself, which now includes the space for a public declaration of faith. It becomes, in fact, an opportunity to make public what has often been an entirely private activity. It is increasingly common, moreover, to baptize an adult candidate immediately before the confirmation, a gesture which is evidence in itself of the fall in infant baptism some 20 to 30 years earlier. Taken together, these events indicate a marked change in the nature of membership in the historic churches which become, in some senses, much more like their non-established counterparts. Voluntarism is beginning to establish itself de facto, regardless of the constitutional position of the institution in question. Or to continue the 'chemical' analogy a little further, a whole set of new reactions are set off which in the *longer* term (the stress is important) may have a profound effect on the nature of European religion.

Two remarks conclude this discussion, which will be re-opened in Part II. The first reflects the public as well as the private implications of 'choosing' religion. As we have seen in Chapter 3, at least some versions of secularization theory (not least Bruce, 1996, 1999) carry with them the notion that chosen religion is necessarily privatized religion; for these commentators, religion has become simply a matter of personal preference or lifestyle. Prompted by discussions with sociologists in the Nordic countries,[5] I am no longer convinced that this is so. Those who opt seriously for religion in European societies will want to make their views heard in public as well as private debate. It is at this point, moreover, that the forms of religion (both Christian and non-Christian) that have arrived more recently within Europe begin to make an impact: they offer positive (at times inspirational) models to the host community – the learning process is running in both directions.

The second remark concerns my own thinking about the nature of religion in modern Europe. In many respects, the shift from obligation to consumption fits easily (gratifyingly so) within the diagram set out in 1994; it articulates exactly the same idea as the earlier formulation, but opens new possibilities in terms of the available choices. Or to put the same point in a different way, I am even more convinced than I was in 1994 that certain forms of the sacred will persist even in Europe, but in order to evaluate these properly Europe – and European forms of modernity – must be set in a wider context. That is the task of the final section of this chapter.

## RELIGION AND MODERNITY: A CONTINUING DEBATE

Before tackling the topic head on, it is important to appreciate the grow-ing corpus of sociological work (both empirical and theoretical) in this field. The amount of available data, for example, has increased signifi-cantly and will continue to do so. The careful reading of these data, moreover, is provoking new and ever more interesting questions about the relationship between religion and modernity. One example, prompted by the findings from the most recent investigations of the European Values Study (EVS), will suffice.[6] As the historic churches of Europe lose the capacity to discipline either the beliefs or the lifestyles of European populations, it is not the case that religion simply disappears. New and somewhat intriguing patterns of belief and behaviour are beginning to emerge, not least among young people.

These patterns are interesting from several points of view. First, they have little to do with traditional forms of religion, where the anticipated relationships hold: namely that older people are more religious than the young in terms of both belief and practice. Nor is there much change where the historic church remains relatively strong (i.e. in countries such as Poland, Ireland or Italy). Here the institution is still able to discipline the beliefs and behaviour of significant sections of the population. Hence a continuing tendency to rebel among young people. But in those parts of Europe where the institutional church is weak, something new is, it seems, occurring. In the data collected in 1999/2000 EVS enquiries, two variables in particular – a belief in an immanent as opposed to transcendent God (a God in me) and a conviction that life continues after death – revealed markedly higher levels of assent among younger generations than among the old, exactly the reverse of what might have been expected (see in particular Bréchon, 2001 and Lambert, 2002). It is still too soon to know whether these shifts are likely to be permanent, but their simultaneous appearance across many parts of Europe at the very least invites reflection. One explanation lies in the possibility that the relationship between at least some measures of belief and belonging might be inverse rather than direct. In other words, as the latter declines, the former increase but in innovative ways – new possibilities open up for newly liberated believers.

The theoretical contributions to the field are equally important. Broadly speaking these can be divided into two groups: first, those whose background and inspiration lie primarily within the sociology of religion but who are taking increasing note of the theoretical trends within the discipline as a whole; and second, those who work within mainstream sociology, but who are beginning, bit by bit, to pay attention to the presence of religion in late-modern societies. Until relatively recently, however, there has been little serious conversation between the two, a point already mentioned and which has preoccupied James Beckford for the best part of two decades. The 'insulation' and 'isolation' of the sociology of religion from the principal currents of sociological thinking formed a principal theme in his *Religion and Advanced Industrial Society* (1989); it continues to penetrate his writing.

Beckford, however, has done more than identify the problem; he has worked harder than most to overcome it, both in the volume already cited and more recently in his very welcome *Social Theory and Religion* (2003) – a constructivist approach to the study of religion, in which the emphasis lies on the processes 'whereby the meaning of the category of religion is, in various situations, intuited, asserted, doubted, challenged, rejected, substituted, re-cast, and so on' (2003: 3). The argument is developed by setting theoretical insights alongside empirical data in order to stimulate new ways of thinking. The technique is then applied to a range of issues in the field, secularization, pluralization, globalization and religious movements, producing a series of helpful, though provocative essays. Chapter 8 of this book, for example, draws very directly on Beckford's discussion of pluralization, noting the degree to which the terms deployed in these increasingly important discussions are themselves social constructions. It follows that effective debate can only begin when the conceptual problems have been fully engaged – the task par excellence of the sociologist.

Beckford is no longer working in isolation. From the mid-1990s on, a clutch of new writing emerged, frequently in the form of edited collections, not least that brought together by Beckford himself, with John Walliss (2006). Other examples can be found in the conference papers assembled by Paul Heelas and colleagues in *Religion, Modernity and Postmodernity* (1998) and – rather differently – in the published sources collected by Heelas and Woodhead in *Religion in Modern Times* (2000). The former addresses very directly the relationship between the forms of religion found in both modernity and postmodernity and their relationship to culture. It has a welcome comparative dimension and includes rather than excludes theological discussion. The latter brings together not only a wide range of authors but an equally impressive range of religions, paying careful attention to how these relate to each other, to the contexts of which they are part and to the forces of modernization that they inevitably encounter. Crucial themes emerge often in the form of tensions; for example, between traditional faiths and new spiritualities; between secularization and sacralization; between the God without and the God within (i.e. external authority and the authority of the self); between exclusivist rejections and tolerant universalisms; between increasing privatization and growing political militancy; and – last but not least – with appropriate attention to gender. One point becomes very clear: more than one thing can happen at once in any given society, indeed in any given group as different religious constituencies seek to reposition themselves in a changing world. There is no need to choose between theories of secularization or sacralization, for example: both can be present.[7] So too can the emphasis on a 'soft' universalism alongside a growing and much 'harder' exclusivism. Interestingly Heelas and Woodhead have themselves begun to explore some of these themes in a series of empirical studies, notably in the Kendal project described in Part II (pp. 149–51 and 170). The work emerging from the Department of Religious Studies in Lancaster has become a touchstone of debate in this field.[8]

Alongside the Lancaster team, Flanagan and Jupp (1996, 2000) have edited two sets of papers emerging from the British Sociological Association's annual meetings, in itself a significant forum for discussion. The first of these addresses the relationship between religion and postmodernity in 11 carefully chosen essays. The emphasis lies on the growing space for religious issues as the confident assertions of modernity or modernism give way to its late, post or new successors (the vocabulary remains complex). The second set of essays takes a further step forward. It is primarily concerned with the concept of 'virtue ethics', through which attempts are made to escape the more disabling effects of postmodern thinking as this is applied to religion. It draws on both the philosophical and sociological classics, paying particular attention to the work of Alasdair MacIntyre. Lyon (2000), finally, offers an original way into the modern/postmodern debate, taking as his starting point a Christian rally held in the headquarters of the Disney empire in Anaheim – the quintessential postmodern experience. *Jesus in Disneyland* becomes, in fact, a metaphor for postmodernity through which a range of issues are addressed, including questions of identity, cyberculture, consumer culture and the notion of time. The spiritual quest does not disappear, but takes new forms in late or postmodern society. Lyon both describes and explains what is happening in a lively, accessible text.

These examples are by no means exhaustive. Rather they have been chosen as illustrations of an increasing body of British writing in the sub-discipline which explores the place of religion in late modernity. Especially welcome are the growing (if slowly) number of references made by these authors to the wider corpus of sociological thinking concerned with the changing nature of modernity as such. Conversely at least some of the sociologists engaged with the latter are beginning to connect with the question of religion – this, however, is more true of some than others. It is also a question that in any developed sense lies beyond the scope of this chapter. With this in mind, the following paragraphs should be regarded primarily as an annotated list or a starting point for the discussion. A much fuller account can be found in Beckford (1996, 2003).

At one end of the scale can be found the social theorists of the mid-postwar decades who have dealt with religion in some detail. Berger, Luckmann and Luhmann exemplify this group – their contributions have been covered in previous chapters. More recently Bryan Turner and Ernest Gellner have, each in their own way, paid significant attention to religion. The contributions of Turner (1991) are largely theoretical;[9] Gellner (1992) combines an analysis of Islam with a trenchant critique of postmodernism. He explores a future for religion that avoids the extremes of relativism on the one hand and fundamentalism on the other, favouring personally an understanding of liberalism committed to the idea of 'truth', but rejecting the possibility that any society might possess such truth definitively. For others, 'religion' undoubtedly exists but is peripheral to the main account. This is most certainly true of Anthony Giddens, for whom fundamentalism becomes a reassertion of ontological security, closely linked to 'tradition in a traditional sense' (1994: 100) – a view that will be challenged in Chapter 9. The core of the debate (Giddens, 1990, 1991, 1994) lies, however, in the nature of modernity itself, including its attendant insecurities, not in the religious responses to these. Bauman's interesting essay 'Postmodern religion?' (1998) is both similar and different. It pays considerable and direct attention to the attitudes (including religious ones) of postmodern people, recognizing their innate diversity. Once again, fundamentalism is identified as a specifically postmodern form of religion – exposing by its very nature the anxieties and premonitions integral to the postmodern condition. The fundamentalist is 'saved', not only from sin, but from the agonies of perpetual choice (1998: 73–4).

The growing awareness of religion amongst mainstream sociologists is indeed welcome, but a consistent thread unites even the most positive of these thinkers. Religion is conceptualized first and foremost as a way of coping with the vicissitudes of late or postmodern life, not as *a way of being modern*.[10] This is a crucial distinction and explains to a large extent the preoccupation with fundamentalism that is found in these accounts. A second, equally significant, point follows from this: the great majority of these authors have assumed that modernity (past, present or future) is a *single* thing – that it is a unitary concept with a definable set of characteristics. It is this assumption that will be challenged in the last section of this chapter, paragraphs which draw extensively on the theoretical framework worked out in *Europe: The Exceptional Case* (Davie, 2002a). If this framework, and the questions that it provokes, are taken seriously, the re-orientation of the agenda and the challenge to sociological thinking will be considerable.

*103*

## NEW APPROACHES TO THE QUESTION OF MODERNITY

The first chapter of *Europe: The Exceptional Case* sets out the parameters of faith in modern Europe, indicating the principal forms of religion that exist in the different parts of the continent, a by now familiar theme. The last chapter approaches the same question from a different perspective – it looks at Europe from the outside rather than from within. The subject matter is similarly reversed: instead of setting out what the patterns of European religion are, it underlines what they are *not*, taking each of the case studies set out in the book (i.e. the United States, Latin America, Africa and two societies from South East Asia) as a point of reference, noting that these case studies cover Christian societies only. The contrasts would be even greater if the Muslim or Hindu worlds were taken into account.

For example, patterns of religion in Europe do not constitute a religious market in the sense that this exists in the United States. The historic churches in Europe are considerably closer to the notion of public utility than they are to a competitive firm. In terms of the material on Latin America, Europe is a part of the world where Pentecostalism does not exist as a widespread and popular movement. Why not will be crucial to the argument of Chapter 10. The material on Africa poses a similar if not identical question. It also introduces the notion of 'reversed mission', an idea that troubles, to put it mildly, the average Europe, accustomed to be a sender rather than a receiver in matters of religion. The forms of religion discovered on the Pacific Rim are equally disturbing. In the Philippines, both the particular nature of Catholicism and the recent Pentecostal growth indicate a degree and intensity in religious life rarely experienced in Europe and at all levels of society. In South Korea, finally, the assumed European trajectory is turned on its head. Here unbelievably rapid modernization is accompanied by an equally extraordinary surge in the nation's religious life. Both Christianity and Buddhism grow exponentially from the 1960s on. It is only at the turn of the millennium that the indicators begin to falter, provoking yet another set of sociological questions.

Two points are immediately apparent from this overview. First, the European observer (whether he or she is a member of one of Europe's churches or simply a spectator) is forced to admit that the familiar is not necessarily the norm in global terms. The assumption that this might be so is radically shaken by the material presented in the case studies (a principal aim of the 2002 book). Second, it is equally important, to avoid jumping to conclusions in terms of value judgements. It may indeed be the case that patterns of religion in Europe are different from those discovered elsewhere in the Christian world, but it does not follow that they are either better or worse; they are simply different. Indeed opinions will vary enormously in this respect. For some Europeans, what we experience in this part of the world is simply reassuringly familiar (there is no real need for change); for others, such changes should be positively resisted (European patterns, not least relative secularity, are to be preserved at all costs); and for a third group, both attitudes are a source of great frustration (there is longing for change and an impatience with those who resist this). All three groups, however, are faced with essentially the same question: how do we *explain* the differences that we have established?

Two studies (or groups of studies) come to mind. The first concerns the empirical testing of some aspects of modernization theory using data from the World Values Survey: that is, the work of Ronald Inglehart and his team in the University of Michigan.[11] The second approach is primarily theoretical; it is associated with Shmuel Eisenstadt at the Hebrew University in Jerusalem, but draws from a wide range of comparative cases embracing, once again, examples from almost all global regions (and indeed almost all world faiths). Eisenstadt's thinking embodies an innovative and crucial concept – that of 'multiple

**104**

modernities'. It moves sharply away from a single or core understanding of either modernity or the modernization process. The case studies together with the theoretical frame have been published in two dedicated issues of *Daedalus* (the journal of the American Academy of Arts and Sciences).[12] These in turn have generated an ongoing and increasingly significant discussion.

## testing modernization theory

Modernization theory evokes strong reactions and has become, more often than not, heavily ideological. In the immediate post-war period, for example, there were those who considered it both necessary and appropriate to bring 'modern' ways of doing things to the developing societies of the world. Such policies rested on attitudes (often well-intentioned) which assumed that traditional values necessarily prevent the proper course of modernization (i.e. effective and inevitable capitalist development); it was right, therefore, that they be replaced. Such views were vehemently opposed, two decades later, by those who saw the lack of modernization of large parts of the world in an entirely different light. It had nothing to do with the value systems of local populations and everything to do with the greed of advanced capitalist societies. The inequalities of the global economy were the outcomes not of 'backward' values but of capitalist exploitation. Unsurprisingly, this too has been criticized by those who perceive advantages as well as disadvantages in capitalist investment on a global scale and not solely for the elite.

Embedded in critique and counter-critique are different understandings of the modernization process. On the one hand, there are those who maintain 'that economic development is linked with coherent and, to some extent, predictable changes in culture and social and political life' (Inglehart and Baker, 2000: 21).[13] On the other hand, there are scholars (mostly dependency theorists and cultural relativists) who reject such a possibility – the relationship between the two sets of variables is essentially random. Data from the World Values Survey are strongly supportive of the former view, but with important modifications to earlier versions of modernization theory (Inglehart, 1997; Inglehart and Baker, 2000; Norris and Inglehart, 2004, 2007).

There are, first of all, two stages to bear in mind in the ongoing process of modernization: the first occurs when societies move from a pre-industrial to industrial economy, and the second as the economy begins to mutate once again – this time to a service-based, post-industrial mode of organization. At each stage, there is an associated shift in the value systems espoused by the populations in question, but not always in the direction anticipated by the early theorists of modernization. It becomes increasingly clear, for example, that it was no longer possible to assume a linear evolution in the development of modern societies: that is, towards an increasingly technical, mechanical, rationalized, bureaucratic, and indeed secular environment in which the values associated with economic and physical security become paramount. Something very different was taking place in many parts of the world. Specifically: as economies moved from the industrial to the post-industrial phase, the populations in question began to place far more stress on *post*-materialist values, not least an increasing emphasis on well-being and the quality of life (something rather more subtle than simple survival).

By this route, we return once again to precisely the same questions (i.e. the long-term evolution of industrial economies) that preoccupied me in the last chapter of *Religion in Modern Britain*, notably the move away from industrial society into new forms of economic and social life. The data from the World Values Survey firmly endorse the latter shift. Across a wide variety of societies, West Europe included, a rather different configuration emerges as industrial economies mutate into post-industrial ones: that is, into societies characterized by growing rather than declining evidence of spiritual concern (indeed of religious belief), though not, it is clear, of institutional commitment. Here, moreover, is further support for the possibility that European patterns of religion (just like any others) will continue to develop: West Europe may be distinctive but it is by no means static.

Working comparatively, Norris and Inglehart (2004) take this debate a stage further, introducing an increasingly observable paradox. They point out that *both* the following statements are true. First, that the publics of virtually all advanced industrial societies have been moving toward more secular orientations in the past 50 years; and second, that the world as a whole now has more people with traditional religious views than ever before – these people constitute a growing proportion of the world's population. The first statement is, in fact, a moderately strong statement of secularization (and, it follows, a refutation of RCT) in so far as it argues that the demand for religion varies systematically with levels of societal modernization, human development and economic inequality. Modernization, for Norris and Inglehart, is associated with increasing levels of existential security; it is this that is likely to bring about a degree of secularization, though not everyone in a society will experience the sense of security equally. Nor do all sociologists agree with their reasoning.[14] But even the process outlined by Norris and Inglehart is self-limiting in so far as exactly the same combination of factors (i.e. modernization associated with secularization) will lead to a decline in fertility. Hence, proportionally speaking, the growth (not decline) of the proportion of the global population that continues to affirm their faith in more rather than less traditional forms of religion.

So much for the longitudinal sequence and the controversies that it brings in its wake. Inglehart and his associates (1997; Inglehart and Baker, 2000; Norris and Inglehart, 2004) then introduce a second and even more important dimension to their argument, namely the diversity between nations, or groups of nations as they engage the modernization process. It becomes increasingly clear, for example, that different societies follow different trajectories even when they are subject to the same forces of economic development. This is a both/and situation. On the one hand, the rise of industrial society and its subsequent mutation into post-industrial forms are associated with coherent and empirically discernible cultural shifts. On the other, the systems that emerge at each stage in this evolution are path dependent: more precisely they reflect Protestant, Catholic, Islamic or Confucian backgrounds, each of which display distinctive value systems. The associated differences, shaped very largely by the cultural (and more specifically religious) heritage in question, persist even after controlling for the effects of economic development. Hence the following conclusion:

> Economic development tends to push societies in a common direction, but rather than converging, they seem to move on parallel trajectories, shaped by their cultural heritages. We doubt that the forces of modernization will produce a homogenized world culture in the foreseeable future. (Inglehart and Baker, 2000: 49)

### multiple modernities

It is at this point that Shmuel Eisenstadt's work on *multiple* modernities becomes significant. It involves, moreover, an entirely different understanding of modernity from that assumed in the corpus of social scientific writing from the time of the founding fathers onwards. The following paragraph sets out the negative agenda; it is unequivocal in its critique:

> The notion of "multiple modernities" denotes a certain view of the contemporary world – indeed of the history and characteristics of the modern era – that goes

against the views long prevalent in scholarly and general discourse. It goes against the view of the "classical" theories of modernization and of the convergence of industrial societies prevalent in the 1950s, and indeed against the classical sociological analyses of Marx, Durkheim, and (to a large extent) even of Weber, at least in one reading of his work. They all assumed, even if only implicitly, that the cultural program of modernity as it developed in modern Europe and the basic institutional constellations that emerged there would ultimately take over in all modernizing and modern societies; with the expansion of modernity, they would prevail throughout the world. (Eisenstadt, 2000: 1)

Right from the start, therefore, Eisenstadt challenges both the assumption that modernizing societies are convergent and the notion of Europe (or indeed anywhere else) as the lead society in the modernizing process.

It is important, however, to grasp the positive as well as the negative aspect of Eisenstadt's idea. In the introductory essay to an interesting set of comparative cases, Eisenstadt suggests that the best way to understand the modern world (in other words, to grasp the history and nature of modernity) is to see this as 'a story of continual constitution and reconstitution of a multiplicity of cultural programs' (2000: 2). A second point follows from this. These ongoing reconstitutions do not drop from the sky; they emerge as the result of endless encounters on the part of both individuals and groups, all of whom engage in the creation (and recreation) of both cultural and institutional formations, but within *different* economic and cultural contexts. Once this way of thinking is firmly in place it becomes easier to appreciate one of the fundamental paradoxes of Eisenstadt's writing: namely that to engage with the Western understanding of modernity, or even to oppose it, is as indisputably modern as to embrace it.

What then is the authentic core of modernity? The question becomes, in fact, very difficult to answer in that modernity is more of an attitude (a distinctive epistemology) than a set of characteristics. In its early forms, it embodied above all a notion of the future which was realizable by means of human agency. As soon as the process was set in motion, however, even the core of modernity was beset by internal contradictions. Were such societies to be totalizing or pluralistic? Or what degree of control/autonomy was considered desirable? Hence, to give an institutional illustration, the very different formulations of the nation-state that emerged even in different parts of Europe – hegemonic in France and the Nordic countries (though differently so in each case) as opposed to the rather more pluralistic pattern adopted in Britain or the Netherlands. Should we be surprised, therefore, at the even greater transformations that took place (both culturally and institutionally) when the idea of modernity transferred itself to the new world, and then, bit by bit, out of the West altogether? Following Eisenstadt, diversity is simply assumed within the modernizing process; it becomes part of modernity itself.

The shifting nature of modernity (or more accurately modernities) is crucial to Eisenstadt's thinking – a point nicely illustrated in his continuing analysis of the state, this time in late- as opposed to early-modern societies. Globalization, in all its diverse forms, has changed dramatically the 'institutional, symbolic, and ideological contours of modern national and revolutionary states' (2000: 16). No longer, for example, can these institutions adequately control much of modern living, whether in economic, political or cultural terms. Despite technologically developed means of restraint, the flows and counter-flows of modern living increasingly transcend political boundaries. The construction of multiple modernities continues nonetheless (that is its nature), but in constantly changing circumstances.

Central to this process in recent decades is the appearance of new actors and new entities, among them a whole range of social movements, who assume responsibility for the emergent problems of the modern world. Feminist or ecological organizations (often transnational in nature) provide excellent examples, but so too do religious movements – even those commonly known as fundamentalist. It is true that the latter are vehemently opposed to 'the West' and to the ideologies embodied therein. Fundamentalist movements are, however, quintessentially modern in the manner in which they set their goals and in the means that they adopt to achieve them: their outlooks, for example, are truly global and their technologies highly developed. Just like their secular counterparts, they are redefining and reconstituting the concept of modernity, but in their own terms. Hence the overlap between this chapter and the one devoted to fundamentalism in Part II.

The crucial point to emerge from Eisenstadt's work is the continued space for religion and for religious movements within the unfolding interpretations of modernity. The forms of religion, moreover, may be as diverse as the forms of modernity. Indeed the examples that follow in the special issue of *Daedalus* offer Christian, Muslim, Hindu and Confucian illustrations. The author of one of these, Nilufer Göle, concludes that the essential core of modernity resides in its potential for self-correction, a capacity that by definition must be ongoing given that the problems that preoccupy us at the start of the twenty-first century could not even be imagined in the early stages of modernization. Thus religion (in Göle's essay this is innovative forms of Islam) becomes one resource among many in the process of continual self-appraisal. More precisely, 'modernity is not simply rejected or readopted but critically and creatively reappropriated' by new religious practices in non-Western contexts (Göle, 2000: 93).

Two conclusions can be drawn from this discussion. First, to underline once again that European versions of modernity are indeed distinct (most notably in their comparative secularity), a possibility underpinned by theoretical as well as empirical considerations. But, second, they are not distinct from a single undifferentiated other. They are simply one modernity among many in the modern world and, like all the others, in the process of continual reconstruction. How then should the European sociologist respond? With humility is the only answer. If Europe is not the global prototype, both Europe and European scholars have everything to learn from cases other than their own. Not least among such lessons is the importance of taking the religious factor seriously, and in public as well as private life. Taking religion seriously, moreover, is greatly facilitated by the assumption that you expect it to be there, as an integral, normal part of modern as well as modernizing societies. That is the assumption embedded in the argument of this book.

## NOTES

1 The Census itself, and the religious question within this, will be discussed in the following chapter.

**110**

2 See pp. 115–17.

3 In 2002, the French left withheld their support for Lionel Jospin, allowing Jean-Marie Le Pen to enter the second round of the presidential election. Jospin's supporters had intended to put down a marker of discontent, but rally to their leader in the second round – that moment never came.

4 Good examples can be found in the countryside march in September 2002 and in the anti-war demonstrations before the invasion of Iraq in March 2003.

5 Notably colleagues in Denmark who are concerned with the influence of Islam in the European context. Privatized Islam makes no sense and the struggle to find appropriate models for Islam in Europe will affect the host society as much as the in-coming communities.

6 Full details of this study will be given in the following chapter, but see www.europeanvaluesstudy.eu (accessed 9 April 2012).

7 Heelas and Woodhead do, however, draw attention to the overwhelming volume of material which is related to secularization – both as an idea and as a process (2000: 476–7).

8 In 2010, the Department of Religious Studies in Lancaster became part of the Department of Politics, Philosophy and Religion.

9 Turner has continued to publish in this field, including a number of important edited texts (see Turner 2010a, 2010b and 2011).

10 An interesting shift can, however, be discerned in the recent writing of critical realists (Archer et al., 2004) and of at least some political philosophers (Habermas, 2006). No longer can the absence of God and/or religion simply be assumed in the social scientific account.

11 See www.worldvaluessurvey.org (accessed 9 April 2012) and the more developed discussion of large-scale surveys in Chapter 6.

12 See 'Early modernities', *Daedalus*, 127/3, summer 1998; 'Multiple modernities', *Daedalus*, 129/1, winter 2000.

13 A second set of questions follow from this position – those that relate to the causal sequence. Do economic changes engender cultural change (the Marxist position) or do cultural values themselves encourage/influence economic endeavour (the Weberian position)? This ongoing debate lies at the heart of social scientific discussion.

14 The argument turns, very largely, on the Japanese case. Is Japan as secular as it first appears? It is at this point that methodologies honed in the West are at their most suspect. Can they capture the forms of religion that continue to exist in Japanese society? The point will be developed in Chapter 6.

# *six*

# methodological challenges

The introductory sections of this book underlined the defining feature of the sociological study of religion: that it is about discerning and explaining the diverse and complex patterns which are found in the religious aspects of human living. In order to accomplish such a task, the discipline draws on a wide variety of methods, some of which have already been mentioned and each of which yields particular kinds of data. Such methods should be considered complementary: taken together they enable the researcher to build up as complete a picture as possible of the phenomenon that he or she is trying not only to describe, but also to explain. The initial task of this chapter is to bring together and exemplify (whenever possible with reference to material presented elsewhere in this book) the principal methodologies found in the sociological study of the religious field. The second, and perhaps more important, undertaking is to encourage more imaginative approaches to the gathering of data – to widen the range of resources and to think carefully about how the data that they yield can be incorporated into the sociological account.[1]

Bearing such diversity in mind, the pros and cons of different methodologies form the core of the chapter. The discussion concludes, however, with an extended note on cognate disciplines and on the overlaps that are to be found with respect to both theory and method in related fields. On the one hand, this section will stress the importance of interdisciplinary work; on the other, it will pay particular attention to the sometimes difficult relationship between the social sciences and theology. It is clear that some theologians are more ready than others to seek help or insights from the social sciences.

Questions about methodology can be provocative in other ways as well. Berger (2002), for example, decries the 'methodological fetishism' of much of post-War sociology – claiming that increasingly elaborate, supposedly scientific, methods have been devised to investigate increasingly trivial issues. Following Berger, the stress on *scientific* method has been counterproductive in that it rules out, almost by definition, the most interesting parts of the agenda. The argument is overstated, but there is truth in it. There are times when the sociologist of religion must go with a hunch, searching for innovative sources of data to support an idea that is difficult to substantiate using more conventional methods. The notion of vicarious religion (Davie, 2000a, 2007a, 2010a) will be used to exemplify this point. How, in other words, can a sociologist document a phenomenon which almost by definition remains stubbornly below the radar, at least in its 'normal' manifestations?

The placing of this chapter at the mid-point of this book bears this discussion in mind; it also reflects the inherent link between theory and method. It is clear, for example, that certain kinds of theorizing lead to the collection of particular kinds of data. Both, moreover, are framed by definitional questions. What exactly is the phenomenon under investigation? How is it conceptualized? How, where and by whom is the enquiry carried out? Substantive and functional definitions of religion lead to different theoretical questions and to different data sets. Likewise, different theoretical frameworks generate different types of hypotheses which are then tested in different ways. This is as true in the field of religion as it is in any other area of sociological enquiry.

113

## EXAMPLES OF QUANTITATIVE METHODOLOGY

### large-scale comparative studies

Both the European Values Study (EVS) and, in more detail, the World Values Survey (WVS) were mentioned in the previous chapter. They offer admirable, though by no means perfect, examples of large-scale comparative surveys which include valuable material for the sociologist of religion. Both, moreover, are 'coming of age' enabling longitudinal as well as comparative studies. The EVS, interestingly, was the brainchild of a generation of scholars whose formative years were deeply coloured by the Second World War – hence a strong motivation to discover *empirically* what Europe and Europeans had in common. The fact that the planning stages of the EVS coincided with the building of the then European Community is no coincidence. The first surveys took place in 1981 in 10 European societies, a second wave was completed in 1990–91, a third set was initiated in some parts of Europe in 1995–96, a more comprehensive fourth set in 1999–2001, and a fifth in 2008. Each tranche of data quite clearly enhances the archive as a whole, which becomes in a very literal sense more than the sum of its parts. It was, moreover, the EVS that gave birth to the WVS (not the other way round). The WVS is a worldwide investigation of ambitious proportions, currently reaching approximately 80 societies in six continents, totalling more than 85 per cent of the world's population. It is organized as a network of social scientists co-ordinated by a central body, the World Values Survey Association. Its relevance to the understanding of the modernization process and the place of religion within this has already been indicated.

The EVS and the WVS are studies of socio-cultural and political change. From a technical point of view, both studies are based on representative national surveys concerned with the basic values and beliefs of a sample of the general population. Questions about religion (indeed many different aspects of religion) form a central part of the survey instrument. Full details of the histories and technical details of each of these surveys, including a copy of the questionnaire, can be found on their respective websites;[2] also listed are the personnel involved and the extensive publications that have emerged from this work. The materials generated from both surveys are widely used, both as a data bank and as a teaching tool; they have become an important resource for the sub-discipline.

They do not stand alone, however. A second source of comparative data can be found in the International Social Survey Programme (ISSP), favoured by some scholars for technical reasons (its stricter social science controls, excellent archiving and the fact that the data are released more quickly than is the case with the EVS).[3] The ISSP works by inserting a 15-minute supplement on a chosen theme into the regular national surveys in almost 50 countries. In 1991 and 1998, the theme was religion, allowing comparison between these dates and between the countries involved in the programme, a process repeated in 2008. Both the WVS (and within this the EVS) and the ISSP cover American data. In terms of the United States itself, however, what was originally known as the American Religion Data Archive (ARDA), generously funded by the Lilly Endowment, offered a growing and admirably organized resource for scholars of American religion. The ARDA existed expressly to preserve quantitative data on American religion, to improve access to these data, to increase their use, and to allow comparisons across the growing number of files. Gaining additional sponsorship, the organization has expanded to become the Association of Religion Data Archives.[4] The archived material now extends well beyond the United States and includes information on churches and church membership, religious professionals and religious groups (individuals, congregations and denominations). The instant availability of such data via the Web permits a significant advance in survey analysis; the potential for teaching is correspondingly enhanced. The ARDA website includes learning modules for exploration and class assignments.[5]

What then are the advantages of this way of working? Above all, these large-scale and cumulative surveys generate ever more sophisticated maps of correlations, about which many questions can be asked. It is possible to make comparisons between increasing numbers of places and, as the longitudinal aspects develop, between different time periods in any one of these locations. Rapidly advancing computer technologies are part of the same story, allowing an almost infinite number of variables to be correlated both with each other and with detailed socio-economic information. The potential is enormous. There is, however, a corresponding need for care with respect both to the data themselves and to the comparisons that are made. Do questions that resonate in Europe, for example, carry the same meaning in the Islamic world or in the Far East? Probably not, leading at times to serious misunderstandings – not least concerning the Japanese case (see p. 111, note 14). And even within Europe, it is important to ask whether comparisons pre- and post-1989 are likely to be valid in terms of the religious sphere. Something that was proscribed under Marxism has become a central feature of the post-1989 democracies, a shift that is bound to influence results, though differently in different places.

In short, surveys supply data that provoke interesting and important questions. They are much less able to give us 'answers' in the sense that answers require explanations as well as data. Why, to use an example already developed in some detail, do the profiles of religion look so different in Europe and America? It is at this point that the need for alternative or additional methodologies becomes apparent – those that take into account cultural specificity, historical trajectory, linguistic nuance and culturally varied motivations.

**115**

## the 2001 British census

For a book concerned with the British contribution to these debates, an interesting variant of the national survey can be found in the 2001 British Census, which for the first time in the history of the census in this country contained a question about religion. Why this was so forms a study in its own right – admirably told by Francis (2003) and Weller (2004). Not only does this story reflect the changing nature of British society, it also reveals a gradual – though controversial – awareness that religion should be seen as a public as well as private category, a shift in perspective with hugely important implications. It is worth noting, for example, that the driving force for the religious question in the Census came from the small but increasingly significant other faith communities in this country, notably the Muslims. The Muslim community in Britain is diverse in terms of ethnicity and nationality. It follows that statistics based on either of these indicators disperse a purely religious identity and downplay for Muslims the most important factor – their faith. British Muslims want to be known as Muslims in public as well as private life, in order that provision for their needs is met on these terms. Appropriate policies should be worked out on a secure statistical base (hence the demand for a specific question in the Census), not on estimates or extrapolations from other variables.

Such a demand should be seen in a wider context. Very similar arguments, for example, can be found in an interesting House of Lords debate on 'Multi-Ethnicity and Multi-Culturalism', illustrating – in terms of a chapter on methodology – an interesting complementarity of sources (in this case, written text reinforces the demand for statistical data). The following quotations exemplify the point perfectly; they are taken from a speech by Baroness Pola Manzila Uddin (20 March 2002), who was the first Muslim in Britain to enter the House of Lords, and who at the time was the only Muslim *woman* in Parliament. The extracts speak for themselves:

> The almost total denial for decades of our identity based on our faith has been devastating psychologically, socially and culturally and its economic impact has been well demonstrated. For years Britain's 2 million or so Muslims ... have been totally bypassed even by the best-intentioned community and race relations initiatives because they have failed to take on board the fact that a major component of their identity is their faith.
>
> Such an identity demanded more than just the stereotypical and lazy imposition of simple cultural labels based on race categorisations. British Muslims, consisting of 56 nationalities and speaking more than 1,000 languages, have never been and shall never be happy about an existence and understanding that rarely goes beyond somosas, Bollywood and bhangra. (Uddin, 2002)

Bearing these 'stereotypical and lazy' impositions in mind, it was hardly surprising that the question on religion proved controversial. It also produced a typically British compromise: a different question emerged in England and Wales from that which was used in Scotland,[6] and both were optional rather than compulsory. Interestingly, the results between the two parts of the United Kingdom were somewhat different, revealing yet again that the formulation of a question has a powerful effect on how people respond, a point underlined by Voas and Bruce (2004).

How then should the findings of the Census be interpreted? The Muslim community was rewarded in so far as its relatively modest presence was recognized as such. The same was true for the other religious minorities present in Britain, revealing their very different demographic profiles and their precise geographical locations. The Jewish community, for example, is significantly different from the more recently arrived religious minorities (see below). Even more striking, however, was a point already mentioned in Chapter 5: that is, the number of people in both populations, but especially in England and Wales, who declared themselves Christian – this was unexpectedly strong evidence of residual attachments. What though did the category 'Christian' mean for those who ticked this box? Did this imply that the individuals concerned were not secular, or did it imply that they were not Muslim (or indeed another world faith), or did it mean something different again – a marker of national identity, for example, as suggested by Voas and Bruce (2004)? It is at this point that more qualitative approaches to methodology become important; or at the very least some rather more detailed questions about religion addressed to a sample of those who answered 'Christian' to the question about religious identity.[7]

**117**

## small-scale surveys

The residually Christian category is addressed in more detail later in this chapter (pp. 128–30). In the meantime, it is important to highlight the in-depth surveys that have been carried out on particular religious communities in Britain. These constituencies are too small for a national survey to do more than indicate their presence. Hence the need for a different kind of enquiry – a survey which gathers information solely on the religious minority with specific questions in mind. The Jewish community offers an excellent example, revealing amongst other things acute sensitivities within a population that is diminishing rather than increasing in size and which is also changing in nature. Simply a glance at the website of the Board of Deputies of British Jews and the constant stream of publications that emanate from its highly effective research department is enough to establish the importance of this work.[8] Such studies should be put into the wider context of European society and the place of Jews within this. They should be read against the accounts of numerical decline provided in Wasserstein (1996), Webber (1994) and more recently in Schoeps et al. (2011).

## QUALITATIVE WAYS OF WORKING

### building a profile

Small-scale surveys bridge the gap between quantitative and qualitative enquiries. The difference in scale also permits a greater degree of flexibility, including the inclusion of interviews (of whatever kind) at an appropriate point in the research design. As ever, there are choices to be made, best seen as a continuum of possibilities. At one end the interview is little more than form filling (the interviewer simply completes a schedule), allowing little room for manoeuvre on either side. At the other, the interview in effect becomes a guided conversation permitting ample time for response and where appropriate additional questions.

More often than not, different elements are brought together in one study. Chambers's excellent analysis of church life in Swansea, for example, began with a survey of all churches within the city – a preliminary mapping of the field. Four cases were developed further in an enquiry which used a combination of interview and observation to discern the particular factors that led to growth and/or decline in church life (Chambers, 2000, 2004). Similar combinations can be found in the Kendal Project. The findings from this study will be referenced in Chapters 7 and 8; at this stage it is sufficient to note the varieties of approach used to build a picture or profile of religious life in a chosen community. These include an initial mapping, attendance counts, congregation counts, selected case studies for more detailed investigation and an in-depth study of one particular street, the goal of which was to learn more about those (the majority) who neither went to church nor became involved in alternative spiritual activities. For the latter, a small but varied area in Kendal was selected for a door-to-door survey. Semi-structured interviews were used to elicit people's beliefs, together with information about their religious and spiritual backgrounds.[9]

To give a comparative illustration, a large-scale study of Welfare and Religion in a European Perspective (WREP) uses a similar range of methods to establish not only the patterns of welfare provision in eight West European societies but the attitudes of different groups within the population regarding these activities.[10] The WREP study is similar to the Kendal Project in so far as each national case is based in a medium-sized town (circa 50,000 people), in order to determine in detail the connections between the secular and religious providers of welfare and how the local population feels about both alternatives.

Interestingly it was clear even from the initial findings that there are more commonalities across Europe at local level than might be supposed from purely national comparisons. The study reveals, however, the complexities of comparative work and the need to pay very careful attention to local resonance. Questions are 'heard' differently in different contexts and apparently similar answers can mean very different things in different places.

## examples of ethnography

In-depth interviewing merges in turn into the classic ethnographic tool: participant observation. The technique has been used to great effect in the sociology of religion. A crucial element is necessary for success in this field: the capacity to see the world from the point of view of the actor. Only then is it possible to understand why an individual becomes a member of a religious movement and why he or she choses or doesn't choose, to remain so. A well-trained ethnographer prioritizes the actor's point of view, however strange this may seem from the outside. Three examples will illustrate the point, all of which have become classics in the field.

*119*

The first is drawn from the extensive work on new religious movements, in which Bryan Wilson's pioneering analysis of three minority groups – Christadelphianism, Elim Pentecostalism and Christian Science – serves as a role model. The study began as a doctoral thesis and was eventually published in 1961 under the title *Sects and Society*. Wilson's sensitivity to religious minorities was revealed at an early stage. In the generation that followed, James Beckford's study of Jehovah's Witnesses stands out (Beckford, 1975); so too does Eileen Barker's careful documentation of the Unification Church, an enquiry that examined in detail and then refuted the accusation of brainwashing as the basis of recruitment to the Moonies (Barker, 1984).

A growing group of studies concerned with congregational life in urban America offers a second set of illustrations. The Religion in Urban America Program (RUAP) covered diverse neighbourhoods in the Greater Chicago area; it is interesting for several reasons, not least the mapping dimensions of the project which reflect very directly the classic studies of the Chicago School. Some 70 years later, the ecology of the city remains central to the RUAP enquiry, but at a very different phase of urban life – *late* as opposed to *early* modernity. The aim is to describe and to explain the 'complex interaction among religion, urban structure, and social change during this extraordinary episode in the history of urban America' (Livezey, 2000: 6). This is achieved by the close study of 75 congregations in eight very different Chicago neighbourhoods. Interestingly several researchers participated in each site, in order to observe the congregations in question 'through each other's eyes', acutely aware of the different capacities of each observer for 'perception and distortion' (2000: ix). The results are impressive.

RUAP brought together a sizeable team of research associates, research assistants and support staff funded by the Lilly Endowment. The work took place from 1992–97, and resulted in an initial volume published in 2000. In every sense, this was a highly professional undertaking. An interesting sequel emerged in Boston in the Metropolitan Congregational Studies Project, where somewhat similar work was achieved, but without the aid of a grant. In Boston the congregational ethnographies were carried out by Masters students as their assignments for the course in 'Religious Agency in the Metropolis'. Clearly an innovative venture, this work invites reflection. In one sense, this is research on the cheap (using students rather than paid researchers); in another, a course of this nature provides an excellent training in methodology in addition to introducing students to the immense variety of religious communities present in urban America.[11] The work is pedagogically as well as methodologically interesting.

Ethnographic methods were equally central to a parallel set of projects concerned with recently arrived immigrant communities in the United States. These included the New Ethnic and Immigrant Congregations Project (NEICP) directed by Stephen Warner from the University of Illinois in Chicago, and the Research on Ethnic and New Immigrant Religion Project (RENIR) centred in Houston, Texas under the direction of Helen Rose Ebaugh. Both projects employed a team of young scholars to complete the fieldwork and both were financed by the Pew Charitable Trusts. Quite apart from the methodology employed, the common emphasis on the religious factor in the identity and assimilation of new communities indicated a welcome recognition of the place of religion in the lives of immigrant people. No longer was this subsumed into ethnicity. The funding, moreover, was part of a 'grantmaking strategy' (a conscious decision) to correct the relative neglect of the religious factor in the academic literature concerned with immigration in modern America.

A third and very different set of examples can be found in the collection brought together by Spickard and colleagues under the title *Personal Knowledge and Beyond* (2002). This is a fascinating collection of chapters, every one of them worth reading for its own sake. The book as a whole, however, digs deeper, in that it contains a short but highly

**120**

perceptive introduction regarding the place of ethnography in the social sciences, paying particular attention to its helpfulness in the study of religion. The paradoxes are many, beginning with the fact that 'scholars of religion have started to adopt what they understand to be "standard" ethnographic practices, just when these practices have come under attack from anthropologists' (2002: 4), primarily for their 'colonial' tendencies. What follows is a *critical* reflection on the use of ethnography in the field of religion, with three aims in mind: first, to encourage the interdisciplinary study of religion; second, to illustrate and reflect on the difficulties as well as the advantages of ethnographic methods (not least the interview that turns into an interrogation of the interviewer); and third, to create a more formalized agenda for the ethnographic study of religion, including a greater sense of responsibility. This is a book to be widely used in the classroom and not only in courses concerned with the study of religion; it is a source of wisdom for all those interested in the sociological task.

## using text as data

Text as a source of data in the social-scientific study of religion has already been mentioned; the parliamentary record concerning the place of Muslims in British society offers an interesting, but by no means isolated example. Indeed it is important to put this illustration in context. A significant marker in this respect can be found in Robert Towler's work on the many thousands of letters sent to John Robinson after the publication of *Honest to God* in 1963. Towler's book *The Need for Certainty* (1984) classified the reactions to Robinson's writing in a series of themes or types, each of which indicated a way of being Christian. The study permitted considerable insight into the nature of believing within the Christian constituency in the 1960s. The findings reveal an evident need for certainty amongst significant groups of people in this notably turbulent decade.

Rather different but equally significant is Callum Brown's *The Death of Christian Britain* (2000), an example of discourse analysis applied primarily to historical material but also to the 1960s. This has become a very widely read book. I would not commend all of its substantive conclusions (see p. 240), but the use of text as an *historical* resource is excellent and deployed to great effect, in order to complement and in some cases to challenge the standard statistical account. A number of recent doctoral theses have followed suit.[12] Jenny Taylor (2001), for instance, scrutinized a set of minutes from a government committee in order to identify the changing nature of discourse relating to racial and religious diversity in the inner-cities of modern Britain. The minutes were those of the Inner Cities Religious Council. Once again they indicate a noticeable shift away from racial or ethnic references, and towards a greater use of religious terminology in public as well as private life, a theme that is asserting itself on both sides of the Atlantic. The more the minorities are allowed to speak for themselves, the more the religious factor is brought to the fore in public as well as private life.

In my own work, I have been drawn to the use of text as data in a fascinating study of reactions to an art exhibition (Davie, 2003a). The facts are simple enough. In the Spring of 2000, the National Gallery in London, with financial support from both the Jerusalem Trust and the Pilgrim Trust, mounted an exhibition entitled 'Seeing Salvation: The Image of Christ'. The exhibition became an important marker of the millennium. It was accompanied by a television series (four 50-minute programmes on BBC2) and two handsome volumes – one the catalogue of the exhibition and the other designed to support the television series. In every sense the venture was a huge success. Over 350,000 people visited the Gallery – the largest number (until then) to visit any Sainsbury Wing exhibition; the television series sustained an impressive BBC2 audience (totalling 2,800,000 across the four programmes); and the catalogue outsold the Highway Code in the final week of the exhibition. The press coverage was extensive and, with one or two exceptions, very positive. Finally, and with particular relevance to this chapter, both exhibition and TV series provoked a considerable correspondence to the National Gallery – the number of letters responding to an exhibition was unprecedented, providing an original, and to some extent innovative, source of data.

So much is straightforward; the problem lies in how to explain this unexpected success. Why was this exhibition – an overtly Christian depiction of the life of Christ – so popular in what is generally thought to be an increasingly secular, or at least multi-cultural society? What, if anything, can we 'read off' from its success in terms of societal attitudes to the Christian narrative and its presentation in a public art gallery? And how, finally, can we integrate the material gleaned from a set of appreciative letters into a broader understanding of religion in modern Britain? Clearly these documents do not tell us everything about the exhibition, nor about those who visited it (the number of letters was large, relatively speaking, but represented but a small fraction of the visitors). They reveal, however, the insights of a particular constituency of people – for the most part a relatively well-educated, older and church-going population – who were touchingly grateful to a member of the secular establishment for promoting an explicitly Christian exhibition at the time of the millennium. These somewhat conservative voices are seldom heard in public debate.

Distinctive themes emerged from these letters which can be analysed in some detail (see Davie, 2003a). One such bridges the gap to the following section; it lies in the letter writers' gratitude to the Director for his skill in revealing the story contained in a painting and his ability to situate this story within a theological as well as an art-historical perspective.

## art and artifacts, place and space

The next step is relatively straightforward: that is, to see the art and artifacts contained in this, or indeed in any other exhibition, as data in themselves. This became, in fact, an important theme within *Religion in Modern Europe* (Davie, 2000a), which looks at the diverse and continually evolving ways in which the religious memory of Europe, in its historic forms, is or is not sustained. The chapter on 'Aesthetic Memory' is particularly relevant to this discussion; it goes beyond the conventional sources of sociological data to examine not only the existence of a wide range of symbolic material that undoubtedly exists in modern Europe (art, architecture, music, literature, etc.), but the capacities of twenty-first century Europeans to appreciate their heritage. An interesting inversion has taken place in this respect. Much of this heritage especially in its visual forms (the stories told in stained glass windows, for example) was created with the intention of bringing familiar stories to mind for a population who were largely non-literate but who were thoroughly acquainted with the Christian narrative. In recent years large sections of a fully literate population are, very often, almost totally out of touch with the narrative and cannot, it follows, interpret the symbols. The consequences for the maintenance of religious memory are serious; only recently have the European churches begun to address these (Davie, 2000a: 173–4).

Art and architecture lead in turn to a consideration of space and place. Learning to 'read' a building or a city can be an instructive exercise in sociological method.[13] Power structures emerge both within buildings and in their relative positions; symbols (or the lack of them) reveal particular understandings of theology. Examples of both can be found in the history of the Protestant community in France. A Calvinist *temple*, for instance, holds within it a distinctive ecclesiology; the lack

123

of adornment and its focus on the open Bible are particularly striking to those who come from a different tradition (a statement that includes most French people). Quite apart from this, the invisibility from the street of Protestant places of worship in most French cities reveals not only a history of persecution when such buildings were proscribed altogether, but a long fight back in order to establish an accepted and visible place in French society. The parallels with Islamic buildings in the current period are only too apparent.

David Martin's essays on the ecology of the sacred, and the elusive, varied and shifting patterns that can be discovered from the built environment set this example into a wider perspective (Martin, 2002b). Martin takes six very different cities in order to illustrate his thesis: five of these are European and one American. Helsinki, for example, exemplifies the state churches of Northern Europe (a dominant confession closely allied to national identity). In Rome, the religious monopoly was eventually challenged by liberal nationalism. In architectural terms the Victor Emmanuel monument blocks out, literally, the view of St Peter's – an opposition now somewhat tempered and symbolized in the aptly named Via della Concilazione, which links the two parts of the city. Bucharest (Orthodox) and Budapest (Catholic) offer examples of ethnoreligion in different parts of post-communist Europe. London, finally, steps towards Boston (the American example) in so far as it embodies moderate pluralism. Westminster Abbey adjoins the Houses of Parliament (signifying an established church); Central Hall Westminster in Parliament Square is the symbol of the gathered church; and Westminster Cathedral (the Catholic cathedral at the *other* end of Victoria Street) embodies the alternative tradition. Both the latter form sizeable minorities in Britain. It is in Boston, however, that pluralism finds its fullest expression, remembering that this came in stages as the Puritan establishment gradually collapsed. A careful reading of Martin – book in hand in the city in question – permits the student to appreciate the ways in which both dominant and subordinate religious traditions have not only influenced the building of the city, but find themselves mirrored within it. Buildings themselves acquire new significance, so too the relationships (spatial and other) between them.

Religious buildings have many uses; central, however, are the requirements of liturgy. Encouraging students to observe and understand liturgy and to use this as a source of data is demanding in a largely unchurched society (especially its younger members). The approach, however, is fruitful: the careful observation of liturgy reveals a great deal, the more so if situated in a Durkheimian perspective. Liturgies associated with special occasions, for example, become choreographies of power. Examples abound in the British case, bearing in mind that some are easier than others to interpret. In the 1953 Coronation, for instance, or more recently in the celebrations of the Golden and Diamond Jubilees, the task is relatively straightforward: the relationships enacted are for the most part what they seem. Much more elusive were the messages that emanated from Princess Diana's funeral and the many different rituals that surrounded her death. Indeed in many respects the ambiguities of this occasion remain unresolved. What, for example, might have happened at Diana's funeral had her then partner – a prominent Muslim – not died in the accident with the Princess? Clearly the whole episode would have been configured in an entirely different way. But how?

Similar contrasts can be found at local level, offering in most places a complete and relatively open laboratory to a student of religion. Almost anything can be observed, from the most formal of cathedral services to the most alternative of liturgies; nor in most places is the choice limited to Christian examples. Careful attention to the ethical aspects of research is, of course, central to questions of access and to the disclosure of identities.

A musical example completes this section. It draws once again on the work of David Martin (2002b) and is, effectively, a study of reception. Martin takes the work of Handel as an example and traces its reception in relation to four interlocking themes: 'the rise and decline of Protestant expansiveness, the rise and decline of Evangelicalism, the twentieth century musical renaissance of the liturgical and the mystical, and the rise and decline of the sort of reverence evoked by the Austrian-German canon' (2002b: 70–1). The argument is complex and at times difficult to follow, especially for those with limited musical knowledge. The underlying question is, however, crystal clear. We can accept that Handel's reputation declined as secularization advanced – that was indeed the case from 1900 to 1960. But why was this trend reversed in the later decades of the twentieth century – 'during the more comprehensive secularization said to have occurred between the 1960s and the present' (2002b: 71)? The two stories quite clearly interlock: Handel emerges in a different guise (in opera as well as oratorio); secularization exists but is not the whole story – sacralization, not least in the world of music, can and does occur at one and the same time. Here in this musical example can be found many of the complexities of modernity outlined in the previous chapter.

## THE COMPLEMENTARITY OF METHODS: SOME EXAMPLES

A first draft of this chapter was written in Northern Spain in the summer of 2004. The date is significant in that 2004 saw the feast of Saint James (25 July) fall on a Sunday, making this a 'holy year' for the city of Santiago de Compostela. Quite apart from the holy year, however, the pilgrim route from various points across Europe to Santiago has become increasingly popular. Year on year since the mid-nineties, the number of 'pilgrims' has risen, prompting a corresponding growth in both interest and facilities. A diverse and growing number of people now make their way to Santiago by various means of transport, many of them on foot. The reasons for this development are complex – economic and political factors must be taken into account alongside religious ones. Significant amounts of European money, for example, have been invested in the infrastructure, not least the path (the *camino*) itself. The Spanish tourist board not only saw an excellent marketing opportunity, but took it, in a decade when Spain was modernizing extraordinarily fast. It is equally clear, however, that the venture caught a moment in the spiritual lives of Europeans – pilgrimage of all kinds is growing.

How though should the phenomenon be studied? The *camino* in is broadest sense offers excellent possibilities for the sociological study of religion. The pilgrims are counted. Who they are, where they came from and for what reasons are carefully documented; so too the break-downs in terms of age and gender. Such information is widely available and reveals that the number of people participating in the pilgrimage is growing fast. Discovering more about the motives and experiences of those who follow the route requires, however, a more probing meth-odology – interviews of various kinds, both with the participants themselves and with the growing numbers of people who support the venture in different ways, whether practically or spiritually. Motives are also revealed in the growing bodies of literature that have arisen from the Santiago phenomenon – first-hand accounts, the comments left in the visitors' book found in every *refugio*, press articles, and prac-tical guides to finding the way and the facilities available en route (such facilities cater for very different markets, economic as well as spiritual). Novels have been written and documentaries made;[14] a whole set of artifacts is available for purchase along the way.

The final step is clear enough: the fullest understanding will come only from those who are prepared to participate, in other words, to do the walk itself. So far I have not seen an ethnographic account of the *camino* written by a sociologist of religion – herein lies an opportunity for an energetic and linguistically gifted doctoral student prepared to walk for the best part of 800 kilometres in a relatively short space of time.[15] Before departure, he or she should read widely in the history of pilgrimage, for much that is occurring now has been seen before – the mixed motives of the pilgrims, the taste for adventure and the growing commercialization of the enterprise as a whole, all of which were as common in the Middle Ages as they are now. None of this invalidates the experience; it calls, however, for a careful and methodologically sophisticated account of a remarkable, and somewhat unexpected, phenomenon in early twenty-first century Europe, bearing in mind that Santiago is but one of several destinations currently sought out by the often young and very modern pilgrim.

A second example of the complementarity of methods was brought to my attention in a different way. One after the other and quite by chance, I was invited to review Robin Gill's *Churchgoing and Christian Ethics* (1999) and Timothy Jenkins's *Religion in English Everyday Life* (1999). Both books are concerned with moral values and the ways that such values are or are not sustained in British society. Gill uses quantitative and primarily longitudinal data to establish the following premise: that church-going is a significant and independent variable in the forming and sustaining of distinct patterns of belief and morality. The next question follows inevitably enough. In most of Western Europe, including Britain, church-going is changing in nature. No longer is it the experience of significant sections of the population; it has become instead a specifically chosen activity within the voluntary sector. What, it follows, will become of the beliefs and values sustained by church-going populations if that constituency declines beyond a certain point?

Jenkins offers a very different, essentially ethnographic account of religion as it operates in the everyday lives of ordinary English people. His account softens, rather than emphasizes, the distinction between church-goers and the community of which they are part, recognizing the myriad links that join one to the other – whether these be personal (chains of relationships) or historical (with a firm emphasis on local rather than national history). 'Respectability', defined as the 'desire to be a full or complete person in the terms of the local society' (1999: 78) emerges as a central theme within his writing, emphasizing the collective rather than individual nature of this quality. Jenkins's analysis should be read alongside Gill's in order to appreciate the intricacies of local life and what these denote in terms of moral values. What you do, where you live and the voluntary organizations (including the churches and chapels) that you join are all important in this process. One of Jenkins's case studies looked in detail at the Kingswood Whit Walk (an annual event in a far from prosperous part of Bristol). Not only was the walk the starting point in Jenkins's analysis, it was also a defining moment in the creation and maintenance of respectability in the neighbourhood as a whole. A purely quantitative analysis will miss this, and possibly other, significant links in the chain.

## uncovering hidden realities: vicarious religion

Such a statement brings to mind Peter Berger's contention that increasingly elaborate, supposedly scientific, methods constrain rather than enhance the sociological agenda. Is this true in the British case? Yes and no is the honest answer. Bearing in mind the regularity with which the relatively small church-going constituency in Britain is quoted as if it were the totality of religion in this country, there are times when I agree with Berger. Such a remark, however, is more true of the popularized accounts of religion to be found in the media; it is less the case in the sociological community as such.

Both constituencies, however, might gain from the concept of vicarious religion and the innovative sources of data that can be used to deploy this concept in sociological enquiry. By vicarious, I mean the notion of religion performed by an active minority but on behalf of a much larger number, *who implicitly at least not only understand but quite clearly approve of what the minority is doing.* That is the crucial point. In terms of my own thinking, the notion of vicarious religion marks a step forward from my earlier distinction between belief and belonging (Davie, 1994). It became a crucial dimension of the argument in my analyses of modern Europe (Davie, 2000a, 2007a, 2010a). The content of both believing and belonging and vicarious religion will be dealt with in Part II; here I am concerned with how we might 'measure' this elusive yet critically important notion.

An iceberg may provide a helpful analogy. It is easy enough both to measure and to take note of the part of the iceberg that emerges from the water. But this is to ignore the mass underneath, which is invisible for most of the time, but without which the visible part would not be there at all. How, though, can a sociologist penetrate more deeply in order to understand what is going on beneath the surface?

One way is to observe societies at particular moments in their evolution when 'normal' ways of living are, for one reason or another, suspended and something far more instinctive comes to the fore. The death

128

of Princess Diana in August 1997 elaborates an example already mentioned
(Walter 1999). In the week following the accident, significant numbers
of British people were instinctively drawn to their churches. This happened in two ways. First, the churches became an important, though not
the only, gathering point for a whole range of individual gestures of
mourning in which Christian and less Christian symbols became inextricably mixed, both materially (candles, playing cards and madonnas)
and theologically (life after death was strongly affirmed, but with no
notion of judgement).

Even more significant, however, was the awareness in the population
as a whole that multiple and well-intentioned gestures of individual
mourning were inadequate in themselves to mark the end of this particular life, as indeed of any other. Hence the need for public ritual or
public liturgy (in other words, a funeral), and where else but in the
established church. The fact that Princess Diana had not led an unequivocally Christian life was immaterial – she, like the rest of us, had a right
to the services of the church at the end of her life. It follows that the
churches must exist in order to meet such demands, ambiguous though
they are.

A second and particularly poignant example of vicarious religion
took place in a small East Anglian town (in England) in August
2002.[16] Two school girls were murdered by a school caretaker in
Soham, Cambridgeshire, at the beginning of the school holidays – an
episode that shocked the nation. The reaction of both the families
and the community was, however, immediate. Once again they
turned to the church, personified in the form of the local vicar, who
emerged as the spokesperson for both the immediate family of each
child and for the population as a whole. The church building became
the focus of mourning, offering both comfort and ritual as the dev-
astated community tried to come to terms with what had happened.
At the end of August, a memorial service took place in Ely Cathedral.
At this point, it was necessary to find a building which offered sufficient space for all those who wanted to take part (the local church
no longer sufficed for even a ticket-only service). Some form of closure, or at least a moving-on, was achieved as the school year recom-
menced: the school community gathered on the playing field as the
vicar (once again his symbolic role is important) released two white
doves into the sky.

The crucial point to grasp in terms of sociological method is the need
to be attentive to episodes, whether individual or collective, in or
through which the implicit becomes explicit. With this in mind, it is

129

equally important to remember that the examples described above are simply large-scale and often media-hyped versions of what goes on all the time in the life-cycles of ordinary people. Individual families and communities regularly pause for thought at critical moments in their existence, frequently marking these with some form of liturgy (Billings, 2004). These are moments when the normal routines of life are suspended, when – to put the same point in a different way – the abnormal becomes normal, in terms of conversation as well as behaviour. Birth (baptism) and death are the most obvious of these events, but confirmation and marriage remain significant for many – though more so in the Lutheran parts of Northern Europe than in Britain itself, a point to be discussed in Part II.

## A NOTE ON COGNATE DISCIPLINES

Sociologists do not work in isolation. The final section of this chapter looks briefly at a range of cognate disciplines and asks what they might contribute to a better understanding of the place of religion in modern societies. It is premised on the following assumptions: first, that the ways in which religion is located in the constitution and development of human societies can never be a matter of final resolution; second, that they can, nonetheless, be gradually uncovered by scholars using a variety of methods and approaches and who come from different disciplinary backgrounds. It follows that a privileged place should be given to those who work at the interstices of conventional disciplines – it is they, very often, who make the most significant steps forward.

Clearly it is important for sociology to pay attention to other branches of social science: to anthropology, psychology, policymaking, demography and to disciplines that are brought together in common topics such as ageing or gender, bearing in mind that different groups of scholars have rather different dispositions towards religion as a subject of study. Many of those interested in gender, for example, have been reluctant to take religion seriously, mostly for ideological reasons – an interesting paradox given the disproportionate presence of women in most forms of Western Christianity (see Chapter 11). Other more practical difficulties also exist, but – once acknowledged – are easier to overcome. Debates in different disciplines, for example, take place in different journals, a fact which all too often inhibits interdisciplinary discussion, though more so in some places than others. In Britain, for instance, there are relatively few psychologists of religion (why is an interesting question) and no dedicated journal for their work. In the United States, in contrast, the *Journal for the Scientific Study of Religion* not only contains extensive work in the psychology as well as the sociology of religion, but offers a truly interdisciplinary forum, at least for those who employ primarily quantitative methods.

The contributions of political scientists – theorists, constitutionalists, internationalists and policymakers – are vital, particularly in terms of law and law-making, constitutional issues and questions of tolerance and human rights. Post-communist Europe has become a veritable laboratory in this respect – unsurprisingly given the need for these societies to come to terms with religion after decades in which this was largely disallowed. Alongside the (uneven) resurgence of historic faith has come, however, a host of new and often less welcome elements from outside. How should these be accommodated? Particularly helpful in this respect are the contributions of scholars trained in both social science and law (a demanding requirement). Such people are able to offer real insight into the debates about religious freedom (itself an ambiguous concept) and how to maintain this in rapidly changing political conditions. A useful and wide-ranging collection has been brought together by Richardson (2004), in which more than 30 studies are arranged geographically. The tensions between tolerance and democracy form an interesting theme within these papers, a point pursued in Part II.

Clearly the list could go on: through international relations (after a long silence);[17] through economics (the Weberian questions still resonate, the market model inspires rational choice theory); through economic history (the modernization process and the mutation to post-industrial society); through geography (the theorizing of cultural geographers and the new technologies of mapping); through area studies (the growing significance of religion in Latin America, South East Asia, China, etc.); and so on. A special place must, of course, be alloted to history given that explanations of difference almost always lie in the past. The recent enlargements of the European Union offer an excellent illustration: what emerged in 2004 was almost exactly coterminous with Western Christianity – the anomalous case being Greece.[18] The more recent extensions of Europe into the Orthodox world are of a different order and need to be seen as such, quite apart from the Turkish question. Interestingly the religious factor in these discussions is now openly expressed; for many years it was subsumed into questions of economy, democracy and human rights. Byrnes and Katzenstein (2006) develop this important point in some detail.

A rather different set of issues arise with respect to philosophy, religious studies and theology, for it is at this point that the insider/outsider question becomes central. Christian Smith's writing addresses these questions very directly (Smith, 2003). If the social sciences are to prosper, we need to be clear about the philosophies of science that underpin both our thinking and our writing. What, in other words, does it mean to be human? And how do our visions of the human shape our theories of social action and institutions? In an argument reminiscent of Luckmann (1967), Smith concludes that being human implies an inescapable moral and spiritual dimension – something (a structure of personhood) that organizes or orders human existence across both time and space. In concluding thus, Smith is making connections between religion as such, with its particular and enduring motivations, and the somewhat different aspirations of social science.[19]

The step to theology is larger still. Indeed for some it is a step too far for the reasons outlined in the introductory pages of this book. Theology is concerned with truth claims and as such is resistant to any discipline which relativizes the religious message. Two rather different points of view have emerged in this respect. The first is held by Milbank (1990), who maintains that sociology and theology are incommensurate discourses. Sociology, an inevitably secular science, should not encroach upon the sublime. Martin (1996b) argues otherwise: that sociology, appropriately understood and carefully deployed, can (and indeed should) contribute to theological understanding without either discipline being compromised.

For Martin, theological insights and the context from which they emerge are necessarily linked. For example, the Christian calling, both individual and collective, is to be 'in the world but not of it'. Or to put this in Martin's socio-theological language, between the specificities of each situation and the exigencies of the gospel lies 'an angle of eschatological tension'. Documenting and explaining the sharpness of the angle are, essentially, sociological tasks. So are suggestions of possible resolution if the tension becomes unbearable. Theologies of baptism provide one illustration, like the shifts in confirmation described in the previous chapter. Modes of initiation that 'fitted' the state churches of Northern Europe are no longer 'fitting', either socially or theologically, as these churches mutate from ascription to voluntarism as the basis of membership. New understandings are required as a result; they are more likely to succeed if the sociological shifts are not only taken into account but properly understood. Hence the need in the second part of this book to concentrate on the empirical realities associated with religion as this is experienced in different parts of the world in the early years of the twenty-first century.

## NOTES

1 Very considerable attention has been paid to methods in relation to the study of religion in the last half decade. See, for example, Stausberg and Engler (2011). See also the relevant sections of the new Preface (pp. 10ff.) – a step change in research has prompted an equivalent leap in methodology.

2 For the European Values Study, see www.europeanvaluesstudy.eu; for the World Values Study, see www.worldvaluessurvey.org/ (both accessed 9 April 2012).

3 See www.issp.org (accessed 9 April 2012).

4 See www.thearda.com (accessed 9 April 2012).

5 Additional sources of information about quantitative work (both in the United States and elsewhere) can be found on the relevant pages of the Pew Forum on Religion and Public Life (www.pewforum.org) and of the Hartford Institute for Religion Research (http://hirr.hartsem.edu). A modest but very accessible British equivalent is known as BRIN: British Religion in Numbers (www.brin.ac.uk). All accessed 9 April 2012.

6 In Scotland, the question was rather more detailed regarding different types of Christianity.

7 Further work has now been done on this question and has yielded very interesting results. See Day (2006, 2011).

8 See www.bod.org.uk/bod/ (accessed 9 April 2012).

9 This information is taken from the Kendal Project website – see www.lancs.ac.uk/fss/projects/ieppp/kendal/methods.htm (accessed 9 April 2012). Interestingly, not all these methodologies are followed through in the publications that have emerged from the project.

10 See www.crs.uu.se/Research/Former_projects/WREP/ and www.crs.uu.se/Research/Former_projects/WaVE/ for the follow-up project on Welfare and Values in Europe (both accessed 9 April 2012). See also Bäckström et al. (2010) and Bäckström et al. (2011). The study is revisited in Chapter 11.

11 In 2003, I saw this programme in action. Something similar followed in New York through the Ecologies of Learning project at New York Theological Seminary. See http://nyts.edu/program-centers/ (accessed 9 April 2012).

12 For a full list, see the examples discussed in Davie (2003a).

13 Taylor (2003) is a helpful, though not primarily sociological, guide in this respect.

14 Note in particular the BBC documentary fronted by David Lodge in March 1997 entitled *Legendary Trails: The Way of St James*. The same theme re-emerges in Lodge's novel *Therapy* (1996).

15 Happily this has now been achieved in a fine piece of doctoral work (Chemin, 2012).

16 A journalistic account of this episode can be found in Gerrard (2004). Davie (2010a) introduces a further example: the rituals and reflections surrounding the premature death of Jade Goody in 2009.

17 See Thomas (2005), Snyder (2011) and Toft et al. (2011).

18 Hence a form of cultural schizophrenia in Greece, admirably illustrated in the debates surrounding the mention (or not) of religion on Greek identity cards (Molokotos-Liederman, 2003, 2007).

19 Interestingly Adam Seligman opens up rather similar themes in *Modernity's Wager* (2003).

# Part II

Substantive issues

## *seven*

# mainstream religions in the western world

This chapter forms a pair with the one that follows, for an obvious reason. What is considered mainstream religion in the Western world is marginal elsewhere and what is marginal in the West is evidently mainstream in other parts of the world. The division of material between the two is determined by the context. This chapter will deal primarily with the forms of religion that are deemed mainstream in Europe and the United States, underlining both the similarities and differences in each case. Berger et al. (2008), of which I was a co-author, develop this discussion further: the title *Religious America: Secular Europe* speaks for itself. It works through the America–Europe comparison under four headings: history, intellectual traditions, institutions and social difference.

## MAINSTREAM RELIGION IN WESTERN EUROPE

The material on West Europe draws on a wide range of published sources, including my own. With this in mind, this section should be read against the data and arguments set out in Davie (1994, 2000a, 2002a, 2006b).[1] The facts and figures found in these publications will not be rehearsed in detail in this chapter. One point is, however, crucial: that is the placing of the British case between continental Europe and the United States. In terms of denominational allegiance, Britain (indeed the whole of the United Kingdom) looks out across the Atlantic and to the English-speaking world, thereby establishing connections that remain as seductive for certain kinds of church people (notably the growing evangelical constituency) as they are for some politicians. In terms of belief, behaviour and institutions, however, Britain is much more like her European neighbours – with low levels of religious activity, but higher levels of nominal allegiance and religious belief. Britain shares with the rest of Europe the common heritage of state church and, historically at least, close connections between religious and secular power. Such patterns have evolved over many centuries with, as we have seen, important implications for sociological understanding. In this chapter the emphasis will lie on the post-war period, outlining in the first instance a series of generational shifts.

## generational shifts

An early chapter in *Religion in Britain since 1945* (Davie, 1994) describes three to four 'generations' or, more accurately, three to four changes in mood, from the end of the Second World War until the mid-1990s; they need only be summarized here. In the immediate post-war decades the emphasis lay on putting back what the war had destroyed, to the point almost of denying that anything had happened to the underlying structures of British society. This was a period in which traditional forms of religion flourished, epitomized more than anything in the rituals associated with the Coronation in June 1953. By the late 1960s everything had changed; attitudes, assumptions, behaviour and institutions associated with earlier decades had been comprehensively swept away. The world in which relatively conservative forms of mainstream religion fitted quite well gave way to a decade in which confidence in secular alternatives dominated the scene – so much so that the churches very frequently followed suit in their efforts to 'catch up' with society. By the mid-1970s, however, secular confidence was itself undermined as the global economy took a turn for the worse and as the negative as well as positive consequences of modernization came to the fore – a shift in perspective in which the oil crisis and its aftermath dominated debate.

These shifts could be seen right across Europe, but made themselves visible in different ways in different places. The French case, for example, is even more dramatic than the British. France industrialized relatively late, but then extraordinarily fast – a shift from rural to urban which effectively took place in the 1950s. May 1968, moreover, is symbolized by the events that took place on the streets of Paris (not London), a moment in which students demanded radical reforms in society as well as in the university system. Such confidence could not last, however, even in France where the reaction was both swift and sharp: De Gaulle won by a landslide in June 1968. A very different mood was beginning to assert itself. Civil unrest – notably in Germany and Italy – became symbolic of wider unease as Europeans began, bit by bit, to come to terms with the downturn in the global economy and rising levels of unemployment. At precisely the same moment, host populations were beginning to realize that the post-war influx of labour from many different parts of the world was to be a permanent rather than temporary feature of European life – one, however, that was much more difficult to manage in straitened economic circumstances than was the case in years of economic boom. The implications for religious life were considerable.

The Thatcher decade, in contrast, was peculiarly British; no other European society experienced the imposition of a market ideology in quite the same way, a fact which once again places Britain on the edge of Europe, looking to the United States rather than to continental neighbours. Interestingly, the churches were in the forefront of resistance at this point, becoming at least for a time the effective political opposition, given the disarray of the Labour Party. The publication of *Faith in the City* (1985) epitomized these relationships. The turn of the millennium saw a reversal in political fortunes about as complete as is possible to imagine, with the Labour Party winning three consecutive terms of office and the Conservatives struggling to emerge from their years in the wilderness. This they did in 2010, but only with the support of the Liberal Democrats. Interestingly, both Margaret Thatcher and Tony Blair claimed Christian inspiration for their political views and in style are closer to each other than they are to many of their political colleagues. The Archbishop of Canterbury, moreover, remains a figure of some importance, in many ways epitomizing the ambiguities of religion in modern Britain. The leader of a supposedly marginal institution finds himself repeatedly on the front pages of the newspapers with respect to political as well as moral discussion. The war in Iraq became a touchstone of debate in this respect.

As indeed in others. The tensions between the United States and 'old Europe' regarding the war became a dominant theme in political discussion, within which the religious factor played an increasingly significant role.[2] The positive interpretation of these events depicted Britain as the bridge between old world and new, minimizing the difference between Europe and the United States (Garton Ash, 2004); others took a more negative stance, seeing Tony Blair as little more than Bush's poodle and emphasizing the need for a distinct and articulate European voice. The political discussion lies beyond the scope of this book; the underlying themes will resonate, however, in the sections that follow – in both the European and the American case.

## conceptual approaches

Quite apart from data themselves, my thinking about the place of religion in European life continues to develop. This will become clear

**139**

in the following paragraphs, which embody three key ideas. The first, 'believing without belonging', was the subtitle of *Religion in Britain since 1945* (Davie, 1994); as a phrase, it caught the attention of significant groups of people – scholars, journalists, church leaders and those with pastoral responsibilities. The second, 'vicarious religion', formed the core concept in *Religion in Modern Europe* (Davie, 2000a). It has already been introduced as a methodological tool, but needs in this chapter to be considered substantively. It provides the key to understanding the present state of religiousness in Europe. The situation continues to evolve, however, prompting questions about the future as well as the past. One way forward in this respect lies in the third idea: in the gradual mutation from a culture of obligation to a culture of consumption – once again a theme introduced in Part I, but which must now be developed in more detail. The section will conclude with reference to the Kendal Project, an in-depth study of religious life in a medium-sized Lake District town. In many respects the findings of the Kendal team concur with my own thinking, but not always.

### believing without belonging

**140**

One of the most striking features of religious life in contemporary Europe is the evident mismatch between different measurements of religiousness. There exists, first of all, a set of indicators that measure firm commitment to (a) institutional life and (b) credal statements of religion (in this case Christianity). All of these display a marked reduction in Europe as a whole, but most of all in the Protestant nations in the North, including Britain. These indicators are closely related to each other in so far as institutional commitment both reflects and confirms religious belief *in its orthodox forms*. The believing Christian attends church to express his or her belief and to receive affirmation that this is the right thing to do. Conversely, repeated exposure to the institution and its teaching necessarily informs, not to say disciplines, belief.

No observer of the current religious scene disputes these facts: that these indicators are both interrelated and in serious decline. There is less agreement regarding the consequences of this situation. The complex relationship between belief (in a wider sense) and practice is central to this discussion, for it is clear that a manifest reduction in the 'hard' indicators of religious life has not, in the short term at least, had a similar effect on rather less rigorous dimensions of religiousness (nominal membership and non-orthodox beliefs). Indeed, the resultant mismatch in the different indicators is the principal finding of the European Values Study; it is supported by most, if not all, empirical investigations of the current religious scene in Europe.[3] It is, moreover, precisely this state of affairs which was captured by the phrase 'believing without belonging', an expression that 'has rapidly spread across the world and beyond the borders of scholarship' (Voas and Crockett, 2005: 11–12).

Some idea of the extent of this discussion can be found by putting 'believing without belonging' into an internet search engine. The phrase appears everywhere: in academic papers all over the world, in more popular writing about the churches in this country and in others, in the statements of religious leaders, in religious journalism, and in student exam papers. Quite clearly, the notion resonates for many, very different, groups of people. Voas and Crockett provide a helpful categorization of this discussion into hard and soft versions of the 'theory' before embarking on a series of empirically based criticisms. These criticisms will not be dealt with here except where they coincide with the argument as a whole; they will be answered in full in the new edition of the 1994 book.[4] At this point, something rather different is required: that is, a clarification of two or three key themes within the 'believing without belonging' debate in order that the concept itself be properly understood.

**141**

The first of these concerns the status of the churches as one type of voluntary organization among many and reflects the argument already introduced in Chapter 5. If it is true that the churches as institutions have declined markedly in the post-war period, it is also true that the same process can be seen in almost all social activities which require people to 'gather' on a regular basis (political parties, trade unions, team sports, etc.). Or to put the same point more directly, believing without belonging is a pervasive dimension of modern European societies, not confined to the religious lives of European people.

The second theme reflects the attitudes of church leaders. Understandably enough, significant numbers of individuals charged with the maintenance of religious organizations have embraced the phrase 'believing without belonging', at least in part to justify their continued existence. Things are not as bad as they seem. As it happens, I do think that the churches have a continuing existence in all parts of Europe, but for reasons that require careful and detailed consideration (see below). In the meantime, it is important that the churches' personnel appreciate that the situation described by this phrase is neither better nor worse than a more straightforwardly (if one may use that term) secular society. It is simply different. Those that minister to a half-believing, rather than unbelieving, society will find that there are advantages and disadvantages to this situation, as there are in any other. Working out appropriate ministerial strategies for this continually shifting and ill-defined context is the central and very demanding task of the religious professional. A firm and necessary grasp of the sociological realities is but the starting point.

Church leaders are not the only group to have adopted the phrase. As was made clear in Chapter 4, American rational choice theorists find in the data marshalled to support the 'believing without belonging' thesis, confirmation of an idea central to one of their principal lines of argument. That is, the notion of a lazy monopoly (i.e. the European state churches) unable either to stimulate or to fulfil the latent religious needs of the populations for which they are responsible. If a free, or freer, market were allowed to develop, Europeans would become as actively religious as their American counterparts; unattached believers would be captured and sustained by active and competitive religious organizations working all over the continent. I am not as convinced as the rational choice theorists that this would, in fact, be the case for the reasons already stated (pp. 87–8).

A third question follows from this and relates to the remark concerning the short and the long term. It is at this point, moreover, that the sociological debate intensifies. They are those (notably Bryan Wilson, Steve Bruce, and to some extent David Voas and Alasdair Crockett) who argue cogently that the mismatch between believing and belonging may well exist, but it is simply a temporary phenomenon; it is only a matter of time before belief, unsupported by regular attendance (i.e. by an institution), diminishes to match the more rigorous indicators of religiousness. In so far as this debate refers to statements of credal religion endorsed by the churches, I would agree with them. I am much less sure, however, about the looser and more heterodox elements of belief. Indeed, following the material introduced in Chapter 5 (pp. 99–100), there are persuasive data emerging from the most recent EVS enquiries, which indicate that the relationship between certain dimensions of belief and belonging may well be inverse rather than direct. Notable here are those aspects of belief that relate to the soul and to life after death. As we have seen, these appear to rise markedly in younger rather than older generations, and in precisely those countries of Europe (mostly but not exclusively in the North) where the institutional capacities of the churches are most diminished.

With this in mind, the future becomes difficult to predict. What seems unlikely, however, is the emergence of a society in which secular rationalism becomes the overriding norm. It is more likely that belief of some sort will go on existing alongside more secular understandings of life.

The relationship between them will be long term and complex, rather than one simply replacing the other. It is at this point, moreover, that the discussion needs to take into account the connections between emergent patterns of belief and the institutional churches themselves, for it is clear that the latter continue not only to exist but to exert an influence on many aspects of individual and collective lives – even in Europe.

## vicarious religion

The separating out of belief from belonging has undoubtedly offered fruitful ways in which to understand and to organize the material about religion in modern Europe. Ongoing reflection about the current situation, however, has encouraged me to reflect more deeply about the relationship between the two, utilizing, amongst other ideas, the notion of vicarious religion.

My thinking in this respect has been prompted by the situation in the Nordic countries. A number of Nordic scholars have responded to the notion of believing without belonging by reversing the formula: in this part of Europe the characteristic stance in terms of religion is to belong without believing.[5] Such scholars are entirely right in these observations. Nordic populations, for the most part, remain members of their Lutheran churches; they use them extensively for the occasional offices and regard membership as part of national just as much as religious identity (more so than in Britain). More pertinently for the churches themselves, Nordic people continue to pay appreciable amounts of tax to their churches – resulting amongst other things in large numbers of religious professionals (not least musicians) and beautifully maintained buildings in even the tiniest village. The cultural aspects of religion are well cared for.

This does not mean, of course, that Nordic populations attend their churches with any frequency, nor do they necessarily believe in the tenets of Lutheranism. Indeed, they appear on every comparative scale to be among the least believing and least practising populations in the world.[6] So how should we understand their continuing membership of and support for their churches? How, in other words, is it possible to get beneath the surface of a Nordic, or indeed any other, society in order to investigate the reflexes of a population that for the most part remain hidden? An answer can be found on pp. 128–30. By paying attention to the place of the institutional churches at the time of personal or collective crises, it is possible to see more clearly the role that religious organizations continue to play in the lives of both individuals and

**143**

communities. Or, to develop the definition of 'vicarious' already offered, it is possible to see how an active religious minority can operate on behalf of a much larger number, who implicitly at least not only understand but quite clearly approve of what the minority is doing. Under pressure, what is implicit becomes explicit.

Two quite different features of Europe's religious life lead in a similar direction: that is, to a better understanding of vicariousness. The first reflects the symbolic importance of the church building both for the community of which it is part and, in many cases, for the wider public. Relatively few Europeans attend their churches with any regularity; that is abundantly clear. Many more, however, feel strongly about the church buildings present in their locality, but only protest (make their feelings explicit) when a building is threatened with closure. The status quo is simply taken for granted until disturbed, when it becomes an issue of considerable importance.[7] Rather more subtle, but equally revealing in this connection, are the reactions of the wider public if they are asked to pay to enter a religious building. In many ways, the 'normal' roles are reversed. The worshipping community, burdened by the maintenance of their building, are anxious both to generate income and to reduce the wear and tear caused by constant visitors; they are frequently in favour of entry charges. The wider public, in contrast, resent being asked for money on the grounds that such buildings, particularly those that belong to the historic churches, are considered public rather than private space, to which everyone (believer or not) should have the right of access. They do not belong exclusively to those who use them regularly.

A second set of issues relates to the complex situation in those parts of Europe previously under communist control. In the years since 1989, considerable attention has been paid to the reconstruction, both in physical and constitutional terms, of the churches in countries where religious institutions had at best an ambiguous legal existence. This has proved a highly contentious topic, the evolution of which reflects a series of shifting moods: from something close to euphoria in the months immediately following the fall of the Berlin Wall to an increasing sense of disillusionment as the years wore on. Conflict, sometimes very bitter, has been part of the story as disputes about money and power have come to the fore. No one, however, has seriously suggested that the churches should not be there – hence the struggle to put them back despite the difficulties. And to concentrate too much on the fact that in some, if not all, of the formerly communist countries church-going rates remain volatile is to miss the point. The real questions lie elsewhere. Why, for example, are the churches so important that they

144

are worth the all-too-evident effort to re-establish them? One reason can be found in the crucial role of the churches in the moments just before the fall of the Wall. In many parts of Europe, a tiny and undoubtedly infiltrated worshipping community had somehow maintained a protected, if marginalized, public space, which became available to the population as a whole at the moment of need and in which protest could become explicit rather than implicit (Martin, 1996a).

In making this point, it is important to bear in mind the Lutheran as well as the Catholic countries dominated by communism until 1989 – notably Estonia and East Germany. Both were and remain some of the most secular parts of the continent. Yet even here the vicarious role was possible, the most notable example being the Nicolaikirche in Leipzig – the chosen venue for those opposed to the Communist regime as the 1989 'revolution' gathered steam. Berger's remarks concerning the Gedächtniskirche in Berlin (Berger, 2001: 195) make exactly the same point, still operative some 10 years later. Vicariousness can, it seems, maintain itself on pretty slim resources. The rather different form of protest that took place in Poland through the 1980s, and in which the Catholic Church undoubtedly played a vital role, was of course much more visible. Quite rightly it has caught the attention of a wide variety of observers; it was not, however, the only way to proceed.

Once the notion of vicariousness has been put in place, a series of sociological questions inevitably follow. It is these that I have explored in considerable detail in Davie (2000a, 2007a, 2010a). It is in this context, moreover, that the nature (as well as the role) of Europe's historic churches becomes apparent, the more so if seen in a comparative perspective. It becomes increasingly clear, for example, that European populations continue to see such churches as public utilities maintained for the common good, a situation quite different from that in the United States. The same point can be approached conceptually: Europeans from all parts of the continent understand the meaning of vicariousness (an understanding that overrides questions of translation). Explaining the notion to an American audience is much more difficult; quite simply it has no resonance. An entirely different ecclesiastical history has led to different understandings of the relationship between church and society, a situation accurately described as a market. The church tax system of Northern Europe exemplifies one relationship, the freely given tithe the other.[8]

With this in mind, I am convinced that vicariousness still resonates in Europe in the early years of the twenty-first century and will do for the foreseeable future. As a concept, it is both more penetrating and more accurate than believing without belonging.[9] The longer term,

**145**

however, is rather more difficult to predict, bearing in mind the complexities in the relationship between belief and belonging already described. A whole range of issues need to be taken into account in this respect, not least an increasingly discernible mutation in the religious lives of Europeans from a culture of obligation to one of consumption or choice.

## from obligation to consumption

The idea as such has been already been introduced (pp. 97–9), with the changing nature of confirmation in the Church of England taken as an example. What until the 1950s was a teenage rite of passage, at least in certain circles, has turned into something very different: a rite requested by a relatively small but very varied group of people, who wish to express publicly what hitherto have been private convictions. Confirmation is often preceded by the baptism that did not take place in infancy. Theologies and liturgies adapt accordingly. Interestingly, very similar shifts can be found in other parts of Europe. In the 1990s, for example, adult baptisms in the Catholic Church in France matched very closely those in the Church of England (Davie, 2000a: 71–2); indeed the similarity in the statistics was almost uncanny given the entirely different ecclesiologies embodied in the two churches.

146

How, then, should these changes be approached? The question can be asked in terms of gains as well as losses. What, in other words, are the forms of the sacred most likely to flourish in late modernity and how can their *relative* success be explained? In the concluding chapter of Davie (1994), two possibilities emerged in this respect: on the one hand, the types of religion that followed or affirmed the fragmentations of late-modern societies, including the many different manifestations of the new age; and on the other, the forms of religion that create islands of security within the uncertainties of rapid economic, social and cultural change, including a tendency towards fundamentalism. Working in terms of a shift from obligation to consumption has enabled me to refine these categories and to understand them better. The discussion will begin in this chapter; it will continue in the two that follow in which both the new age and the notion of fundamentalism will be discussed in more detail.

The first point to grasp is that the gains and losses run through the denominations, not between them. What follows, therefore, can be applied, in Britain, to Catholics, Anglicans, Methodists, Presbyterians, Baptists and so on, keeping in mind that the other faith populations are rather different (see Chapter 8). Within the mainstream, broadly speaking, any congregation that relies on a sense of obligation or duty to bring people to church (or similar institution) is likely to be in trouble. No longer are European populations 'obliged' to go to church if they do not want to; nor do they attend for the kind of reasons that compelled them in the past (to get a job, to get a house, for social standing or for political influence). Equally changed are the internal disciplines – the sense that church-going was the right and proper thing to do, a sentiment enforced by common values or shared beliefs. It is these pressures, both external and internal, that have very largely collapsed in modern Europe. The idea, for example, that employment or housing should depend on evidence of religious activity is no longer acceptable. Respectability, moreover, has little to do with church-going.[10] Such changes are hardly surprising given that the imperatives of Christian belief, including the injunction to attend worship, are no longer shared by most people in the population.

Hence a new situation. Church-goers have ceased to be a relatively large group of people who attend worship for a wide range of motives, some religious and some not. They have become instead a noticeably smaller but still significant group, whose reasons for attending church are still diverse but derive less from habit or custom and rather more from individual choice. The freedom from constraint is, surely, a good thing. There are, however, unintended consequences. Among them is the erosion of a common religious narrative – a body of knowledge shared by the population as a whole and in many respects crucial for the understanding of European culture. Great swathes of European art, architecture, literature and music are largely incomprehensible without it, a fact that is widely recognized and frequently lamented in educational circles (Hervieu-Léger, 1990). Conversely the readiness with which some people will attend church in order that their children may go to a church school remains a feature of English life; likewise the presence in church of a politician (local or national) at key moments in the political process.

**147**

The next step in the argument follows logically. What are the choices made by the reduced but still significant church-going minority? In the British case, two very different options stand out, which at first glance appear contradictory. On closer inspection, however, they have an important and very interesting feature in common – the key perhaps to understanding the nature of religious life in twenty-first century Britain.[11] The first is the conservative evangelical church, the success story of modern church-going, both inside and outside the established Church. These are churches which draw their members from a relatively wide geographical area and work on a congregational rather than parish model. Individuals are invited to make a conscious decision about joining, and membership implies commitment to a certain set of beliefs and behavioural codes. Such churches offer firm boundaries and protection from the vicissitudes of life – features that are increasingly attractive in times of uncertainty (whether economic, social or cultural). Such findings fit well both with the predictions that I made in 1994 and, interestingly enough, with a central tenet of RCT (i.e. that churches which demand more from their members are themselves in greater demand).

On closer inspection, however, it is clear that some kinds of evangelical church are doing better than others – notably those that incorporate a charismatic element (Guest, 2004, 2007; Chambers, 2004; Heelas and Woodhead, 2004). Old-fashioned biblicism is less popular. The evangelical success story is clearly epitomized in the Alpha course, a formula which brings together firm biblical teaching, warm friendship and an emphasis on the Holy Spirit in a strikingly successful combination (Hunt, 2004). The appeal of this movement is extraordinary, a fact admitted by friend and foe alike. Whether you like Alpha or not, it is hard to think of an equivalent movement (religious or secular) of parallel proportions. A secular training programme that claimed a throughput of some 1.5 million volunteers and which grew through the 1990s from four courses to more than 10,000 would find itself the focus of extensive media attention.

Very different and less frequently recognized in twenty-first century Britain is the popularity of cathedrals and city centre churches. These are places that offer a distinctive but rather different product, which characteristically includes traditional liturgy, first-rate music and excellence in preaching, all of which take place in an historic and often very beautiful building. A visit to a cathedral is an aesthetic experience – sought after by a wide variety of people, including those for whom membership or commitment present difficulties. 'I go to a cathedral confident that I will not be obliged to share the Peace or stay for coffee' is a common sentiment; the implied criticism of the evangelical church can be read between the lines. Cathedrals, moreover, deal with very diverse constituencies. Working from the centre outwards it is possible to identify regular and irregular worshippers, pilgrims, visitors and tourists, bearing in mind that the lines between these categories are frequently blurred. The numbers in all these categories are considerable and in many cases rising, the more so on special occasions (Platten, 2006). The links with pilgrimage (see pp. 126–7) are particularly interesting (Hervieu-Léger, 1999; Davie, 2000a: 157–62; Chemin, 2012).

Is there a common feature in these very different stories? There is little sociological evidence on which to draw at this point, but it is, I think, the experiential or 'feel-good' factor, whether this be expressed in charismatic worship, in the Alpha weekend, in the tranquillity of Cathedral evensong or in the special occasion – Greenbelt or Spring Harvest on the evangelical side, a candle-lit mass for the cathedrals or prominent parish church. The point is that we *feel* something. We experience the sacred or the set-apart in a way that echoes an essentially Durkheimian insight – that religion (the sacred) awakens in us something beyond the realities of everyday life without which we remain dissatisfied. Hence a possible hypothesis: late-modern Europeans are much more likely to go to places of worship in which an *experience* of the sacred is central to the occasion. The purely cerebral (the biblical exposition or liberal Protestantism) is much less seductive.

One question remains to be asked: do these changes add up to an incipient rational choice model? There have been hints that this might be so. It is important, however, to put the shift from obligation to consumption into a broader context. A distinctive constituency is undoubtedly emerging, whose religious choices are beginning to reflect the ideas set out by the rational choice theorists. Such sentiments are encouraged by a growing religious market, particularly in the larger cities of Europe where parish boundaries most easily erode. Far more Europeans still operate, however, on an older model: one in which latent belief and nominal membership dominate the scene, sentiments that are activated at particular moments in individual or collective life or for particular, sometimes unexpected, reasons. Hence the complexity of the current situation: the two models are in partial tension but they also overlap. All churches, moreover, are increasingly exposed to pressures from outside Europe as well as within, a point that will resonate repeatedly in the following chapters.

**149**

### the Kendal Project – a worked example

A moderately recent case study offers a worked example of some of these ideas. The Kendal Project looked at 'religion' in all its manifestations in a particular community in England – Kendal, a town of 28,000 people in the Lake District (i.e. in a rural and moderately traditional part of the country where other faith populations are relatively rare). The project has generated very interesting theoretical as well as empirical material (Heelas and Woodhead, 2004).

Broadly speaking, the facts and figures confirm the national pattern: in any one week, 7.9 per cent of the Kendal population are active in a Christian congregation of some kind, whereas 1.6 per cent take part in the holistic milieu. (Regrettably, there are no data for monthly figures, which would give a better idea of the size of the pool in both cases.) More generally, the evidence from Kendal clearly suggests that the holistic groups are growing fast, while the Christian congregations continue to decline. The implications of these changes for the twenty-first century becomes the crucial question. Is this evidence, as the authors claim, of a momentous shift in the sacred landscape of modern Britain or is this something rather more modest? I suspect the latter, but only time will tell. The results of the street survey are similarly provoking. In one sense these are very clear: only two people (out of 56 interviewed) declared a definite lack of belief or anti-church sentiments. But how the rest of the figures are configured depends a good deal on how the 'grey' areas of belief are categorized – as support for relatively high levels of belief in its most general sense or as a marked drift from the Christian norm. Either could be argued from these data.

Even more provocative are the theoretical currents underpinning the Kendal Project. The authors are convinced both of significant shifts in the religious landscape of Britain and of what Charles Taylor calls the 'massive subjective turn of modern culture' (Taylor, 1992, 2007). The importance of the inner voice, the authenticity of the self, the God in me are the watchwords of our culture, never mind our religion – a finding that fits nicely with the data emerging from the 1999–2000 European Values Study (see above). The evidence from Kendal should be seen in this light, noting not only the shift from the congregational domain to the holistic, but the very similar mutation found *within* the congregational sphere itself (i.e. in the forms of Christianity that, relatively speaking, are doing well). It is clear, for example, that the charismatic churches in Kendal are holding up better than the liberal Protestants, confirming the interpretation already suggested: that the successful churches in modern Britain are those which offer an experiential or feel-good element in their worship.

Woodhead (2004) sets these shifts into a long-term and more theological perspective. Clearly the tensions between the inner life, the mystical and the spiritual on one side and mainstream Christian teaching on the other are nothing new; they have been present within the Christian tradition since its earliest days but, Woodhead claims, in a somewhat uneasy relationship. Modern culture, moreover, very much favours the former. The next question cannot be avoided: will this be at the expense of mainstream Christianity as such or only to certain parts of this?

In other words, do the churches have the option of responding positively to the subjectivization of modern culture, or will this necessarily undermine their raison d'être altogether? For Woodhead, the evidence from Kendal suggests the latter – arguing that there is a deep and increasingly destructive incompatibility between two very different ways of thinking. I am not so sure. Somewhat similar questions will arise in the tensions between the spiritual and the religious introduced in a later section of this chapter and in the material on the new age pursued in the next. Before turning to either, however, the similarities and differences with the American case require attention.

## MAINSTREAM RELIGION IN THE UNITED STATES

The preliminary sections of the chapter on rational choice theory make it quite clear that the forms of religion that obtain in the United States both grew and exist in an entirely different social space from their European counterparts (i.e. in a quasi-public space that no single group could dominate). How a whole series of immigrant communities, each with their own form of (mostly) Christianity came to inhabit this space and learnt gradually to live together constitutes a core theme in American history and one in which the differences from Europe are immediately apparent. Precisely these differences provide the starting point for Warner's seminal contribution to the rational choice debate (Warner, 1993). In terms of this chapter, the important point to grasp is that two very different histories lead to two very different outcomes: in Europe, an incipient market is beginning to overlay a still present, though weakened, historical monopoly; in the United States an almost unbelievable range of denominational groups compete with each other for the attentions of a population that, with very few exceptions, believes in God and regards church-going as normal rather than abnormal behaviour. In the former, religion is thought of as a public utility by most, if not all, of the population; in the latter, the analogy of the market comes naturally.

**151**

### facts and figures

For Europeans, one 'fact' stands out above all the others in their observations of religion in the United States: that is, the seemingly high levels of religious activity. Approximately 40 per cent of Americans declare that they attend church weekly and even more once a month, figures that have displayed remarkable stability over several decades. Indeed across a whole range of indicators, Americans emerge as not only more religious but noticeably more orthodox (in the sense of endorsing credal statements) than almost all European populations (Ester et al., 1994: 37–52; Stark and Finke, 2000; Pew Forum on Religion and Public Life, 2008a). Attendance and orthodoxy remain, therefore, mutually reinforcing in the American case, exactly the reverse of what is happening in Europe.[12]

But not all Americans do what they say – a point already raised in connection with RCT and the methodologies employed to test this (Hadaway et al., 1993, 1998; Hadaway and Marler, 2005). There is no need to go over this material again except to underline the inescapable conclusion: Americans want to be seen as church-goers, even if many attend less frequently than they say. Europeans do the reverse.[13] The pressures to conform are, however, more effective in some parts of the United States than others, a point that reflects Martin's observations that levels of attendance are markedly higher in the South and centre of the country (in the Bible Belt) than they are on the coastal sides of the mountain ranges. The difference between men and women is a further significant variable, just as it is in Europe; women are noticeably more religious than men, over a wide range of indicators and in very different types of churches – a point to be developed in Chapter 11. The age factor is more complex. It is true that young Americans leave their churches, just like young Europeans, and disproportionate numbers of younger people appear in the growing 'non-religious' category of American surveys (Smith, 1998: 80), but significant numbers of these individuals return to the churches later in life, complicating the overall picture (Roof, 1993, 2000). In short, there is still a marked difference in levels of religious activity between America and most (if not quite all) European countries. More importantly, the difference is qualitative; it is not simply a question of degree.

A second point follows from this: in the United States, there is continual movement between denominations, or 'switching' to use the American term. Towards the end of the twentieth century, the cumulative effects of these decisions amounted to a major re-alignment of American religion: a shift from the liberal Protestant mainstream towards more conservative forms of religion (Wuthnow, 1990; Smith, 1998; Wolfe, 2003). The gainers in these exchanges are the many varieties of evangelical faith, both black and white – an increasingly vocal constituency. The case of the Catholic churches is more complex. The proportion of Catholics in the American population remains solid, despite a decline in mass attendance in the 1960s and 1970s. This decline has been offset, however, by a rise in the overall numbers of Catholics, boosted by significant arrivals from Central and Latin America.[14] As a result, Catholic churches find themselves on both sides of the switching equation. Taking both Catholics and Protestants together, the crucial point is the following: there is in the United States growth to compensate for decline in the historically dominant denominations, a feature which so far is absent in Europe.

The overall levels of religious activity and the growth in conservative forms of religious life lie behind one of the most controversial features of American religion: the New Christian Right. The controversy, moreover, is as much sociological as political.[15] One point, however, is beyond dispute. In Europe there is nothing that can realistically be called a New Christian Right in the sense of a social movement of conservative Christians that has an effect on the political or electoral map of the nation in question. It *is* true that a relationship exists between religious allegiance and political predilections in much of Western Europe – by and large there is a correlation between religious activity (of all forms) and conservative political leanings (S. Berger, 1982; Medhurst, 2000), but in ways that are very different from those that exist in America. It is also true that most European politicians would be wise not to offend too directly the religious sensitivities of both the minorities in their populations that do attend their churches with reasonable regularity and the very much larger numbers of nominal members. But the capacities of religious activists to lobby their governments over matters of policy is not a matter of concern (or from another point of view of approval) in most parts of Europe, whether these be evangelical Protestants in the North or Catholic political parties in the South. Indeed in Catholic Europe the restructuring of the political scene in recent decades has largely resulted in a loss of power on the part of the Christian Democrats.[16]

An article that brought home to me the truly radical divergence in thinking between Europeans and Americans on the presence of a politico-religious lobby can be found in the quintessentially American journal *The National Interest* (Muller, 1997). In this the author (the President Emeritus of Johns Hopkins University) not only draws attention to the fact that the New Christian Right does not exist in Europe, but implies that the European political scene is the poorer because of this. Religion survives in America as a serious force in politics, not least in the form of a conservative religious movement – explicitly committed to traditional Christian values and vigorously opposed to social and political liberalism (including, amongst other things, the promotion of social justice through 'big government'). In Muller's view, this is a good thing.

The key difference between Europe and the United States in this regard is twofold: nothing comparable to the American religious right is in evidence in Europe, and the liberal orthodoxy is institutionalized more deeply in the structures of the welfare state – and indeed in the churches – in Europe than it is in America. Most Europeans, conversely, are profoundly supportive of the status quo, in so far as it underpins social justice in the form of a moderately comprehensive welfare system (the principal theme of Muller's article). Bearing this and indeed many other reasons in mind, the absence of a religious right is for them quite clearly an advantage, something that many Americans (including Muller) find difficult to understand. The implications for policy, both domestic and foreign, are considerable.

The place of televangelism is part and parcel of the same story. If the New Christian Right provides the political arm of particular forms of American religion, televangelism fulfils the same function in terms of the media. It is abundantly clear, for example, that televangelism resonates with a particular kind of Protestant Christianity that flourishes in North America, though more in some places than in others; its sociological patterns have been worked over by a variety of scholars employing a range of socio-political perspectives (Hadden, 1987; Hoover, 1988; Bruce, 1990; Peck, 1993). Unsurprisingly, these scholars conclude differently concerning the scope and influence of televangelism in American life. In 1987, for example, Hadden considered televangelism a highly significant social movement with ongoing influence in American life. A year or two later, Bruce stressed the limited influence of televangelists outside their immediate and already committed constituency; this is a classic case of preaching to the converted. Such differences of opinion are important and need to be taken into account in an overall assessment of the phenomenon in question. Of a totally different order, however, is the more or less complete failure of the televangelistic enterprise on this side of the Atlantic, despite numerous efforts on the part of American evangelists to break into the European market (Elvy, 1986, 1990; Schmied, 1996).

This 'failure' has been covered in some detail in Davie (2000a). Essentially it revolves around the fact that the constituency with which the televangelists find a resonance in the United States does not exist in Europe and no amount of trying by means of increasingly deregulated radio and television networks can make good this fact. This is an area in which the power of the media has proved itself surprisingly limited, with the result that a European visitor to the United States, coasting the channels in any hotel room at almost any time of the day or night, is simply astonished when they discover the examples of televangelism on

154

offer. Who, they ask, is watching this kind of thing? That person does not exist in Europe.

## explanations

If this is the case, how can these differences between Europe and America be explained? Nancy Ammerman's (1997, 2005) magisterial work on religious congregations is crucial in this respect. Ammerman's publications reflect not only the variety but the sheer resilience of religious congregations in American life, despite the multitude of vicissitudes that some of them face. It is true that many of these congregations (perhaps the majority) face decline, whether in the long or short term (1997: 44), but even the Contents page of Ammerman's volume gives an impression of persistence, relocation, adaptation and innovation in combinations that would be hard to match in Europe. There is, in other words, more of a forward movement in the United States than would be possible on this side of the Atlantic and in an astonishingly wide variety of communities. Exactly the same feeling emerges from Livezey's work on Chicago Metropolitan area (see pp. 119–20); in the 75 congregations studied in this project, there is the same emphasis on survival and adaptation to the surrounding context. More than this, in fact, there is an emphasis on how the congregations themselves 'reflect, resist, or influence' the changes going on around them or order to be pro-active as well as reactive to what is happening in their neighbourhoods (Livezey, 2000: 6). Any number of further examples could be found from a growing sociological literature on American congregationalism.[17]

155

Such evidence leads irrevocably to the apparent advantages of a system based on *voluntarism* (the very essence of the congregations that Ammerman and Livezey describe) over a relatively immobile state church (the common feature of Europe's religious heritage), seeing in the principle of voluntarism the fundamental reason for the continuing vitality of religion in American civic life. Herein lies the core of the rational choice approach to religious life. A second set of arguments are, however, important – deriving this time from perspectives contained within the secularization paradigm. David Martin (1978), for example, argues that religion cuts *vertically* into American society as each group of new arrivals brings with it its own religious package, and maintains or adapts this way of working as the generations pass. A glance round any American city confirms this impression, revealing a huge diversity both within and between denominations. Irish, Italian and Polish Catholics, to name but the most obvious, each have their own centres of worship and community – now joined by increasing numbers of Latino congregations. Protestants, given their fissiparous nature, are even more diverse. An essentially similar pattern, moreover, can be found in the different 'interest groups' of American religion as families, singles, professionals, seniors, activists and so on create and sustain forms of religion that are suited to their particular lifestyles – a central theme of Ammerman's and Livezey's work and of the growing number of projects and publications devoted to more recent waves of immigration.

In Europe, in contrast, the insertion tends to be *horizontal*, a pattern which derives ultimately from the collusions of religion and power over many centuries, a direct legacy of the 'official' status of Christianity as a state religion. As European populations began, some more radically than others, to reject the political dominations of the past, they discarded some, if not all, of the religious connotations that went with these. The result, however, is complex – a point well-illustrated in the subtle combinations of vicarious religion and religious choice described in the earlier sections of this chapter. Be that as it may, the default positions are quite clearly different in each case: in Europe residual membership of the historic tradition remains the norm (both upheld and contradicted by the commitments of an active minority); in the United States, active voluntary membership of a free-standing religious group is the dominant model for large sections of the population.

There is nothing particularly new in this analysis. Indeed it was precisely this feature of American life – the commitment to a voluntary association – that formed the core of Alexis de Tocqueville's observations about American democracy in the mid-nineteenth century, in which religion had a central place. The implications, however, go very deep. The independence of religious organizations from any kind of state support is both embedded in the American Constitution and integral to American self-understanding – attitudes that colour a whole series of subsequent issues, not least the manner in which religion as such enters the public square. One illustration of the latter can be found in the notion of civil religion, a concept famously developed by Bellah in the American context (Bellah, 1970), but with roots in European political discourse, notably in the work of Jean-Jacques Rousseau. Bellah, working in a Durkheimian perspective, seeks above all to identify the features that bind Americans together. Prominent among these are the allusions to a shared Judaeo-Christian heritage, taking care to emphasize commonality rather than difference. Despite the formal separation of church and state, phrases such as 'One nation under God' or 'In God we trust' resonate throughout the nation, the more so since 9/11 and the 'war on terror'. Such phrases are consciously deployed by American politicians at key moments in American life. They are, of course, entirely compatible with organizational independence, in that no single church or denomination is privileged above others. The attempts to return the concept of civil religion to the European context have already been considered (see p. 43).

## MAINSTREAMS AND MARGINS: A PRELIMINARY DISCUSSION

It is at this point that questions relating to immigration and the increasing diversity of religious life both in the United States and in Europe need to be introduced into the discussion, which is premised on the following assumption: that the position of a religious minority can only be fully understood if the characteristics of the host society are taken into account. (The detail of who these minorities are and where they come from will be outlined in the following chapter.)

Clearly both the United States and Europe are faced with a similar question: how does a culture dominated for the majority of its history by Judaeo-Christian understandings come to terms with minorities whose values are rooted in an entirely different politico-cultural environment? But it does, surely, make a difference if that history is measured in centuries rather than millennia and if immigration has always been the norm (at least since the arrival of the first European settlers). In the United States, for example, it is largely a question of extending an already existing religious diversity – a situation that is easier for some minorities than for others (e.g. those who can adapt more easily to the congregational model). Conspicuously absent, however, are two distinctive features: first, the legacy of Europe's imperial connections; and second, a dominant state church. Both, moreover, are implicated in the two quite separate movements which come together in the mid-post-war decades – for which, very confusingly, the same term is applied.

The first concerns the flows into Europe in the 1960s and 1970s. At precisely the moment when the historic churches were losing control of both the belief systems and lifestyles of many modern Europeans, substantial other faith populations began to arrive, primarily for economic reasons and, mostly, from parts of the world that were formerly colonies. Religious *pluralism*, in this understanding of the term, is a crucial aspect of late-modern European life; it is largely dominated by the existence within Western Europe of approximately 17 million Muslims. In coming to Europe, most of these communities moved from the

157

mainstream to the margins of religious life, a process to be described in Chapter 8.

Religious pluralism has, however, an entirely different meaning (in both popular and sociological discourse); it refers to the increasing fragmentation of belief systems already identified as one of the likely manifestations of religion in late modernity, not least in Kendal. Once again it is explained by the loss of control on the part of the historic tradition – a fact that is more developed in some parts of Europe than in others, but it is evident all over the continent. So far, such decline has not resulted in large numbers of conversions to secular rationalism. It has, however, encouraged a growing diversity of religious belief, as the disciplines associated with regular attendance diminish and the market in spiritual goods continues to increase with the growing mobility of European populations. The new age, itself extraordinarily diverse, is but one of the new spiritualities on offer (pp. 167–70). Other versions (i.e. of the 'spiritual' as opposed to the religious) permeate institutions as well as individual living: almost all publicly funded bodies in Britain, for example, are required to have policies on spirituality, explaining how the institution (a school or a hospital) will cater for the increasingly diverse populations that come through its doors. In short, spirituality has become a pervasive feature of modern European societies; it is a word with strongly positive connotation, but multiple and notoriously imprecise meanings (Flanagan and Jupp, 2007; Harvey and Vincett 2012).

Interestingly, recent work in the United States reveals a similar tendency towards spiritual seeking, despite – or alongside – relatively high levels of church-going (Roof, 1999, 2000; Wuthnow, 1999; Pew Forum on Religion and Public Life, 2008b). The context is different, however. For a start, the links with organized religion are very much stronger in the United States, where seeking takes place within the churches as well as outside them and where specific forms of religious institutions emerge to meet the needs of the questing population. Once again the market is responding to demand and with considerable success.[18] Bearing this in mind, 'spirituality' becomes a category to be scrutinized by sociologists on both sides of the Atlantic, carefully distinguishing this understanding of religious pluralism from that which relates to competing and well-organized religious organizations. The confusion between these areas of study has lead to persistent and damaging misunderstandings, notably amongst groups whose religious commitments form the very core of their existence and for whom a 'pick and mix', 'live and let live' kind of attitude simply will not do. It is precisely this contrast that provides the starting point for the discussion of religious minorities in the following chapter.

158

# NOTES

1 A new edition of Davie (1994) is planned for 2014. Additional material on Britain can be found in Bruce (1995a), Jenkins (1999) and Gill (1999), and on Europe in Rémond (1999), Greeley (2003), McLeod and Ustorf (2003), Robbers (2005) and in the publications emerging from the European Values Study. These are listed on the frequently updated EVS website: www.europeanvaluesstudy.eu/evs/ publications/ (accessed 16 April 2012), and include both the overviews of European society and publications pertaining to particular societies. See also the material referenced in the Preface to this edition, noting especially Woodhead and Catto (2012) – a major output of the Religion and Society Programme.

2 The 'excessive' religiousness of some Americans is seen as a problem by many Europeans; the 'excessive' secularity of much of Europe is viewed in similar light by some Americans.

3 Much of the debate turns on the manner in which the terms 'believing' and 'belonging' are operationalized. Belief, for example, is sometimes taken to mean belief in a 'personal God' and sometimes understood more broadly. Interpretations differ accordingly.

4 See note 3. If the terms are interpreted too rigidly, the original meaning of the phrase is distorted.

5 One commentator, Anders Bäckström, puts this point even more subtly: what Swedish people, in fact, believe in is belonging. Greeley (2003) argues in a rather similar way with reference to Norway.

6 In the Swedish case, the findings of the European Values Study are supported by a number of national studies, including Skog (2001), Bäckström et al. (2004) and Winsnes (2004).

7 Note, for example, the furore surrounding the temporary closure of St Paul's in the autumn of 2011 in connection with the Occupy London movement.

8 These systems are, of course, mixed in practice, especially in Britain where there is no church tax, a certain amount of inherited wealth and a marked reluctance to give generously.

9 In this respect at least I largely agree with Voas and Crockett that 'believing without belonging' might 'enter honourable retirement' (2005: 25). Note, however, the valuable work of Day (2011), which has opened up the notion of believing without belonging in new ways. More recently, Voas – this time working with Bruce – has critiqued the notion of 'vicarious religion' (Bruce and Voas 2010).

10 But see the reference to Jenkins (1999) in Chapter 6.

11 Interestingly, somewhat similar 'choices' can be discovered in the French case, a point which is nicely captured in the ideal types presented by Hervieu-Léger in *Le Pèlerin et le converti* (1999). Hervieu-Léger underlines an additional, very valuable point – that both the pilgrim and the convert indicate mobility and movement. Conversely the somewhat static categories of church-goer (*pratiquant*) and non-church-goer (*non-pratiquant*) no longer resonate in late-modern society.

12 Chaves (2011) offers a recent, succinct and rather more nuanced overview of religious trends in the United States.

13 In Europe, the over-zealous church-goer may well run the risk of being called a hypocrite, especially in working-class communities (Ahern and Davie, 1987).

14 Huntington (2004) offers a controversial interpretation of these changes.

*159*

15 See, for example, Bruce (1988), Lienesch (1993) and Wolfe (2003). The discussion of the New Christian Right as a political movement will be developed in Chapter 9; here it is simply its presence that is noted.

16 It is worth noting, however, that it was precisely this constituency that provoked the debate about religion in the Preamble of the European Constitution. The results were ambiguous: the attempt failed, but the fact that the debate took place at all took many people by surprise.

17 An excellent source for this material can be found on http://hirr.hartsem.edu/cong/congregational_studies.html, maintained by the Hartford Institute for Religion Research (accessed 16 April 2012).

18 Some churches in Europe have also responded to this phenomenon; Holy Trinity Brompton, the home base of Alpha, offers an excellent example.

# *eight*

## minorities and margins

This chapter begins where the previous one ended – with a brief note on religious pluralism and the confusions surrounding this term. It draws on the work of Beckford (2003). The discussion then turns to the field in which the idea of religious pluralism was first explored in socio-logical debate: that is, the extensive corpus of work on new religious movements and their significance for modern societies. The emphasis lies on the need to pay attention to the host society as well as to the new religious movements themselves. The subsequent section has a rather different focus; it develops the remarks on spirituality already intro-duced in Chapter 7, looking in particular at the new age. The relation-ship of the latter to more orthodox forms of religion and indeed to modernity itself provides the framework for this analysis.

These, necessary though they are, are the preliminaries. The core of the chapter lies in a developed discussion of a numerically far more significant section of Western populations: that is, the growing other faith communities now present in Europe and the United States and the gradual process of accommodation, or otherwise, as these communities become part of their chosen societies. Once again the *relationship* between newcomer and host society constitutes the pivot of the argu-ment, which turns on the tensions between pluralism and democracy. It is this section, moreover, which links this chapter to the two that follow. The arrival within the West of significant other faith populations is part of the ongoing movement of labour associated with globalization (Chapter 10). Attitudes towards these mobile populations are influ-enced not only by events that are taking place on the other side of the world, but also by their portrayal in the Western media. The concept of fundamentalism is central to both (Chapter 9).

With this in mind, the conclusion returns once again to the twin notions of mainstream and margins. We live in a world in which the flows of people and knowledge become less and less easy to corral within specified geographical or social spaces. Given such tendencies, the thinking associated with the idea of mainstream and margin becomes correspondingly complex. Is it the case that the terms no longer resonate in an increasingly interdependent world? Or do they, despite everything, continue to dominate both human and social relationships? Either way, the implications are considerable – for the establishment of hierarchies in any given society and for the construction of identities, individual as well as collective.

## conceptual clarity: the different meanings of religious pluralism

James Beckford's work has already been introduced, not least as an advocate of constructivism in sociological account. How then does this apply to religious pluralism? Beckford goes straight to the heart of the matter: in public as well as sociological discourse several ideas have been conflated in one term. Not only is the term used to describe markedly different things (e.g. those introduced at the end of Chapter 7), it is also used to evoke the moral or political values associated with religious diversity. The inference is clear enough: there is a persistent confusion between what is and what ought to be, and until we get this straight, there are bound to be misunderstandings in public as well as sociological debate.

162

Equally diverse are the ways in which different societies accommodate religious diversity. Legal or constitutional arrangements provide the starting point – analyses that call on a range of different disciplines, including a knowledge of law. Rather more penetrating, however, are Beckford's remarks concerning the 'normal' or 'taken for granted' in any given society's acceptance or regulation of religion. The examples from France outlined in the following section will exemplify this point; they also reveal the importance of paying careful attention to the chain of events through which the 'default positions' have been, consciously or unconsciously, put in place. An inevitable question follows from this: can they be changed and if so, by whom? Who, in other words, has the right to recognize or to reject the parameters of religious life in any given society? Definitional issues are central to these discussions.

'Tolerance' opens another Pandora's box. Like pluralism, it means different things to different people – along a continuum which runs from a tacit acceptance of a restricted list of religious activities to a positive affirmation of forms of religion very different from the norm. Tolerance, moreover, operates at different levels: individuals who are tolerant of religious differences may exist in societies that have difficulty with the idea, and vice versa. Nor is there any direct correlation between pluralism (in its various forms) and toleration, though it is at least likely that those who affirm that religious diversity is beneficial rather than harmful are more likely to be tolerant of forms of religion that are able to co-exist. They will be less happy with forms of religion that aspire to monopoly status. The converse is equally true.

The discussion could continue. Enough, however, has been said to alert the reader to the pitfalls. How then do these ideas work out in practice?

## NEW RELIGIOUS MOVEMENTS

Sociologists of religion were among the first to pay attention to new religious movements: that is, to acknowledge their presence, to explain their growth and to endorse their right to exist. So much so that the work on new religious movements began to assert a disproportionate presence in the sociological literature devoted to religion. Case studies proliferated, often in the form of doctoral theses, alongside handbooks, encyclopaedias and thematic analyses. This story has been told many times and provides material for at least one, if not more, chapters in a standard textbook in the sociology of religion. It need not be told again. The following paragraphs will stress selected points only – those that relate to process rather than substance.

The first is brief and reflects the discussion of methodology in Chapter 6. The best of these case studies became classics in the field, as examples of patient and careful ethnography (p. 119). The second is rather different and concerns the motivations for sociological work in this area. Why were sociologists of religion so taken with movements that, numerically speaking, attract so few people? One reason lies in the pre-occupations of the 1960s, at least in Britain and America. This was the decade of radical questioning in which the mainstream, both religious and secular, was called to account. In Britain, moreover, it was the decade in which the historic churches began to lose members at a truly alarming rate. To look elsewhere for spiritual satisfaction, to experiment with new things and to take note of influences coming from outside, notably those from the East, was entirely 'normal'; so too the tendency for sociologists to follow suit. At times, however, the attraction to new forms of religion went a little too far – to the point of abandoning the reduced but still significant numbers that remained in the mainstream churches. Sociologists were beginning to know more about the 'edge' than they did about the centre.

Third, this was an Anglo-Saxon industry – one that fitted well with American denominationalism, and reasonably well with the more moderate pluralism (in both a descriptive and normative sense) of

*163*

Britain. In Latin Europe, sociological work in the 1960s had a rather different emphasis; it too was concerned with non-standard beliefs and practices, but in the form of popular religion – more precisely of popular Catholicism. Interesting regional studies were central to this endeavour (Hervieu-Léger, 1986). Some 30 years later, the situation has changed considerably. New religious movements remain a crucial aspect of the sociological agenda, but in different parts of the world – notably in France and in the post-communist countries of Europe.[1] The reasons are clear enough and reveal an entirely positive feature of sociological attention to this field: an awareness of the issues that such movements raise, not so much for themselves but for the societies of which they are part. The questions, moreover, go to the core of the sociological debate, in which the careful conceptualizations of Beckford resonate at every stage.

Clearly the presence of new religious movements indicates an increase in religious diversity. But even a cursory glance at the data reveals both that new religious movements take root more easily in some places than in others, and that they are treated in very different ways. By and large, societies that have been religiously plural from the start or which have learnt over time to accommodate diversity simply extend this to new forms of religious life (albeit more easily to some than to others). Conversely societies that once enjoyed a religious monopoly, or quasi-monopoly, react rather differently; here the resistance to new religious movements raises important issues of religious freedom. Normative questions can no longer be avoided – indeed in many parts of Europe, they dominate debate. The French case is not the only European society where this occurs, but it has become something of a cause célèbre. It offers an interesting illustration of the themes set out above.

A first step in understanding the specificity of the French situation was taken by Beckford himself in 1985, an account which draws directly on Martin's analysis of secularization (Martin, 1978). Just as the historic churches form different 'patterns' across Europe in terms of their modes of secularization, so too do the minority groups, including new religious movements – and for exactly the same reasons. Particular features can be identified which have predictable effects both for the process of secularization and for the management of new forms of religious life. One such is the state. In France the state assumes a moral quality, becoming itself an actor in the religious field; no other European society exhibits this tendency to quite the same degree. The particular difficulties facing new religious movements in France derive very largely from this situation. In effect they are hemmed in on two sides, by a monopoly church (historically speaking) and a monopoly state – they are victims of a classic 'double whammy'. The reasons, as ever, can be found in the past.

A full account of the historical process is beyond the scope of this chapter.[2] Here the story will begin in 1905, the culmination of a notably acrimonious separation of church and state. The 1905 law has iconic status in France; it symbolizes the moment when 'church' finally gives way to 'state' as the dominant institution in French society. Two parallel organizations emerge, one Catholic and one secular, each with its own set of beliefs, institutions and personnel. Even more important, however, are the default positions set in place in the course of this process: what did and what did not count as religion in the French context? The system that was worked out at the beginning of the twentieth century was predicated on a particular understanding of religion, one which could encompass the Catholic Church, the historic forms of Protestantism and Judaism, but not much else.[3]

The situation at the beginning of the twenty-first century, examined in some detail by Hervieu-Léger (2001a, 2001b), is markedly different. Innovative forms of religious belief, including new religious movements,[4] have exploded in France just as they have everywhere else, causing immense strain on the system. More precisely, the checks and balances so carefully worked out in 1905 are thrown into disarray. A model that has served France well for the best part of a century cannot cope, either conceptually or institutionally, with the forms of religion that are presenting themselves at the turn of the new millennium. Hervieu-Léger puts this as follows:

> [T]he system topples when the mesh of the confessional net is strained by the multiplication of groups and movements claiming religious status and demanding the benefits of a freedom taken for granted in democratic societies. In reaction to the anarchic proliferation of self-proclaimed and extradenominational religious groups, *laïcité*'s deep-rooted suspicion that religious alienation poses a constant threat to freedom is tending to resurface. (2001b: 254)

A whole range of factors come together in these sentences: the frameworks (both legal and conceptual) set in place in 1905, the quintessentially French notion of *laïcité* (itself related to French understandings of the Enlightenment), the transformation of the religious scene in the late twentieth century, and the clearly normative reactions of French officialdom and the French public to these changes. These reactions reveal the fundamental points: first, the definitional issue – what can and cannot count as religion and who should decide; and second, a persistent and at times worrying reflex – a widespread and very French belief that religion as such might be a threat to freedom.

**165**

The size of the questions is, it seems, inversely related to the size of the movements in question; equally striking are the contrasts with the United States.

Interestingly, very similar debates are now happening in other parts of Europe, notably those that were under communist domination in the post-war decades. Here the historic forms of religion had themselves been pushed to the margins, never mind the minorities. Post-1989, the structures and ideologies of communism imploded, releasing spaces for religion that had not existed for several generations. In most places the mainstream churches have re-emerged to fill the gaps, some more successfully than others, but new forms of religion have also flooded in through open borders. The questions that follow are by now familiar: which forms of religion are to be welcomed and which are not, and who is to decide? The debate has repeated itself in one country after another in the search not only for democratic institutions, but for the philosophies that underpin these. Just as in France, it is the rapid deregulation of the religious field that has prompted the discussion; the catalyst is the same in each case.

The place of the mainstream churches within these debates is interesting. Paradoxically, or perhaps not, in those parts of Europe where the mainstream churches themselves were victims of pressure or worse, there is in many places a marked resistance to new forms of religious life. The historic churches, having reclaimed the centre, are reluctant to share their hard-won freedoms with a multitude of competing denominations. Instead these essentially territorial institutions conspire to 'protect' both the physical spaces of which they are part and the populations who live therein. Looked at from a different point of view – and one that is central to this book as a whole – there is, once again, an evident clash between European understandings of religion and American congregationalism. In the minds of some European church leaders, especially those emerging from decades of resistance under communism, there is little to choose between the more enthusiastic Protestant missionaries (many of which come from the United States) and new religious movements as such. Both challenge the territorial 'rights' of indigenous forms of religion.

Attempts to manage these encounters are fraught with difficulty. They involve, amongst other things, the writing of constitutions and the administration of finance and property, the details of which impinge on many vested interests, calling into question centuries-old assumptions about local as well as national power. A detailed discussion of these issues cannot be pursued here, except to remark that Beckford's

166

conceptual clarity is not always as present in these discussions as it ought to be.[5] Given the tumultuous circumstances in which such arrangements were worked out, this is hardly surprising; at times, however, the attempts to find solutions to these very difficult issues create almost as many problems as they solve – debates that will continue well into the twenty-first century.

## THE NEW AGE OR SELF-SPIRITUALITIES

The sociological debates surrounding the new age (and the many associated ideas) are rather different. This is an area of enquiry in which the emphasis is personal rather than corporate – individuals are free to explore a wide diversity of beliefs and practices guided by internal motivations rather than external constraint. It follows that questions concerning the institutional forms of religion are less relevant. The flash points, if any, occur in the encounters with organized religion (notably in its more dogmatic versions). Are these or are these not compatible with new age teaching? A second set of issues concerns the relationships between the new age and mainstream society, themes that are central to the writing of Paul Heelas (1996, 2008).[6]

It is important, first, to grasp the nature of the topic. New age or self-spiritualities include a diverse, ill-defined and somewhat amorphous set of ideas held together by a relatively small number of consistent and crosscutting themes – notably an emphasis on the self and self-discovery, and a tendency to 'connect'. The former provides the essence of self-spirituality (the God in me, reaching fulfilment, realizing potential, 'I did it my way' and so on). The latter can be found at a variety of levels: it reflects both the interconnected person (mind, body and spirit) and the interconnected universe (each individual is part of a cosmic whole). The fields in which such ideas both germinate and grow are diverse: they range along a continuum, which at the 'hard' end includes new forms of capitalism and management training (the self as a business leader) and at the other, somewhat 'softer' end, displays a range of mostly holistic therapies (the self in need of healing). In between can be found outlets in publishing (huge ones), in alternative forms of education (those which emphasize the self-discovery of the child), in green issues (the connected universe) and in alternative forms of medicine (the connected person).

The relationship with the religious mainstream is complex: self-spiritualities are both friend and foe of more conventional forms of religion. They are 'friend' in the sense that they reject the emphasis on materialism as the primary goal of human existence. Happiness does not lie in the accumulation of possessions, whether big (investments, houses and holidays) or small (shopping). Excessive consumption, in fact, is an indication of unmet need rather than fulfilment. They are a 'foe' in so far as traditional understandings of Christian teaching normally emphasize a transcendent rather than immanent God – a God to whom the Christian submits, rather than the God within (a central tenet of new age teaching).

The distinction, however, is less than clear-cut. There are, and always have been, different – indeed contradictory – lines of thinking within the corpus of Christian doctrine, some of which make more room for the self than others (a point already made, pp. 150–1). Hence a variety of reactions to the new age. At one end of the spectrum are the churches that affirm many, if not all, aspects of new age teaching as a source of inspiration or wisdom for the Christian; St James's Piccadilly offers an obvious example.[7] At the other end are congregations that see new age ideas in a far more negative light. More than mistaken, such ideas are dangerous – something to be avoided at all costs. Significant sections of the evangelical constituency take this view, but not all. Paradoxically, it is precisely the kinds of Christianity that adopt some if not all aspects of self-spirituality – the form, if not the content – which are currently doing well: that is, the charismatic churches described in the previous chapter, and admirably exemplified in the Kendal Project (Woodhead's subjectivized Christianity). Those, however, which reject both form and content – the more rigid, biblically based churches – are not only overtly hostile to the new age, but are finding themselves in trouble.

Such reactions should be seen against the mutations of modern society. Here Paul Heelas's work becomes central to the argument. Heelas has been a close observer of alternative religions for at least two decades. Not only have his own ideas evolved; so has the field itself. In Heelas (2008), for example, an interesting set of generational changes are established. First can be found a set of historical antecedents to the new age as such; these need not concern us here, except to remark that the ideas themselves are by no means 'new'. They come and go periodically. But why, in the late twentieth century, have they moved centre stage? Following Heelas, the first breakthrough came in the 1960s, a decade in which spiritual discovery coincided with the proliferation of new religious movements already described. Both were indicative of counter-cultural trends as traditional institutions, including religious ones, came under attack.

Each innovation, moreover, encouraged the other. Some forms of self-spirituality became effectively new religious movements (the human potential movements for example). Others, it is clear, eschewed any form of organization altogether.

But just as the mainstream evolves, so too do the margins. As the 1960s gave way to a rather less confident decade, new forms of self-spirituality appeared on the scene. Heelas uses the term 'seminar spirituality' to describe these shifts, which themselves turn bit by bit into the 'soft production capitalism' of the 1980s. The crossings over into other disciplines are immediately clear – into social psychology and management training, for instance, as the stress falls increasingly on releasing human potential for the benefit of business as well as leisure. Life and work are reconnected as each individual discovers the different ways in which he or she can contribute, and to very different goals (some of them linked to capitalist endeavour, others opposed to this). The 1990s suggest a further chapter in this story, with a growing emphasis on well-being. At this point the many different strands already introduced are drawn together in the notion of 'being yourself only better'. It is also the decade in which the ideas associated with self-spirituality become ever more visibly part of society's mainstream, a theme to be developed in Chapter 11. No longer is it necessary to seek the products of the new age in alternative outlets or specialized shops; they are increasingly found in the high street.

What then is the position in the first decades of the twenty-first century? Is it the case that Western populations are happy to embrace spirituality (including the new age) as more traditional forms of religion begin to fade? And does the process always take place in the same way? It is at this point that we rejoin the discussion in the previous chapter, returning once more to the Kendal Project – more precisely to its comparative dimensions. Its authors look in some detail at the American case, concluding that the shift from the congregational to the holistic domain is not only taking place in the United States but is rather more advanced than it is in Britain (Heelas and Woodhead, 2004: 60). Why is this so? The answer lies, as ever, in the capacity of the American market to adapt to the changing needs of the population. New spaces open up, just as they do here, but the institutional responses are different. In America such spaces are filled with new age, holistic or 'seeker' churches; in Britain that is less likely to be the case. It *is* possible for a Church of England parish to adopt at least some aspects of the new age or holistic experience: St. James's Piccadilly offers one solution, the charismatic churches another. It is rather more difficult for the average church to follow suit, even if they wanted to, given the constraints of the parish system.

**169**

Hence, on this side of the Atlantic, a rather different scenario. Clearly the British seek spiritual satisfaction, just like their American counterparts. But they do this in different ways, affected as ever by the context of which they are part. Once again Princess Diana offers an interesting and very poignant illustration with which to conclude this section. Like many English people, Diana was baptized and nurtured in the Church of England, where her marriage to Prince Charles took place. As her marriage began to collapse, Diana sought solace in a number of places, including alternative forms of spirituality – a side of her nature to which the public readily responded, not least at the time of her death. Diana's 'self' and evident mortality found expression in the laying of flowers, the lighting of candles and the signing of books. Any element of judgement, conversely, was noticeable by its absence. Her funeral, however, took place in the church in which she started, publicly in Westminster Abbey, and more privately at her home in Northamptonshire, a decision quite clearly endorsed by the population as a whole (Davie and Martin, 1999). Interestingly, exactly the same point is made by Billings (2004) in a parallel account of religion in Kendal. The author, an experienced parish priest, pays careful attention to the occasional offices and their continuing role in the lives of the local population – a feature missing from the more sociological Kendal Project. Indeed for a rounded view of religion in this unusually well-studied English town, both these sources should be carefully noted.

## OTHER FAITH COMMUNITIES

New religious movements and the new age raise important issues for the sociologist of religion. In both cases, however, the numbers involved are relatively small. Very much larger are the religious minorities that have arrived in Europe for economic reasons. Distinctive patterns have emerged across Europe in this respect as, once again, the incoming minority interacts with the host society to produce different formulations. Issues that cause a problem in one society do not do so in another – contrasts which more often than not are explained by the strains and tensions of the receiving society, not the minority in question. It is this relationship that forms the crux of the following section.

It is important first to sketch out the facts and figures. A helpful summary table, at least of Muslims, can be found in a report sponsored by the Pew Forum on Religion in Public Life (2010); it is reproduced below in Table 8.1.[8] Additional accounts can be found in a growing list of titles, among them Maréchal (2002), Allievi and

Nielsen (2003), Esposito and Burgat (2003), Cesari (2004), Nielsen (2004), Cesari and McLoughlin (2005), Klausen (2005), Buijs and Rath (2006) and Garton Ash (2006). For obvious reasons – a number of them elaborated in the Preface to this edition – this remains a burgeoning field of scholarship.[9]

The bare bones of the story are clear enough. As the dominant economies of West Europe – that is Britain, France, West Germany and the Netherlands – took off in the mid-post-war decades, there was an urgent need for new sources of labour. Unsurprisingly, each of the societies in question looked to a different place in order to meet this need, and wherever possible to their former colonies. Hence in Britain there were two quite distinct inflows: one from the West Indies and one from the Indian sub-continent. In each case, the implications for the religious life of Britain were different. Afro-Caribbeans were Christians – in many ways more 'formed' in their Christianity than the British; but also more exuberant, leading to tensions with the churches of the host society. Whether for racial or liturgical reasons, these new arrivals found themselves increasingly excluded from the religious mainstream, forming in consequence Afro-Caribbean churches for Afro-Caribbean people – churches that

Table 8.1  *Number of Muslims in Western Europe*

| Country | Estimated 2010 Muslim Population | Percentage of Population that is Muslim |
|---------|----------------------------------|------------------------------------------|
| Austria | 475,000 | 5.7 |
| Belgium | 638,000 | 6.0 |
| Denmark | 226,000 | 4.1 |
| Finland | 42,000 | 0.8 |
| France | 3,574,000 | 5.7 |
| Germany | 4,119,000 | 5.0 |
| Greece | 527,000 | 4.7 |
| Ireland | 43,000 | 0.9 |
| Italy | 1,583,000 | 2.6 |
| Luxembourg | 13,000 | 2.7 |
| Netherlands | 914,000 | 5.5 |
| Norway | 144,000 | 3.0 |
| Portugal | 22,000 | 0.2 |
| Spain | 1,021,000 | 2.3 |
| Sweden | 451,000 | 4.9 |
| Switzerland | 433,000 | 5.7 |
| United Kingdom | 2,869,000 | 4.6 |
| **Total** | **17,094,000** | |

Pew Research Center's Forum on Religion & Public Life • Forthcoming Pew Forum Report, 2010
*Source:* Pew Research Center's Forum on Religion & Public Life, 'Muslim Networks and Movements in Western Europe', © 2010, Pew Research Center. http://pewforum.org/.

have become vibrant and active Christian communities, the envy of the religious mainstream. Incomers from South Asia were entirely different. Muslims from Pakistan and Bangladesh came together with Hindus, Sikhs and more Muslims from India, bringing with them the religious tensions all too present in the sub-continent in the years following partition. Populations that had been separated on the other side of the world found themselves side by side in British cities. Interfaith issues are an inevitable part of this story and do not mean simply relationships with a predominantly Christian host society.

A similar process took place across the Channel, bringing into metropolitan France a rather more homogeneous population from North Africa. In France, the words 'Arab' and 'Muslim' are (rightly or not) used interchangeably in popular parlance to describe these communities. This could not happen in Britain where Muslims are rarely Arabs, and represent a huge variety of nationalities, ethnicities and languages. West Germany looked in a different direction to meet the need for labour in the post-war economy – this time to Turkey and the former Yugoslavia, but in each case creating a distinctive Muslim constituency. Post-1989, the influx of cheap labour from the former East brought new tensions to the German situation. The Netherlands, finally, encouraged immigration from colonial territories, notably Surinam, but also from Turkey and more recently from Morocco. The overall numbers in the Netherlands are smaller, but then so is the country – markedly so, leading to very specific resentments. One further fact is important: in each of the cases set out above, the incoming populations are now in their third or fourth generation, enabling longitudinal as well as comparative studies. Each generation, moreover, presents particular issues – specific combinations of assimilation and difference.

In the last decade of the twentieth century something rather different happened. European countries that traditionally were places of emigration – notably Spain, Italy and Greece – became countries of immigration, as did the Nordic societies. Once again an expanding economy and falling birthrates generated a need for labour, but particularly in the North of Europe, a comprehensive welfare state is clearly a pull factor for some, including a growing number of asylum seekers. Distinguishing the genuine from the less genuine among the latter has become a 'hot' political issue in societies where the host population is inclined to overestimate the total number of immigrants, and within them asylum seekers, by a considerable figure.

Demographic shifts are important in this connection; they are also complex. In most West European societies there is a growing awareness that the ratio between the working and the dependent sections of the population is shifting to the extent that the former is no longer able to support the latter, including a growing number of retired people. This, moreover, is as true in the countries of Southern Europe as it is in the North. Hence the need to find alternative sources of labour – not only to do the work itself, but to increase the proportion of working people. Distinctive patterns emerge in this respect, not least in terms of gender. In North Italy, for example, Italian women are liberated from their domestic tasks by Filipino or Albanian women, who then leave a 'gap' in the family at home. Interestingly (Catholic) Filipino populations are more easily absorbed into Italy than (Muslim) Albanian ones, despite the smallness of the Albanian population overall.

But what will happen when those who work today in order that Europeans may enjoy either professional careers or a relatively prolonged retirement, become themselves dependent in one way or another on the welfare system? And what will happen when the economic situation implodes as it did in 2008? It is at this point that the tensions begin to show, just as they did in Britain, France, West Germany and the Netherlands, as the 1960s merged into the rather less prosperous decade that followed. Two things happened at once in the 1970s. On the one hand, groups of people who were initially viewed as migrant workers – people who came and went as the economy required – were becoming, along with their families, a permanent feature of European societies. At precisely the same moment, however, the economic indicators turned downwards, unemployment rose and the competition for jobs, houses and school places became increasingly acute. Unsurprisingly those Europeans whose economic positions were most vulnerable resented the newly arrived populations, leading in the 1970s and 1980s to extensive urban unrest in which racial and ethnic tensions played a significant role. The situation post-2008 was very similar.

**173**

The economic story has been told many times and is not in itself central to this chapter. Here the emphasis will lie on the religious dimensions of the 'problem', paying attention not only to the religious communities themselves, but to the wider questions that they raise for the understanding of religion in modern Europe – notably the challenge that they bring to the notion of privatization. The focus will lie on three case studies: Britain, France and the Netherlands; that is, all countries that have had a moderately long-term experience of other faith communities but which have come to terms with these changes in different ways. The Danish case will be taken up in the Conclusion (Chapter 12).

## three catalysts

All three case studies revolve around a particular episode. Two of these date from the late 1980s and, at least in their earlier stages, were covered in the appropriate chapter of *Religion in Modern Europe* (Davie, 2000a). These are the Rushdie controversy in Britain and the *affaire du foulard* in France. To an extent, the former has been partially resolved, though the points at issue still resonate and the *fatwa* is still formally in place. The latter has proved rather more intractable, revealing exactly the same issues as the discussion of new religious movements: that we learn as much about France from this episode as we do about Islam and that the understandings of religion set in place by the 1905 law still operate some 100 years later. The problem lies in the largely unanticipated circumstances of the twenty-first century. The Dutch example is rather different. Here the spark can be found in two very violent episodes: the murders of Pim Fortuyn and Theo Van Gogh in 2002 and 2004 respectively. A country for which tolerance was a primary virtue has been thrown into disarray as it attempts to come to terms with these events.

First then the British case. The facts can be summarized in a sentence or two:[10] *The Satanic Verses*, a novel by Salman Rushdie, was published in 1988; Muslim protests followed quickly, including public book burnings. In February 1989, the Ayatollah Khomeini proclaimed a *fatwa* (declaring the author guilty of blasphemy) and Rushdie was forced into hiding. In December 1990 Rushdie 'claimed' to embrace Islam – a key moment in the chain of events, but not one that was reciprocated by the religious authorities in Iran who re-affirmed the *fatwa*. Lives were lost in violent episodes outside Britain, including the stabbing to death of the translator of the Japanese edition. In short, this is an episode which appears to violate almost every assumption of a modern, liberal and supposedly tolerant society. The fact that Rushdie was himself of Indian and Islamic origin simply makes the whole episode more bizarre.

What then lies beneath these events and how should we understand them some 20 years after the novel was published? Here I return to the paragraphs that I wrote some twelve years ago – the essential points have not changed. It is important to grasp, first of all, why *The Satanic Verses* was so deeply offensive to Muslims. Why, in other words, did the Muslim community feel so strongly about a 'blasphemous' book which no one had to read unless they wanted to? It is these questions that the average Briton (or European) finds almost impossible to answer. A huge imaginative leap is required by the European mind – not only to master a different set of assumptions but to empathize with the emotional impact that *The Satanic Verses* made on an already vulnerable community. It is at this point, moreover, that the logic of the Enlightenment imposes itself. Europeans think in ways that separate subject from object and have difficulty with a world view that cannot make the same distinction. This is as true for Christians as it is for non-believers. Christians nurtured in a post-Enlightenment climate may not like works of art or literature that mock or make light of Christianity, but have nonetheless the capacity to distance not only themselves but their beliefs from such onslaughts. For most (not quite all) Christian believers, such episodes may lack both taste and discretion; they do not, however, damage 'faith' itself.[11] For the believing Muslim, this distinction is altogether more difficult – hence a rather different understanding of blasphemy. For many Europeans this concept is barely relevant in a new millennium; for Muslims it is central to daily living.

Rushdie no longer dominates the headlines; the underlying issues, however, still remain. An interesting sequel, for example, can be found in a combination of events that came together at the end of 2004 – both in many ways are quintessentially British. In December, Birmingham's Repertory Theatre put on a play entitled *Behzti*, meaning 'Dishonour', written by a Sikh playwright (a woman). The Sikh community was disturbed by particular scenes within the play which depicted both sex and violence in a Sikh temple. Peaceful protests and requests for minor changes in the text turned into more violent expressions of disapproval, leading eventually to the play being taken off, primarily for safety reasons, and renewed public discussion about freedom of speech in a multi-cultural society. Sikhs are rarely involved in this kind of controversy: they are a respected community in Britain and the turban totally accommodated – even in those professions (e.g. the police) where uniform is required. The point at issue remains, however, exactly the same as it was a decade or so earlier: to what extent can a minority prevent the publication or depiction of material in a democratic society if that material is deemed offensive to their religion? Conversely, can the majority afford simply to ignore the feelings of small, but nonetheless significant groups, whose religious views are different from the mainstream? Both views if pushed to the extreme are not only intolerant, but non-viable. And neither will be resolved by superficial recourse to the privatization thesis, the more so if the faith of the minority has no concept of the public/private distinction in the first place.

Enter, somewhat surprisingly, the Queen who – coincidentally with the Sikh unrest – made religious tolerance in the United Kingdom the central theme of her 2004 Christmas broadcast.[12] Immediately acclaimed by the faith communities in Britain, the speech endorsed not only the presence of different religions in this country, but the positive values associated with religious diversity (this was clearly a normative statement). Religious diversity is something that enriches a society; it should be seen as a strength, not a threat. The broadcast, moreover, was accompanied by shots of the Queen visiting a Sikh temple and a Muslim centre. It is important to put these remarks into context. The affirmation of diversity as such is not a new idea in British society; what *is* new is the gradual recognition that religious differences should be foregrounded in these affirmations, a point that returns us to the discussion of methods and the statements of Baroness Uddin in the House of Lords (p. 116). Paradoxically these bastions of privilege (the Monarchy and a half-reformed House of Lords) turn out to be the positive opinion-formers in this particular debate. Less democratic than most institutions, they appear, in this sense at least, to be more tolerant (Davie, 2007b).[13]

They are both, of course, intimately connected to the established church, a significant player in its own right. Here the crucial point lies in appreciating the difference between an historically strong state church, which almost by definition becomes excluding and exclusive, and its modern, somewhat weaker equivalent. A weakened state church is in a different position, frequently using its still considerable influence to include rather than exclude, becoming de facto the umbrella body of all faith communities in Britain. This gradual shift from exclusion to inclusion should be read against the changing nature of both society as a whole and the religious communities now present within it. Multiple realignments have taken place (as ever in a pragmatic and piecemeal manner) leading to a growing, if gradual, divergence between those with faith and those without. Rather more positively, quite apart from a convergence between different 'people of faith', there is a growing recognition that faith *communities* (i.e. collectivities) are, and must remain, an integral part of a tolerant and progressive society.

The situation in France could hardly be more different. Here the *affaire du foulard* provides the catalyst, played out in a series of incidents that once again begins in the late 1980s, when three girls attending a state school in a suburb to the north of Paris were sent home from school for wearing the Muslim headscarf. The reasons lie in the history already outlined in the section of this chapter concerned with new religious movements – notably the emergence in France of both a secular ideology (*laïcité*) and a set of institutions (the state and the school) through which this ideology is created, sustained and transmitted. The parallels to the Catholic Church are obvious and have already been developed. As a result both religion and religious symbols have been proscribed from the state system – hence the problem with the Muslim headscarf, which is seen as a religious artifact (similar, in fact, to a nun's habit). More difficult is the question of why, for most of the post-war period, Christian and Jewish artifacts (the cross and the yarmulke) have been tolerated. Why is the Muslim headscarf regarded as qualitatively different and why has this provoked not only a series of expulsions, deliberations, ministerial decrees, commissions and legislation, but a heated and continuing public controversy?

Clear accounts of this sequence of events and of the ideologies that lie behind these can be found in English as well as French.[14] Such accounts include a real attempt to grasp the principles of *laïcité*, together with a careful listing of the chronology from 1989 onwards, including the expulsion of the Muslim girls from school, the various and not always consistent attempts to find a solution to the problem, the evident difficulty in establishing what constituted an 'ostentatious' religious symbol, the establishment of the Stasi Commission in July 2003, its report at the end of the year, and finally the promulgation (by a huge majority) of the new law in March 2004, which unequivocally excluded religious symbols from the state school system. 'In public elementary schools, *collèges* and *lycées* [senior schools], students are prohibited from wearing signs or attire through which they exhibit conspicuously a religious affiliation.'[15] The law, moreover, has the support of the French population – in approving this piece of legislation, France was acting with admirable internal consistency, enforcing codes that are entirely understandable within the logic of the French democratic system. Exactly the same consistency was seen in the reactions to extensive urban unrest in France in the autumn of 2005, within which the discontent of the Muslim community was clearly a central factor.

Until relatively recently,[16] conveying the seriousness of these issues to British students was difficult – the more so when at least some in the group had spent large parts of their school lives in a classroom alongside Muslim girls wearing the headscarf. What, therefore, is the problem? The answer lies in the evident tensions between pluralism, tolerance and democracy. Both constitutionally and institutionally France is undoubtedly the more democratic society – no monarchy, half-reformed House of Lords or state church here. The political philosophies underlying this democracy, moreover, strongly encourage assimilation into French culture, with the entirely positive goal that all citizens should enjoy similar

**177**

rights. Hence a mistrust of alternative loyalties – whether to religion or to anything else. In France, it follows, *communautarisme* is a pejorative word, implying a less than full commitment to the nation embodied in the French state. In Britain, the equivalent word (together with the idea that it represents) is viewed more positively; in other words, group identities, including religious ones, are affirmed. The result is a less democratic system (in any formal sense), but a markedly more tolerant one, *if by tolerance is meant the acceptance of group as well as individual differences* and the right to display symbols of that group membership in public as well as private life.

Will such tolerance endure following the bombings of 7/7 (2005) and further 'scares' just one year later? The situation is noticeably less positive than it was when the first edition of this book went to press. Clearly the bombings in London sharpened yet further the debate about faith and faith communities in British society. The question became urgent. On the negative side, the incidents undoubtedly provoked a marked rise in the level of harassment, if not violence, experienced by the Muslim communities in Britain, at least in the short term. More positively, there have been repeated and well-informed attempts by almost all public figures involved in this debate (Muslim and other) to draw a sharp line between both the violence of these attacks and the teachings of Islam, and between the attitudes of the perpetrators and the peaceful intentions of the vast majority of Muslim people. A BBC poll conducted in August 2005 provided a more quantitative basis for comment. Its findings affirm considerable support for multi-culturalism – more precisely that 62 per cent of the population believe that 'multiculturalism makes Britain a better place to live'.[17] By 2011, however, the situation was rather more ambiguous: all over Europe, politicians have challenged both the theory and the practice of multiculturalism.

The Dutch case is different again. Once again the chain of events was sparked by two very violent episodes, the murders of a prominent politician and of a rather less-known film producer. Both incidents occurred in broad daylight in public places; the latter was particularly brutal. Such events would be shocking in any democratic society, but particularly so in the Netherlands, a point that becomes clear as soon as the background is put in place. Dutch society, like its neighbour Belgium, dealt with pluralism in a particular way – by constructing pillars in which different sections of the population lived from the cradle to the grave (Goudsblom, 1967; Martin, 1978). In the Dutch case, there were Catholic, Reformed (including Re-reformed) and secular pillars, divisions that pervaded education, politics, social services, medical care, journalism, leisure activities and so on. This system persisted well into the post-war period, resisting for longer than most European societies the pressures of secularization. The obvious parallel in North America is Québec (see pp. 37–8). But when secularization came to the Netherlands, the change was dramatic. Regular church-going collapsed along with the pillars, leading amongst other things to new political alignments. The crucial decades in this respect are the 1970s and 1980s: that is, precisely the moment when new forms of religious life (notably Islam) were beginning to embed themselves in Dutch society.

A second point is equally important: that is, the long established tradition of tolerance in Dutch society, a sensitivity epitomized in the Anne Frank museum in Amsterdam. Not only is this a poignant memorial to a remarkable young woman and her family, it also offers a de facto seminar in tolerance, related primarily (at least when I saw it) to the gay issue. Concerning the latter, Dutch people have been at the forefront of change, as they have in the legalization of soft drugs and in their attitudes towards a wide range of ethical issues (notably euthanasia). The acceptance of difference is considered a primary virtue in Dutch society.

Pim Fortuyn's own position is complex in this respect. In 2002, this flamboyant, controversial and sociologically trained politician burst on to the public stage. Gay himself, he defended Dutch acceptance of his lifestyle. Much more controversial were the means to the end: that is, the suggestion that those opposed to this view (notably the growing Muslim population) should be excluded from Dutch society. Such views shocked certain people, but by no means all. Despite the country's celebrated reputation for liberalism and religious tolerance, Fortuyn's anti-Muslim views, his calls for an end to all immigration and promises to crack down hard on crime quite clearly struck a chord with the electorate. Hence the creation of a new political party and considerable interest as the election approached. The dénouement was dramatic: 10 days before the election, Pim Fortuyn was shot as he left a radio station by an animal rights activist, an act that bewildered the Dutch.

In terms of this chapter, the essential point is the following: to what extent can you defend liberal values with illiberalism, i.e. by excluding from society those who do not share the views of the majority? Hence the rather specific and very Dutch combination of acceptance and exclusion, distinguishing Fortuyn from other right-wing populists. Both in his person and in his views, he was different, for example, from Jean-Marie Le Pen in France or Joerg Haider in Austria. His goal was the recreation of a Dutch consensus: stable (in population), ethically 'advanced', permissive, accepting of less conventional lifestyle – but excluding of those whose values contravened the majority. Fortuyn's policy on immigration derived precisely from the socially tolerant nature of the Netherlands, a quality he valued and wanted to preserve. It is equally clear that this position resonated with a significant proportion of the Dutch electorate: condemned by the conventional political class, Fortuyn was riding high in the pre-election polls.

His sudden and violent death complicated the issue: shocking in itself, it turned Fortuyn into a martyr. It also unleashed currents of opinion in the Netherlands that had been suppressed for decades. Indeed some of the most interesting work being done in the Netherlands concerns the present state of opinion, both religious and political, in a society where the conventional carriers or constraints (the pillars) have collapsed. It is true that the Netherlands has secularized, late and very fast; it is less true that this has produced a nation of secular rationalists.[18] What emerges is rather more complex, within which a new pillar is clearly visible: that of Islam itself. Paradoxically the system itself has encouraged what the Dutch find so difficult: the independent existence of a growing Muslim community, itself the victim of growing discrimination. It is this juxtaposition of de- and re-pillarization that needs to be grasped by those trying to comprehend Dutch society in the first decades of the twenty-first century.

**180**

Just over two years later a yet more violent murder took place, in which the clash between liberalism and multi-culturalism was even more clear – devastatingly so (Buruma, 2006). Theo van Gogh, a film producer known, at least amongst aficionados, for his ferociously anti-Muslim (and indeed anti-Semitic) views, was stabbed, shot dead and beheaded in broad daylight in an Amsterdam street – this time by a young Dutch-born Moroccan Muslim. The trigger was strikingly similar to the Rushdie controversy: van Gogh had produced a film that portrayed violence against women in Muslim societies. Some scenes were considered insulting to Islam, a point that calls for the same imaginative leap for Europeans as had been required with *The Satanic Verses*. But the outcome this time was even more shocking. And quite apart from the episode itself, Dutch people were left coming to terms with the fact that the assassin had been brought up in the Netherlands, but had failed – manifestly – to absorb the essentially 'tolerant' values of Dutch society. Something, it seems, had gone very wrong.

What then is to be done? How is it possible to accommodate within modern European democracies populations whose values are, apparently, so very different from the mainstream? The Dutch reaction has been sharp and not always indicative of tolerance. Two policies have emerged: the first expressed in the enforced repatriation of asylum seekers (even those that have been in the Netherlands for some time); the second can be found in the renewed emphases on the need to instil Dutch values in the immigrant populations that remain. Very little has been said about how Dutch society might accommodate itself to a more diverse population, a lacuna which is revealing given the messages quite clearly 'given off' (in the Goffmanian sense) in the Anne Frank museum. The debate is the same as that which took place in Britain following the events of 7/7, but framed by Dutch as opposed to British preoccupations.

### a note on America

European societies are becoming steadily more diverse in religious terms; so too is the United States, where an already extant and much talked about religious diversity is beginning to include faiths other than Jewish and Christian. There is not space in this chapter to develop the American case in detail except to recognize that any religion putting down roots in the United States has to come to terms with a congregational model rather than a state church – a situation which is easier for some faith groups than for others.

Some examples of the role and significance of religion in immigrant communities in the United States were given in Chapter 6; this is a rapidly expanding research field. More precise indications of the material available on Islam can be found in the continuing publications of the Pluralism Project at Harvard, of the Prince Alwaleed Bin Talal Center for Muslim-Christian Understanding at Georgetown University and of the Macdonald Center for the Study of Islam and Christian-Muslim Relations at Hartford Seminary.[19] Haddad and Smith (1994, 2002), J. Smith (1999) and Geaves et al. (2004) provide helpful overviews of both the Muslim minority itself and the issues that it raises. Cesari (2004) offers a useful comparative perspective between Europe and America. Necessarily, work in this area, especially the Christian–Muslim dialogue, has been prioritized since 9/11, a pivotal moment in this debate.

**181**

## CONCLUSION

Europe and America have very particular histories which colour their reception of new religious constituencies, just as the different parts of the Islamic world welcome Westerners variously. It is equally important to remember that it is the mainstream in any given place which continues to fashion the religious discourse taken as a whole. With this in mind, it is more sensible to work within these parameters than to pretend or assume that they no longer exist – in other words, to admit from the outset that in Western societies the religious playing field is not level, nor is it likely to become so in the foreseeable future. It is irrevocably 'formed' by its Christian past.

That said, both the increasing mobility of labour and the even more rapid exchange of information have profoundly altered the situation within which debates about religion take place. It is simply not possible for Western societies, and the Muslim communities within them, to live in isolation from events that are taking place in other parts of the world. Concepts such as pluralism, tolerance and democracy should be considered in this light. The cataclysmic shock of 9/11 and the subsequent bombings in Bali (twice), Madrid, London and Mumbai (India) have altered our lives for ever, and with them our understandings of the concepts in question. The wars in Iraq and in Afghanistan have had a similar effect, so too the troubled situation in the Middle East. Sadly, it is not only the Muslim communities in the West that have suffered as a result; anyone 'not white' or 'not Christian' has at some point been at the receiving end of prejudice and at times of physical violence. Post-9/11, it has become harder rather than easier to assume goodwill in our attempts to build an accepting and mutually considerate society.

These are huge issues claiming the attention of many disciplines. In a rather more modest conclusion to this chapter, two sets of ideas deserve particular attention, one being effectively a subset of the other. First, religion has become an increasingly salient factor in public debate, both in the West and elsewhere. That is abundantly clear. Whether this is considered a 'good' or a 'bad' thing depends largely on the point of view of the observer – a discussion that reflects once again the constructivist perspective articulated by Beckford. In terms of the argument of this book, it is a fact to be observed and documented with some care. It must also be explained – a shift that makes considerable demands on a profession unused to thinking in such terms. The second set of ideas follows from this. The salience of religion in public as well as private life has undermined a long-standing Western assumption: that is, the distinction between the public and the private. Many of those now arriving in the West, not least the growing and frequently vulnerable Muslim populations, do not operate in these terms. Hence, in many respects, the difficulty in finding a resolution to all three episodes outlined above. Had it been possible to separate the public and

182

private, the Rushdie controversy would have had little or no resonance, young Muslim women in France would simply wear their veil sometimes but not at others, and the depictions of Islam in Theo van Gogh's films could have been safely ignored by those who found them distasteful. Such was not the case.

Who will give way to whom in these problematic debates becomes a difficult question to answer. On the one hand, there are those who take the 'when in Rome, do as the Romans do' approach. Muslims, or indeed members of a new religious movement, who want to live in the West must behave as Westerners. This is fine in theory, but pushed too far it effectively means that such people can no longer practise their faith in any meaningful way. At the other extreme, a few (very few) religious enthusiasts want, it seems, to hold Western society to ransom in demanding special privileges for themselves and the communities that they represent. Here there is a whole spectrum of possibilities, including, it must be said, acts of terrorism. Most people, of course, lie somewhere between the two, though exactly where will vary from place to place to place, group to group and person to person. Finding a way through these dilemmas in terms of policymaking has become an urgent and very demanding task. It is more likely to be successful if careful attention is given to the concepts underpinning the debate and if the communities most closely involved are heard with respect and on their own terms (the discussion must be about religion, not about 'something else'). In short, issues involving religious identities become more, not less, difficult to solve if religion is disallowed as a category in public discussion.

**183**

## NOTES

1 That is not to say that work in this field has disappeared in Britain and the United States, but it has certainly diminished relatively speaking.

2 More detailed accounts can be found in Davie (1999a, 2003b). A rash of commemorative events and publications were timed to coincide with the centenary of the 1905 separation of church and state.

3 Recognition of these minorities came gradually in France. Centuries of persecution predated gradual acceptance during the eighteenth century, which was formalized at the time of the Revolution.

4 New religious movements are still known as 'sects' in the French case.

5 See in particular the case studies brought together in Richardson (2004).

6 Paul Heelas is not the only author working in this field. The work of Marion Bowman (Sutcliffe and Bowman, 2000) and Michael York (1995) is also important. A recent overview of 'Alternative spiritualities' can be found in Harvey and Vincett (2012).

7 See www.st-james-piccadilly.org (accessed 17 April 2012).

8 This table is reproduced with kind permission from the Pew Foundation. See http://features.pewforum.org/muslim/number-of-muslims-in-western-europe.html for an interactive version of the table (accessed 17 April 2012). See also the following BBC website, which includes statistics for most European countries and is regularly updated: 'Muslims in Europe: Country Guide', http://news.bbc.co.uk/1/hi/world/europe/4385768.stm (accessed 17 April 2012).

9 The *Yearbooks of Muslims in Europe*, edited by Nielsen et al. from 2009 onwards, are excellent sources for this material. See also the plethora of research projects referred to in the new Preface. Gilliat-Ray (2010) offers an excellent overview of the British case.

10 For a more detailed account, see Davie (2000a: 126–30) and Weller (2009).

11 A partial exception can be found in the furore surrounding *Jerry Springer: The Opera* (January 2005). Interestingly this production was acceptable in the West End, but not, it seems, on mainstream television.

12 See www.sim64.co.uk/queens.html (accessed 17 April 2012).

13 Quite apart from the Queen herself, Prince Charles has become an outspoken champion of Islam.

14 See, for example, Freedman (2004), Gemie (2004), Laurence and Vaisse (2005) and the extensive press reports surrounding the law implementing the principle of *laïcité* in March 2004. Jean Baubérot (1990, 1997, 2005) is the principal authority on *laïcité* in France. In 2011 the discussion focused on the complete ban of the burqa or face veil in public. Once again the parliamentary vote was overwhelmingly in favour of the ban.

**184**

15 'Dans les écoles, les collèges et les lycées publics, le port de signes ou de tenues par lesques les élèves manifestent ostensiblement une appartenance religieuse est interdit', Law 2004–228, 15 March 2004.

16 An extensive debate about Muslim dress took place in the United Kingdom in the Autumn of 2006. British students are now far more aware of this issue than they were just a few years ago.

17 Interestingly, the Muslim minority is often more affirming of the basic tolerance of British society than the population as a whole. See http://news.bbc.co.uk/1/hi/uk/4137990.stm (accessed 17 April 2012).

18 In this connection it is interesting to note the material emerging from the research initiative, 'The Future of the Religious Past: Elements and Forms for the Twenty-first Century', funded by the Netherlands Organisation for Scientific Research. See www.nwo.nl/nwohome.nsf/pages/NWOP_59HJMQ_Eng (accessed 17 April 2012).

19 See www.pluralism.org; http://acmcu.georgetown.edu/about/; and http://macdonald.hartsem.edu/ (all accessed 17 April 2012) for further details of this work. Note in particular the papers brought together in the 'New Religious Pluralism and Democracy Conference' at Georgetown University, which offer interesting comparisons between Europe and America. These are published in Banchoff (2007).

## *nine*

## demanding attention: fundamentalisms in the modern world

Fundamentalism is a word much used in popular parlance to describe forms of religion that are prevalent in the modern world. As a term, however, it is as much abused as used, and not only in popular writing – the misuse is equally evident in sociological discourse. With this in mind, the engagement with fundamentalism marks both a step forward for the sociology of religion (the inclusion within the discipline of forms of religion outside the West) and a step back (the misinterpretations of what is going on). Both advantages and disadvantages will be made clear in this chapter.

On the positive side, the attention paid to fundamentalism has indeed expanded the horizon, both geographically and conceptually – a shift driven by the changing nature of global affairs within which the religious factor has become increasingly evident. Observers of all kinds – scholars of religion in a variety of disciplines, journalists, politicians and policymakers – are obliged to take the presence of religion into account, whether they like what they see or not. The turning point in this respect came in the late 1970s, a decade that saw both the election of a new Pope (who brought with him a distinctive and politically urgent agenda) and the overthrow of the Shah of Iran (a Western figurehead forced to flee before a very different and religiously motivated regime). Not all of these movements are correctly described by the term 'fundamentalist', a point to be considered in the sections below, but they do reveal a change in mood. A 1990s commentator described this as follows:

Around 1975 the whole process [of secularization] went into reverse. A new religious approach took shape, aimed no longer at adapting to secular values but at recovering a sacred foundation for the organization of society – by changing society if necessary. Expressed in a multitude of ways, this approach advocated moving on from a modernism that had failed, attributing its setbacks and dead ends to separation from God. The theme was no longer *aggiornamento* but a 'second evangelization of Europe': the aim was no longer to modernize Islam but to 'Islamize modernity'. Since that date this phenomenon has spread all over the world. (Kepel, 1994: 2)

And if 1979 marked one turning point, 2001 marked another; the trends are intensifying rather than diminishing in the early years of the new century.

A second point is equally significant: scholars of all disciplines, including sociologists of religion, failed to anticipate these shifts in perspective and were, as a result, seriously unprepared for what was happening: that is, the appearance on a large scale across several continents of new, and frequently conservative, forms of religion. Not only were the data themselves increasingly evident, they led to awkward questions concerning theoretical frameworks. At the very least, the changes that were taking place questioned very directly the widely held view that the world would become a more rather than less secular place as the twentieth century drew to a close. On the contrary, the evidence not only of religion but of apparently 'unreasonable' forms of religion was growing all the time. How then was the Western-trained scholar to understand what was happening and what tools and concepts were available to assist with the task?

One requirement became clear almost immediately: a need for care with respect to terminology. Hence the emphasis in the early sections of this chapter on the attempts to clarify the ways in which the term 'fundamentalism' has been used, and to appreciate why conceptual precision is so important. An ideal type of fundamentalism provides the answer, reflecting a way of working central to the Fundamentalism Project established by the University of Chicago in the late 1980s – in itself a crucial feature of the sociological story. The Fundamentalism Project gathered a distinguished team of scholars from different parts of the world, brought together to understand the rapid and unexpected growth in distinctive forms of religious life in almost every global region. The details of the team, their working methods and their impressive series of publications are easily documented.[1] More important are the motivations that lie behind the project and the finance made available to execute the task. Clearly this hugely expensive endeavour was indicative of concern on the part of American academia, and the foundations that resource them, about the forms of religion that were increasingly visible on a global scale. Berger (1999b) is even more

186

provocative in his comments: the assumption that we need both to document and to understand the nature of fundamentalism by means of a research project of this stature tells us as much about American academics as it does about fundamentalism itself.[2]

Central to the Fundamentalism Project is the idea of an ideal type or a set of family resemblances, against which the realities of the world, in this case supposedly fundamentalist movements in different parts of the world, can be measured. It is this idea that will be developed in the following section. Certain points must, however, be made clear before starting. First that the term 'fundamentalist' should not be used in a negative or pejorative sense: that is, as a label for beliefs of which the commentator disapproves. (The fact that the reverse is so often the case simply makes the social scientific task harder.) Nor should there be a slippage in meaning which implies that all members of one particular faith group might come into this category. In Britain, for instance, fundamentalism is too often seen as synonymous with Islam, with the strong implication that this world faith in particular is prone to fundamentalist tendencies. This is not the case. Strictly speaking fundamentalism is a descriptive term used to portray a distinctive type of religious movement in the world of the twentieth and twenty-first centuries and its relationship with modern societies. The interaction with modernity provides the key to what is happening and hence the *fil conducteur* for this chapter which is structured as follows.

The first section elaborates both definition and ideal type, paying attention to the pitfalls already set out. The second will scrutinize in more detail the relationship between fundamentalism and modernity. These paragraphs are crucial. They build very directly on to the discussion of modernity in Chapter 5 and raise a question central to this book as a whole: that is, the assumed incompatibility between being religious (in whatever way) and being modern. For a second time, the work of Eisenstadt will be used to clarify this point, as will the case studies that follow. The first of these develops the material on the New Christian Right already introduced; the second presents the Iranian case. The final section turns in a rather different direction, inviting the possibility that the notion of fundamentalism might extend beyond the religious sphere, taking into account a range of secular ideologies. Despite the range, the same questions resonate throughout: under what circumstances are both ideologies and movements, secular as well as religious, prone to fundamentalist tendencies and how might these be avoided? The implications for policymaking are immediately clear.

187

## DEFINITION AND IDEAL TYPE

Fundamentalism is notoriously difficult to define. The editor of a 1980s collection of papers on the subject admits as much in his introduction, declaring that 'fundamentalism' will be defined anew by practically every one of the book's authors (Kaplan, 1992). He offers, nonetheless, a working definition: 'For the purposes of this introduction, fundamentalism can be described as a world view that highlights specific essential "truths" of traditional faiths and applies them with earnestness and fervor to twentieth-century realities' (1992: 5). Both parts of this definition are crucial – the existence of essential truths and their application to twentieth-century realities. Indeed the word fundamentalism should not be used to describe the traditional elements of religions that have been left undisturbed by the modern world, nor does it mean the creation of entirely new ideas. It involves the re-affirming of essential truths within a situation that has been disturbed, sometimes very profoundly, by the pressures of an expanding global economy and the effects that this has on social, political or ideological life.

The term itself emerges from the debates among American Protestants in the years immediately following the First World War. In this case the focus lay on re-establishing what were felt to be the traditional truths of Protestant teaching, beliefs which had been threatened by more liberal interpretations of the Bible. The Protestant 'fundamentals' were set down once and for all, and underlined more than anything else the absolute truth of scripture (Ammerman, 1987, 1994; Bruce, 1988). An important question follows from this: is it possible to transfer this kind of thinking – developed in a distinctively Western and Protestant culture – to other world faiths which embody utterly different thought processes? Answers to this question vary, but even those who wish to proceed within a comparative framework should do so with caution. Indeed the study of fundamentalisms demands very particular skills on the part of the sociologist. It requires, first of all, a capacity to empathize: what does it feel like to be in a situation in which patterns of belief and practice established for centuries are under attack? It demands in addition a sensitivity to world views other than the sociologist's own. This is an area of sociological study in which a little knowledge of other world faiths can at times be a dangerous thing.

It *is* possible, nonetheless, to proceed. One of the most constructive ways forward has been to make use of an ideal type analysis. There are various examples of this approach (Caplan, 1987; Kaplan, 1992), often taking the form of an introductory chapter to a collection of case studies. The one elaborated here is taken from a relatively early exposition of the topic by Martin Marty[3] and is titled, aptly enough, 'The fundamentals of fundamentalism'. Recognizing – indeed underlining – that fundamentalisms may well have little or nothing in common with each other from a substantive point of view, Marty proceeds to delineate the common elements from a whole range of fundamentalist movements: 'Such elements need not be present in all such movements, but they should be characteristic of most of them' (1992: 15). In other words, the enquiry starts with a range of empirical examples from which it is possible to construct a Weberian ideal type. The following paragraphs describe its essential features.

Fundamentalisms usually occur on the soil of traditional cultures; cultures that over long periods of time have been relatively protected from disturbance either from within or from outside. The seeds of fundamentalism are sown when such a situation is challenged or disturbed (the point already made). The threat may be constructed in a variety of ways: sometimes it comes from outside the group in question and is given a code word such as 'Westernization' or 'modernity' or 'invasion'; other threats may come from within (e.g. when particular individuals or sub-groups begin to incorporate new or different ideas). The development of liberal interpretations of scripture amongst American Protestants provides a good illustration of the latter.

A vague sense of threat is insufficient in itself to provoke a response; to be effective it requires focus. Hence the crucial importance of the leader in the emerging fundamentalist group – an individual able to translate unease into action. The next stage is clear:

> [T]he term 'fundamentalist' is first applied when leaders and followers take steps consciously to react, to innovate, to defend, and to find new ways to counter what they perceive as threats to the tradition that they would conserve. ... Reaction, counteraction, revanchist action: these are characteristic. If they are not present, observers continue to call movements or cultures simply 'traditional' or 'conservative'. (Marty, 1992: 19)

The nature and form of these reactions are important for they almost always make use of selective retrieval from the past, for which particular authority is sought. Such authority is often discovered in the form of a sacred text or book – a point, however, that is likely to exclude from the definition the clearly conservative forms of religious life that rely more on the tradition of the church than on textual authority. Traditionalist movements in the Catholic Church offer an obvious example.

The subsequent actions of fundamentalist movements aim to draw attention to the group in question. They are, quite frequently, aggressive actions, calculated to shock, to intimidate and in some cases to violate both property and people. The 'us and them' mentality that emerges supplies a further characteristic of fundamentalism; it is constructed quite deliberately both to create and to maintain an impenetrable boundary between the constituency in question and its surrounding context. One further point is crucial. In order to achieve such ends, fundamentalists make maximum use of modern technology. Hence the paradox: groups that perceive themselves as resistors not only to modernity itself, but to its philosophical foundations, make optimal use of its technological outputs. The final step of the argument follows naturally enough: that fundamentalisms are themselves products of modernity, in so far as they are born out of the clash between modernity and traditional cultures. Such a statement needs immediate qualification for not all such encounters end in a fundamentalist reaction; they seem, nonetheless, to constitute a necessary, if not sufficient, condition for the emergence of fundamentalist movements.

It is this way of working that lies at the heart of the Fundamentalism Project. The ideal type is set out in the first volume – as a five-finger exercise at the beginning and in more detail in the final chapter – and becomes effectively a working definition for the project as a whole (Marty and Appleby, 1991). Interestingly, in the fifth and concluding volume of the initial series (Marty and Appleby, 1995), the authors of the final section (Almond et al., 1995a, 1995b, 1995c) return to the definitional question, taking great care to distinguish between the thing to be described (i.e. the 'genus' called fundamentalism) and the explanations for its existence. The latter are discovered in the historical and contextual variables that are found in the different cases and will be dealt with below.[4] Within the genus further precisions are made, revealing five ideological and four organizational properties in the material established by the project, by this time a very extensive database. The next step follows logically and takes the form of a welcome refinement of the working definition, correcting what for many is the major criticism of the Fundamentalism Project: that is, a tendency to include within it rather too much.

The *exclusions* are worth noting. Among them are a series of religious movements which rely more on ethno-national identities than on reactions to modernization or secularization as such. Interestingly, Ulster Protestants are included in this category. A second exclusion, though less definitive than some scholars would like, can be found in the Pentecostal Protestants of Latin America – a group to be discussed in

Chapter 10. Regarding Pentecostals, the definitional issue had already been raised at an earlier point in the Fundamentalism Project, including a chapter that examines 'the Christian family portrait now emerging in Latin America' (Levine, 1995: 155). Levine pays particular attention to what he calls 'liberationist Catholicism and fundamentalist Protestantism'. It becomes increasingly clear, however, that Pentecostal forms of religious life south of the Rio Grande do not display the 'family resemblances' or common features of fundamentalism as these are set out in the ideal type. In short, eliding Latin American Pentecostalism with fundamentalism is a serious category mistake and raises important methodological questions.[5] If existing terms and concepts do not enable us to see clearly what is happening in the religious field in many parts of the world, we need to think carefully about alternatives.

Running right through the Fundamentalism Project, in fact, is a series of tensions between ideal type or family resemblance (both of which are forms of generalization) and the historical specificity found in each of the case studies described – a problem inherent in the methodology employed. To a certain extent, these tensions can be resolved by means of typology (a set of sub-types) within which the relationship with 'the world' becomes central. Four sub-types emerge from this analysis: world conquerors, world transformers, world creators and world renouncers. It is important to bear in mind, however, that fundamentalist movements move between these categories at different moments of their existence and that the 'world' can be conceptualized in many different ways. Hence the complexity of the task.

A second set of issues runs parallel – those which explain the emergence of fundamentalism in the first place. These are divided into three groups: the structural factors (i.e. the long-term contextual conditions and changes from which fundamentalism movements evolve); the contingent, much less predictable factors which very often become the catalyst; and, finally, what the authors call 'human' factors (i.e. the choices that are made regarding leadership). Almond et al. conclude: '[T]o explain fundamentalist movements means to show how structure, chances, and choice combine to determine their formation, growth, and fate – and their shifting patterns of relation to the world' (1995c: 445). Or to be more precise, that is how these authors *begin* the chapter that looks at the influence of all these factors on the emergence, growth and decline of the many case studies covered in the project, whilst at the same time taking into account their ideological and organizational characteristics and strategies. These very detailed analyses mark a significant stage in an undertaking which, despite its imperfections, has become a touchstone for future debate.

*191*

## THE CHANGING NATURE OF MODERNITY

Essentially the same connections – the relationship between a particular context and a particular movement – can be approached in a different way. More precisely the emergence across the globe of a whole series of fundamentalist movements from the 1970s onwards appears to link such movements to a critical moment in the evolution of the modern world order – one, moreover, that embodies contradictory features. On the one hand there is a continuing expansion in economic scale as the forces of globalization assert themselves; on the other can be found a *loss* of confidence of parallel proportions. Examples of the latter are easy to find: they include a growing concern about environmental matters, a revision of economic aspirations as the oil crisis began to bite, and a marked change in outlook as full employment – and all the assumptions that went with this – gave way to patterns of life more dominated by uncertainty. Hence the emergence of a very different mood from that which prevailed in the immediate post-war period, a situation in which religion takes on new, diverse and at times unexpected roles.

This does not mean, of course, that examples of fundamentalism do not predate this moment. Indeed we have seen already that the word itself emerges out of American Protestantism some 50 to 60 years earlier. But it does help to explain the rapid spread of such movements across a diversity of world faiths towards the end of the twentieth century, to which this same term – rightly or wrongly – has been applied. The *contradictory* pressures of the economic and cultural spheres offer an important clue. First, there are the inevitable and necessary demands of trade, economic stability and power, factors which require larger and larger economic units in order to survive, where the movement of capital as well as labour leads to innovative modes of production and new markets, and in which a whole range of actors (economic as well as political) look to the international order for security and justification. But for many people precisely the opposite inclinations – the reassertion of local and national identities and the need for psychological security and rootedness – are correspondingly strengthened: in other words, 'the need to know that we and our heritage, our language and our culture, count in the scheme of things, and that we are free to make our own choices' (Habgood, 1992). Habgood continues with reference to the European debate, but his perceptions have a wider application. Interestingly these words were written in 1992, at the time of the Maastricht Treaty. They are equally applicable to the debates surrounding the ratifications of the European Constitution a decade or so later:

192

> These conflicting pressures, manifesting themselves in local earthquake and continental drift, are shaping the new world. It is not about whether individual politicians like or dislike Europe. It is about the forces at work in an era of world interdependence, easy communication and disorienting change. (Habgood, 1992)

Seeing religious fundamentalism as one response to this particular combination of pressures locates it firmly within wider sociological debates about modernity. It becomes, moreover, a rather more understandable phenomenon, even if its particular manifestations continue to shock and to bewilder.

The last section of Chapter 5 took the discussion a step further, asking whether modernity should be considered in the singular or the plural. Eisenstadt's analysis was central to this issue; it is equally important with respect to fundamentalism. Not only was Eisenstadt involved himself in the Fundamentalism Project (Eisenstadt, 1995), he has published since a book-length monograph on the subject. *Fundamentalism, Sectarianism and Revolutions* (1999) places the study of fundamentalism in a long-term historical perspective. Modern fundamentalisms are preceded by proto-fundamentalist movements which themselves arose in the Axial Civilizations of pre-modern times. The distinctiveness of the modern phenomenon and the key to our understanding of this both lie in the relationship between fundamentalist movements and what Eisenstadt calls the 'crystallization of modernity', a tension which distinguishes the true fundamentalist movement from its precursors. The following extract summarizes the argument:

*193*

> Modern fundamentalist movements, despite their seemingly traditional flavor and their affinity to proto-fundamentalist movements, can – perhaps paradoxically – best be understood against the background of the development of modernity and within the framework of this development … They constitute one possible development within, or component of, the cultural and political program and discourse of modernity, as it crystallized above all with the Enlightenment and with the Great Revolutions, as it expanded through the world and has continually developed with its different potentialities, contradictions, and antinomies. (1999: 39)

For Eisenstadt, fundamentalism is at one and the same time an anti-modern utopia and a modern, distinctively Jacobin, social movement – or, more accurately, a set of social movements. Fundamentalisms represent a new phase in the tensions that must always emerge between different aspects of modernity (i.e. between the Jacobin or totalizing elements and the tendency towards modern constitutional pluralism). Such tensions have occurred before: they emerged, for example, in the early part of the twentieth century. Indeed, for Eisenstadt, there is an important link between the totalitarian movements of the 1920s and 1930s and modern forms of fundamentalism. Both exhibit anti-modern and anti-Enlightenment tendencies, including a negative attitude to the autonomy of the individual and the sovereignty of reason (the central components of the Enlightenment), but in their phenomenology of vision and action, both are profoundly modern 'bearing within themselves the seeds of very intensive and virulent revolutionary, utopian Jacobinism' (1999: 206).

The final chapter of Eisenstadt's text closes the loop, making explicit the link to the work on multiple modernities on which we have drawn already. Interestingly it is in teasing out the relationship between fundamentalism and modernity, both conceptually and empirically (the book contains a huge range of examples), that the nature of modernity itself becomes clearer. Modern cultural programmes are not always the same, nor do they remain static. Hence the need for a radical reappraisal of both the concept of modernity itself and the nature of the modernization process. Particularly interesting in this context are the forms of modernity in which, for one reason or another, fundamentalism is absent rather than present; the parts of the world where this is so include Japan and West Europe. In the study of fundamentalism, the explanation of absence is as important as the explanation of presence, a statement which turns many of the assumptions of sociological thinking on their head.

**194**

## TWO EMPIRICAL EXAMPLES

In order to illustrate this primarily theoretical approach, the following examples have been drawn from two very different contexts. The first is taken from the United States and develops the ideas on the New Christian Right (NCR) set out in Chapter 7. The second, the Iranian case, offers an example from the Muslim world.[6] Both continue to evolve. In November 2004, George Bush was elected to a second presidential term by an electoral coalition that included within it very significant numbers of conservative Protestants, some of whom would claim the label 'fundamentalist' with pride – bearing in mind that the question of definition is difficult even here. In modern America, the line between evangelical and fundamentalist is increasingly difficult to draw: the categories are distinct but quite clearly overlap (Smith, 2002: 17). And if the beliefs of those at one end of the spectrum are little different from the mainstream of American life, the beliefs at the other would undoubtedly reflect the views of those who first coined the term 'fundamentalist' – a group for whom a series of black and white moral issues have come to dominate not only the presidential election but the agenda as a whole. Attitudes towards abortion, towards gay marriage and (much more surprisingly for Europeans) towards stem cell research are, it seems, of much greater importance than the economy, and for some if not all of their proponents, of sufficient gravity to legitimate law-breaking.

But more significant than either moral issues or the economy was the question of security, a matter of paramount importance to Americans since 9/11 – the moment when American territory was in a very real sense 'invaded' and with devastating effect. One result of this episode has been the emergence of an 'us and them' mentality. The dangerously bifurcating categories that have appeared, moreover, are grist to the mill of the fundamentalist who can persuade significant sections of the more moderate middle ground to join them, at least for electoral purposes. The fact that other sections of the evangelical constituency are moving in a rather different direction – towards a more expressive individualism and away from doctrinal certainty (Wolfe, 2003) – is indeed important, but not the whole story. The point already made in Chapter 7 is abundantly clear; no politician or would-be President of the United States can afford to ignore this constituency and its role in modern America.

Hence the bewildered cry of someone like Jim Wallis whose book became the number one best seller on Amazon even before it was published. Its title *God's Politics: Why the Right Gets It Wrong and the Left Doesn't Get It* (2005) sums up the dilemma. The political right (the Republican Party) have not only seized the religious vocabulary but have used this to considerable effect. In 2004, the liberals (the Democratic Party) were simply wrong-footed in that they failed, until too late, to appreciate the significance of religion in the electoral process. To argue as does Bruce (1988) that the religious right should be discounted given its inability to turn America as a whole into a morally conservative nation is to miss the point. America is a society in which religion remains a decisive factor in the political process, a situation fully appreciated by the NCR and to which it has responded with skill. Aided and abetted by the Republican Party (the mutual attraction is clear), the NCR has become a sophisticated political player. The aim of Jim Wallis, meanwhile, was to set an alternative, religiously inspired agenda – one that draws on religious values (a sense of social justice) to promote the common good. The election of Barack Obama in 2008 is noteworthy in this respect. Obama and his team fully appreciated Wallis's argument

**195**

and deployed it with considerable success – thus challenging the assumption that the religious vote is necessarily a Republican one. Davie (2010b) considers the sociological implications of this pivotal episode.

In the longer term, the work of two scholars is particularly helpful in understanding the place of religious conservatives in modern America and the questions that follow from this – both for the actors themselves and for the scholars who observe them. In 1987, Ammerman published what has become a classic in the field. At one level, *Bible Believers* (1987) is an exemplary case study of a fundamentalist church – a model not only for further studies of conservative churches but for congregational studies more generally. The discussion, however, goes further than this. Not only does Ammerman clarify the distinction between 'evangelical' and 'fundamentalist', she places her case study within a wider sociological context. Regarding the former, Ammerman emphasizes the separation from the world that characterized fundamentalists – 'compromise' and 'accommodation' are the dreaded words (1987: 4). Regarding the latter, she is particularly concerned with both the power of fundamentalists and the limits to that power: in other words, what they can and cannot achieve within a necessarily pluralist society. Interestingly, Ammerman comes herself from a fundamentalism background, enabling a degree of empathy that is absent in many studies of this constituency. She was, in addition, a major contributor to the Fundamentalism Project.

Christian Smith (1998, 2002) pursues these questions further, but this time in relation to the much wider category of evangelicals rather than to fundamentalists as such. Drawing on an impressive range of empirical data, he and his team examine the tensions between American evangelicals and the wider society. Smith explodes the myth that evangelicals are a marginalized community seeking refuge from the modern world in their own congregations. They are instead a relatively well-educated, upwardly mobile constituency, well able to *exploit* the potential of American pluralism rather than withdraw from this. In a very real sense they are 'in the world but not of it'; or following the suggestive title of the 1998 volume, they are both embattled and thriving. Holding this tension becomes the crucial point: evangelicals must resist the retreat into isolation (the fundamentalist trap), but at the same time they must avoid becoming so engaged with secular society that they are indistinguishable from it (the fate of the liberal mainstream). How then do they do this? The answer becomes clear very quickly: evangelicals resolve this dilemma in different ways. Smith (2002) explores the considerable diversity within the evangelical constituency. These 20 million or so people do not speak with one voice – they embrace very different views with regard to the family, to the school system or to political life more generally. Smith's scholarly, yet accessible work has become essential reading in the sociology of religion; it unites careful empirical investigation and creative theorizing in order to understand better a constituency which is becoming ever more significant in the life of modern America.

The Iranian case could hardly be more different.[7] Here the adherents of Shi-ite Islam wanted neither to change Western society nor to succeed within this; they despised the West altogether – an attitude displayed in abundance in 1979. The crucial events can be summarized in a sentence or two. In this tumultuous year, what became known as the 'Islamic Revolution' in Iran swept away the pro-Western Shah and brought to power a conservative religious leader, the Ayatollah Khomeini. What happened not only took the West entirely by surprise, but became a symbolic moment for the understanding of religion in the modern world. It was this incident above all others that Kepel had in mind when he suggested that the process of secularization seemed for many to go into reverse (Kepel, 1994).

To be properly understood, the events of 1979 need to be placed in a broader context, both in Iran itself and in the shifting world order. Arjomand (1998) supplies the historical background for Iran, seeing the 1979 insurgency as the last of four revolutions in which the religious factor has played a major part[8] – more precisely in which the gradual assertion of Shi-ite teaching provides a linking theme. This necessarily long-term process culminated in the upheavals of 1979 with the establishment of an Islamic theocracy, the point at which the superiority of the hierocracy (the clerical class) is finally asserted:

197

> This logical possibility was actualized when Ayatollah Ruholla Khomeini (1900–1989) transformed a sizable section of the Shi-ite hierocracy into a revolutionary political party. The projected final stage of the growth of Shi'ite clerical authority then became the blueprint for the militant clerics who overthrew the shah in 1979. (Arjomand, 1998: 378)

Why then was this possible, and why did it happen at this particular time? The answer can be found in a complex mix of economic, political, cultural and religious factors.

The Shah had been in power since 1941 (with a brief interruption in the early 1950s). His rule was autocratic; this was a regime in which opposition was crushed by violence. It was also a regime in which the extremes of wealth and poverty were all too visible. An expanding economy and a rise in the value of oil exacerbated rather than reduced these differences, which were ostentatiously displayed in 1971 during the festivities surrounding the 2,500th anniversary of the founding of the Persian Empire. Such excess was resented by large numbers in the population; it also invoked criticism by the Islamic authorities on moral grounds. Criticisms, however, produced a reaction: a series of anti-Islamic reforms, including the abolition of the feudal system (which removed property from some Shia clergy), a reduction of clerical influence in education and in family life, and in 1976, the prohibition of the lunar calendar. The extension of the vote to women was seen as a further challenge to clerical authority.

The dissatisfaction grew worse, leading to protests against the Shah, beginning in 1977 and escalating in the following year. They came, moreover, from different quarters: from the Muslim clerics, but also from the liberal secularists and more radical Marxists, some of whom combined their Marxism with Shia orthodoxy. Towards the end of 1978, a series of massive demonstrations in the capital bought the crisis to a head. Last-minute attempts to compromise failed and in January 1979 the Shah fled from Iran; Khomeini arrived some two weeks later. In itself, his arrival did not guarantee an Islamic republic. Gradually, however, the clerically dominated Assembly of Experts asserted its authority, establishing Iran as the first theocratic republic in the modern world. The provisional government (both more liberal and more secular) of Mehdi Bazargan came to an end in a series of events that included the storming of the American Embassy and the taking of hostages – a moment of revenge and of profound humiliation for the world's superpower.[9] Khomeini became the new regime's *rahbar*, that is its head of state and supreme religious jurist with powers over the armed forces and the judiciary, a post held until his death in 1989. It was, moreover, Khomeini who pronounced the *fatwa* on Salman Rushdie following the publication of *The Satanic Verses* (see pp. 174–5).

Subsequent decades have seen both a gradual liberalization in the regime and a conservative reaction.[10] Rajaee (1993) describes these tensions, the engagements with modernity, in more detail. Iran has also experienced a long and costly war with its neighbour Iraq (1980–88). The aftermath of the war and the unhappy sequence of events that have unfolded in this part of the world since its end lie beyond the scope of this chapter, which needs at this point to recall the essentials (the ideal type) of fundamentalism and its relevance to the Iranian case. The family resemblances are clear. This is a nation, indeed a whole region, where traditions of all kinds have been disturbed by Western influence. Generalized unease, moreover, found a focus: first

198

in an attack on the Shah and then in the establishment of a strong, Islamic and anti-Western regime. And in justifying his position as leader, Khomeini appealed to an earlier tradition in Shi-ite teaching: the Rule of the Jurist. Appleby puts this as follows: 'This innovative interpretation of Shi-ite theology justified the establishment of an Iranian government run by Muslim religious scholars and presided over by the grand ayatollah, Khomeini himself' (1998: 286). The fact, finally, that this regime could humiliate the United States under the gaze of the world's media is critical to the narrative: Khomeini quite deliberately shocked the world.

## EXTENSIONS BEYOND THE RELIGIOUS SPHERE

It is important at this point to move the debate in a rather different direction – this time from the religious to the secular sphere, a shift in which the distinction between the early and late phases of modernity set out in Chapter 5 becomes, once again, a helpful tool of analysis. The argument can be summarized as follows. The Enlightenment, a crucial element in the emergence of modern society, took different forms in different places – of that there can be no doubt (Himmelfarb, 2004). But in Europe, and most notably in eighteenth-century France, Enlightenment thinkers very often found themselves in opposition to the hegemony of the Catholic Church, and in their more extreme forms in opposition to any religious tradition whatsoever. Simultaneously, a belief in progress, alongside an increased reliance on the benefits of science and human reason, began to pervade the atmosphere – characteristics that spilled over into every aspect of human life.

199

It was inevitable that such approaches should enter, sooner or later, the science of theology itself. Particularly in Germany, biblical criticism was gradually transformed as the tools of critical reason were applied to sacred texts, subjecting them to detached and systematic inquiry. It followed that the Bible was no longer simply the 'word of God'; it became instead a text like any other. It was, moreover, the reaction of certain groups of American Protestants to this situation – specifically to the questioning of the biblical text and the foundations on which this rested – that led to the concept of 'fundamentalism' in the first place. Congregations emerged which found their raison d'être in affirming above everything else the literal truth of scripture. Fundamentalism was born out of a reaction to hostile or critical ideas that had encroached on the certainties of particular groups of believers.

Towards the end of the twentieth century, however, the terms of the debate altered radically. In a rapidly changing intellectual climate, the philosophies that had seemed so threatening to the early American fundamentalists were themselves subject to attack. No longer was the Enlightenment Project beyond question; it too, like the biblical text, was subject to ever greater scrutiny. Hence a very different set of alignments in which the competition between opposing creeds (i.e. secular versus religious) gives way to a pervasive questioning *on each side* of the classic divide. The whole nature of the debate alters as each profession or ideology struggles with the disturbing and seemingly uncontrollable situation of post- or late modernity, and its associated loss of confidence. An illustration will clarify the argument. It is taken from Harvey's classic, though difficult, discussion of the subject – from a passage which portrays very aptly the changing relationship between three narratives: theology, liberal secularism and Marxism (Harvey, 1989).

Harvey reviews the various fields in which postmodern influences have been visible in the later post-war decades, for example art, architecture and literature. He then turns to the philosophical debate taking place in Paris following the 1968 *événements*. Here a striking change has taken place: no longer are the protagonists convinced by the power of abstract reason. On the contrary, they are expressing considerable unease about any project that claims 'universal human emancipation' through the powers of technology, science and reason itself. In other words, precisely those elements that had been the source of so much confidence in earlier decades – a belief in progress and in the benefits of science – have become the focus of philosophical unease. Harvey continues the argument with the following remarkable statement:

> Here, also, no less a person than Pope John Paul II has entered the fray on the side of the postmodern. The Pope 'does not attack Marxism or liberal secularism because they are the wave of the future' ... but because the 'philosophies of the twentieth century have lost their appeal, their time has already passed'. (1989: 41)[11]

The essential point is clearly made: the secular certainties, the former competitors of religious truth, are themselves struggling for survival. They are, to use a different metaphor, past their sell-by date.

If this is the case, it has crucial implications for the argument set out above. For precisely those ideologies which have threatened (and to some extent continue to threaten) the traditional certainties of a whole range of religious groups become, at least potentially, the victims rather than the perpetrators of economic and cultural change. No longer are they seen as the confident alternatives, but become instead – like the religious certainties they once sought to undermine – the threatened tradition, themselves requiring justification and, at times, aggressive rehabilitation. A good illustration of 'aggressive rehabilitation' can be found in the dangerous combinations that have broken out in parts of the former Soviet Union, where ambitious nationalisms become linked to the reassertion of tradition (including the Orthodox Church), and where communism itself has become a seriously, possibly terminally, threatened creed. In this part of the world, frameworks of thought established for decades, and held in place by institutional structures at every level of society, collapsed almost overnight in the *annus mirabilis* of 1989, creating a vacuum in which many different philosophies have emerged to replace the dominant tradition. In a situation of permanent flux, compounded by severe economic hardship, a retreat into certainty – whatever its nature – is an entirely understandable reaction and fits, almost exactly, the analysis of fundamentalism established above. The dramatic, speeded-up quality of this particular historical moment reveals in unusually sharp focus a process that normally takes much longer.

A second example, also reflecting the uncertainties following 1989, can be discovered in the Balkans where, in the tragic events of the 1990s, newly acquired and fragile nationalities sought in a variety of ways to bolster their positions with appeals for religious justification. In this case a *secular* ideology (nationalism) very clearly interacted with a *religious* one in order to justify its actions. One such action, ethnic cleansing or the purification of territory, is an obvious consequence of such policies. Once again it fits the analysis of fundamentalism already offered, manifesting in particular the desire for clear-cut solutions, in this case for unambiguous boundaries, territorial or otherwise. It follows, perhaps, that the *interaction* of varieties of fundamentalisms across the globe should become an increasingly important area for sociological study, noting in particular the overlapping reassertions of identity (i.e. where one vulnerable creed is used, or manipulated, to reinforce another). It is interactions such as these that are likely to become particularly dangerous realities.

In both these cases, the collapse of Marxism as a political philosophy, a master narrative, has been both dramatic and visible; on the whole the loss of confidence in liberal secularism has taken a different path. The latter, however, has flexed its muscles in certain parts of Europe both before and after the millennium. One example can be found in the *affaire du foulard*, described in the previous chapter. The *affaire* culminated in the law of 2004 banning all religious symbols – whether Christian, Jewish or Muslim – in French schools, an illustration surely of a threatened ideology (in this case *laïcité*) re-asserting its dominance.[12] Something rather similar happened, and not only in France, in response to the suggestion that the Preamble to the 2004 European Constitution[13] might contain an explicit reference to Christianity. Once again, or so it appeared, European secularists closed ranks against a resurgence, or rather more modestly, a reappearance of religion in the public square in twenty-first century Europe. No longer can the privatization of religion simply be assumed. In this case the 'threat' often comes from Islam, but not always. It was, for example, Rocco Buttiglione's conservative Catholicism that called into question the secular norms of the European Parliament in November 2004 (see note 11, p. 205). The reaction was swift: the Parliament demanded that the membership of the Commission be rethought. But which group of people – the conservative Catholic restating conservative moral norms or the threatened secular liberal insisting that such norms be proscribed from the public square – conforms most closely to the ideal type of fundamentalism set out in the earlier sections of this chapter? It is, I think, the latter, though popular parlance might have it otherwise. The decision turns on a careful distinction between seriously held conservative beliefs and something more sharply reactive.[14]

Two rather different examples of non-religious fundamentalisms complete this section.[15] The first concerns the animal rights movement, which quite clearly contains within it an extremist element, which in turn reflects the ideal type of fundamentalism set out above. More difficult in this respect is the question of a 'sacred' text. Does such a text exist or not? There are clearly 'iconic' publications in the field (Singer, 1976 for example), but the analogy should not be pushed too far. And whatever the case, the crucial point lies elsewhere. Most supporters of animal rights are entirely 'reasonable'; despite their firmly held convictions about the rights of all sentient beings they remain within the law. Such people are prepared to modify their diet or clothing and try hard to persuade others of their views, but would stop short at acts of sabotage or violence. A small minority, however, go further, revealing a familiar set of characteristics: a tendency to think in black-and-white terms (i.e. of us and them), a desire to shock and at times a willingness to inflict harm in the name of a higher cause. In Britain, there are two flashpoints of such activities: the hunt saboteurs and the violence perpetrated against individuals and institutions who use animals for the testing of medical products. In both cases they have been remarkably successful.[16]

It has been suggested, finally, that certain types of feminism may be subject to fundamentalist pressures. As an idea, this may seem particularly provocative given that one motive for the emergence of religious fundamentalisms in many parts of the globe has been their rejection of new and different roles for women in the modern world. The changing role of women is seen as an aspect of modernity that disturbs and confuses accepted religious outlooks. The reaction sets in: traditional female roles become, very often, one of the 'fundamentals' that must be re-established, justified by appeal to the sacred text. An excellent discussion of the significance of gender in relation to fundamentalism can be found in Hawley (1994). The essays collected in this volume assert that control over women – their sexuality, reproductive power, and social and economic roles – is central to a fundamentalist agenda. Looking in detail at four representative cases, the authors argue that fundamentalist movements are concerned with establishing islands of certainty against what is experienced as social and cultural chaos.

Rather more striking are the arguments of feminists themselves including those considered mainstream. The following example is one such. It is all the more interesting in that it reflects very closely the essence of this chapter:

**203**

> I don't like the term 'feminist fundamentalism' – feminism isn't a religion – but it does seem to me that there is a parallel between religious fundamentalism, with its clear distinction between the saved and the damned, and those brands of feminism which contrast women's essential, innate female goodness with men's moral turpitude. Women are good by biological fiat, virtuous because of our XX chromosomes, and our reproductive capacity. Women are the genetically superior race. (Kitzinger, 1990: 24–5)

Not all feminists would, of course, agree with the view paraphrased here. Indeed most feminists, like most adherents to any ideology, including the major world faiths, are not accurately described by the word 'fundamentalist' at all. But the quotation illustrates the essential point: religious movements are not the only ones that succumb to fundamentalist tendencies, a situation greatly exacerbated by the uncertainties of the late-modern or postmodern world; a world in which the reassertion of certainty or truth become inherently attractive.

Hence the structure of this chapter. The discussion began by locating the study of fundamentalisms in the relationship between a religious tradition and the nature of modernity; it was then extended to include secular as well as religious ideologies. Two points have been crucial in this shift: first, the changing nature of modernity itself, and second, the effect of these changes on the nature of intellectual confidence. With this in mind, it is possible to see more than one stage in the emergence of fundamentalisms through the course of the twentieth century. Initially *religious* fundamentalisms emerged to counteract, among other things, the threat of alternative ways of thinking, particularly in cases where the latter encroached on the religious sphere itself. Secular rationalism in both its Western and Eastern (communist) forms was in the ascendant. More recently the alternative ideologies themselves have found themselves prone to similar pressures as secular as well as religious creeds have begun to fragment. Fragments, however, can be rebuilt into certainties – artificial ones perhaps – which provide a bulwark against the corrosiveness of perpetual change.

Such certainties can be described as competing fundamentalisms – the plural is important. They should be seen as a normal rather than abnormal feature of late-modern societies, for they provide coping mechanisms in times of uncertainty. Interestingly in her analysis of religion as a chain of memory, Hervieu-Léger comes to exactly the same conclusion: she considers the growth of fundamentalisms as one example of alternative or recreated memories in a situation in which societies have forgotten or lost their sense of historic tradition (Hervieu-Léger, 2000). They are not necessarily harmful, though they may in certain circumstances become so, particularly in situations where opposing fundamentalisms compete for disputed territory, whether such territory be geographical or moral. Discerning the particular situations in which fundamentalisms of whatever kind become destructive is, therefore, a crucially important area of study. In this and other ways, the study of fundamentalism in its broadest sense must move rapidly up the sociological agenda, for it confronts an essential, perhaps expanding, feature of the modern world. It does not, conversely, exhaust the religious field, a point that will become abundantly clear in the remaining chapters of this book.

## NOTES

1 See, for example, the introductory material contained in the first volume that appeared (Marty and Appleby, 1991). In the end, five volumes were published in the original series; a further volume appeared in 2003 (i.e. post 9/11), which drew on the material of the project as a whole (Almond et al., 2003).

2 The following quotation sums up Berger's argument:

> The concern that must have led to this Project was based on an upside-down perception of the world, according to which 'fundamentalism' ... is a rare, hard-to-explain thing. But a look either at history or at the contemporary world reveals that what is rare is not the phenomenon itself but knowledge of it. The difficult-to-understand phenomenon is not Iranian mullahs but American university professors – it might be worth a multi-million dollar project to try to explain that! (Berger, 1999b: 2)

3 The volume in which this essay first appeared was initially published in 1988.

4 In this respect, the Project adopts the framework set out in this book: that is, to distinguish between reportage and explanation. There is also a great deal of material in the Fundamentalism Project which attempts to understand the world view of the fundamentalist individual or community, including a remarkable chapter on fundamentalist humour (Aran, 1995).

5 Ammerman makes this point very strongly in her contribution to *Accounting for Fundamentalisms*. Pentecostals in Latin America may indeed be conservative and evangelical, but 'relative to their own culture, they are not fundamentalist' (Ammerman, 1994: 151). Martin (2002a: 1) is even more direct in his critique (see Chapter 10).

6 In order to place this illustration in its proper context, it should be read against the more moderate forms of Islam described on pp. 223–8.

7 In the 1980s the Iranian case captured the attention of the world. Shi-ite Muslims are, however, considerably less numerous than Sunnis who have produced their own versions of extreme or fundamentalist movements.

8 The first of these revolutions occurs in the third century with the rise of the Sassanian dynasty, the second in the sixteenth century with the emergence of the Safavid movement, and the third much more recently in the constitutional reforms of 1906–11.

9 Provoked, it is argued, by the admission of the Shah into an American hospital for treatment. The hostages were not released until 1981.

10 The unexpected victory of Mahmoud Ahmadinejad in the Iranian presidential election in June 2005 became a defining moment, setting Iran on an ultra-conservative and anti-Western track.

11 Here, interestingly, Harvey is quoting from Rocco Buttiglione, whom he describes as a theologian close to the Pope. In 2004, Rocco Buttiglione was proposed as European Union's new commissioner for Justice, Freedom and Security, but his remarks on homosexuality and the role of women sparked an institutional crisis that led to him withdrawing his candidacy. Large numbers of MEPs demanded that he be stripped of his portfolio. Italy, however, expressed outrage and the Vatican complained of a 'new inquisition'.

12 As indicated in Chapter 8, this situation has since repeated itself in the ban on wearing the burqa in public in France (see note 14, p. 184).

13 Further information about European Union legislation and treaties can be found on http://europa.eu/documentation/legislation/index_en.htm accessed 17 April 2012.

14 The Buttiglione case is both ambiguous and politically complex. Many people would agree that his appointment as commissioner for Justice, Freedom and

Security was inappropriate; equally it was challenged for the 'wrong' – primarily religious – reasons. It is the latter point that is stressed here. It can also be turned into a question: what would have happened had Buttiglione been a Muslim? The answer is far from clear.

15 A third – the emergence of new atheism – is addressed in the Preface to this edition.

16 The final revisions to the first edition of this book coincided with the closure of a Staffordshire farm which bred guinea pigs for medical research after prolonged intimidation by animal rights activists. Their tactics included death threats and the exhumation of the body of an elderly relative of the farm's owners.

# *ten*

# globalization and the study of religion

## A PAPAL FUNERAL

At the beginning of April 2005, Pope John Paul II died, bringing to an end an unusually long papacy. His death came after several years of illness in which his physical strength was clearly diminished, but not his mental or spiritual stature. The moment had been anticipated – the obituaries were ready, so too the commemorative programmes to which suitable concluding statements were added before they were broadcast. The tone of these tributes was revealing. John Paul II was universally acclaimed for his resistance to communism in East Europe. Both his presence and his frequent visits to Poland in the 1980s were recognized as a powerful catalyst in the chain of events that led, extraordinarily fast, to the collapse of communism as a political system. Rather more nuanced were the reactions to his thinking, and evident moral courage, regarding the growing relativism of the modern world. Here respect was tempered by criticism for John Paul II's uncompromising views on birth control, a 'problem' inextricably connected in many people's minds to the AIDS epidemic in Africa.[1]

In terms of the argument of this chapter, however, one point stands out. The Pope was a global figure in every sense of the term: probably the best-known individual in the modern world, instantly recognized wherever he went, totally in command of the world's media, and strikingly adept in using the latter to drive a global agenda. No one was surprised, therefore, when the world turned towards Rome as it became clear that the Pope was dying. Few people, however, anticipated the scale of the reaction that followed, as almost every country suspended 'normal' activities in order to mark the event. Rome became the centre of attention for heads of state, for religious leaders, for journalists of all kinds, and for hundreds of thousands of individuals (Catholic and other), many of whom converged on the city in the week preceding the funeral. Here there is overwhelming evidence of the continuing presence of religion in the modern world and of the relationship between religion and globalization. The data speak for themselves: the influence of the Pope transcended every imaginable boundary, political as well as religious. Not everyone liked what they saw, but few could deny the impact of this remarkable man.

The strange juxtaposition of events in Britain in the first week of April is instructive in this respect, not least for the paradoxes that this reveals. Here, a second, and as it happens secular, marriage of the heir to the throne was postponed in order that Prince Charles himself, Tony Blair (as Prime Minister) and Rowan Williams (as Archbishop of Canterbury) should attend the funeral of the Pope in Rome. But no Prime Minister or Archbishop of Canterbury or heir to the throne has ever been to such a funeral before, never mind prioritizing this over a royal wedding – a gesture that symbolizes the wholly different configurations that are emerging in the twenty-first century. Increasingly the links (or indeed the antagonisms) between faiths and peoples of faith become the dominant factor; domestic agendas (royal weddings, the calling of a general election and even the 2005 Grand National) were simply re-arranged.

## THE BROADER CONTEXT

The discussion, however, takes different forms in different parts of the world. Indeed one of the most striking features of the Pope's death – and even more of the decisions that followed from this – is the growing tension between North and South in global terms in the articulation of religious priorities. It is becoming increasingly clear, for example, that the great majority of the world's believers (both Christian and Muslim) now live in the global South, forming not only a considerable mass of people but a significant source of power (Jenkins, 2002). This huge and growing population has, moreover, an entirely different agenda from that which exists in the North, both inside and outside the churches. Or to put the same point more forcibly, the liberals of Northern Europe, religious as well as secular, are increasingly discomfited as, one by one, their expectations of the future, premised on the principles of the Enlightenment, are called into question.

So constructed, the points of tension lie between a religious and populous South and a rather more secular North. There is certainly truth in this statement. Looked at more closely, however, such tensions exist as much *within* the churches as they do between different global regions. Hence the speculation surrounding the appointment of a successor to John Paul II: should the new Pope be a European or someone from the developing world, a liberal (in terms of sexual ethics) or a conservative? And how, precisely, do these attributes align themselves? The answer came quickly: the College of Cardinals elected Cardinal Ratzinger as Pope to follow John Paul II. Benedict XVI is a European and a respected scholar, but known above all for his rigorously conservative views – able therefore to win more easily than most the support of Catholics in the Southern hemisphere.

Casanova (1997, 2001b) places these debates into a longer-term historical context, in which the paradoxes are revealing. At precisely the moment when European expressions of Catholicism begin to retreat almost to the point of no return – as the convergence between state and church through centuries of European history becomes ever more difficult to sustain – Catholicism takes on new and global dimensions. No longer confined, it becomes increasingly a *trans*national religious movement, and as such has grown steadily since 1870 (the low point of the European Church).[2] There are twin processes at work in these changes: the Romanization of world Catholicism and the internationalization of Rome. Regarding the former, transnational Catholic movements begin to grow at the expense sometimes of the national churches (Opus Dei offers an excellent example); regarding the latter, both the College of Cardinals and the Curia are increasingly populated with non-Europeans (hence the growing capacity for transnational networks). There have, of course, been negative as well as positive reactions to these changes, including difficult tensions between Rome and the national churches. That is to be expected but is not the crucial point, which is to be found in the following statement: '[T]he combination of globalization, nationalization, secular involvements, and voluntary disestablishment has led the Catholic Church to a significant change of orientation from nation-state to civil society' (Casanova, 1997: 137). Civil society, moreover, is global in its reach.[3]

The tensions between North and South can be seen equally in the Anglican Communion, more especially in the heated debate relating to homosexuality within this worldwide grouping of churches with its centre in Canterbury.[4] In 2003, two events raised the temperature of this discussion: a controversial appointment in the Church of England[5] and the decision in the Episcopalian Church (in the United States) to appoint as Bishop an openly gay priest.[6] Much of the notably acrimonious exchanges which ensued lies beyond the scope of this chapter, but not the central theme: that is, the desire of the more conservative churches in the South to resist the more 'advanced' positions of the North in terms of their acceptance of homosexuality. To what extent, in other

*209*

words, can the demographic power of the South (the part of the world where the churches are growing) challenge the historic power of the North (where the churches are, for the most part, in decline)? For those in the South, homosexuality remains a sin; for those in the North, there has been a gradual – if somewhat uneven – acceptance of different forms of sexuality, though a marked reluctance until very recently to test the application of such freedoms in senior church appointments. The result has been painful to say the least. An offer of a senior post in the Church of England was withdrawn, and those responsible for the appointment of an openly gay Bishop in the United States have been asked to repent.

There is a further twist in this still unfinished story: that is, the readiness with which some, though by no means all, representatives of conservative opinion in the North will make use of the North/South tension to advance their own cause. Observers of the controversy are of one mind in this respect: that minority sections of the Anglican churches in the North – minorities, however, which are growing both in size and confidence (see Chapter 7) – have worked with (some would say exploited) their colleagues in the South to challenge the power of a liberal elite. Hence the significance of the issue, which is ultimately about power. For centuries, power has resided in the North; indeed to a considerable extent it still does – in terms of tradition, precedent, knowledge or, more immediately, of money. The current challenge reflects a new source of power. It comes from numbers, more precisely from the growing mass of believers in the South – aided and abetted by a minority in the North who feel that their more conservative views have been marginalized for too long.

The outcome of these complex and painful debates is far from clear despite the evident flexibilities of Anglicanism if this is compared with the Catholic Church. One thing, however, is certain. The Church of England can no longer ignore what is happening elsewhere; nor can the churches in the North dominate the agenda. Interestingly the secular press is beginning to grasp this point. It is as ready to pay attention to these discussions as its religious equivalents. One reason for this lies in the issue itself: homosexuality attracts attention both inside and outside the churches. Another can be found in a growing, if gradual, awareness of the religious factor in the modern world order and its capacity to influence the domestic as well as the global agenda.

Sociologists should be equally attentive. Questions about power, and within these about the growing tensions between North and South, are central to the enquiry. They need, however, to be set into a broader context – the principal aim of this chapter. This deals first with the various theoretical perspectives that have emerged in the study of globalization, paying particular attention to the place of religion with these. The examples that follow offer substantive illustrations of at least some of these ideas. Both sections are necessarily selective. This has to be so given the most striking features of the modern world: that is, the existence in almost every continent of every imaginable form of religion – abundant, varied and constantly changing (Beckford, 2003), only some of which can be included in the present discussion.

## THEORETICAL PERSPECTIVES

### contrasting approaches

The place attributed to religion in the process of globalization depends essentially on how that process is understood. The word 'globalization' means different things to different people. If, for example, the term is used to denote a primarily economic movement, driven by a particular ideology (i.e. more rigorous forms of market principles), the place given to religion is likely to be minimal. Globalization is something that takes place at the level of macro-economic change. Individuals and communities, religious or otherwise, can do little about it except retreat and at times react; they are victims of a process that they cannot control.

Certain kinds of religious people (notably theologically liberal Christians) very frequently articulate this approach. Quite properly, their analyses pay careful attention to the devastating effects that Western (mostly American) driven economic forces are likely to have for huge numbers of people in the developing world. If religion is significant at all, it is in the provisions of havens for those in retreat from the globalization process. In one reading of the term, fundamentalist forms of religion constitute examples of such havens.

This, however, is not the only story. If, as an idea, globalization includes not only economic change but a whole range of developments in the modern world (economic, political, social and cultural) – shifts that bring with them an entirely new set of global actors, both collective and individual – then the place for religion becomes far more significant. Indeed those engaged in religious activities very often have access to impressive transnational networks and make maximum use of modern forms of communication both to establish and to develop these relationships. Without doubt they are global actors. Examples abound in, for example, the metamorphoses of the Catholic Church already described; in the global ecumenical movement (see below); in an ever increasing number of globally connected religious organizations, institutions, churches, denominations, groups and movements; and, finally, in the bewildering variety of activities subsumed under the heading of 'mission'.

The last of these can be taken as an example; it offers an excellent 'image' of globalization in the last 100 years. For much of modern history, mission (at least in its Christian forms) has been understood as a movement from North to South, as significant numbers of Europeans, and later Americans, moved across the world in an initiative closely (and sometimes dubiously) associated with the development of empire.[7] In the mid post-war decades, however, the language began to alter. Bit by bit the notion of 'sending' gave way to a discourse of 'partnership', as the churches in the developing world began increasingly to assert their presence as equal partners of their European or American equivalents. No longer were these churches simply recipients; increasingly they were becoming centres of Christianity in their own right, notably larger in many cases than the churches 'back home'. Organizational changes followed. Partnerships evolved between dioceses and parishes (with one partner in the North and another in the developing world) and began gradually to complement, if not to replace, the voluntary society as the focus of mission in many Western societies.

A further stage in this evolution is becoming ever more evident; it is also complex. On the one hand, there is a growing tendency to reverse the North/South flow as increasing numbers of missionaries are now arriving in Europe from the developing world – a constituency motivated by a combination of economic and more purely religious factors.[8] On the other, the North/South axis is collapsing altogether as mission becomes increasingly a series of movements from everywhere to everywhere else. Brazil offers an interesting example – both in the growing number of Brazilian missionaries working abroad and in the Portuguese-speaking churches of the Brazilian diaspora (in the United States, Europe, Japan and Paraguay).[9] Even more numerous, however, are the South Koreans, who are found all over the world; an initiative greatly intensified by the lifting of restrictions relating to currency exchange – the sending bodies could now keep missionaries in the field for much longer periods (Clark, 1997; Park, 1997). Destinations include Asia, Eurasia (including Russia), Latin America, Europe, the Pacific, the Middle East, the Caribbean and North America.

One further point is important. Are missionaries as such crucial to the enterprise of mission, or is the movement of people more important? Mobility, moreover, is central to globalization: whether of capital, markets or labour. And once populations begin to move in significant

212

numbers, ideas (including religious ideas) will move with them. Precisely that happened in Africa in the late nineteenth and early twentieth centuries, a factor which accounts for the very rapid Christianization of the region (Hastings, 1994; Sundkler and Steed, 2000). Interestingly the same question is currently being asked of China, though in somewhat different terms. It can be formulated as follows. Is it possible for the Chinese to have the economic advantages of the market without the deregulation of culture that goes with this? The religious element is particularly important in this case, given the aggressive secularization of the communist period in China and the forcible removal of the missionary presence that occurred as a result. Exactly what forms of religious life will emerge and take root in the new century are still uncertain, but one thing is sure: they will be closely related to the movement of people both within and from outside this vast and relatively unknown territory.[10]

## theories and theorists

In terms of theory, one fact is clear: until relatively recently a great deal of sociological work in the field of globalization paid no attention to religion at all. That point is underlined firmly by both Robertson (2001) and Beckford (2003), together with its consequences for mainstream sociology. This section will deal, however, with three very notable exceptions to this generalization: Roland Robertson himself, Peter Beyer and David Lehmann, bearing in mind that these scholars often work in collaboration with others and that the list is by no means exhaustive.[11] Indeed the situation is beginning to change noticeably as scholars in many different parts of the world examine from their particular perspectives the meaning of globalization for the forms of religion most familiar to them. Global religion requires global endeavour, found among other places in a rash of publication in this field. Two very timely encyclopaedias come particularly to mind: the first includes the study of religion in the work on globalization (Robertson and Scholte, 2006); the second focuses on the concept of global religion itself (see Juergensmeyer and Roof, 2011).[12]

Robertson's interest in globalization is long term; it begins as early as the 1960s and pays increasing attention to religion as the decades pass. He starts from the following assumption: that working within a global perspective transforms the study of religion. More specifically it reconnects religion to the mainstream of economic and social life, overcoming the isolationist assumptions embedded in the Western experience of

213

modernity. There is, therefore, an immediate resonance with the dominant theme of this book – the need to escape from the view of religion as 'a sequestered and relatively inconsequential aspect of twentieth-century societies' (Robertson, 2001: 4). As Robertson so rightly says, that perspective has been seriously challenged by recent events – not once but several times. The transformations of the modern world demand that we do better: new areas of enquiry generate new ways of thinking, the formulation, in fact, of a different – radically different – sociological canon.

The consequences of thinking in these terms are spelled out at the end of Robertson's contribution to an important collection of papers published in 2001 (Beyer, 2001a). They go straight to the heart of the matter. Thinking globally makes us think differently: about religion itself; about the contributions of the classics (both their strengths and weaknesses); about the relationship between sociology and its cognate disciplines; about comparative perspectives; about the capacities of religion to initiate as well as respond to changes; and about the interconnections with culture, ideology, politics, economics and so on. Above all, it challenges the assumptions of the secularization thesis, breaking any necessary connection between modernization and secularization. No longer is religion cast in the role of inhibitor – the factor that prevents the emergence of a fully modern society; nor is it simply an epiphenomenon, dependent on an increasingly interconnected global economy. It becomes instead an infinitely varied subject that interacts in a myriad different ways with the cultural, ideological, political and economic systems which surround it. Between the lines, Robertson's critique of world systems theory is abundantly clear. Globalization is not uni-dimensional, as Wallerstein (1979) and others maintain. It is a 'multi-dimensional and multi-centred historical development' within which religion has a central place. The principal task of the sociology of religion, indeed of the sociologist *tout court*, is to take this phenomenon seriously, document what is happening and create the necessary theoretical frameworks to understand these things properly.

Peter Beyer is one who has responded to this challenge. Able to draw from an extensive theoretical resource in three languages and equally at home in Europe and North America, he is well placed to do this. Interestingly, however, his single-authored account of *Religion and Globalization* (1993) begins not with the theory but with an incident: the *fatwa* pronounced by the Ayatollah on Salman Rushdie in 1989. Beyer uses this to illustrate both the global nature of the world that we inhabit and the place of religion within this, noting in particular: the immediacy of the reaction to this episode (the media followed it minutely), its truly global dimensions, its capacity to perplex, and the initiative taken by a non-Western leader. The Rushdie affair becomes, in fact, the spring-board for Beyer's argument, which interprets the *fatwa* in two rather different ways. At one level the Muslim reaction to Rushdie's novel demonstrates the link between religious faith and particularist identity (there are no real surprises here). At another, it reveals a much more troubling response: the notion that Muslims are being asked to surrender the core of their faith – the *immutable sacredness* of the Qur'an – 'as the price for full inclusion in a global system currently dominated by non-Muslims' (1993: 3). Hence on one hand the profound unease of the Muslim community (its assumed marginality), and on the other the incomprehension of the secular response (representative of the dominant global system). Neither is reassuring.

Given such a challenge, Beyer's principal aim is to know more about the 'institutionally specialized and systemic' forms of religion that are present in the modern world and the different ways in which these find expression (1993: 12). The purely private (in its many and diverse forms) is of less significance for this analysis, though it most certainly continues to exist. For Beyer it is the place of religion in the public, indeed political, arena that demands attention. Here religion can operate in two rather different ways, revealing on one hand a tendency towards particularism and cultural distinctiveness (as already described), but on the other a form of 'ecumenism' (i.e. forms of religion that make links with the issues that emerge from a global, functionally differentiated society). Hence the case studies found in his writing, three of which illustrate the conservative option (including the New Christian Right and the Islamic Revolution outlined in the previous chapter) and two of which reveal rather more liberal ways of doing things (liberation theology in Latin America and religious environmentalism).

**215**

Some seven years later, Beyer goes further still, stating his goal in the introduction to the collection of papers mentioned above (Beyer, 2001a); it is to understand globalization by means of religion, not the other way round. Hence the following logic:

> [J]ust as the capitalist economic system represents a specifically modern, specialized, instrumental, and now globalized form of doing economy; just as the system of nation-states is likewise a modern, specialized, instrumental, and now globalized form of doing polity; so it makes sense at least to ask if there exists a corresponding globalized and systemic form of doing religion. (Beyer, 2001b: xxvii)

In order to answer this question, Beyer draws extensively on Luhmann's theoretical frames, notably his systems theory of society. More substantively Beyer looks first at the evolution of religion in Europe, from the unifying system of medieval Europe to the very different and more plural forms of religion that exist today. Part of this story relates to the expansion of Europe across the globe and a growing awareness that there are many different forms of religion in the modern world; it is these, taken together, that 'constitute and define a global religious system' (2001b: xxix). But what 'counts' as religion will change over time, just as what 'counts' as a nation is frequently contested. The model, therefore, must constantly adapt; so too the research agenda. Both, for example, must take into account that there are not one, but many forms of modernity in the modern world, and thus of religion. For Beyer, the focus lies on a constant process of formation and reformation in the religious field as new public entities emerge both alongside and in place of those that already exist.

Lehmann (2002) takes a somewhat different view. No longer is religion seen as part of the globalization process (i.e. the spreading of standard, homogenized forms across the world or conversely as a reaction to this). Religion is seen instead as the *original* globalizer, but expressed once again in two ways. Lehmann uses the term 'cosmopolitan' to describe the first of these; a form, or forms of religion characteristic of elites and which involve 'attempts to introduce into the clash of religious systems a historical and contextualized "theory" of other cultures' (2002: 299). Thoughtful leaders of the world's faiths 'take into account' the exigencies of local culture and act accordingly, an approach epitomized in the movement which has become known as 'liberation theology'. Highly trained intellectuals live among the poorest people of Latin America in an attempt to understand their world view. Together such leaders and the communities of which they were part strive for both economic and social improvement through the transformations of structures – a necessarily long-term process.

Somewhat in competition with these efforts are the much more disorganized forms of global religion, driven this time by a mass of independent actors who adhere lightly to the disciplines imposed by elites or hierarchies. It is here that the proliferations of fundamentalist[13] or charismatic religions find their place, remembering that these are as much the carriers of modernity as reactions to it. Indeed it is modernity that offers the means for what Lehmann calls 'promiscuous propagations', as innovative forms of religion cross and re-cross boundaries. Here is the mobility of people described in the previous section and indeed in the next, as both individuals and groups move from everywhere to everywhere else making full use of what modernity can offer – including the ever more rapid forms of communication across the globe, the techniques of management and marketing, and the emergence of English as a universal language.

Lehmann's own career is instructive in this respect (Lehmann, 1996). As a scholar of Latin America for some 30 years, Lehmann failed initially to take the religious factor into account at all. The first step towards a remedy led to a study of liberation theology and base communities in so far as these related to both economic and political (democratic) development (Lehmann, 1990). By the time, however, that he came to do detailed fieldwork in Brazil in the early 1990s, it was clear that the innovative forms of Protestantism springing up all over the place demanded equal attention. What emerges, in consequence, is a developed analysis of the religious field in Latin America, envisaged as an arena in which contending forces 'struggle for the spirit' – hence the title of the 1996 book. Macro as well as micro questions come to the fore:

> The big questions are very big: do the people feel more faithfully represented by, or identified with, the revolutionary priests and nuns in their jeans and sandals, promising a long period in the wilderness travelling towards an uncertain Promised Land, and offering a diet of agonized self-questioning, of seminars and consciousness-raising combined with mini-projects, to sustain the People of God on their journey? Or will they be drawn towards the pastors, uniformly respectable in their suits, white shirts and black ties, as they proclaim the tangible happiness that will follow from a fulminating conversion experience, a herculean effort to get their lives and their families under control, and the financial discipline of a weekly contribution to church funds? (Lehmann, 1996: 3–4)

The research questions that follow operationalize Lehmann's two types of global religion, contrasting the 'option for the poor' articulated by liberation theologians with the 'option of the poor' in the form of individual choices in favour of Pentecostalism. Each possibility – the membership of a base community or Pentecostal conversion – is set out in terms of its relationship to the history, culture and institutions of Latin America in general and of Brazil more particularly. Theme and counter-theme are repeatedly set against one another: one modality, for example, seeks insertion into the highly valued culture of the people (the Catholic mode of inculturation); the other continually confronts what are construed as the evils of local behaviour (i.e. the feasts, celebrations, rituals and rhythms, to follow Lehmann's own list), offering the convert a new and 'better' way. The stakes, quite clearly, are very high – indeed.

The following, necessarily selective, illustrations exemplify in more detail some of the possibilities put forward by these authors. The first develops the material on Pentecostalism – a quintessentially modern form of religion. The second looks at the global ecumenical movement, paying particular attention to the World Council of Churches, a post-war institution now coming to terms with a very different global context. The final examples are taken from the Muslim world to illustrate the role of Islam in the formation of distinctive types of modernity. They ask a crucial and often repeated question: to what extent is it possible in the twenty-first century for a society to be both authentically Muslim and fully democratic?

## EXAMPLES OF GLOBAL RELIGION

### pentecostalism: a global success story

It is hard to comprehend both the overall figures and the changes that have taken place in the Christian populations of the Southern hemisphere.[14] To say, for example, that approximately 13 per cent of the Latin American population is now Pentecostal fails to convey either the size of the shift or the significance of what has happened. A concrete example may help. In Rio de Janeiro between 1990 and 1992, a new church was registered every weekday, as a result of which '[i]n one Catholic diocese there were over twice as many Protestant places of worship as Catholic, and in the poorest districts the ratio was seven to one' (Freston, 1998: 338). It is also important to recall the absolute numbers. Brazil (with circa 200 million inhabitants) is not only the largest country in Latin America but the fifth largest country in the world. For this reason, percentages can be deceptive. Pentecostals in Brazil now number some 25 million people; there are in addition some 15 million 'historic' Protestants, whose presence is boosted in some cases by adopting Pentecostal characteristics (Neri, 2011). In Britain, in contrast, less than 10 per cent (i.e. 5 to 6 million people) are seriously active in *any* religious denomination. By any standards these statistics are impressive – they could be repeated many times over. There is, however, a parallel need for caution. It would be unwise to assume that these growth rates will necessarily continue. It is also important to appreciate regional variations both within Brazil and within Latin America as a whole.

That said, something remarkable has happened and time as well as place is important. Paradoxically, the take-off point for Pentecostalism in Latin America can be located at precisely the moment when the secularization thesis peaked among Western sociologists, the mid-1960s. Unsurprisingly the latter were slow to see what was happening.

And when the facts themselves could no longer be denied, explanations were sought in American influence – more precisely in the supposed imposition of American forms of Protestantism on to an unwilling population south of the Rio Grande. Such was not the case. Such misinterpretations, deliberate or otherwise, are nonetheless revealing in that they offer a telling illustration of the assertion of theory over data. It was the theoretical assumptions of Western social science that 'required' an external explanation for the unanticipated growth in religious activity in Latin America, not the data themselves.[15]

Why, though, did it happen? Why did the Pentecostal forms of Protestantism begin to grow exponentially in the Southern hemisphere towards the end of the twentieth century – first in Latin America, then in Africa and finally all over the Pacific Rim? For many different reasons, is the obvious response. Freston (following Droogers, 1991) is undoubtedly right to draw attention to this diversity:

> Pentecostalism is flexible and there is unlikely to be a single grand reason for its success. An eclecticism based on the ambivalence of religion must take into account not only political and economic, but also social, cultural, ethnic and religious factors; not only the macro level (which social characteristics favour conversion) but also the micro level (why only some people with those characteristics convert); not only the appeal of Pentecostalism to men but also (especially) to women; not only the demand side (why are people ready to convert) but the supply side (what Pentecostals do to maximize their potential public). And it must ask not only why Pentecostalism grows so much, but why does it not grow more, and why some types grow more than others. (Freston, 1998: 347–8)

Some points are clear, however. Pentecostalism grows fastest among groups of people who find in this particular form of Christianity both a vision for themselves and a means of support for their families. Both are important. Pentecostal communities look up and out. Theologically, they offer a vision for the individual Christian who has been redeemed from past experience, blessed by the spirit and opened to new opportunities. But in a much more tangible sense, such communities are linked to an ever expanding network of churches and organizations that, by their very nature, transcend boundaries, whether national, political or ethnic. The fact that these chains of communication are frequently English-speaking is of significance in itself. Equally important, however, are the capacities of Pentecostalism to provide a refuge. This is true in terms of teaching (conservative readings of scripture) and of practice (protection from the vicissitudes of life). Hence a set of communities that are freely joined but firmly directed – leadership is often authoritarian. In the fragile economies of the developing world,

219

where alternative sources of welfare are conspicuous by their absence, this has proved a winning combination.

Significant changes in lifestyle occur in consequence. It is at this point, moreover, that the question of gender becomes central. Here Brusco's work amongst Pentecostals in Colombia can be taken as an example. Her data are striking. No longer, following Brusco, is 20 to 40 per cent of the household budget consumed by the husband in the form of alcohol. Nor are 'many of the extra household forms of consumption that characterize masculine behavior in Colombia, such as smoking, gambling and visiting prostitutes' allowed to continue (Brusco, 1993: 14; 1995). More positively, the men withdraw from the (public) street and, alongside their wives, begin gradually to assume responsibilities in both the church and the home (the private sphere). Hence, at the very least, a rather more secure economic existence for the family and, crucially, an education for the children – itself a decisive factor in intergenerational mobility. The household becomes an effective corporate group.

So far so good. Few would dispute that Latin American women are advantaged by such changes. This, however, is not the whole story; nor is it 'liberation' in the Western sense of the term. The men in question may indeed withdraw from the street but they maintain with vigour the traditional headship role, both in the family and in the churches. In an article entitled very aptly 'The Pentecostal gender paradox', Bernice Martin (2000) explores this tension further. Her conclusions are not only provocative, but central to the argument of this book. In relation to the Pentecostal experience, Western feminist perspectives (rather like the traditional versions of secularization) are not only inappropriate, they are themselves part of the problem, in so far as they have blinded many Western academics to much that was happening in the developing world. Interestingly, the observers *sur place* (anthropologists and missiologists) were quicker to appreciate the changes taking place – not least their very positive effects for the women in question.

These effects, moreover, are cumulative. For growing numbers of people in the global South, the resources of Pentecostalism have enabled not only survival but real, if modest, improvement. This is not a question of hard-headed capital accumulation; nor, as some have argued, is it a direct application of the Weber thesis. It is a considerably more modest enterprise. But given the precariousness of both economic and political context, the basic qualities of honesty, thrift, self-discipline and organizational talent stand out, becoming sought after skills in the local economy. Networks of trust, reciprocity and betterment begin both to emerge and to grow. As people move from the countryside into the city looking for better jobs and educational opportunities (especially for

220

their children), Pentecostal communities become in a very practical sense 'havens and way stations in the journey up the socio-economic ladder' (Maldonado, 1993: 235).

The same process, moreover, can work across continents as well as countries. Hence, for David Martin, the significance of Pentecostalism as a 'global option' (Martin, 2002a). The characteristics already described come into their own. On the one hand, Pentecostals are freed from the ascribed categories that bind people to place, whether socially or geographically; on the other, they can put down roots. The same network that nurtured you in one place can do so in another, both creating and sustaining the disciplines necessary for survival in a mobile world. Such accounts should not be romanticized. At times, these are long and difficult journeys, demanding many sacrifices. Nor do Pentecostals always live up to expectations (their own or anyone else's). These ever expanding networks capture, nonetheless, the combination of movement and discipline which have given Pentecostals a very particular place in a global world. At the very least they are deserving of sustained sociological attention.[16]

## two examples of global ecumenism

221

The World Council of Churches (WCC) could hardly be more different.[17] Unquestionably a global institution, it exemplifies very clearly the second of Beyer's types; it reflects a form of religion that makes links with the questions that arise from a functionally differentiated society (Beyer, 1993: 93). Its staff are diverse in origin, highly qualified, and able to engage effectively with different aspects of the global agenda.

Officially founded in 1948, the WCC became the channel through which the varied streams of ecumenical life that already existed were brought together. From the start it was clear about its goal: this was *not* to build a global 'super-church', nor to standardize styles of worship. It was rather to call both Christians and churches 'to visible unity in one faith and in one eucharistic fellowship, expressed in worship and common life in Christ, through witness and service to the world, and to advance towards that unity in order that the world may believe' (WCC Constitution). Such aims are laudable and, in many respects, much progress has been made; it is not the fault of the WCC that 'visible unity' remains as yet an aspiration. In the context of this chapter, however, it is the emphasis on Christian service that is of particular interest. It is here that the resistance to globalization *as an economic doctrine* is at its most evident. A truly global movement has become sharply critical of the economic consequences of capitalism, advocating instead a global order based on justice rather than growth.

To understand both the positive and negative aspects of this statement, an historical perspective is important. The motives and aspirations of the post-war generation can be clearly seen in the early years of the WCC. Its creation in 1948 reflected a whole series of initiatives aimed at establishing and maintaining world peace.[18] In its early years, the WCC was deeply influenced by the Cold War and its consequences for church life. The movement looked for ways to overcome the divisions between East and West, especially in Europe – encouraging, as far as this was possible, contacts with the churches in countries dominated by communism. With this in mind strong support was given to those who brought together the insights of Marxism and Christianity, including the advocates of liberation theology. Post-1989, however, the context has altered radically and to the surprise of many – not only the devotees of the ecumenical movement – it is the conservative, even reactionary forms of religion (both Christian and non-Christian) that have been growing fastest in the final decades of the twentieth century, not those which lean towards the political left. Pentecostalism offers an obvious example, and whilst some Pentecostal churches have become members of the WCC, others have not; the latter resist any form of co-operation that might compromise their understanding of truth.

222

Hence the dilemma for an organization founded on two assumptions: first, that the world would become an increasingly secular place; and second, that the best way forward in this situation was for the churches most open to change and most attentive to the modern world (notably the liberal Protestants) to group together, in order to sustain each other in a necessarily hostile environment. The churches that resisted 'the world' would automatically consign themselves to the past. Both assumptions were incorrect. The world is not 'an increasingly secular place'; it is full of very different forms of religious life, many of which are expanding rather than contracting. It is, moreover, the forms of religion least interested in ecumenism that are developing with the greatest confidence. Coming to terms with such shifts constitutes a major, and as yet unresolved, challenge to the WCC. Equally challenging is the changing nature of the organization itself, as it gradually evolves from a modern, bureaucratic and centralized institution into what is best described as a late-modern, dispersed and global network.

A very different, and in some ways more 'organic', example of ecumenism can be found in modern Europe. In many respects, the development of ecumenical contacts and 'widening' of the European Union are two sides of the same coin. In both cases, Europeans are invited to consider what they have in common rather than what divides them. And the fact that some churches, just like some nations, find this easier than others is of itself significant. The Scandinavian, British and Greek examples are interesting in this respect. All of them display ambivalent attitudes towards the European Union and in all their hesitations the religious factor as an exemplar of particularity plays a significant role. The Greek case is the most striking, and problematic, of the three.[19] Europe, however, is a rapidly changing place, not least in terms of religion. As a continent, it now houses significant groups of Muslims, Sikhs, Hindus and Buddhists in addition to the Jewish communities which have played such a crucial role in Europe's history. Concepts alter accordingly: 'European religion' must give way to the 'religions of Europe'. It is paradoxical that at precisely the moment when Europe, and to some extent the Christian churches of the continent, are attempting to draw themselves back together, new forms of demographic and religious diversity are beginning to appear. The tension between unity and diversity *re*-presents itself in new and different ways, in forms that are peculiar to late-modern rather than early-modern pressures. The case studies elaborated in Chapter 8 were designed to illustrate this point.

A final and very poignant example concludes this section. One of the finest exemplars of both peace-making and ecumenism in Europe can be found in Brother Roger, the founder of the Taizé community in Burgundy.[20] The community was established in the aftermath of the Second World War as a symbol of reconciliation in a village close to the border between Occupied and Vichy France. It has become a major centre of pilgrimage for mostly young people from all over Europe and beyond, who come to Taizé in order that they may share a simple lifestyle and learn more about each other. The numbers visiting are impressive by any standard (between 3,000–6,000 visitors are there every week in the summer). In August 2005, the very elderly Brother Roger was murdered during a service attended by some 2,000 people. His assailant was clearly mentally disturbed, but the shock was considerable for many people. It prompted a moment of recollection in the national papers of most European countries regarding a modest but very effective symbol of unity in a troubled world.

*223*

## Islamic modernities

Martin (2002a: 1) draws a distinction between Pentecostalism and resurgent forms of Islam. Both are parts of the self-conscious awakening of a part of the world that has been excluded from the mainstream in so far as this is expressed by Western forms of development, but they do this in different ways. The fissiparous and essentially mobile aspects of Pentecostalism have already been discussed. So too have the forms of Islam that display most notably the 'family resemblances' of fundamentalism set out in the previous chapter. Not all Islamic societies, however, conform to this model. In the final section of this chapter, two rather different examples will be introduced: first, the Indonesian case, paying particular attention to the policy of Panca Sila; and second, the changes taking place in Turkey. The latter has crucially important implications for Europe, revealing once again the continuing significance of religion in even this, relatively secular, corner of the globe.

Indonesia is the largest Muslim nation in the modern world with a population of 240 million, 88 per cent of which are Muslim – hence its significance both for the global region of which it is part, and for an understanding of religion in a global context. The economic background is important: from conspicuous poverty in the immediate post-war period Indonesia became in a very short time an industrial giant (an Asian tiger). In the 1990s, however, the country experienced extreme instability as the financial markets of South East Asia plunged into crisis; it has not yet fully recovered. Equally significant are the religious changes that have taken place in the same period. These include the conversion of some 2 million Muslims to Christianity and Hinduism following the violence of the mid-1960s (the largest mass conversion from Islam in modern times), but in the 1980s an Islamic revival of considerable proportions. Hefner (2000a) provides a detailed account of these events, taking as his organizing theme the relationship between Islam and the gradual and at times very demanding process of democratization in this huge and overwhelmingly Muslim nation.

The crucial point to grasp in this narrative is the plural nature of Islam. Pluralism as such has always been the case for Muslims, just as it has for Christians; it is nothing new in conceptual terms (Hefner, 2000a: 7). The notion, however, found particular resonance in Indonesia in the later decades of the twentieth century. Not only did the reformist groups play a significant role in the revival of Islam in the region, they also helped to build a well-educated Muslim middle class – a group of people, that is, who began 'to raise questions about a host of characteristically modern concerns, including the status of women, the challenge of pluralism, and the role of morality in market economies' (Hefner, 1998b: 395). It is these politically aware and very diverse individuals who have been active in finding new ways forward for the Indonesian state. They became, among other things, a crucial element in the overthrow of President Suharto in May 1998.

Their presence can be seen equally in the debates surrounding Panca Sila, the official doctrine underlying the Indonesian state. Panca Sila means 'five principles': belief in one supreme God, humanitarianism, nationalism expressed in the unity of Indonesia, consultative democracy and social justice.[21] The first of these principles, moreover, is central to political discussion, though not without controversy. How should this 'one supreme God' be understood? Clearly different formulations are pleasing to different religious groups which ebb and flow in their influence. Polytheistic religions pull in one direction, Muslims (especially more conservative ones) in another. Religion as such, however, is seen as a public good, actively promoted by the state which formally recognizes five religions. These are Islam, Protestantism, Catholicism, Hinduism and Buddhism, bearing in mind the overwhelming majority of Muslims in the population – this is hardly a dialogue of equals. But given this imbalance, Panca Sila represents a genuine attempt to incorporate and to affirm the cultural and religious differences that are present in a huge and heterogeneous population. It offers a constructive way forward for a nation that endorses neither a Muslim state nor an entirely secular institution. The fact that the process towards democratization has not always been easy and that the results are less than perfect should not detract from these efforts. To what extent they will be allowed to continue, however, is more difficult to say.[22]

**225**

Hefner's work on Indonesia should be seen in a broader context. In the final decades of the twentieth century, political debate has foregrounded two possibilities. On the one hand, Western forms of democracy have exerted a universalizing tendency (the claim that this is the right and proper way to do things); on the other, a whole series of ethnic and regional conflicts have emerged to counter this trend. No one has put this more forcibly than Samuel Huntington in his *Clash of Civilizations* (1997), a book that has generated a huge secondary literature. The title itself is revealing in so far as it conceptualizes the evolution of the modern world in a series of violent encounters, within which Islam becomes a particular focus for conflict. An inevitable question follows from this: is it the case that Islam and democracy are by definition incompatible? Or is it possible for *both* Islam and democracy – the dual emphasis is important – to adapt, in order to permit a constructive conversation between them (Hefner 2001)? It is these questions that are central to the comparative project set up by Hefner at the Institute on Culture, Religion and World Affairs in Boston. The project was dedicated to understanding better the prospects for democracy and pluralism in the Muslim world.

A subsequent volume offers an example of this work (Hefner, 2004). Twelve very different case studies are outlined, within which particular attention is paid to the social origins of 'civil democratic Islam' and its implications for a better understanding of religion and politics in the modern world. Turkey, as well as Indonesia, is included in this project. It too is of crucial significance in the global order, given its strategic position between East and West. Of itself, this is nothing new; Turkey's role as a bridge between Europe and Asia has always been important. It has, however, a particular resonance in the early years of the new century, not least with respect to religion. The ongoing negotiations between Turkey and the European Union should be seen in this light.

The modern Republic of Turkey emerged in 1923 from the ruins of the Ottoman Empire. The leader of the independence movement, Kemal Atatürk, was universally regarded as the father of the Turkish nation and still revered as such. Under Atatürk, Turkey experienced a rigorous programme of reform and, effectively, of Westernization. The process included the abolition of both sultanate and caliphate; the prohibition of the fez; the adoption of the Western calendar, the Latin alphabet and the Swiss Civil Code; and, finally, the removal of Islam as a state religion from the constitution. Even more emphatically, in 1937 the constitution was amended to declare Turkey 'a republican, nationalist, populist, statist, secular, and revolutionary state' (Mardin, 1998: 744). Interestingly the nascent republic was closely modelled on France: Turkey is one country where the quintessentially French notion of *laïcité* has immediate resonance. Unsurprisingly many of the same problems ensue – the wearing of the headscarf in public life, for example, has been as contentious in Turkey as it has been in France, despite the fact that Turkey remains a predominantly Muslim society.

Indeed the key question follows from this: how can a rigorously secular state accommodate the manifestation of Islam in public as well as private life? The gradual emergence within the political system of an Islamicist Party is one expression of this debate. The initiative began in the 1960s within the centre-right Justice Party. Subsequent formulations came and went in the decades that follow (the name of the party changes constantly), leading bit by bit to electoral success. In 1995, the National Salvation Party achieved some 20 per cent of the vote; this lead one year later to participation in government. The reaction, however, was swift: in 1998 both the Welfare Party and its leader Nejmettin Erkaban were banned from politics for five years, on the grounds that they had participated in anti-secular activities. Despite such setbacks, the AKP finally gained power in 2002. Both the Prime Minister (Recep Tayyip Erdogan) and the then Foreign Minister (Abdullah Gul, who

**226**

became President in 2007) have a strongly Islamicist background, indicating a significant shift in Turkey's political life. The implications of this shift for the protracted negotiations between Turkey and the European Union are not only interesting in themselves, they present a profound paradox.

In order to qualify as a candidate for European Union membership, Turkey has had to satisfy certain criteria – these include institutional stability, guarantees of democracy, the rule of law, human rights, and the respect and protection of minorities. Huge advances have been made in these various fields, the details of which lie beyond the scope of this chapter. The gradual emergence of the religious factor as a central issue within these negotiations is, however, important. The debate moves in stages. Initially the insistence on secularism, both ideologically and in practice, was seen as a necessary step towards Europe; this was strongly supported by the military. Gradually, however, it became apparent that too strong an emphasis on secularism was running the risk of violating, rather than protecting, the place of the actively Muslim minority in the democratic process. The latter, moreover, were themselves beginning to grasp that accession to Europe was likely to enhance rather than impede their role in Turkish society. It was, therefore, the AKP that began to edge Turkey towards membership of the European Union; conversely the military – the strongest advocates of secularism – became more resistant, appreciating that becoming part of Europe might for them be detrimental, limiting rather than supporting their position within the Republic. Hence an unlikely logic: 'Christian' Europe turns out to be more generous to the Islamicists than 'secular' Turkey.

For Europe itself, the accession of Turkey to the European Union poses many questions – many of them similar to the ones engaged in Chapter 8 and for exactly the same reason: the presence of Islam both inside and outside Europe remains disturbing. More profoundly they reveal a growing awareness at different levels of European society that the 'problem' of religion has not been resolved in the way that many had assumed to be the case. Seen in this light, the accession of Turkey becomes, in fact, a trigger for a larger and unresolved debate concerning the identity of Europe. Should this or should this not include a religious dimension? And if so, how should this be expressed? The questions are perplexing in themselves; so also are the reasons for ignoring them for so long. Both are confronted in Byrnes and Katzenstein (2006). The final irony concerning the accession of Turkey lies in the French case. The nation on which the Turkish constitution is modelled becomes one of the nations most implacably opposed to Turkish entry. No one expressed this more forcibly than Giscard d'Estaing, the former French

**227**

President and architect of the European Constitution. For Giscard, Turkey's capital is not in Europe and 95 per cent of its population live outside Europe; it is not, therefore, a European country. It follows that those who persist in backing Turkey's accession are quite simply 'the adversaries of the European Union'.[23]

## NOTES

1 The debate centred on the Pope's refusal to condone the use of condoms in countries where the AIDS epidemic is widespread. All too often the argument was over-simplified – to the point of accusing John Paul II of causing the epidemic itself. The reality is infinitely more complex.

2 Not all scholars would agree with this reading of decline – indeed in many respects 1870 marks the high point of religious practice in both France and Britain. It is, however, the date associated with the loss of temporal power by the Vatican.

3 See the special issue of *Sociology of Religion* on 'Religion and globalization at the turn of the millennium', 62, 2001.

4 More information about the Anglican Communion is available on www. anglicancommunion.org. The background to the debate about homosexuality can be found on the same website (see 'The Listening Process' on www.anglicancommunion. org/listening/index.cfm). (Both sites were accessed on 21 April 2012). The debate is also covered in Jenkins (2002).

5 In May 2003, the appointment of Jeffrey John as Bishop of Reading was announced. In July of the same year, he was asked to step down given the controversy that this decision provoked.

6 See the sections of the Anglican Communion website devoted to the Lambeth Commission on Communion and its associated documents: www.anglicancommunion.org/commission/index.cfm (accessed 21 April 2012).

7 The history of mission is a fascinating and complex story. Its detractors are reluctant to acknowledge the enormous cost paid by those who went to the developing world. Not very many came home.

8 See Davie (2002a) for a further discussion of this point, especially Chapter 4.

9 I am indebted to Paul Freston for this information. See Freston (2008) for further information on the Brazilian diaspora in the United States.

10 Interesting collections of papers on this topic can be found in the special issues of *Social Compass*, 50/4, 2003, in Yang and Tamney (2005), and in Yang (2011).

11 See, for example, the authors brought together in Beyer (2001a).

12 The French contributions to this debate are interesting in themselves. The French frequently use their own term *mondialisation* rather than 'globalization' for their analyses. See Beckford (2003: 145).

13 Once again the use of this term is difficult. See the discussion in Lehmann (2002: 305).

14 At one stage, the literature on Pentecostalism was growing almost as fast as the communities themselves (Corten, 1997). This section draws on the longer discussion in Davie (2002a) and the bibliography contained therein. It also draws on the Pew Forum's (2006) *Pentecostal Resource Page*, which brings together a huge amount of data (including statistics) and other material. There is a burgeoning literature in

English (including some notable contributions from the Dutch), in French, and increasingly in Spanish (in a growing community of Latin American sociologists). A notable and interesting development is the literature about Pentecostalism by Pentecostals – in, for example, the work emanating from Fuller Seminary in California.

15 An account of this tension can be found in David Martin (2000).

16 Interestingly this is an area where different European scholars have addressed the debate in different ways, reflecting the themes articulated in Chapters 1 and 2 of this book. See Davie (2002a: 62–5) for a fuller discussion of this point.

17 The website of the World Council of Churches (www.oikoumene.org, accessed 21 April 2012) contains comprehensive information about the WCC, including a copy of its constitution. See also Davie (2006c).

18 The most obvious parallel can be found in the United Nations, an organization which – some 65 years after its inauguration – is coming under considerable strain. It too must adapt to changing circumstances.

19 Molokotos-Liederman (2003, 2007) provides a clear and sociologically informed account of this case.

20 See www.taize.fr (accessed 21 April 2012).

21 These are set out in the Preamble to the 1945 Constitution of the Republic of Indonesia.

22 Hefner (2004) admits that recent tensions have put the pluralist experiment under considerable strain; so too have the Bali bombings, a view echoed by Barton (2004). The latter offers a very accessible account of the different factions that make up Indonesian life – small shifts in the balance of power can have disproportionate effects.

23 These sentiments appeared in *Le Monde*. An English version can be found on http://news.bbc.co.uk/2/hi/europe/2420697.stm (accessed 21 April 2012).

# *eleven*

## religion and the everyday

This chapter introduces a very different perspective; it is concerned with the place of religion in the everyday lives of modern, primarily Western people. How, in other words, do such people relate to what they perceive as religious or spiritual and what difference does this make to their lives? These questions are, and always have been, central to the anthropological agenda. Until recently, however, sociologists had rather lost sight of them, assuming that modern people had not only other interests, but also other frameworks by which to orient their existence. Such is not always the case.

A consistent theme runs though the material: that is, a tendency towards 'de-differentiation' in the late-modern world, bearing in mind that this somewhat clumsy term questions many of the assumptions articulated so far, notably Casanova's firm assertion that '[T]he differentiation and emancipation of the secular spheres from religious institutions and norms remains a modern structural trend' (1994: 212). That idea was central to the discussion of secularization in Chapter 3, but it is not the only story. For a start, it was never complete, a fact already acknowledged (p. 50). Towards the end of the twentieth century, however, a whole series of factors came together to suggest that policies grounded on the notion of institutional separation, and taken for granted for much of the post-war period, might be re-examined. The provision of welfare will be taken as an example, drawing extensively on a comparative European project.

Health and healthcare are similar. Here, they will be accessed through a discussion of birth and death – frequently regarded, with some justification, as the most sacred moments of human existence. Are these moments to be defined solely in medical terms or do they still have a religious resonance? And to what extent are they conditioned by the environment in which they take place? Who, finally, is in control? Answers to these questions will be used to exemplify and to extend the discussion of modernity in Chapter 5. Firmly modernist answers about the beginning and end of life are progressively giving way to ever more searching questions, in an environment in which the institutional boundaries are less and less clear. De-differentiation, finally, is as much an individual as an institutional matter. The concept of 'well-being' – an idea already introduced in the paragraphs on holistic forms of religion – will be central to this discussion, in which body, mind *and* spirit all play their part.

The later sections of the chapter evoke similar questions, but they begin from a different perspective. The first of these concerns gender. References to the difference between men and women in terms of their religious lives have been scattered through this book. It is important to gather these together, recognizing that a topic that for several decades was largely ignored in the sub-discipline is now, quite rightly, demanding attention. Indeed the shift in the priorities of the discipline is as important as the topic itself. A similar shift has occurred with respect to age – one that opens a fresh range of possibilities concerning, amongst other things, religious change. Should this be considered in terms of the individual (the life-cycle) or in terms of society (generational shifts), or both? Either way, the discussion of age leads once again to the question of death and the rapidly increasing sociological activity that surrounds this. Death and the existential questions that it raises have, more than anything else, resisted the secular. Is there any reason why this should not still be the case in late modernity? Probably not.

*231*

## DIFFERENTIATION AND DE-DIFFERENTIATION: A RANGE OF ILLUSTRATIONS

### Welfare and Religion in a European Perspective (WREP)[1]

Significant sections of this book have been concerned with the differences between Europe and America, not least the existence of a state church in the former and its absence in the latter. A second point follows from this: in the United States, there is not only no state church, but to a considerable extent, no state in the sense that this is understood in Europe. For Europeans, moreover, the state is responsible for welfare, or so we have come to believe. The separating out of welfare as a distinct area of activity is central to the process of secularization in European societies and it is to the state that we look for support in time of need. That is much less the case in America. But even in Europe, the process takes place differently in different societies, leading to distinctive welfare regimes. Specialists in social policy will immediately recognize these differences and categorize them in various ways (Esping-Andersen, 1990).[2] For the sociologist of religion, however, one point is immediately clear: the patterns that emerge relate very closely to the differences observed by Martin in his work on secularization. Each, in fact, is the mirror of the other.

The material that follows reflects this theme and is drawn very largely from a comparative project on religion and welfare in eight European societies. It is used first to exemplify the different situations regarding these issues in different parts of Europe. In the Nordic countries, for example, the Lutheran churches embrace the doctrine of 'two kingdoms', which ascribes a particular role to the state in the organization of social welfare.[3] It follows that the ceding of welfare to the state was achieved relatively easily in this part of Europe. In France, in contrast, the process has been noticeably more acrimonious as the state claims for itself not only the functions of welfare, but the moral authority that once belonged to the Church. Hence a situation of conflict rather than co-operation, in which the boundary between church and state is firmly policed, in welfare as in so much else. Elsewhere in Catholic Europe, Catholic social teaching has been influential in a different way – this time through the concept of subsidiarity.[4] Welfare (as indeed all social policy) should be delivered at the lowest effective level of society, usually the family. Hence, historically, the heavy responsibilities of women as the traditional providers of welfare, supported by the churches rather than the state; the latter, in fact, fills the gaps left by the family and the church, not the other way round – the reverse of what happens in Northern Europe. Something rather similar can be found in Greece, bearing in mind that the Greek situation is framed by Orthodox rather than Catholic theology, bringing with it a noticeably different body of social teaching. Britain, finally, is *sui generis* in European terms; it relies far more than its continental neighbours on the voluntary sector, understanding 'voluntary' in every sense of the term.[5]

Hence the complexity of the situation: a similar goal (the separating out of welfare from the influence of the churches and the creation of an autonomous sphere with its own institutional norms) is achieved, or semi-achieved, in markedly different ways. One point is clear, however. European populations are of one mind in thinking that the state *should* take responsibility in this area. That finding emerges from all of the case studies in the WREP project. The fact that the churches are still doing much of the work is seen as a necessary feature of European life, but not 'how it should be'. The project's respondents are, nonetheless, realistic:[6] given that the situation is less than perfect, it is just as well that the churches are there, if only to fill the gaps. It follows that their contributions are welcomed rather than rejected even in societies where the welfare state is more rather than less developed.

Towards the end of the twentieth century, however, a number of factors have come together to question many of these assumptions. Some of these come from outside. European societies are as subject to the swings in the global economy as anyone else and from the 1970s on, almost all European nations experienced both a downturn in economic growth and a corresponding rise in unemployment – a situation which became acute following the 2008 financial crisis. Coincidentally, demographic profiles are altering, leading (as in all advanced economies) to an increase both in the numbers and in the proportion of elderly people. Taken together, these trends are beginning to undermine the assumptions on which European societies based their provision of welfare: not only with respect to the adequacy of the services themselves but, more radically, how these services will be financed. The question is simple: will the proportion of people active in the economy remain sufficient to support those who, for whatever reason, are not able to work? Add to this the marked prolongation of education that is part and parcel of a post-industrial economy and the implications are clear. No longer is it possible for most European societies to meet the obligation of welfare as these were understood in the immediate post-war period.

A noticeable change in political philosophy – a rowing back from the notion that the state is responsible for the provision of welfare from the cradle to the grave – is one reaction to these shifts. As ever, European societies have set about this in different ways, the most striking of which occurred in Britain in the 1980s. As we saw in Chapter 7, the Thatcher government not only instigated radical reforms, it developed an ideology to legitimate such changes. The debate, however, is not only ideological. If the state is no longer able, or even willing, to provide a comprehensive system of welfare for its citizens, who is to be responsible for this task? It is clear that the churches, amongst others, have a role to play in these changes.

Observations from the WREP project reveal an interesting theme: that the factors which were present when the initial differentiation of responsibilities took place are still in place as the new situation begins to emerge. Or to put the same point in a different way, the process of de-differentiation is as culturally specific as its predecessor. Hence the possibility of a relatively easy resumption of the welfare role on the part of the churches in some parts of Europe, and a much more difficult one in others. Three examples will suffice. In Italy or Greece, a very incomplete separation of powers in the first place has meant that the line between state and church remains essentially fluid. It can move back and forth as the situation demands. In France, in contrast, the secular state remains firmly in control, so much so that the researcher engaged on the

French case had difficulty persuading the public authorities to co-operate at all in a project that paid attention to religion. In Finland, finally, the very particular conditions of the recession in the early 1990s, as the Russian market collapsed, have led not only to a noticeable increase in the welfare roles undertaken by the churches but to a increase in their popularity as a result.

Considerably more could be said with respect both to this project and to its successor, which extended the work in two ways: first, to the minority religions of Europe, paying particular attention to the Muslim population; and second, to the selected countries in the formerly communist parts of Europe where the positions of state and church are necessarily different.[7] Both are central to the debates about inclusion and exclusion that are current in European life.

## health, healthcare and the visibility of the sacred in modern societies

Welfare, however, is not the only example of differentiation and de-differentiation. The same is true in health and healthcare, where the residues of history are equally present. Originally religious foundations – St Bartholomew's and St Thomas's in London, for example – have become in the twentieth century centres of cutting-edge medicine, funded primarily by state. The debate about health and healthcare will be approached, however, from a different perspective, taking as a starting point the moments of human existence when the sacred is at its most visible: birth and death. The understandings of modernity set out in Chapter 5 form a background to these discussions.

Childbirth was a dangerous process in pre-modern societies and remains so in much of the developing world. In Europe, the evidence can be found in almost every churchyard or parish register, which display in a strikingly visible form the fact that tens of thousands of young women lost their lives when giving birth to children.[8] So much so that preparation for birth for many women implied preparation for their own death. It was hardly surprising, therefore, that the process was surrounded as much by religious ritual as it was by medical knowledge. The religious rite commonly known as the 'Churching of Women' offers a poignant illustration of this fact, in which the giving of thanks for safe deliverance from 'the great pain and peril of Child-birth' is the dominant theme.[9] Safe deliverance could not be taken for granted. The development of modern medical techniques – notably the combination of antibiotics and safe surgery – has transformed this situation. Here, if nowhere else, can be seen the 'modern' solution: the application of scientific knowledge to a problem of human existence, and with great effect. In the West at least, the death of a mother in childbirth is now so rare as to be a deeply shocking event. This revolution in the lives of women is entirely welcome; few would relish a return to the sufferings of previous generations.

That is one version of the story. The second is more ambiguous and centres on the progressive loss of control on the part of the woman herself (or indeed women more generally), who complain that the experience of giving birth is little different from the assembly line found in a Fordist factory. Hence the reaction, the 'postmodern' response, in which women – mostly middle-class women, it must be said – regain their control, asking to give birth at home rather than in hospital, and insisting that both themselves and their babies be at the centre of the event, rather than the routines of the hospital or the requirements of the medical profession. Such re-appraisals have become an important body of literature in their own right in which comparative research plays an interesting role (Moscucci, 1990; Marland and Rafferty, 1997; Marland, 2004).

A searching set of questions lie beneath these shifts: how in late modernity should the moment of birth be understood and who or which agency is to decide? Is this a medical, administrative, moral or deeply personal – some would say sacred – event? Or all of these? Interestingly, exactly the same questions are revealed in the debates surrounding abortion in the United States.[10] No-one can deny the significance of this issue both for the American political class and for the various lobbies that put pressure on the decision-making process – not least the New Christian Right. Senior appointments (e.g. to the United States Supreme Court) are frequently reduced to this question.[11] Even more immediate from a sociological point of view is the gradual re-location of the abortion debate in American understanding, from an issue that was primarily one of justice for all women regardless of their socio-economic status (in the 1970s), to one that has become a central plank of the 'right to life' movement. That in turn reflects the changes which have taken place in American society as a whole. To an increasing extent, moral rather than socio-economic issues have come to dominate the agenda. Why is an interesting, and somewhat perplexing, question.

A further example of these shifts can be found in the sad story of Terri Schiavo – an episode that continued for more than a decade.[12] In February 1990, Schiavo suffered a cardiac arrest at the age of 26, which led to irreversible brain damage, following which she required constant care – first in a rehabilitation centre and then in a nursing home. In 1998, her

235

husband petitioned the courts for the first time, asking that the feeding tube be removed on the grounds that his wife was in a persistent vegetative state. The sequence of events that followed was both long and complex as different family members disagreed about what should or should not be done, as the case moved from court to court, and as senior political figures not only took an interest in the case but became actively involved. The decision-making process reached a climax in March 2005 (i.e. a full 15 years after the cardiac arrest) when the legal options open to Schiavo's parents to obstruct the process were finally exhausted; the feeding tube was removed for the third and last time – leading to her death a few days later.

So much for the case itself. Equally arresting is the extent to which it became a focal point of the media and a touchstone for political debate. In the later stages of the story, for example, the Bush Administration intervened repeatedly, not least in an attempt to change the federal court ruling by a 'private bill' applying to the Schiavo case. President Bush flew to Washington from Texas on Palm Sunday expressly to sign the bill. Church groups became equally involved, demanding that Schiavo be granted the 'right to life'. The vocabulary employed becomes increasingly emotive, reflecting the religious as well as moral aspects of the case. Churches held 'vigils' and Schiavo became a 'martyr' – themes picked up in the media and played and re-played on television. Boundaries were crossed and re-crossed repeatedly as political, religious and moral issues became increasingly intertwined, not to mention the evident confusions of the private and public sphere.

The whole episode, in fact, flies in the face of institutional separation, whether this is understood in terms of the separation of powers in the United States (bearing in mind that the attempts to overrule the court eventually failed), or more generally of the institutional specializations associated with modernization – themselves a central theme of the sociological canon. In assessing this material, moreover, one point needs very firm underlining. That is, to remember that the Schiavo case is simply an American, unusually public and very litigious version of a much larger issue: how late-modern societies come to terms with the difficult moral questions that are increasingly posed as medical techniques permit the continuation of physical life after the brain has ceased to function, or equally the sustaining of a premature baby in one room of a hospital while in another a late abortion is taking place. The cover of the issue of *Time* devoted to the Schiavo case says it all: 'The End of Life. Who decides?'[13] Who indeed? The question will be re-opened in the final section of this chapter.

236

## from welfare to well-being

So much for de-differentiation in terms of institutions – the same is true with respect to individuals. At this point, moreover, there is an obvious link with the material on the new age and self-spirituality introduced in Chapter 8, bearing in mind (following Heelas) that there are generational shifts in this field just as there are in mainstream religions (pp. 168–9). In the last of these generations (our own) can be found what Heelas terms the 'well-being spirituality' of modern consumer culture. Well-being becomes increasingly a lifestyle choice as people shop for the goods and services that they feel will be beneficial to body, mind *and* spirit. Health foods, beauty products, organic produce of all kinds, spa treatments, holidays, alternative remedies, self-help manuals, counsellors, classes and such like have become part of our everyday lives – easily available in either the well-stocked supermarket or book shop or their online equivalents. This is a rapidly expanding field. What might be termed the 'de-differentiation of the person' is part and parcel of these shifts. No longer is the emphasis on the separation of spheres, home and work, body and mind, mind and spirit and so on. The crucial point lies in the development of the *whole* person.

Hence the seeking of a healer rather than, or as well as, a medical practitioner. The insertion of 'as well as' is significant in this respect. Here, as elsewhere, boundaries are softening as increasing numbers of alternative practices are both recognized by the medical profession and paid for by private insurance. Healing, moreover, merges into therapy, undertaken in order that we may be more effective citizens or (more sharply) more effective capitalists – as our energies are directed towards economic as well as spiritual goals. What, in fact, is the difference in a world where the market invades the spiritual and the spiritual invades the market (Woodhead, 2012)? Spiritual goods can be bought and sold like any others. One point remains clear, however: women are considerably more involved in this enterprise than men (Heelas and Woodhead, 2004; Harvey and Vincett, 2012). In this respect at least, the search for well-being is very similar to more conventional forms of religious life – a point that must be examined in more detail.

*237*

## THE SIGNIFICANCE OF GENDER

One caveat is important before embarking on this discussion. What follows applies only to the Christian West, not to the other faith communities now present in both Europe and America, nor to the parts of the world dominated by different religious traditions. This is not to say that gender differences are not important for a proper understanding of these populations. They are. They take, however, significantly different forms, the understanding of which requires both theological and sociological insight that go beyond this chapter.

In terms of the Christian West, the difference between men and women with respect to their religious lives is one of the most pervasive findings in the literature. It is true of practice, of belief, of self-identification, of private prayer and so on, and can be found in almost every denomination – large or small, traditional or innovative, Catholic or Protestant. Early reviews of this literature can be found in Francis (1997) and Walter and Davie (1998); more recent summaries are contained in Woolever et al. (2006) and Trzebiatowska and Bruce (2012). All of these include extensive references to the available data. Indeed the significance of gender is a point on which almost every commentator agrees, whether their approach be quantitative (the hardest of hard statistics) or qualitative (the most impressionistic of religious sources). It is equally true for those forms of religion which appear on first reading to be hostile in many respects to the welfare of women. It was precisely this point, for example, that Bernice Martin was exploring with respect to the position of women in the Pentecostal communities of Latin America. It is also discovered in communities that would properly be described as 'fundamentalist'.

Two questions immediately present themselves: why is this so and – equally important – why was the question ignored for so long? For such it was, a fact that becomes increasingly difficult for students to grasp given the preoccupations of those currently engaged in the field. Here, in fact, is a timely and very positive example of the discipline catching up with reality. But why did it take so long? There are two rather different reasons for the delay: the first can be found in the churches themselves, the second in the limitations of sociology as a discipline. Within the churches – or more precisely within significant sections of the Protestant churches – a major debate about leadership took place in the second half of the twentieth century. Central to this debate was the possibility, or otherwise, that women should become ordained priests or ministers, assuming thereby the full responsibilities of leadership. The debate itself is interesting, but is not the primary point in this chapter.[14] This lies in the fact that a strong focus on leadership led to a relative lack of attention regarding the place of women in the pews of not only the Protestant churches themselves but of the much larger Catholic constituency which (like the Orthodox) remains immune to the possibility of change regarding the priesthood.

Only gradually did the pendulum begin to swing revealing disproportionate numbers of women among the faithful in practically all Christian churches in the West, not only now but in the past. Historians just as much as sociologists began to adjust their spectacles.

The second reason for the delay can be found in the point already noted in Bernice Martin's discussion of Pentecostalism. Here the responsibility lies squarely in the theoretical frameworks of the discipline, notably the concept of patriarchy. More precisely, on some readings of the sociological agenda, women of all people should be leaving the churches, given that it is the teaching of these 'patriarchal' institutions that has not only disadvantaged the women who have remained within the fold, but – much more insidiously – has legitimated their subordination throughout society. Women even more than men, it follows, should be anxious to jump ship. Awkwardly for the protagonists of these theories, the data suggested something different – that the women might be leaving but the men were leaving faster still. Not only was there a persistent gender imbalance in the Christian churches, it was getting larger rather than smaller (Brierley, 1991). In the short term, however, it was easier to ignore the topic than to rethink the theories that would be immediately vulnerable if the issue was tackled head on.

Happily the data triumphed. So much so that the number of articles addressing the question of *why* women are or appear to be more religious than men grows year on year – articles which engage the issue in a variety of ways. A relatively early marshalling of these explanations can be found in Walter and Davie (1998). Essentially these can be divided into two groups: those that explain the differences between the religious behaviour of men and women in terms of 'nature' and those that favour explanations based on 'nurture'; that is, on the different roles that men and women perform in society and, it follows, the different patterns of socialization associated with these roles. Is it the case, in other words, that women are more religious than men because of what they are, or because of what they do?

Important implications follow. They can be found first in the possibility that women are, or think themselves, to be more vulnerable than men – whether economically, socially or physically. Religion, it follows, is a compensator, an answer to a problem that in some respects at least is specific to women. The logic of the argument demands, however, a supplementary question. Is the position of women changing in modern societies and in ways that overcome these difficulties or do they – despite everything – endure? One aspect of this debate is frequently referenced in the literature (De Vaus, 1984; De Vaus and McAllister, 1987; Becker and Hofmeister, 2001) and concerns the increasing tendency for women to participate in the labour force on an equal footing with men, a fact that not only reduces their economic dependence but at the same time distracts women from their domestic responsibilities – and within this, their primary role as the bearers and carers of children. It is the latter tasks, moreover, that are most closely associated with stronger indices of religious activity. They also relate to vulnerability in a much more physical sense, a discussion which draws directly on the material on childbirth set out in the previous section. Women – for most of human history – were acutely vulnerable every time that they gave birth, a situation that has transformed only very recently. Hence the complexities of the issues. A whole series of *interrelated* factors need to be kept in mind in assessing the religiousness of women: their distinctive role in childbearing, the ways in which this has changed in recent decades, new opportunities in the labour force and the re-ordering of women's lives in consequence – not to mention the families of which they are part.

Broadly speaking, two ways of thinking emerge in the sociological responses to these questions. The first argues that the roles of women have changed very significantly in the twentieth century, leading to a corresponding reduction in their need for religion – a conclusion favoured very largely by secularization theorists. Callum Brown (2000) exemplifies this point of view. Brown, in fact, rests his entire account of *The Death of Christian Britain* on the transformation of gender roles that took place in the 1960s. Not only have women ceased to be noticeably more religious than men, they have ceased dramatically to fulfil their traditional function of handing on the faith to the next generation – hence, from the point of view of the churches, the extreme seriousness of this situation. There are others, however, who take a different view, arguing that something much more profound is at stake in the religiousness of men and women than has been indicated so far. A differential need for religion is embedded in the nature and personalities of male and female and is, therefore, unlikely to change in the foreseeable future, if at all. Interestingly, the rational choice theorists are at least hinting that this might be the case in so far as they rest their argument on the fact that women are more risk averse than men (Miller and Stark, 2002; Stark, 2002). It is the risk-taking aptitudes of men that permit them, relatively speaking, to live without religion – or, in terms of RCT, to make different 'rational' choices.

It is unwise, in my view, to dichotomize these choices: this is a both/ and rather than an either/or situation. Societies, moreover, continue to evolve. It is true that childbearing has become not only safer but more efficient in the Western world: relatively few years are now spent in pregnancy and childrearing, leaving more time for employment within a life-span that is getting longer rather than shorter. But precisely this (a marked increase in longevity) is creating new burdens for women as they become, or more accurately remain, the primary carers of elderly people, whether in the home or in an institution (a major finding of the WREP study). It echoes, in fact, a point made by Walter and Davie (1998: 654) at an earlier stage: namely that it is important to look at the *nature* of women's employment as well as the fact that increasing numbers of women are now engaged in the labour force. One very obvious example can be found in the disproportionate numbers of women in the relatively low-paid service sector, in which the care of the very young and the very old remains a noticeable and persistent feature.

With this in mind, a number of ideas that have been introduced in this chapter can be brought together. The first reflects the presence of women in the caring professions, however these are organized. The second concerns the continuing visibility of the sacred in modern societies, noting in particular the difficult decisions that relate to the beginning and end of life. The third reflects the marked differences between men and women in terms of their religious lives, whether the forms of religion are traditional or rather less so. Hence a somewhat tentative conclusion: is it possible that these factors are related to each other? Might it be the case, in other words, that one reason for the disproportionate religiousness of men and women lies in the fact that women are closer, both physically and emotionally, to the sacred than men – in so far as the sacred is exposed in late modernity, just as it was in earlier forms of society, at the most critical moments of the life-cycle: birth and death?

It is hard to dispute that this is so in terms of the former – it is, after all, women who give birth. Here the argument stands or falls on the capacities of modern medicine to eliminate the sacred in what might be termed the progressive 'routinization' of childbirth. This elimination is, at best, partial; indeed the non-medical nature of childbirth, if not the sacred as such, is being steadily reclaimed in late modern, de-differentiated societies.[15] In terms of death, the situation is a little different and will be discussed in more detail in the final paragraphs of this chapter. At this stage it is sufficient to note that the medicalization of death is as much part of the modernization process as the medicalization of birth, but it is still the case that those who care for, and sit with, the dying are more likely to be women than men, even if they are paid to do this – a situation reinforced by the fact that women live longer than men, a consequence in itself of the transformation in childbirth already described. These factors become cumulative.

One further contribution to the literature on gender is worth noting before closing this discussion. It can be found in Woodhead's short but very careful analyses of the contrasting ways in which different groups of women engage with religion in different parts of the world (Woodhead, 2000, 2001). Rejecting the possibility that religion is necessarily a 'good' or a 'bad' thing for women, Woodhead emphasizes the fact that women, just like men, are very diverse, as indeed are the societies of which they are part. With this in mind, she looks first at the societies of the modern West, noting in particular the distinction between the private and the public sphere. Broadly speaking, women who remain in the private sphere (in the home) find it easier to affirm their religiousness than those who straddle both public and private. Such a conclusion echoes the labour-force argument cited above, but is, possibly, less persuasive in late or postmodern societies than it was in the mid-post-war decades, in so far as these are societies in which de-differentiation is increasingly present. This is certainly true in terms of the labour market. It may also be true in terms of religion. Here Woodhead's argument quite clearly reflects the dominant theme of this chapter; it also evokes the emphasis on holistic spirituality found in the Kendal project (bearing in mind that the project postdates the chapters on 'Women and religion'). Interestingly, it is older women who are disproportionately found in the 'spiritual' domain, just as they are in more traditional forms of religion.

242

In the less developed parts of the world, following Woodhead, the process of differentiation is, and always has been, less marked. Here women have found both in religious teaching and in religious organizations a space to develop their talents, in public as well as in private life. Religion becomes a resource, a way forward – a way to curb the excesses of their menfolk, and to develop the habits that are necessary for stability or even modest improvement in parts of the world where welfare in any developed sense is lacking (an argument that draws on the work of both David and Bernice Martin). Hence Woodhead's conclusion: no one should doubt the importance of gender to the sociological study of religion. Nor, as both Woodhead and Bernice Martin affirm, is it enough for sociology simply to take note of the differences between men and women in terms of religion and to embed these distinctions into existing bodies of theory. The theories as such must evolve in order to include the many, varied and subtle ways in which men and women, themselves very diverse, both shape and are shaped by the religious dimensions of the societies of which they are part. The chapters brought together by Aune et al. (2008) constitute an excellent starting point for this discussion.

## AGE AND THE LIFE-CYCLE

The reluctance of sociologists to engage the question of gender in relation to religion has been discussed in some detail. The question of age is
rather different, given that the inclusion of 'age' as a sociological category came relatively late into almost every aspect of the discipline. This
was a shift driven by the demographic changes that were taking place in
industrial societies in the late twentieth century and their likely impact
on existing societal structures. The issue has already been addressed in
relation to welfare.

Once 'age' is included in the analyses of religious data, however, distinctive and in many ways predictable patterns begin to emerge (Davie
and Vincent, 1999; Davie, 2000a). Older people are more religious
than the young on all the conventional indicators, a fact that interacts
with the differences in gender already observed to produce a preponderance of older women in almost every denomination or congregation
both in Europe and the United States. In this sense the analyses of social
science simply reinforce a stereotype – one, moreover, which is frequently regarded as a 'problem'. So much so that institutions which
perform admirably on important indices of inclusion or widening participation are regarded as failures in many Western societies.

How, though, should these marked differences in age be understood? **243**
Once again there are two possibilities: on the one hand, there are explanations that relate to the life-cycle, and on the other, there are those that
reflect the notion of the generation or cohort. The first is straightforward enough: it rests on the premise that the closer an individual comes
to death, the greater the concern with matters of mortality and therefore
with the issues that, in most societies, come under the rubric of religion.
The second is rather different and underlines the markedly different
outlooks of the age-cohorts or generations which are found in any society. In Europe, an obvious example can be found in the generations born
before or after the Second World War. More recently, the epithets 'baby
boomers' and 'generations X and Y' pervade both popular parlance and
social science, not to mention the more economically driven world of
marketing.

Generations, moreover, are as different in their religious lives as they
are in everything else – an argument that lies at the heart of Callum
Brown's analysis (see above). His work is very largely based on the *generation* of women that came of age in the 1960s and their reluctance to
engage with religion in the same way as their mothers or grandmothers.
If Brown is right, the present preponderance of older women in the

churches will be a temporary rather than permanent feature. The present 'cohort' is unlikely to be replaced.

This, however, is not the whole story. Quite apart from the generational shifts and life-cycle changes, there is a third factor to take into account: an awareness that the life-cycle itself is changing and in ways that have important implications for religion. Three of these will be dealt with here, in a discussion that builds on to the material presented in *Religion in Modern Europe* (Davie, 2000a).[16] The first concerns the sharp decline in infant mortality that has taken place in all modern societies; the second engages the notion of adolescence and its marked prolongation in late modernity; and the third opens the discussion of old age itself and the ways in which this is understood by modern people – in so doing it forms a bridge to the final section of this chapter. These are not exhaustive discussions; they should be seen rather as indicative of the questions that need to be asked, and in many respects of the sociological work that needs to be done, in this clearly expanding field.

The decline in infant mortality is an index of modernization in itself. As such it is closely related to the transformation of childbirth already discussed – the evidence from churchyards or parish registers is equally persuasive in either case. The particular combinations of improved economic conditions and medical advance that brought these changes about are crucially important in historical terms. They lie, however, beyond the scope of this chapter, which will focus on a specific but very revealing issue: that is, the implications of these changes for the understanding of baptism – the rite of passage associated in almost all of Europe with the birth of a new child. Indeed for many centuries, Europe's historic churches were effectively the registrars of birth and death. This is no longer so – a change brought about for many different reasons. Among them can be found the following: first, the process of institutional separation that has produced a professional class trained to deal with the registration of citizens at various points in their lives; second, the mutation in the religious life of European societies described in Chapter 7 (best described as a shift from contracting-out to contracting-in); and third, a marked change in the 'status' of the newborn child (an infant who is almost certain to live to maturity is less in need of divine blessing in either the short or the longer term). Taken together, these factors have transformed the rite of baptism in the course of twentieth century – a point with considerable implications for both sociological and theological study, not least for comparative work.

It is here, in fact, that many of the themes of the previous chapters converge, both methodological and substantive. In terms of the former, for example, it is simply not possible to compare baptism figures across time (more precisely across different generations) without an awareness that you might not be comparing like with like – a point underlined by Bernice Martin in her trenchant critique of social scientific methodology (Martin, 2003).[17] Here too can be found the 'angle of eschatological tension' evoked by David Martin in his discussion of the relationship between sociology and theology (p. 132). Liturgies alter to fit new situations; theologies follow suit. But here, thirdly, can be found noticeable and persistent differences between neighbouring European societies: the Church of England, for example, has seen a dramatic decline in its figures for baptism; so too has its Catholic equivalent in France;[18] not so the Lutheran churches of Northern Europe. The rates of baptism in the Nordic churches remain extraordinarily high *for specifically Nordic reasons* – exactly the same reasons, in fact, that encourage Nordic people to pay substantial amounts of tax to their churches despite the fact that they rarely attend. Membership of the national church, denoted by baptism, remains despite everything a central plank of Nordic identity.

Relatively speaking, this is also the case with confirmation, a rite traditionally associated with adolescence. But adolescence itself has changed. No longer is it a relatively brief period of transition between childhood and becoming an adult, marked for a man by getting a job and for a women by a move from her father's household to that of her husband. It has become instead a prolonged period for both men and women, associated (at least for some) with an extended period of education, a somewhat piecemeal entry into the labour market, and a marked tendency to delay marriage and childbearing until a much later stage (chronologically speaking). Almost everything, in fact, is different, including attitudes to religion. What at one stage was a brief and somewhat rebellious transition is now almost a way of life. At this point, however, it is important to recall the recent findings of the European Values Study (pp. 99–100). It is true that younger generations are less religious than the old in terms of the more conventional religious indicators. Conversely, today's adolescents are those most likely to experiment with new forms of religion – this, in other words, is the generation most attracted to the idea of an immanent God (a God in me) and to the conviction that there is some sort of 'life after death'. As we have seen, this is most evident in the parts of Europe where the historic churches are relatively weak: that is, when conventional forms of religious transmission are much less likely to take place (Fulton et al., 2000).[19]

Whatever the case, the notion of 'life after death' is somewhat remote for today's adolescents, given the increase in longevity in the developed world – a fact of considerable significance for the churches. The issues, moreover, can be looked at from a variety of perspectives. The first is entirely positive: religious organizations cope well with older people and are expected to do so (a conclusion firmly endorsed by the WREP study and likely to continue for the foreseeable, if not indefinite, future). Indeed for significant sections of the elderly population – most notably women and those who live in rural areas – the churches constitute the *only* effective network. Rather more complex, however, are the implications of ageing for the economic lives of religious institutions. They, just like their secular counterparts, are financially stretched by the need to pay pensions for an extended period, a point discussed in Davie (2000a). Once again different situations are revealed in different countries – financial arrangements, including pension schemes, become a sensitive indicator of the place of the church in any given society. Financial strain, however, lies behind the increasing use of volunteers in many, if not all, European societies – bearing in mind that volunteers are themselves a mutating species. No longer primarily married women, they have become instead an army of 'early retired'.

It is in this context, finally, that we should place the bodies of empirical material that relate to religion and the elderly, in all senses of the term. Two ways of working come particularly to mind. First, there is a series of studies that seek to establish a link between religious activity (variously defined) and longer living (see, for example, Levin, 1994 and Koenig et al., 1996). The links may be direct or indirect – in the sense that religious commitment (prayer, Bible reading, fellowship and so on) may be good in themselves, but at the same time they encourage lifestyles that are conducive to good health.[20] The second group of studies is exemplified in the excellent work undertaken by Williams (1990) in Aberdeen. Now some 20 years old, this has become a classic in the literature. Williams considers a generation of Aberdonians brought up in a strongly Protestant tradition, examining the link between personal biography, including its religious elements, and the ways in which his subjects deal with illness and death. Three things become clear in this study: first, that this is a 'generation' unlikely to be repeated; second, the Protestant tradition is but one element in the overall picture – work and wealth are equally significant; and third, that this tradition is more significant for some of Williams's respondents than it is for others. Indeed the picture that emerges is both subtle and complex: not only do the respondents in this painstaking enquiry have very different understandings of what it means to be religious, they make use of the resources that religion offers them in contrasting ways.

## DEATH AND THE STUDY OF DEATH

In September 2005, the University of Bath established a Centre for Death and Society in its Department of Social and Policy Sciences.[21] The Centre has four aims: to further social, policy and health research; to provide education and training for academics and practitioners; to enhance social policy understanding; and to encourage community development. Here, in other words, is a Centre firmly committed to interdisciplinarity (de-differentiation) not only in relation to the academic work carried out in this field, but to the practical applications of this. De-differentiation, moreover, was well exemplified in the conference that inaugurated the new venture.[22]

An obvious example can be found in the plenary session of the conference devoted to the hospice movement (Hartley, 2005). The story itself is well known: the hospice movement grew out of a dissatisfaction with medical provision, where in the early post-war period dying was seen more as a failure of modern medical techniques than as the natural end of life. Interestingly, the early promoters of the movement were almost all women (notably Cicely Saunders and Elizabeth Kubler-Ross). Hartley's plenary address, however, underlines not so much the early history of hospice care as the renewed emphasis on partnership with the National Health Service – increasingly the care of the dying is being taken back into the mainstream. This is interesting in two respects: first, that institutional separations (of whatever kind) reflect a particular stage in a process – they are not necessarily the final goal; and second, that initiatives which begin by splitting off from the mainstream can in the course of time return, bringing with them new-found skills and insights. In terms of the hospice movement, one such insight is clearly the importance of caring for the dying person, not simply the alleviation of symptoms. Such care is multi-faceted and includes body, mind and spirit, bearing in mind that the latter may present in a wide variety of forms.

The creation of an interdisciplinary and specialist Centre for Death and Society marks in a very visible way the emergence of a new sub-discipline, one which brings together the contributions of scholars from many different fields: medicine, history, sociology, psychology, social policy, counselling, religious studies and so on (the full list would be a long one). But quite apart from this very welcome collaborative activity, there has been a noticeable revival of *sociological* interest in 'death, dying and disposal' over the last two decades, a period in which the subject itself has re-emerged into public consciousness.[23] This re-emergence is, in fact, part of the story, which has caught the attention of main-stream sociologists as much as those interested in religion – notably those who engage with the nature of modernity (Bauman, 1989; Giddens, 1991). In this necessarily selective account, two themes exemplify the implications for religion: first, the reflections of Walter concerning the pre-modern, modern and postmodern ways of death; and second, the evidence that the study of death brings to the vexed question of secularization. Both ideas resonate strongly with the broader themes of this book.

Walter's seminal work in this field (1990, 1994 and 1995) relates directly to the discussion of modernity in Chapter 5. In *The Revival of Death*, for example, Walter traces the evolution of death and death prac-tices in different societal forms, noting in each case the key authority that deals with these questions and the body of knowledge that frames the discourse. In pre-modern societies, authority lay with the church (sometimes one, sometimes more than one), whose personnel supported their claims by reference to religious texts. In modern societies, there is a marked shift towards the medical or scientific, both organizationally and in terms of discourse. The medical and scientific, however, have repeatedly been called into question – a by now familiar point. Increas-ingly they are seen as a necessary and in many ways beneficial aspect of modern societies, but not a *sufficient* one – particularly when it comes to the difficult moral questions surrounding the beginning and end of life. As Walter argues, the only authority that counts in these circum-stances is the self, who must decide how he or she wishes to die and the particular nature of the support required. That, however, is a lonely position, the more so in societies in which the body and its maintenance have become ever more important notions. Hence the huge variety of practices and personnel that have emerged in the Western world to engage these issues.

Are these changes evidence of secularization or are they not? It is true that the Christian churches have lost their monopoly of death and death practices in most Western societies? They remain, however, key players – not least for the sections in the population who rarely attend them. To withdraw the services of the church at the moment of death would cause considerable offence to the great majority of European citizens. For some, it is true, a secular funeral has become an attractive option, though not yet for that many (uptake is limited, though more likely to grow than to recede). A much more popular solution lies in the gradual evolution of the religious ceremony, which increasingly contains ele-ments that are specific to the individual who has died but which lie outside the religious tradition that takes responsibility for the ceremony.

Once again an excellent example can be found in the ceremonies that took place following the death of Princess Diana, a point of reference for funerals in the following decade.

Hence the connection between this chapter and the notion of vicarious religion (pp. 143–6) in which the reactions of a society to collective or unexpected deaths played an important role. Such reactions support an increasingly evident fact: namely that there are effectively two economies in the traditional churches of modern Europe. The first of these concerns birth and baptism and is changing moderately fast, though more in some places than in others; here is the model of choice. The second relates to death and the role of the churches within this, which is noticeably more resilient; it reflects the persistence of vicarious religion. An informed discussion of the secularization process must take both, and the inevitable tensions between then, firmly into account. Such is not always the case.

## NOTES

1 Details of the Welfare and Religion in a European Perspective project can be found at www.crs.uu.se/Research/Former_projects/WREP/?languageId=1 (accessed 23 April 2012). See also Bäckström and Davie (2010), Bäckström et al. (2011) and Davie (2012). This is a European story. There is not space in this chapter to develop the American equivalent; it is admirably told in Cnaan (2002).

2 Rather more recently, scholars have come to realize that religion, in both its form and content, is an independent variable in this process. Manow (2004), for example, both examines and refines Esping-Andersen's typology.

3 To all intents and purposes the Lutheran Church became itself a department of state – a public utility financed through the tax system.

4 Multiple definitions of subsidiarity exist, all of which articulate the key principle, i.e. that in the European Union decisions of all kinds should be taken as closely as possible to the citizen. The term as such finds it origins in Catholic social teaching.

5 'Voluntary' can be understood in two ways: as the voluntary (non-state) sector of the economy, and as voluntary (unpaid) work.

6 These were divided into three categories: those working for the churches; those working for the local authority or equivalent; and representatives of the general public.

7 WREP's successor is known as WaVE (Welfare and Values in Europe); the project was financed though the Framework 6 Programme of the European Commission. See www.crs.uu.se/Research/Former_projects/WaVE/ (accessed 23 April 2012).

8 Equally pertinent is the ambiguous presence of the step-mother in popular culture as the bereaved father re-married, often to provide a mother for his children. An historically informed account of this state of affairs, the numbers of deaths that occurred and the attempts to escape from it can be found in Loudon (1992, 2000).

9 See also its alternative title: 'The Thanksgiving of Women after Child-birth'. The text can be found in the 1662 *Book of Common Prayer* and in almost all

subsequent revisions. There are, of course, alternative readings of this rite – those which relate to the need for 'purification' after childbirth. Hence the negative response of many feminists both to the rite itself and to what it signifies.

10 The section that follows owes a great deal to the knowledge and perceptions of an outstanding graduate class that I taught at Hartford Seminary in June 2005.

11 An excellent example can be found in the debates surrounding the nominations of John Roberts, Harriet Miers and Sam Alito to the Supreme Court in 2005. Miers subsequently withdrew; despite the support of President Bush, her views on the abortion question failed to satisfy the pro-life enthusiasts.

12 See http://en.wikipedia.org/wiki/Terri_Schiavo (accessed 23 April 2012) for the various stages in this extremely complex case.

13 See *Time*, 4 April 2005, 165/14.

14 A clear account can be found in Dowell and Williams (1994).

15 It is important to remember that this is *not* a return to conventional religiousness; it is rather a moving on from the modernist position.

16 Especially Chapter 4.

17 A point of view challenged in turn by David Voas in his painstaking work on religious demography (see Voas, 2003a and 2003b).

18 Figures for baptism in the Church of England can be found on www.churchofengland.org/about-us/facts-stats/research-statistics.aspx (accessed 23 April 2012).

19 Having said that, a recent study of young people in Britain found that 'Generation Y' (i.e. those born since 1982) were very largely indifferent to religion (Savage et al., 2006). In a substantial edited text, Collins-Mayo and Dandelion (2010) bring together a large amount of information concerning religion and youth.

20 See also the work of psychogerontologist Peter Coleman (2011).

21 See www.bath.ac.uk/cdas/ (accessed 23 April 2012) for details of the Centre. The journal *Mortality* is closely associated with this venture.

22 See in addition the contents page of any issue of *Mortality*.

23 The press attention to the establishment of the new Centre was evidence in itself of this interest.

# *twelve*

## conclusion: revisiting the agenda

The primary task of this relatively short conclusion is to revisit the central question set out at the beginning of this book: namely the noticeably imperfect relationship between the debates that pervade the sociology of religion and the realities of religious life in the modern world. The question, moreover, is closely related to a series of crosscutting themes that have emerged in the preceding chapters. Two examples will be taken as starting point for this discussion: the ever-increasing mobilities of the modern world and the ongoing tensions between mainstream and margins in the religious field. They are closely interrelated.

The second section approaches similar issues, but from a different angle – the shifts within sociology itself. Particular attention will be given to what has become known as the 'cultural turn'. To what extent does this disciplinary adjustment assist the study of religion and where, conversely, are the pitfalls? Where, secondly, are the parallel fields in sociology and what can be learnt from these? The final paragraphs of this section recall the cognate disciplines set out at the end of Chapter 6. Not only can sociologists of religion learn from related fields in the discipline, they can also contribute to broader social scientific debates.

Two examples bring the chapter to a close. The first takes a further look at the vexed issue of homosexuality in the Anglican Communion – a discussion in which the 'truth' is claimed by many people. What can a sociologist bring to this debate and how might this contribute if not to a solution, then at least to a better understanding of the issues? The second relates to the Danish 'cartoons', a particularly vehement episode which burst on to the international scene when the first edition of this book was in its final stages. Both have been chosen to ground in reality – sometimes a very painful reality – the themes set out in the previous chapters.

### THEORY AND DATA: AN UNEASY RELATIONSHIP

Mobilities of all kinds pose new and complex questions for every aspect of sociology as the movement of people, together with the flows of capital, goods and ideas, becomes an increasingly pervasive feature of late-modern capitalism. Religion, or more accurately religions, are part and parcel of these movements, and in a myriad of different ways. Religions can encourage or discourage movement; they can push and pull; they can transcend boundaries or impose them; they can welcome or reject. Religions that are majorities on one side of the world become minorities on the other, and vice versa. Those that were recipients of missionary endeavour become missionaries themselves; the marginalized move centre stage. Predictions, finally, are overturned – the unexpected can and does happen: in Iran in 1979, in the Soviet Union in 1989, in the United States in 2001 and so on.

These constantly changing scenarios have been documented in some detail in the preceding chapters; they form a major part of the agenda relating to religion in the modern world. How then has the sociology of religion responded? Unevenly is the honest answer. In one sense, sociologists of religion have been attracted by these changes, frequently paying more attention to minorities than to majorities. On the whole, the exotic (whether at home or abroad) is more interesting than the everyday. There are many more books written about Muslims in Europe than there are about the mainstream churches, and events on the other side of the world frequently take precedence over those at home. Conversely – and herein lies the paradox – the theories of the sub-discipline remain relatively fixed. So much so that, in some cases at least, they have inhibited rather than enabled the imaginative response that is so evidently required.

Such a statement requires elaboration. The early sections of this book looked at three bodies of theory: those that relate to secularization, those that draw from rational choice, and those that seek a better understanding of both the notion and nature of modernity. Considerable attention was paid to the genesis of these theories in terms of place as well as to the argument as such. There is no need to go over this material again except to note that both the advocates of secularization and those of rational choice theory have considerable justification for their ways of working in the parts of the world in which these theories first emerged; the problems arise when the ideas are applied elsewhere – and the more indiscriminate the application, the worse the problem gets. To some extent, the work on modernity is similar: modernity (in the singular) works well in the West. This is unsurprising in so far as modernity in this sense expresses the self-understanding of Western societies (philosophical as well as sociological). Once again, it is the application of the concept elsewhere that causes the difficulty – a way of working which leads very quickly to the conclusion that any society or group of societies that does not conform to the patterns of Western modernity is in some sense less than modern.

The 'problem', moreover, is compounded in so far as Western modernity (at least in its European forms) includes as one of its attributes a degree of secularization – a fact that brings at least two of these bodies of theory into alignment. Or, rather more negatively, the prejudices of one type of theorizing at times reinforce those of the other. But whichever way round the question is put, it goes straight to the heart of the matter: *is secularization intrinsic or extrinsic to the modernization process?* The question itself is important – the fact that it is being asked at all is a consequence of the ever more obvious presence of religion in the modern (twenty-first century) world. It provokes, however, very different answers. There are those, like myself, who feel increasingly that secularization is *extrinsic* to the modernization process. It is possible, and indeed entirely 'normal', to be both fully modern and fully religious – hence the need for paradigms that take this into account. There are others who maintain that the present state of affairs is simply transitional. In the fullness of time (how long isn't easy to say), to be modern will necessarily mean to be secular. The fact that relatively few parts of the globe have achieved this status does not detract from the *intrinsic* and therefore necessary connection between the two ideas. This is more than a semantic debate; it represents a fundamental difference in approach to the sociological agenda. Who, then, is setting this agenda and for whom? It is important to spell out the issues in more detail.

**253**

One point of departure can be found in the final chapter of *Europe: the Exceptional Case* (Davie, 2002a), in which I explored these differences using the notion of conceptual maps. Secularization theory, in these terms, is a conceptual map helpful for exploring European issues; it is, if you like, an excellent aid for climbing the Alps. It is much less appropriate for trips to the Rockies – where rational choice theory (another conceptual map) is likely to come into its own. Neither are much help when it comes to the Andes where, it is clear, the application of the 'wrong' map is not only misleading but positively dangerous – the investigator fails to see the most obvious features of the landscape. David Martin's anecdote about Guatemala illustrates the point perfectly:

> The power of the ruling paradigms came home to me most forcibly on a bus full of Western academics in Guatemala. When told that 66 percent of the population was Catholic they asked no questions about where the rest might be, even though the answer shouted at them from texts on huts in remote El Petén, storehouse churches called 'Prince of Peace', and buses announcing 'Jesus is coming'. (Martin, 2000: 27)

I have a feeling that the same story – with suitably adjusted content – could be told many times over, a problem that will remain as long as sociologists of religion retain a certain rigidity in their theorizing when the data are multiplying at an exponential rate.

I do not want to give a negative impression. There is an enormous amount of excellent work being done, and in some areas of the sociology of religion huge efforts have been made to bring theory and data into a new and more positive alignment. The work on globalization is a case in point – religion came late to the understanding of globalization, but it is now coming very fast (see Chapter 10). Equally important are the attempts to understand the Muslim world. The same, eventually, has been true of gender – a point discussed in Chapter 11. What emerges, in fact, is a kind of leapfrog. Just as the thinking catches up, the subject matter moves again – ever faster as the events of the modern world reveal aspects of religion that the founding fathers, let alone their successors, never thought of. Nor could they have done given the parameters of the European context. Hence the crucially important element in any successful theorizing: that is, to build into the model itself the possibility that things may change, and in unexpected directions. Change must be integral to thinking, not an optional extra.

It is for these reasons that I am attracted to the notion of modernities being multiple. Not only does this build diversity into the theory from the outset, it incorporates an understanding of 'modernity' itself as a process rather than an object. One such process can be found not only in the mobilities of the modern world themselves, but in the complex interactions that take place when both individuals and groups transplant their cultures to new and very different situations. A whole series of factors need to be taken into account in these continually evolving relationships, including the fact that some people can move more easily than others, and some – quite definitely – cannot move at all. The organization of an international conference or workshop in order to explore these questions further will immediately reveal the difficulties: some delegates will be able to come and some will not, prevented either by finance (specifically by non-convertible currencies) or by ever more stringent visa regulations. And if this is true for an academic meeting, how much more does it apply to 'real life'?

A second point is equally clear. One person's mainstream is indeed another person's margin and, frequently, remains so in the place of destination. Physical proximity does not lead to equality of treatment despite, in many cases, constitutional stipulation and institutional provision. Exactly how these relationships work out in practice, and who will influence whom in the longer term, is an empirical rather than theoretical question, within which the norms, history and institutions of the host society play a crucial role. Religious minorities in the United States have a different experience from religious minorities in Europe, and even within Europe the variations continue – the European Union notwithstanding. Muslims who arrive in Britain, France, Germany and the Netherlands will all too often remain on the margins of all these societies. So much is clear. Less clear, very often, is the fact that the margin will be constructed in different ways. In Britain, for example, a 'group' existence has been possible, in France it has not. And in the Netherlands, to the dismay of the host population, the mentalities of pillarization not only endure but have been taken up by the Muslim community itself. How could it, in fact, be otherwise?

## THE RESOURCES OF THE MAINSTREAM: THE CULTURAL TURN

For too long, the sociology of religion has been both insulated and isolated from the parent discipline – that point has been made more than once. But assuming that there is, increasingly, the will to overcome such separation, what resources might be available in the parent discipline to facilitate this task? One possibility in particular will be developed in this section: the notion of the 'cultural turn' and its implications for the study of religion.

**255**

The cultural turn has generated a huge literature in the social sciences, most of which lies beyond the scope of this chapter.[1] Its essence, however, is relatively simple: sociologists who support this approach will place 'meaning-making processes' (of which religion is a classic example) at the centre of sociological understanding and will analyse these processes on their own terms. The phrase 'on their own' terms is crucial – here, definitively, is an escape from reductionism, in which religion is 'really something else'. The stress on culture and its independent and free-standing existence allows ample space for religious ideas and religious motivations. Both can be explored in two ways. First, culture can be seen as constitutive of social relations and identities as such; and second, culture can be examined in so far as it influences the social relations and identities of any given society.

Examples of both abound. Some of these were brought together in the sessions devoted to 'the cultural turn' at the 2003 meeting of the Association for the Sociology of Religion held in Atlanta – they have subsequently been published in a special issue of the *Sociology of Religion*.

The first two have already been referenced in Chapter 2, not least Martin's essay on 'The Christian, the political and the academic' – a piece of sociological writing that draws directly on Weber (pp. 42–3). The opening sentence of this essay makes the link with the cultural turn abundantly clear:

> If for the sake of argument we agree there has been a return in sociology to culture and cultural analysis, then we are once again given full permission to visit the classical sites excavated by Max Weber concerning the great issues of Christian civilization. The issue I raise here could hardly be more fundamental: the language of Christianity about power, politics and violence in the context of secularization. (Martin, 2004: 341)

The crucial point of the essay lies, however, not so much in the appeal to culture as such, as in the need to appreciate the specific constraints of the political role when this is compared with others – a point that will resonate at several junctures in this chapter. It is, in fact, a valuable corrective to the dangers of taking the cultural turn too far: that is, to put so much emphasis on culture that the structures of societies and the constraints they impose (for good or ill) are simply brushed aside.

Exactly the same point was articulated by Mellor in his contribution to the special issue. Following Mellor, this is a classic 'baby and the bathwater' exercise. In terms of the sociology of religion, its implications are clear. It is indeed important to give sufficient space to culture, but it is equally important to remember that ideas are carried by people, and that people have roles – very varied ones. Hence the connection with Martin's essay: some individuals are leaders and some are followers; political leaders, moreover, are different from religious ones and both are different from academics. Roles, moreover, come together in institutions which vary in nature and take different forms in different places. In terms of religion, some institutions are inclusive and some are not so; some relate easily to the wider society and some do not. In short, all the old questions – the nature of leadership, questions of authority, organizational types, church and sect and so on – cannot simply be abandoned in favour of 'culture'; they need careful and constant interrogation. Interestingly, in resolving these tensions, Mellor reaches back not this time to Weber but to the social realism of Durkheim for a more balanced approach to the complex realities of human, social and cultural life (see pp. 43–4).

Two other contributions to the special issue require attention in terms of the themes of this book. Jean-Paul Willaime articulates the cultural turn from the point of view of French scholarship. In France the influence of both Marxism and structuralism was particularly strong – leading to a philosophical as well as sociological attachment to the idea of secularization (i.e. to a 'strong' version of the Enlightenment). Even in France, however, there is visible change as cultural and religious identities are beginning to invade the public sphere. As a result, French sociologists of religion have turned increasingly to the approaches of anthropology and the political sciences, to reveal both the structures and the dynamics of religious identities in ultra-modernity (a peculiarly French construction). So much so that French *laïcité* is increasingly questioned – the more so given the pressures of the European context. No longer, in other words, 'is the sociological study of religious phenomena simply an analysis of social determinants; it becomes instead, in France as elsewhere, the study of symbolic mediations, examining their influence on both social bonds and the formation of individuals as active subjects' (Willaime, 2004: 373). The fact that the advocates of *laïcité* have regrouped to defend both the concept and the policy is part of the same story.

Neitz (an American sociologist) considers the cultural turn in relation to gender, providing a further example of interest in this area. There is, it is clear, a certain congruence between aspects of feminist theory and a shift towards culture – both, for instance, have distinctive views about the Enlightenment and the role of the autonomous (male) individual within this. Neitz (2004) considers two alternatives to these views: the self as relational and the self as constituted through narrative. The implications of her thinking for the study of religion are plain. Sociologists of religion should pay more attention to practice and the ways in which structure and culture are brought together in the everyday lives of people. Religious practice, moreover, is both embodied and gendered, and lies at the core of religious identification. This notion of doing sociology of religion from the bottom up is strongly endorsed by others in the field, not least in the recent writing of Ammerman (2006). Its focus lies on 'lived religion', not on the categories imposed by the social researcher. Interestingly Ammerman indicated precisely this in her response to the papers presented at the Atlanta conference.

In short, the cultural turn in sociology is, in itself, as socially patterned as the phenomena it seeks to address; it means different things in different places. And taken too far it can create as many problems as it solves. Used judiciously, however, it permits innovative understandings of the religious field. At the same time, it opens up the links to parallel fields in sociology. Two types of illustration will be used to explore these connections: the first is drawn from the sociology of the arts, of sport and of the military; the second from European Studies.[2]

Sociological work on music and the arts is central to an interest in religion, a point that was brought home to me as I prepared the chapter in *Religion in Modern Europe* (Davie, 2000a) devoted to the aesthetic aspects of religious life across the continent. The discussion – already referenced in Chapter 6 – centred on the ways in which the religious memory of Europe is maintained and transmitted through architecture, art, artifacts and music, bearing in mind the importance of 'reception' to a proper understanding of this field. Hence the two emphases in this work: the first lies in appreciating the economic, social and cultural contexts that enabled such marvels as the basilica of La Madeleine in Vézelay in Burgundy – to take but one example; the second can be found in the efforts required of modern populations in order to interpret the symbolism both of the building itself and of the artifacts contained within it. That, however, is not the end of the story. It was in Vézelay, interestingly, that I first encountered the Communautés d'Accueil des Sites Artistiques – a voluntary movement that exists expressly to *re*-introduce the European public not only to their cultural heritage as such, but also to its spiritual dimensions. A generation that is rapidly losing touch with a foundational narrative of the European continent requires help in order to do this (2000a: 173–4).

258

In many respects, the parallels between religion and sport are even more striking. All over Britain, for instance, small, traditional, locally based football clubs struggle for people (spectators) and therefore for money, just like small, traditional parishes. The larger clubs thrive at the expense of the smaller; so too do some churches, if not quite so dramatically. Patterns of attendance are transforming in both cases. Both, for example, saw a marked decline in the post-war period as the voluntary activities associated with one form of society gradually gave way to something very different. Interestingly attendance at professional football matches is now recovering, but more in some divisions than in others. Those responsible for the churches would do well to reflect on this upturn; so far they have not followed suit.[3] Comparisons with the military are similarly instructive. In most (if not all) European societies, a conscript army has given way to a highly trained professional corps. In the churches, obligation (conscription) has given way to a self-selecting constituency (not always highly trained, but very different from its predecessor) – a point developed at some length in Chapter 7. In both cases, membership and with it recruitment are constructed in new ways that, in turn, transform the institution in question. The same thing is happening right across the continent. The crucial point to grasp is that the churches, sporting organizations and the military are all exposed to the wider transformations that are taking place in European societies. None of them are free from these pressures.

But Europe itself can be constructed variously. Definitions include the geographical, historical-political, contemporary political, historical-economic, contemporary economic, social, cultural (both high and low), linguistic, and security-focused conceptions of the continent. Europe can also be viewed from the outside (from the United States, from the Far East, from the Middle East and from the margins of Europe itself – not least from Turkey). All of these must be properly explored if 'Europe' is to be fully understood. The 'coincidence' between the shape of the European Union (post-May 2004) and the parameters of Western Christianity was nonetheless striking and can be explained as follows. European nations that have shared for centuries the experience of the Renaissance, of the Reformation, of the scientific revolution, of the Enlightenment, of Romanticism and so on are likely to have more in common than those that were excluded from this cycle of events (i.e. the Orthodox and Muslim worlds).[4] These are explanations within which culture, and more precisely the religious factor, is not only important but enduring; religion, moreover, is becoming more rather than less salient in European debate in the early years of the twenty-first century.

These interdisciplinary approaches raise a further question. It is not only the paradigms of the sociology of religion that must alter if the pressures and constraints of the modern world order are to be adequately grasped. Even more important is the need for social science *as a whole* to take on board the religious factor as an independent as well as a dependent variable. Religion continues to influence almost every aspect of human society – economic, political, social and cultural. No longer can it be relegated to the past or to the edge of social scientific analysis. Hence the challenge for the economic and social sciences: to rediscover the place of religion in *both* the empirical realities of the twenty-first century *and* the paradigms that are deployed to understand this. The implications for policy are immense.

## PAINFUL REALITIES

So much is clear, but in order to end this book on a note of realism, it is important to return to the difficult decisions of everyday life. Two episodes, one Christian and one Muslim, demonstrate just how intractable these can be. The first builds on to an illustration introduced in Chapter 10: that is, the acute tensions within the Anglican Communion concerning the acceptance or otherwise of homosexuality. The second introduces the Danish 'cartoons'.

A multiplicity of factors must be kept in mind in even an elementary understanding of the former. Most have already been put in place, not least the major demographic shifts of Christianity in the modern world.[5] The consequent tensions between historic power in the global North and demographic power in the global South are all too evident – so also is the tendency of some in the North to manipulate this situation to their own advantage. With some justification this has been presented as a clash of cultures *within* Christianity: a theologically conservative South versus a theologically liberal North, which has come to a head over the acceptability or otherwise of openly acknowledged homosexuality in the lives of religious professionals.

Caught in the middle are those responsible for keeping the Anglican Communion intact – a point at which it is helpful to recall David Martin's depictions of the Christian, political and academic roles, all of which can be clearly detected. The politician in the secular sense is, it is true, largely absent. Not so the ecclesiastical politician whose job it is to hold together different factions in the Anglican Communion. Here the goal is not only a solution to the question of homosexuality in itself, but the continuation of the Communion in a viable form. He or she must live with the consequences of both actions and decisions. Prophets, in contrast, are differently placed: that is, those (and there are many) who have definitive views on the issue but who are free to express these without the responsibilities of those already mentioned. They become, in fact, the academics or journalists captured in Martin's analysis. Both the advocates of greater liberalism[6] and its opponents, however, are convinced that they have right on their side. Both are claiming to speak 'the truth' – articulating, in their own terms, an unequivocally 'Christian' voice.

Most difficult of all is the position of the Archbishop – the pivotal figure of the Anglican Communion whose role is in itself 'an instrument of communion'.[7] Here the 'Christian' and the 'politician' are compressed into one figure who is obliged on a daily basis, on this issue as on others, to decide between what is right and what is expedient. He is obliged, moreover, to take into account not only the very different cultures that are represented in the Anglican Communion, but the cumbersome structures through which decisions can be made in both the Communion itself and in its constituent churches. Ignoring the latter will be as disastrous as ignoring the former. Hence a debate in which the commensurate nature of theology and sociology is clearly displayed. Both have contributions to make to an issue that will only progress if observers as well as protagonists can 'imagine' the role of the other. All those involved must ask themselves where it might be possible to ask for compromise and where, for the time being at least, this is simply out of the question.

The Danish cartoons are both similar and different.[8] In the autumn of 2005, the Danish newspaper *Jyllands-Posten* – in an effort to help out the illustrator of a children's book – commissioned 12 cartoonists to draw images of Mohammed. Their work was published in the paper on 30 September. Particularly offensive for Muslims was the depiction of Mohammed with a bomb in his turban (the fuse was clearly lit). It was hardly surprising that protests followed, remembering that these were initially peaceful – an apology was sought alongside a request for the cartoons to be withdrawn. Neither happened. Instead, the opposition hardened: on one hand were those who refused to compromise on the freedom of speech, a stance that provoked yet more radical forms of protest on the other – not only in Denmark but in many parts of the Muslim world. Without doubt the episode became Denmark's most difficult foreign relations affair since the war. It has had extensive political and economic consequences – lives were lost, embassies burnt and Danish goods were subject to costly economic boycott.

In terms of the themes of this book, two points stand out: the role of the Danish Prime Minister (Anders Fogh Rasmussen), and the decision by the press in some countries to reproduce the offending images. In October 2005, ambassadors from 11 Muslim countries requested a meeting with the Prime Minister, asking him to distance himself from the cartoons in *Jyllands-Posten*. The Prime Minister refused this request, on the grounds that it was not possible for a political figure such as himself to interfere in the decisions of a free press. This was a statement of principle for which Rasmussen was greatly admired in some quarters. Others, however, felt that the refusal to receive the ambassadors amounted to a further insult to the Muslim world; it made matters worse, not better. Equally provocative was the decision by editors all over Europe (and indeed beyond) to re-publish the cartoons – a process that escalated in the early months of 2006. Some justified this gesture by saying that the publics in question have a right to know what the controversy was about. Others clearly felt that the very act of publishing was an affirmation of free speech – there was no need to explain further. The interesting point lies in the fact that re-publication was more likely in some places than others (it occurred disproportionately in continental Europe and hardly at all in Britain and the United States) and in itself provoked further reactions. In some places editors were fired for their decisions to publish; in others journalists walked out where publication was prevented.

In short, the affair proves as intractable as its most obvious predecessor – the Rushdie controversy. Clearly, very little had changed in the 15 years between them, including, once again, the seeming impossibility for one side in the encounter to make the imaginative leap that is required in order to understand the concerns of the other, a refusal that leads in turn to a dangerous escalation. One point, however, remains crystal clear. If social science is to contribute at all to these debates, there is an urgent need to grasp the continuing and public significance of religion in the modern world order – including Western democracies – and to establish a social-scientific discourse that is capable of taking this into account. Without such, very little can be done.

## NOTES

1 Good summaries of this work can be found in Bonnell and Hunt (1999) and Edwards (2006).

2 In selecting these illustrations, I should acknowledge my debt to colleagues at the University of Exeter, notably Robert Witkin, Tia DeNora, Tony King (in Sociology) and Chris Longman (in European Studies).

3 See Chapter 7 for a detailed discussion of these changes. It is worth noting in this connection that from 1990 on the indices of both membership (electoral rolls) and attendance began to rise rather than fall in the Church of England's Diocese of London (Jackson and Piggot, 2011). Cinema-going offers a further example of a dramatic fall in numbers, followed by a modest rise. Statistics on sport and cinema-going can be found in the annual issues of *Social Trends*.

4 The later (2007) inclusions of Bulgaria and Romania raise new questions in this respect – questions that can also be applied to the Greek case as it struggles to emerge from financial crisis.

5 The references to source material can be found in Chapter 10.

6 See, for example, the contributions brought together in Linzey and Kirker (2005).

7 See www.anglicancommunion.org/communion/index.cfm (accessed 23 April 2012).

8 This episode was covered extensively in the press and media, notably in the early months of 2006. A Wikipedia account can be found on http://en.wikipedia.org/wiki/Jyllands-Posten_Muhammad_cartoons_controversy (accessed 23 April 2012). This contains a very helpful timeline.

# bibliography

Ahern, G. and Davie, G. (1987). *Inner City God: The Nature of Belief in the Inner City*. London: Hodder & Stoughton.

Allievi, S. and Nielsen, J. (eds) (2003). *Muslim Networks and Transnational Communities in and Across Europe*. Leiden: Brill.

Almond, G., Appleby, R.S. and Sivan, E. (2003). *Strong Religion: The Rise of Fundamentalisms Around the World*. Chicago, IL: University of Chicago Press.

Almond, G., Sivan, E. and Appleby, R.S. (1995a). 'Fundamentalism: genus and species', in M. Marty and R.S. Appleby (eds), *Fundamentalisms Comprehended* (pp. 399–424). Chicago, IL: University of Chicago Press.

Almond, G., Sivan, E. and Appleby, R.S. (1995b). 'Explaining fundamentalisms', in M. Marty and R.S. Appleby (eds), *Fundamentalisms Comprehended* (pp. 425–44). Chicago, IL: University of Chicago Press.

Almond, G., Sivan, E. and Appleby, R.S. (1995c). 'Examining the cases', in M. Marty and R.S. Appleby (eds), *Fundamentalisms Comprehended* (pp. 445–82). Chicago, IL: University of Chicago Press.

Ammerman, N. (1987). *Bible Believers: Fundamentalists in the Modern World*. New Brunswick, NJ: Rutgers University Press.

Ammerman, N. (1994). 'Accounting for Christian fundamentalists: social dynamics and rhetorical strategies', in M. Marty and R.S. Appleby (eds), *Accounting for Fundamentalisms* (pp. 149–72). Chicago, IL: University of Chicago Press.

Ammerman, N. (1996). 'Religious choice and religious vitality: the market and beyond', in L. Young (ed.), *Rational Choice Theory and Religion: Summary and Assessment* (pp. 119–32). London: Routledge.

Ammerman, N. (1997). *Congregation and Community*. New Brunswick, NJ: Rutgers University Press.

Ammerman, N. (2005). *Pillars of Faith: American Congregations and their Partners*. Berkeley, CA: University of California Press.

Ammerman, N. (ed.) (2006). *Everyday Religion: Observing Modern Religious Lives*. New York: Oxford University Press.

Appleby, R.S. (1998). 'Fundamentalism', in R. Wuthnow (ed.), *Encyclopedia of Politics and Religion* (pp. 280–88). Washington, DC: CQ Press.

Aran, G. (1995). 'What's so funny about fundamentalism?', in M. Marty and R.S. Appleby (eds), *Fundamentalisms Comprehended* (pp. 321–52). Chicago, IL: University of Chicago Press.

Archer, M., Collier, A. and Porpora, D.V. (2004). *Transcendence: Critical Realism and God*. London: Routledge.

Arjomand, S. (1998). 'Iran', in R. Wuthnow (ed.), *Encyclopedia of Politics and Religion* (pp. 376–8). Washington, DC: CQ Press.

Aune, K., Sharma, S. and Vincett, G. (eds) (2008). *Women and Religion in the West: Challenging Secularization*. Farnham: Ashgate.

Bäckström, A. and Davie, G., with Edgardh, N. and Petterson, P. (eds) (2010). *Welfare and Religion in Europe, Volume 1: Configuring the Connections*. Farnham: Ashgate.

Bäckström, A., Davie, G., Edgardh, N. and Petterson, P. (eds) (2011). *Welfare and Religion in Europe, Volume 2: Gendered, Religious and Social Change*. Farnham: Ashgate.

Bäckström, A., Edgardh Beckman, N. and Pettersson, P. (2004). *Religious Change in Northern Europe: The Case of Sweden*. Stockholm: Verbum.

Baker, C. and Beaumont, J. (eds) (2011). *Postsecular Cities: Religious Space, Theory and Practice*. London: Continuum.

Banchoff, T. (ed.) (2007). *Democracy and the New Religious Pluralism*. New York: Oxford University Press.

Barker, E. (1984). *The Making of a Moonie: Choice or Brainwashing*. Oxford: Blackwell.

Barton, G. (2004). *Indonesia's Struggle; Jemaah Islamiyah and the Soul of Islam*. Sydney: University of New South Wales Press.

Bastian, J.-P. and Collange, J.-F. (eds) (1999). *L'Europe à la recherche de son âme*. Geneva: Labor et Fides.

Baubérot, J. (1990). *Vers un nouveau pacte laïque?* Paris: Seuil.

Baubérot, J. (1997). *La Morale laïque contre l'ordre moral*. Paris: Seuil.

Baubérot, J. (2005). *Histoire de la laïcité en France*. Paris: Presses Universitaires de France.

Bauman, Z. (1989). *Modernity and the Holocaust*. Ithaca, NY: Cornell University Press.

Bauman, Z. (1998). 'Postmodern religion?', in P. Heelas, with D. Martin and P. Morris (eds), *Religion, Modernity and Postmodernity* (pp. 55–78). Oxford: Blackwell.

Becker, G. (1976). *The Economic Approach to Human Behavior*. Chicago, IL: University of Chicago Press.

Becker, P.E. and Hofmeister, H. (2001). 'Work, family, and religious involvement for men and women', *Journal for the Scientific Study of Religion*, 40: 707–22.

Beckford, J. (1975). *Trumpet of Prophecy: Sociological Study of Jehovah's Witnesses*. London: Blackwell.

Beckford, J. (1985). *Cult Controversies: The Societal Response to New Religious Movements*. London: Tavistock.

Beckford, J. (1989). *Religion and Advanced Industrial Society*. London: Routledge.

Beckford, J. (1996). 'Postmodernity, high modernity and new modernity: three concepts in search of religion', in K. Flanagan and P. Jupp (eds), *Postmodernity, Sociology and Religion* (pp. 30–47). Basingstoke: Palgrave Macmillan.

Beckford, J. (2003). *Social Theory and Religion*. Cambridge: Cambridge University Press.

Beckford, J. (2012). 'Public religions and the postsecular: critical reflections', *Journal for the Scientific Study of Religion*, 51: 1–19.

Beckford, L. and Demerath, J. (eds) (2007). *The Sage Handbook of the Sociology of Religion*. London: Sage.

Beckford, J. and Walliss, J. (eds) (2006). *Theorising Religion: Classical and Contemporary Debates*. Farnham: Ashgate.

Bellah, R. (1970). *Beyond Belief*. London: Harper & Row.

Berger, P. (1967). *The Sacred Canopy: Elements of a Sociological Theory of Religion*. New York: Doubleday.

Berger, P. (1970). *A Rumor of Angels: Modern Society and the Rediscovery of the Supernatural*. New York: Anchor.

Berger, P. (1980). *The Heretical Imperative: Contemporary Possibilities of Religious Affirmation*. London: Collins.

Berger, P. (1992). *A Far Glory: The Quest for Faith in an Age of Credulity*. New York: Free Press.

Berger, P. (ed.) (1999a). *The Desecularization of the World: Resurgent Religion and World Politics*. Grand Rapids, MI: Eerdmans.

Berger, P. (1999b). 'The desecularization of the world: a global overview', in P. Berger (ed.), *The Desecularization of the World: Resurgent Religion and World Politics* (pp. 1–18). Grand Rapids, MI: Eerdmans.

Berger, P. (2001). 'Postscript', in L. Woodhead, with P. Heelas and D. Martin (eds), *Peter Berger and the Study of Religion* (pp. 189–98). London: Routledge.

Berger, P. (2002). 'Whatever happened to sociology?', *First Things*, 126: 27–9.

Berger, P. and Huntington, S. (2002). *Many Globalizations: Cultural Diversity in the Contemporary World*. New York: Oxford University Press.

Berger, P., Davie, G. and Fokas, E. (2008). *Religious America: Secular Europe*. Farnham: Ashgate.

Berger, S. (1982). *Religion in West European Politics*. London: Frank Cass.

Beyer, P. (1993). *Religion and Globalization*. London: Sage.

Beyer, P. (1998). 'Canadian study of religion', in W. Swatos (ed.), *Encyclopedia of Religion and Society* (pp. 70–1). Walnut Creek, CA: Alta Mira Press.

Beyer, P. (ed.) (2001a). *Religion in the Process of Globalization*. Würzburg: Ergon.

Beyer, P. (2001b). 'English-language views of the role of globalization', in P. Beyer (ed.), *Religion in the Process of Globalization* (pp. vii–xliv). Würzburg: Ergon.

Billings, A. (2004). *Secular Lives, Sacred Hearts*. London: SPCK.

Blasi, A. (1998). 'Definition of religion', in W. Swatos (ed.), *Encyclopedia of Religion and Society* (pp. 129–33). Walnut Creek, CA: Alta Mira Press.

Bocock, R. and Thompson, K. (1985). *Religion and Ideology*. Manchester: Manchester University Press.

Bonnell, V. and Hunt, L. (eds) (1999). *Beyond the Cultural Turn: New Directions in the Study of Society and Culture*. Berkeley, CA: University of California Press.

Boulard, F. (1945). *Problèmes missionnaires de la France rurale*. Paris: Cerf.

Boulard, F. and Rémy, J. (1968). *Pratique religieuse urbaine et régions culturelles*. Paris: Éditions Économie et humanisme, les Éditions ouvrières.

Bréchon, P. (2001). 'L'évolution du religieux', *Futuribles*, 260: 39–48.

Brierley, P. (1991). *Christian England: What the English Church Census Reveals*. London: MARC Europe.

**265**

Brown, C. (2000). *The Death of Christian Britain*. London: Routledge (a revised edition appeared in 2009).

Bruce, S. (1988). *The Rise and Fall of the New Christian Right*. Oxford: Oxford University Press.

Bruce, S. (1990). *Pray TV: Televangelism in America*. London: Routledge.

Bruce, S. (ed.) (1992). *Religion and Modernization*. Oxford: Oxford University Press.

Bruce, S. (1995a). *Religion in Modern Britain*. Oxford: Oxford University Press.

Bruce, S. (1995b). 'The truth about religion in Britain', *Journal for the Scientific Study of Religion*, 34: 417–30.

Bruce, S. (1996). *Religion in the Modern World: From Cathedrals to Cults*. Oxford: Oxford University Press.

Bruce, S. (1997). 'The pervasive world view: religion in pre-modern Britain', *British Journal of Sociology*, 48: 667–90.

Bruce, S. (1999). *Choice and Religion: A Critique of Rational Choice Theory*. Oxford: Oxford University Press.

Bruce, S. (2001). 'The curious case of the unnecessary recantation: Berger and secularization', in L. Woodhead, with P. Heelas and D. Martin (eds), *Peter Berger and the Study of Religion* (pp. 87–100). London: Routledge.

Bruce, S. (2002a). *God is Dead: Secularization in the West*. Oxford: Blackwell.

Bruce, S. (2002b). 'Praying alone. Church-going in Britain and the Putnam thesis', *Journal of Contemporary Religion*, 17: 317–28.

Bruce, S. (2003). *Politics and Religion*. Cambridge: Polity Press.

Bruce, S. (2011). *Secularization: In Defence of an Unfashionable Theory*. Oxford: Oxford University Press.

Bruce, S. and Voas, D. (2010). 'Vicarious religion: an examination and critique', *Journal of Contemporary Religion*, 25: 243–59.

Brusco, E. (1993). 'The reformation of machismo: asceticism and masculinity among Colombian evangelicals', in D. Stoll and V. Garrard-Burnett (eds), *Rethinking Protestantism in Latin America* (pp. 143–58). Philadelphia, PA: Temple University Press.

Brusco, E. (1995). *The Reformation of Machismo: Evangelical Conversion and Gender in Colombia*. Austin, TX: University of Texas Press.

Buijs, F. and Rath, J. (2006). *Muslims in Europe: The State of Research*. A revised version of an essay prepared for the Russell Sage Foundation, New York and presented to a planning meeting of the Social Science Research Council and the Russell Sage Foundation on 'Islam and Muslims in Europe and the United States: Processes of Accommodation' in 2003. (See http://dare.uva.nl/document/144737, accessed 23 May 2012.)

Buruma, I. (2006). *Murder in Amsterdam: The Death of Theo Van Gogh and the Limits of Tolerance*. Harmondsworth: Penguin.

Byrnes, T. and Katzenstein, P. (eds) (2006). *Religion in an Expanding Europe*. Cambridge: Cambridge University Press.

Cameron, H. (2001). 'Social capital in Britain: are Hall's membership figures a reliable guide?' Paper presented to the 2001 ARNOVA Conference, Miami, FL.

Cameron, H. (2003). 'The decline of the Church in England as a local membership organization: predicting the nature of civil society in 2050', in G. Davie, P. Heelas and L. Woodhead (eds), *Predicting Religion: Christian, Secular and Alternative Futures* (pp. 109–19). Farnham: Ashgate.

Cameron, H. (2004). 'Are congregations associations? The contribution of organizational studies to congregational studies', in M. Guest, K. Tusting and L. Woodhead (eds), *Congregational Studies in the UK: Christianity in a Post-Christian Context* (pp. 139–51). Farnham: Ashgate.

Caplan, L. (ed.) (1987). *Studies in Religious Fundamentalism*. Basingstoke: Palgrave Macmillan.

Casanova, J. (1994). *Public Religions in the Modern World*. Chicago, IL: University of Chicago Press.

Casanova, J. (1997). 'Globalizing Catholicism and the return to the "universal church"', in S.H. Rudolph and J. Piscatori (eds), *Transnational Religion: Fading States* (pp. 121–43). Boulder, CO: Westview Press.

Casanova, J. (2001a). 'Secularization', in N. Smelser and P. Baltes (eds), *The Encyclopedia of Social and Behavioral Sciences* (pp. 13786–91). Oxford: Elsevier.

Casanova, J. (2001b). 'Religion, the new millennium, and globalization', *Sociology of Religion*, 62: 455–73.

Casanova, J. (2003). 'Beyond Europe and American exceptionalisms', in G. Davie, P. Heelas and L. Woodhead (eds), *Predicting Religion: Christian, Secular and Alternative Futures* (pp. 17–29). Farnham: Ashgate.

Casanova, J. (2006). 'Rethinking secularization: a global comparative perspective', *The Hedgehog Review*, 8: 7–23.

Cesari, J. (2004). *Islam in the West*. Basingstoke: Palgrave Macmillan.

Cesari, J. and McLoughlin, S. (eds) (2005). *European Muslims and the Secular State*. Farnham: Ashgate.

Chambers, P. (2000). 'Factors in church growth and decline'. Unpublished PhD thesis, University of Wales, Swansea.

Chambers, P. (2004). *Religion, Secularization and Social Change: Congregational Studies in a Post-Christian Society*. Cardiff: University of Wales Press.

Chaves, M. (2011). *American Religion: Contemporary Trends*. Princeton, NJ: Princeton University Press.

Chaves, M. and Cann, D. (1992). 'Regulations, pluralism, and religious market structure: explaining religion's vitality', *Rationality and Science*, 4: 272–90.

Chemin, E. (2012). 'Pilgrimage in a secular age: religious and consumer landscapes of late modernity'. Unpublished PhD thesis, University of Exeter.

Chesnut, A. (1997). *Born Again in Brazil: The Pentecostal Boom and the Pathogens of Poverty*. New York: Oxford University Press.

Chesnut, A. (2003). *Competitive Spirits: Latin America's New Religious Economy*. New Brunswick, NJ: Rutgers University Press.

Cipriani, R. (1998). 'Desroche, Henri', in W. Swatos (ed.), *Encyclopedia of Religion and Society* (p. 137). Walnut Creek, CA: Alta Mira Press.

Clarke, D. (1997). 'History and religion in modern Korea: the case of Protestant Christianity', in L. Lancaster and R. Payne (eds), *Religion and Society in*

*Contemporary Korea* (pp. 169–214). Berkeley, CA: Institute of East Asian Studies, University of California.

Clarke, P. (ed.) (2008). *The Oxford Handbook of the Sociology of Religion*. Oxford: Oxford University Press.

Cnaan, R. (2002). *The Invisible Caring Hand: American Congregations and the Provision of Welfare*. New York: New York University Press.

Coleman, P. (2011). *Belief and Ageing: Spiritual Pathways in Later Life*. Bristol: Policy Press.

Collins-Mayo, S. and Dandelion, B.P. (eds) (2010). *Religion and Youth*. Farnham: Ashgate.

Corten, A. (1997). 'The growth of the literature of Afro-American, Latin American and African Pentecostalism', *Journal of Contemporary Religion*, 12: 311–24.

Cox, H. (1968). *The Secular City*. Harmondsworth: Penguin.

Cox, J., Campbell, A. and Fulford, B. (eds) (2006). *Medicine of the Person: Faith, Science and Values in Health Care Provision*. London: Jessica Kingsley.

Davie, G. (1994). *Religion in Britain since 1945: Believing Without Belonging*. Oxford: Blackwell.

Davie, G. (1999a). 'Religion and laïcité', in M. Cook and G. Davie (eds), *Modern France: Society in Transition* (pp. 195–215). London: Routledge.

Davie, G. (1999b). 'Europe: the exception that proves the rule', in P. Berger (ed.), *The Desecularization of the World: Resurgent Religion and World Politics* (pp. 65–83). Grand Rapids, MI: Eerdmans.

Davie, G. (2000a). *Religion in Modern Europe: A Memory Mutates*. Oxford: Oxford University Press.

Davie, G. (2000b). 'The sociology of religion in Britain: a hybrid case', *Swiss Journal of Sociology*, 26: 193–218.

Davie, G. (2001). 'The persistence of institutional religion in modern Europe', in L. Woodhead, with P. Heelas and D. Martin (eds), *Peter Berger and the Study of Religion* (pp. 101–11). London: Routledge.

Davie, G. (2002a). *Europe: The Exceptional Case – Parameters of Faith in the Modern World*. London: Darton, Longman & Todd.

Davie, G. (2002b). 'Praying alone. Church-going in Britain and social capital: a reply to Steve Bruce', *Journal of Contemporary Religion*, 17: 329–34.

Davie, G. (2003a). 'Seeing salvation: the use of text as data in the sociology of religion', in P. Avis (ed.), *Public Faith: The State of Religious Belief and Practice in Britain* (pp. 28–44). London: SPCK.

Davie, G. (2003b). 'Religious minorities in France: a Protestant perspective', in J. Beckford and J. Richardson (eds), *Challenging Religion: Essays in Honour of Eileen Barker* (pp. 159–69). London: Routledge.

Davie, G. (2004a). 'New approaches in the sociology of religion: a Western perspective', *Social Compass*, 51: 73–84.

Davie, G. (2004b). 'Creating an agenda in the sociology of religion: common sources, different pathways', *Sociology of Religion*, 65: 323–40.

Davie, G. (2005). 'From obligation to consumption: a framework for reflection in Northern Europe', *Political Theology*, 6/3: 281–301.

Davie, G. (2006a). 'Is Europe an exceptional case?', *The Hedgehog Review*, 8/1–2: 23–35.

Davie, G. (2006b). 'Religion in Europe in the 21st century: the factors to take into account', *Archives européennes de sociologie/European Journal of Sociology/ Europaeisches Archiv für Soziologie*, 47: 271–96.

Davie, G. (2006c). 'World Council of Churches' and 'Ecumenical movement', in R. Robertson and J.A. Scholte (eds), *Encyclopedia of Globalization* (pp. 363–6 and 1271–3). New York: Routledge.

Davie, G. (2007a). 'Vicarious religion: a methodological challenge', in N. Ammerman (ed.), *Everyday Religion: Observing Modern Religious Lives* (pp. 21–36). New York: Oxford University Press.

Davie, G. (2007b). 'Pluralism, tolerance and democracy: theory and practice in Europe', in T. Banchoff (ed.), *Democracy and the New Religious Pluralism*. New York: Oxford University Press.

Davie, G. (2010a). 'Vicarious religion: a response', *Journal of Contemporary Religion*, 25: 261–67.

Davie, G. (2010b) 'Religious America, secular Europe: framing the debate', in E. Ben-Rafael and Y. Sternberg (eds), *World Religions and Multiculturalism: A Dialectic Relation* (pp. 41–62). Leiden: Brill.

Davie, G. (2012). 'A European perspective on religion and welfare: contrasts and commonalities', *Social Policy and Society*, 11: 989–99.

Davie, G. and Martin, D. (1999). 'Liturgy and music', in A. Walter (ed.), *The Mourning for Diana* (pp. 187–98). Oxford: Berg.

Davie, G. and Vincent, J. (1999). 'Progress report. Religion and old age', *Ageing and Society*, 18: 101–10.

Day, A. (2006). 'Believing in belonging: a qualitative analysis of being Christian for the 2001 census'. Paper presented to the 2006 Conference of the British Sociological Association Sociology of Religion Study Group, Manchester.

Day, A. (2011). *Believing in Belonging: Belief and Social Identity in the Modern World*. Oxford: Oxford University Press.

De Santa Ana, J. (ed.) (2005). *Religions Today: Their Challenge to the Ecumenical Movement*. Geneva: WCC Publications.

De Vaus, D. (1984). 'Workforce participation and sex differences in church attendance', *Review of Religious Research*, 25: 247–56.

De Vaus, D. and McAllister, I. (1987). 'Gender differences in religion', *American Sociological Review*, 52: 472–81.

Demerath, J. (1965). *Social Class in American Protestantism*. Chicago, IL: Rand-McNally.

Dillon, M. (ed.) (2003). *Handbook of the Sociology of Religion*. Cambridge: Cambridge University Press.

Dobbelaere, K. (1981). 'Secularization: a multi-dimensional concept', *Current Sociology*, 29/2.

Dobbelaere, K. (2002). *Secularization: An Analysis at Three Levels*. Frankfurt am Main: Peter Lang.

Douglas, M. (1982). 'Environments at risk', in B. Barnes and D. Edge (eds), *Science in Context: Readings in the Sociology of Science* (pp. 260–75). Milton Keynes: Open University Press.

Dowell, S. and Williams, J. (1994). *Bread, Wine and Women: Ordination Debate in the Church of England*. London: Virago.

Droogers, A. (1991). 'Visiones paradójicas sobre una religión paradójica: modelos explicativos del crecimiento del pentecostalismo en Brasil y Chile', in B. Boudewijnse et al. (eds), *Algo más que ópio: Una lectura antropológica del pentecostalismo latinoamericano y caribeño* (pp. 14–42). San José, Costa Rica: DEI.

Durkheim, E. (1976). *The Elementary Forms of Religious Life*. London: HarperCollins (first published in French 1912).

Edwards, T. (ed.) (2006). *Cultural Theory: Classical and Contemporary Positions*. London: Sage.

Eisenstadt, S. (1995). 'Fundamentalism, phenomenology, and comparative dimensions', in M. Marty and R.S. Appleby (eds), *Fundamentalisms Comprehended* (pp. 259–76). Chicago, IL: University of Chicago Press.

Eisenstadt, S. (1999). *Fundamentalism, Sectarianism and Revolutions: The Jacobin Dimension of Modernity*. Cambridge: Cambridge University Press.

Eisenstadt, S. (2000). 'Multiple modernities', *Daedalus*, 129: 1–30.

Elvy, P. (1986). *Buying Time: the Foundations of the Electronic Church*. Great Wakering: McCrimmons for the Jerusalem Trust.

Elvy, P. (1990). *The Future of Christian Broadcasting in Europe*. Great Wakering: McCrimmons for the Jerusalem Trust.

Esping-Anderson, G. (1990) *The Three Worlds of Welfare Capitalism*. Cambridge: Polity Press.

Esposito, J. and Burgat, F. (eds) (2003). *Modernising Islam: Religion in the Public Sphere in the Middle East and Europe*. New Brunswick, NJ: Rutgers University Press.

Ester, P., Halman, L. and de Moor, R. (eds) (1994). *The Individualizing Society: Value Change in Europe and North America*. Tilburg: Tilburg University Press.

*Faith in the City: A Call for Action by Church and Nation* (1985). A Report of the Archbishop of Canterbury's Commission on Urban Priority Areas. London: Church House Publishing.

Fenn, R. (ed.) (2000). *The Blackwell Companion to the Sociology of Religion*. Oxford: Blackwell.

Ferrari, S. and Cristofori, R. (eds) (2010). *Law and Religion in the 21st Century: Relations between States and Religious Communities*. Farnham: Ashgate.

Finke, R. (1996). 'The consequence of religious competition', in L.A. Young (ed.), *Rational Choice Theory and Religion: Summary and Assessment* (pp. 46–65). London: Routledge.

Finke, R. and Stark, R. (1992). *The Churching of America, 1776–1990: Winners and Losers in Our Religious Economy*. New Brunswick, NJ: Rutgers University Press (a revised edition appeared in 2005).

Finke, R. and Stark, R. (2003). 'The dynamics of religious economies', in M. Dillon (ed.), *Handbook for the Sociology of Religion* (pp. 96–109). Cambridge: Cambridge University Press.

Flanagan, K. and Jupp, P. (eds) (1996). *Postmodernity, Sociology and Religion*. Basingstoke: Palgrave Macmillan.

Flanagan, K. and Jupp, P. (eds) (2000). *Virtue Ethics and Sociology: Issues of Modernity and Religion*. Basingstoke: Palgrave Macmillan.

Flanagan, K. and Jupp, P. (eds) (2007). *A Sociology of Spirituality*. Farnham: Ashgate.

Francis, L. (1997). 'The psychology of gender differences in religion: a review of empirical research', *Religion*, 27: 81–96.

Francis, L. (2003). 'Religion and social capital', in P. Avis (ed.), *Public Faith: The State of Religious Belief and Practice in Britain* (pp. 45–64). London: SPCK.

Freedman, J. (2004). *Immigration and Insecurity in France*. Farnham: Ashgate.

Freston, P. (1998). 'Pentecostalism in Latin America: characteristics and controversies', *Social Compass*, 45: 335–58.

Freston, P. (2001). *Evangelicals and Politics in Asia, Africa and Latin America*. Cambridge: Cambridge University Press.

Freston, P. (2008). 'The religious field among Brazilians in the United States', in L.J. Braga and C. Jouët-Pastré (eds), *Becoming Brazuca: Brazilian Immigration to the United States* (pp. 255–68). Cambridge, MA: Harvard University Press.

Froese, P. and Pfaff, S. (2005). 'Explaining a religious anomaly: an historical analysis of secularization in eastern Germany', *Journal for the Scientific Study of Religion*, 22: 397–422.

Fulton, J., Dowling, T., Abela, A., Borowik, I., Marler, P. and Tomasi, L. (2000). *Young Catholics at the New Millennium: The Religion and Morality of Young Adults in Western Countries*. Dublin: University College Dublin Press.

Garton Ash, T. (2004). *Free World: Why a Crisis of the West Reveals the Opportunity of our Time*. London: Allen Lane.

Garton Ash, T. (2006). 'Islam in Europe', *New York Review of Books*, 5 October: 32–5.

Geaves, R., Gabriel, T., Haddad, Y. and Smith, J. (2004). *Islam and the West post September 11th*. Farnham: Ashgate.

Gellner, E. (1992). *Postmodernism, Reason and Religion*. London: Routledge.

Gemie, S. (2004). 'Stasi's Republic: the school and the "veil", December 2003–March 2004', *Modern and Contemporary France*, 12: 387–98.

Gerrard, N. (2004). *Soham: A Story of Our Times*. London: Short Books.

Giddens, A. (1971). *Capitalism and Modern Social Theory: An Analysis of the Writings of Marx, Durkheim and Max Weber*. Cambridge: Cambridge University Press.

Giddens, A. (1990). *The Consequences of Modernity*. Berkeley, CA: University of California Press.

Giddens, A. (1991). *Modernity and Self Identity: Self and Society in the Late Modern Age*. Cambridge: Polity Press.

Giddens, A. (1994). 'Living in a post-traditional society', in U. Beck, A. Giddens and S. Lash (eds), *Reflexive Modernization: Politics, Tradition and Aesthetics in the Modern Social Order* (pp. 56–109). Cambridge: Polity Press.

Gill, A. (1998). *Rendering unto Caesar: The Roman Catholic Church and the State in Latin America*. Chicago, IL: University of Chicago Press.

Gill, A. (1999). 'The struggle to be soul provider: Catholic responses to Protestant growth in Latin America', in C. Smith and J. Prokopy (eds), *Latin American Religion in Motion* (pp. 17–42). London: Routledge.

Gill, R. (1993). *The Myth of the Empty Church*. London: SPCK.

Gill, R. (1999). *Churchgoing and Christian Ethics*. Cambridge: Cambridge University Press (a revised edition appeared in 2003).

Gilliat-Ray, S. (2010). *Muslims in Britain: An Introduction*. Cambridge: Cambridge University Press.

Godin, H. and Daniel, Y. (1943). *La France, pays de mission*. Paris: Cerf.

Göle, N. (2000). 'Snapshots of Islamic modernity', *Daedalus*, 129: 91–118.

Goudsblom, J. (1967). *Dutch Society*. New York: Random House.

Greeley, A. (2003). *Religion in Europe at the End of the Second Millennium: A Sociological Profile*. London: Transaction.

Guest, M. (2004). '"Friendship, fellowship and acceptance": the public discourse of a thriving evangelical congregation', in M. Guest, K. Tusting and L. Woodhead (eds), *Congregational Studies in the UK: Christianity in a Post-Christian Context* (pp. 71–84). Farnham: Ashgate.

Guest, M. (2007). *Evangelical Identity and Contemporary Culture: A Congregational Study in Innovation*. Milton Keynes: Paternoster.

Guest, M., Tusting, K. and Woodhead, L. (eds) (2004). *Congregational Studies in the UK: Christianity in a Post-Christian Context*. Farnham: Ashgate.

Habermas, J. (2006). 'Religion in the public sphere', *European Journal of Philosophy*, 14: 1–25.

Habgood, J. (1992). 'Viewpoint', *Independent*, 12 March.

Hadaway, K. and Marler, P. (2005). 'How many Americans attend worship each week? An alternative approach to measurement', *Journal for the Scientific Study of Religion*, 44: 307–22.

Hadaway, K., Marler, P. and Chaves, M. (1993). 'What the polls don't show: a closer look at church attendance', *American Sociological Review*, 58: 741–52.

Hadaway, K., Marler, P. and Chaves, M. (1998). 'A symposium on church attendance', *American Sociological Review*, 63: 111–45.

Haddad, Y. and Smith, J. (eds) (1994). *Muslim Communities in North America*. Albany, NY: State University of New York Press.

Haddad, Y. and Smith, J. (eds) (2002). *Muslim Minorities in the West: Visible and Invisible*. Walnut Creek, CA: Alta Mira Press.

Hadden, J. (1987). 'Religious broadcasting and the mobilization of the New Christian Right', *Journal for the Scientific Study of Religion*, 26: 1–24.

Hak, D. (1998). 'Rational choice theory', in W. Swatos (ed.), *Encyclopedia of Religion and Society* (pp. 402–4). Walnut Creek, CA: Alta Mira Press.

Hamberg, E. and Pettersson, T. (1994). 'The religious market: denominational competition and religious participation in contemporary Sweden', *Journal for the Scientific Study of Religion*, 33: 205–16.

Hartley, N. (2005). 'Re-vision: challenges and responsibilities for the third generation of hospice care'. Paper presented to The Social Context of Death, Dying and Disposal Conference, University of Bath, September.

Harvey, D. (1989). *The Condition of Postmodernity*. London: Blackwell.

Harvey, G. and Vincett, G. (2012). 'Alternative spiritualities: marginal and mainstream', in L. Woodhead and R. Catto (eds), *Religion and Change in Modern Britain* (pp. 156–72). London: Routledge.

Hastings, A. (1994). *A History of African Christianity*. Oxford: Clarendon Press.

Hawley, J. (ed.) (1994). *Fundamentalism and Gender*. Oxford: Oxford University Press.

Heelas, P. (1996). *The New Age Movement: Religion, Culture and Society in the Age of Postmodernity*. Oxford: Blackwell.

Heelas, P. (2008). *Spiritualities of Life: From the Romantics to Wellbeing Culture*. Oxford: Blackwell.

Heelas, P. and Woodhead, L. (eds) (2000). *Religion in Modern Times: An Anthology*. London: Blackwell.

Heelas, P. and Woodhead, L. with Seel, B., Szerszynski, B. and Tusting, K. (2004). *The Spiritual Revolution: Why Religion is Giving Way to Spirituality*. Oxford: Blackwell.

Heelas, P. with Martin, D. and Morris, P. (eds) (1998). *Religion, Modernity and Postmodernity*. Oxford: Blackwell.

Hefner, R. (1998a). 'Indonesia', in R. Wuthnow (ed.), *Encyclopedia of Politics and Religion* (pp. 372–4). Washington, DC: CQ Press.

Hefner, R. (1998b) 'Islam, South East Asia', in R. Wuthnow (ed.), *Encyclopedia of Politics and Religion* (pp. 393–7). Washington, DC: CQ Press.

Hefner, R. (2000a). *Civil Islam: Muslims and Democratization in Indonesia*. Princeton, NJ: Princeton University Press.

Hefner, R. (ed.) (2000b). *The Politics of Muticulturalism: Pluralism and Citizenship in Malaysia, Singapore, and Indonesia*. Honolulu, HI: University of Hawaii Press.

Hefner, R. (2001). 'Public Islam and the problem of democratization', *Sociology of Religion*, 62: 491–514.

Hefner, R. (ed.) (2004). *Remaking Muslim Politics: Pluralism, Contestation, Democratization*. Princeton, NJ: Princeton University Press.

Hervieu-Léger, D. (1986). *Vers un nouveau christianisme: Introduction à la sociologie du christianisme occidental*. Paris: Cerf.

Hervieu-Léger, D. (ed.) (1990) *La Religion au lycée*. Paris: Cerf.

Hervieu-Léger, D. (1993). *La Religion pour mémoire*. Paris: Cerf.

Hervieu-Léger, D. (1999). *Le Pèlerin et le converti. La religion en mouvement*. Paris: Flammarion.

Hervieu-Léger, D. (2000). *Religion as a Chain of Memory*. Cambridge: Polity Press (translation of *La Religion pour mémoire*, 1993).

Hervieu-Léger, D. (2001a). *La Religion en miettes ou la question des sectes*. Paris: Calmann-Lévy.

Hervieu-Léger, D. (2001b). 'France's obsession with the "sectarian threat"', *Nova Religio*, 4: 249–58.

Hervieu-Léger, D. (2003). *Catholicisme, la fin d'un monde*. Paris: Bayard.

Hervieu-Léger, D. and Willaime, J.-P. (2001). *Sociologies et religion: Approches classiques*. Paris: Presses Universitaires de France.

Himmelfarb, G. (2004). *The Roads to Modernity: The British, French, and American Enlightenments*. New York: Knopf.

Hoover, S. (1988). *Mass Media Religion: The Social Sources of the Electronic Church*. London: Sage.

Hunt, S. (2004). *The Alpha Initiative: Evangelism in a Post-Christian Age*. Farnham: Ashgate.

Huntington, S. (1993). 'The clash of civilizations', *Foreign Affairs*, 72: 22–50.

Huntington, S. (1997). *The Clash of Civilizations and the Remaking of the World Order*. New York: Simon & Schuster.

Huntington, S. (2004). *Who Are We? America's Great Debate*. New York: Simon & Schuster.

Iannaccone, L. (1992). 'Sacrifice and stigma: reducing free-riding in cults, communes, and other collectives', *Journal of Political Economy*, 100: 271–91.

Iannaccone, L. (1994). 'Why strict churches are strong', *American Journal of Sociology*, 99: 1180–211.

Iannaccone, L. (1996). 'Rational choice: framework for the scientific study of religion', in L. Young (ed.), *Rational Choice Theory and Religion* (pp. 25–44). London: Routledge.

Inglehart, R. (1997). *Modernization and Postmodernization: Cultural, Economic and Political Change in 43 Societies*. Princeton, NJ: Princeton University Press.

Inglehart, R. and Baker, W. (2000). 'Modernization, cultural change and the persistence of traditional values', *American Sociological Review*, 65: 19–51.

Isambert, F.-A. and Terrenoire, J.-P. (1980). *Atlas de la pratique religieuse des catholiques en France*. Paris: Editions du CNRS.

Jackson, R. and Piggot, A. (2011). 'Another capital idea: church growth in the Diocese of London 2003–10)'. (See www.london.anglican.org/CapitalIdea, accessed 23 April 2012.)

Jenkins, P. (2002). *The Next Christendom: The Coming of Global Christianity*. New York: Oxford University Press (a third edition appeared in 2012).

Jenkins, T. (1999). *Religion in English Everyday Life: An Ethnographic Approach*. London: Berghahn.

Juergensmeyer, M. and Roof, W.C. (eds) (2011). *Encyclopedia of Global Religion*. Thousand Oaks, CA: Sage.

Kaplan, L. (ed.) (1992). *Fundamentalism in Comparative Perspective*. Amherst, MA: University of Massachusetts Press (1st edn 1988).

Karlenzig, B. (1998). 'Berger, Peter L.', in W. Swatos (ed.), *Encyclopedia of Religion and Society* (pp. 52–4). Walnut Creek, CA: Alta Mira Press.

Kepel, G. (1994). *The Revenge of God*. Philadelphia, PA: Pennsylvania State University Press.

Kitzinger, C. (1990). 'Fundamentally female', *New Internationalist*, August: 24–5.

Klausen, J. (2005). *The Islamic Challenge: Politics and Religion in Western Europe*. Oxford: Oxford University Press.

Koenig, H., Larson, D. and Matthews, D. (1996). 'Religion and psychotherapy with older adults', *Journal of Geriatric Psychiatry*, 29: 155–94.

Laermans, R., Billiet, J. and Wilson, B. (eds) (1998). *Secularization and Social Integration: Papers in Honour of Karel Dobbelaere*. Leuven: Leuven University Press.

Lambert, Y. (2002). 'Religion: l'Europe à un tournant', *Futuribles*, 277: 129–60.

Laslett, P. (1983). *The World We Have Lost: Further Explored*. London: Methuen (1st edn 1965).

Laurence, J. and Vaisse, J. (2005). *Integrating Islam: Political and Religious Challenges in Contemporary France*. Washington, DC: Brookings Institution.

Lechner, F. (1998). 'Parsons, Talcott', in W. Swatos (ed.), *Encyclopaedia of Religion and Society* (pp. 352–5). Walnut Creek, CA: Alta Mira Press.

Lehmann, D. (1990). *Democracy and Development in Latin America: Economics, Politics and Religion in the Post-war Period*. Cambridge: Polity Press.

Lehmann, D. (1996). *Struggle for the Spirit: Religious Transformation and Popular Culture in Brazil and Latin America*. Cambridge: Polity Press.

Lehmann, D. (2002). 'Religion and globalization', in L. Woodhead, P. Fletcher, H. Kawanami and D. Smith (eds), *Religions in the Modern World* (pp. 299–315). London: Routledge.

Lepenies, W. (1991). 'Grudge match as Marx ruled off side', *The Higher*, 4 October: 14.

Levin, J. (ed.) (1994). *Religion in Aging and Health: Theoretical Foundations and Methodological Frontiers*. Thousand Oaks, CA: Sage.

Levine, D. (1995). 'Protestants and Catholics in Latin America: a family portrait', in M. Marty and R.S. Appleby (eds), *Fundamentalisms Comprehended* (pp. 155–78). Chicago, IL: University of Chicago Press.

Lienesch, M. (1993). *Redeeming America: Piety and Politics in the New Christian Right*. Chapel Hill, NC: University of North Carolina Press.

Linzey, A. and Kirker, R. (2005). *Gays and the Future of Anglicanism*. Oakland, CA: O Books.

Livezey, L. (ed.) (2000). *Public Religion and Urban Transformation: Faith in the City*. New York: New York University Press.

Lodge, D. (1996). *Therapy*. Harmondsworth: Penguin.

Loudon, I. (1992). *Death in Childbirth: An International Study of Maternal Care and Maternal Mortality 1800–1950*. Oxford: Clarendon Press.

Loudon, I. (2000). *The Tragedy of Childbed Fever*. Oxford: Oxford University Press.

Lübbe, H. (1975). *Säkularisierung*. Freiburg: Alber.

Luckmann, T. (1967). *The Invisible Religion: The Problem of Religion in Modern Society*. New York: Macmillan.

Lyon, D. (2000). *Jesus in Disneyland: Religion in Postmodern Times*. Cambridge: Polity Press.

Maldonado, J. (1993). 'Building "fundamentalism" from the family in Latin America', in M. Marty and R.S. Appleby (eds), *Fundamentalisms and Society* (pp. 214–39). Chicago, IL: University of Chicago Press.

Manow, P. (2004). 'The good, the bad and the ugly: Esping-Anderson's regimes typology and the religious roots of the Western welfare state'. Paper presented to a workshop on Religion and the Western Welfare State, at the Max-Planck Institute, 30 April–1 May.

Mardin, S. (1998). 'Turkey', in R. Wuthnow (ed.), *Encyclopedia of Politics and Religion* (pp. 742–6). Washington, DC: CQ Press.

Maréchal, B. (ed.) (2002). *L'Islam dans l'Europe élargie: Radioscopie. A Guidebook on Islam and Muslims in the Wide Contemporary Europe*. Louvain-la-Neuve: Academia-Bruylant.

Marland, H. (2004). *Dangerous Motherhood: Insanity and Childbirth in Victorian Britain*. Basingstoke: Palgrave Macmillan.

Marland, H. and Rafferty, A. (eds) (1997). *Midwives, Society and Childbirth: Debates and Controversies in the Modern Period*. London: Routledge.

Martin, B. (2000). 'The Pentecostal gender paradox: a cautionary tale for the sociology of religion', in R. Fenn (ed.), *The Blackwell Companion to the Sociology of Religion* (pp. 52–66). Oxford: Blackwell.

Martin, B. (2003). 'Beyond measurement: the non-quantifiable religious dimension in social life', in P. Avis (ed.), *Public Faith: The State of Religious Belief and Practice in Britain* (pp. 1–18). London: SPCK.

Martin, D. (1965). 'Towards eliminating the concept of secularization', in J. Gould (ed.), *Penguin Survey of the Social Sciences* (pp. 169–82). Harmondsworth: Penguin. Reprinted in Martin, D. (1969).

Martin, D. (1967). *A Sociology of English Religion*. London: Heinemann.

Martin, D. (1969). *The Religious and the Secular*. London: Routledge.

Martin, D. (1978). *A General Theory of Secularization*. Oxford: Blackwell.

Martin, D. (1990). *Tongues of Fire: The Explosion of Protestantism in Latin America*. Oxford: Blackwell.

Martin, D. (1991). 'The secularization issue: prospect and retrospect', *British Journal of Sociology*, 42: 466–74.

Martin, D. (1996a). *Forbidden Revolutions*. London: SPCK.

Martin, D. (1996b). *Reflections on Sociology and Theology*. Oxford: Clarendon Press.

Martin, D. (1996c). 'Remise en question de la théorie de la sécularisation', in G. Davie and D. Hervieu-Léger (eds), *Identités religieuses en Europe* (pp. 25–42). Paris: La Découverte.

Martin, D. (2000). 'Personal reflections in the mirror of Halévy and Weber', in R. Fenn (ed.), *The Blackwell Companion to the Sociology of Religion* (pp. 23–38). Oxford: Blackwell.

Martin, D. (2002a). *Pentecostalism: The World Their Parish*. Oxford: Blackwell.

Martin, D. (2002b). *Christian Language and Its Mutations*. Farnham: Ashgate.

Martin, D. (2004). 'The Christian, the political and the academic', *Sociology of Religion*, 65: 341–56.

Martin, D. (2005a). *On Secularization: Towards a Revised General Theory*. Farnham: Ashgate.

Martin, D. (2005b). 'Secularization and the future of Christianity', *Journal of Contemporary Religion*, 20: 145–60.

Martin, D. (2011). *The Future of Christianity*. Farnham: Ashgate.

Marty, M. (1992). 'The fundamentals of fundamentalism', in L. Kaplan (ed.), *Fundamentalism in a Comparative Perspective* (pp. 15–23). Amherst, MA: University of Massachusetts Press.

Marty, M. and Appleby, R.S. (eds) (1991). *Fundamentalisms Observed*. Chicago, IL: University of Chicago Press.

Marty, M. and Appleby, R.S. (eds) (1993a). *Fundamentalisms and Society: Reclaiming the Sciences, the Family and Education*. Chicago, IL: University of Chicago Press.

Marty, M. and Appleby, R.S. (eds) (1993b). *Fundamentalisms and the State: Remaking Polities, Economies, and Militance*. Chicago, IL: University of Chicago Press.

Marty, M. and Appleby, R.S. (eds) (1994). *Accounting for Fundamentalisms: The Dynamic Character of Movements*. Chicago, IL: University of Chicago Press.

Marty, M. and Appleby, R.S. (eds) (1995). *Fundamentalisms Comprehended*. Chicago, IL: University of Chicago Press.

Marx, K. and Engels, F. (1975). *Collected Works*. London: Lawrence & Wishart.

McLeod, H. (1997). *Religion and the People of Western Europe, 1789–1990*. Oxford: Oxford University Press.

McLeod, H. (2000). *Secularisation in Western Europe, 1848–1914*. Basingstoke: Palgrave Macmillan.

McLeod, H. and Ustorf, W. (eds) (2003). *The Decline of Christendom in Western Europe*. Cambridge: Cambridge University Press.

Medhurst, K. (2000). 'Christianity and the future of Europe', in M. Percy (ed.), *Calling Time: Religion and Change at the Turn of the Millennium* (pp. 143–62). Sheffield: Sheffield Academic Press.

Mellor, P. (2004a). 'Religion, culture and society in the "information age"', *Sociology of Religion*, 65: 357–73.

Mellor, P. (2004b). *Religion, Realism and Social Theory*. London: Sage.

Mellor, P. and Shilling, C. (1997). *Re-forming the Body: Religion, Community and Modernity*. London: Sage.

Mellor, P. and Shilling, C. (2001). *The Sociological Ambition: The Elementary Forms of Social Life*. London: Sage.

Micklethwait, J. and Wooldridge, A. (2009). *God is Back: How the Global Rise of Faith is Changing the World*. London: Allen Lane.

Milbank, J. (1990). *Theology and Social Theory: Beyond Secular Reason*. London: Blackwell.

Miller, A. and Stark, R. (2002). 'Gender and religiousness: can socialization explanations be saved', *American Journal of Sociology*, 107: 1399–423.

Molendijk, A., Beaumont, J., and Jedan, C. (eds) (2010). *Exploring the Postsecular: The Religious, the Political and the Urban*. Leiden: Brill.

Molokotos-Liederman, L. (2003). 'Identity crisis: Greece, Orthodoxy and the European Union', *Journal of Contemporary Religion*, 18: 291–315.

Molokotos-Liederman, L. (2007). 'The Greek ID cards controversy: a case study on religion and national identity in a changing European Union', *Journal of Contemporary Religion*, 22: 187–203.

Moscucci, O. (1990). *The Science of Woman: Gynaecology and Gender in England, 1800–1929*. Cambridge: Cambridge University Press.

Muller, S. (1997). 'Time to kill: Europe and the politics of leisure', *The National Interest*, 48: 26–36.

Neitz, M.-J. (2004). 'Gender and culture: challenges to the sociology of religion', *Sociology of Religion*, 65: 391–402.

Neitz, M.-J. and Mueser, P. (1996). 'Economic man and the sociology of religion: a critique of the rational choice approach', in L. Young (ed.), *Rational Choice Theory and Religion: Summary and Assessment* (pp. 105–19). London: Routledge.

Neri, M.C. (ed.) (2011). *Novo Mapa das Religiões*. Rio de Janeiro: FGV/CPS.

Niebuhr, H.R. (1929). *The Social Sources of Denominationalism*. New York: New American Library.

Nielsen, J. (2004). *Muslims in Western Europe*. Edinburgh: University of Edinburgh Press (1st edn 1992).

Nielsen, J., Akgönül,S., Alíbašiⵗ, A., Maréchal, B. and Moe, C. (eds) (2009). *Yearbook of Muslims in Europe, Volume 1*. Leiden: Brill. This is an annual publication: Volume 2 appeared in 2010, Volume 3 in 2011 and Volume 2 in 2012. From 2012 onwards, the former article and review section of the *Yearbook* will be published as the new *Journal of Muslims in Europe*.

Norris, P. and Inglehart, R. (2004). *Sacred and Secular. Religion and Politics Worldwide*. Cambridge: Cambridge University Press.

Norris, P. and Inglehart, R. (2007). 'Sellers or buyers in religious markets? The supply and demand of religion in the US and Western Europe', in T. Banchoff (ed.), *Democracy and the New Religious Pluralism*. New York: Oxford University Press.

O'Toole, R. (1996). 'Religion in Canada: its development and contemporary situation', *Social Compass*, 43: 119–34.

O'Toole, R. (2000). 'Classics in the sociology of religion: an ambiguous legacy', in R. Fenn (ed.), *The Blackwell Companion to the Sociology of Religion* (pp. 133–60). Oxford: Blackwell.

Pace, E. (2011). *Religion as Communication*. Farnham: Ashgate (translation of *Raccontare Dio: La religione come comunicazione*, 2008).

Park, S.W. (1997). 'A survey on mission work in the Korean churches', *International Review of Mission*, 342: 329–44.

Peck, J. (1993). *The Gods of Televangelism: The Crisis of Meaning and the Appeal of Religious Televangelism*. Creskill, NJ: Hampton Press.

Pérez Vilariño, J. (1997). 'The Catholic commitment and Spanish civil society', *Social Compass*, 44: 595–610.

Pew Forum on Religion and Public Life (2006). Pentecostal Resource Page. (See www.pewforum.org/Christian/Evangelical-Protestant-Churches/Pentecostal-Resource-Page.aspx, accessed 21 April 2012.)

Pew Forum on Religion and Public Life (2008a). US Religious Landscape Survey. (See http://religions.pewforum.org/reports, accessed 16 April 2012.)

Pew Forum on Religion and Public Life (2008b). US Religious Landscape Survey: Update. (See www.pewforum.org/Religion-News/Survey-More-have-dropped-dogma-for-spirituality-in-US.aspx, accessed 16 April 2012.)

Pew Forum on Religion and Public Life (2010). Muslim Networks and Movements in Western Europe. (See www.pewforum.org/Muslim/Muslim-Networks-and-Movements-in-Western-Europe.aspx, accessed 17 April 2012.)

Platten, S. (ed.) (2006). *Dreaming Spires: Cathedrals in a New Age*. London: SPCK.

Pollack, D. and Olson, D. (eds) (2008). *Religion in Modern Societies: New Perspectives*. London: Routledge.

Putnam, R. (1995). 'Bowling alone: America's declining social capital', *Journal of Democracy*, 6: 65–78.

Putnam, R. (2000). *Bowling Alone: The Collapse and Revival of American Community*. New York: Simon & Schuster.

Rajaee, F. (1993). 'Islam's modernity: the reconstruction of an alternative Shi'ite Islamic worldview', in M. Marty and R.S. Appleby (eds), *Fundamentalisms and Society: Reclaiming the Sciences, the Family and Education* (pp. 103–25). Chicago, IL: University of Chicago Press.

Rémond, R. (1999). *Religion and Society in Modern Europe*. Oxford: Oxford University Press.

Richardson, J. (ed.) (2004). *Regulating Religion: Case Studies from Around the Globe*. New York: Kluwer Academic/Plenum.

Robbers, G. (ed.) (2005). *State and Church in the European Union*. Baden-Baden: Nomos.

Robertson, R. (1992). *Globalizations: Social Theory and Global Culture*. London: Sage.

Robertson, R. (2001). 'The globalization paradigm: thinking globally', in P. Beyer (ed.), *Religion in the Process of Globalization* (pp. 3–22). Würzburg: Ergon.

Robertson, R. and Garrett, W. (1991). *Religion and the Global Order*. St Paul, MN: Paragon House.

Robertson, R. and Scholte, J.A. (eds) (2006). *Encyclopedia of Globalization*, 4 vols. New York: Routledge.

Robinson, J. (1963). *Honest to God*. London: SCM Press.

Roof, W.C. (1993). *A Generation of Seekers*. San Francisco, CA: Harper San Francisco.

Roof, W.C. (1999). *Spiritual Marketplace: Baby Boomers and the Remaking of American Religion*. Princeton, NJ: Princeton University Press.

Roof, W.C. (2000). 'Spiritual seeking in the United States: report of a panel study', *Archives de Sciences Sociales des Religions*, 109: 49–66.

Runciman, W. (1983). *A Treatise on Social Theory: The Methodology of Social Theory, Vol. 1*. Cambridge: Cambridge University Press.

Rushdie, S. (1988). *The Satanic Verses*. London and New York: Viking-Penguin.

Sacks, J. (2002). *The Dignity of Difference*. London: Continuum.

Savage, S., Collins-Mayo, S., Mayo, B. and Cray, G. (2006). *Making Sense of Generation Y: The World View of 15- to 25-year-olds*. London: Church House Publishing.

Schmied, G. (1996). 'American televangelism in German TV', *Journal of Contemporary Religion*, 11: 95–9.

Schoeps, J. and Glöckner, O. with Kreienbrink, A. (eds) (2011). *A Road to Nowhere: Jewish Experiences in Unifying Europe*. Leiden: Brill.

Séguy, J. (1972). 'Max Weber et la sociologie historique des religions', *Archives de Sociologie des Religions*, 33: 71–104.

Seligman, A. (2003). *Modernity's Wager: Authority, the Self, and Transcendence.* Princeton, NJ: Princeton University Press.

Sharot, S. (2001). *A Comparative Sociology of World Religions.* New York: New York University Press.

Simpson, J. (1990). 'The Stark–Bainbridge theory of religion', *Journal for the Scientific Study of Religion,* 29: 367–71.

Singer, P. (1976). *Animal Liberation.* London: Cape.

Skog, M. (2001). *Det religiösa sverige.* Örebro: Bokförlaget Libris.

Smith, C. (1998). *American Evangelicalism: Embattled and Thriving.* Chicago, IL: University of Chicago Press.

Smith, C. (2002). *Christian America? What Evangelicals Really Want.* Berkeley, CA: University of California Press.

Smith, C. (2003). *Moral, Believing Animals: Human Personhood and Culture.* New York: Oxford University Press.

Smith, C. (2005). *Soul Searching: The Religious and Spiritual Lives of American Teenagers.* New York: Oxford University Press.

Smith, C. and Prokopy, J. (eds) (1999). *Latin American Religion in Motion.* London: Routledge.

Smith, J. (1999). *Islam in America.* New York: Columbia University Press.

Snyder, J. (ed.) (2011). *Religion and International Relations Theory.* New York: Columbia University Press.

Spickard, J., Landres, J. and McGuire, M. (eds) (2002). *Personal Knowledge and Beyond: Reshaping the Ethnography of Religion.* New York: New York University Press.

Stark, R. (1996). 'Bringing theory back in', in L. Young (ed.), *Rational Choice Theory and Religion: Summary and Assessment* (pp. 3–24). London: Routledge.

Stark, R. (1997). 'German and German American religiousness: approximating a crucial experiment', *Journal for the Scientific Study of Religion,* 36: 182–93.

Stark, R. (1999). 'Secularization, R.I.P.', *Sociology of Religion,* 60: 249–70.

Stark, R. (2002). 'Physiology and faith; addressing the "universal" gender difference in religious commitment', *Journal for the Scientific Study of Religion,* 41: 495–507.

Stark, R. and Bainbridge, W. (1980). 'Towards a theory of religion', *Journal for the Scientific Study of Religion,* 19: 114–28.

Stark, R. and Bainbridge, W. (1985). *The Future of Religion.* Berkeley, CA: University of California Press.

Stark, R. and Bainbridge, W. (1987). *A Theory of Religion.* New York: Peter Lang.

Stark, R. and Finke, R. (2000). *Acts of Faith: Explaining the Human Side of Religion.* Berkeley, CA: University of California Press.

Stark, R. and Iannaccone, L. (1994). 'A supply-side reinterpretation of the "Secularization of Europe"', *Journal for the Scientific Study of Religion,* 33: 230–52.

Stausberg, M. and Engler, S. (eds) (2011). *The Routledge Handbook of Research Methods in the Study of Religion.* London: Routledge.

Sundkler, B. and Steed, C. (2000). *A History of the Church in Africa.* Cambridge: Cambridge University Press.

Sutcliffe, S. and Bowman, M. (eds) (2000). *Beyond the New Age: Exploring Alternative Spirituality*. Edinburgh: Edinburgh University Press.

Swatos, W. (ed.) (1998). *Encyclopaedia of Religion and Society*. Walnut Creek, CA: Alta Mira Press. (This encyclopedia is available online at http://hirr.hartsem.edu/ency/index.html, accessed 23 May 2012.)

Swatos, W., Kivisto, P. and Gustafson, P. (1998). 'Weber, Max', in W. Swatos (ed.), *Encyclopedia of Religion and Society* (pp. 547–52). Walnut Creek, CA: Alta Mira Press.

Taylor, C. (1992). *Sources of the Self: The Making of Modern Identity*. Cambridge: Cambridge University Press.

Taylor, C. (2007). *A Secular Age*. Cambridge, MA: Harvard University Press.

Taylor, J. (2001). 'After secularism: inner-city governance and the new religious discourse'. Unpublished PhD thesis, SOAS, University of London.

Taylor, R. (2003). *How to Read a Church*. London: Rider.

Thomas, S. (2005). *The Global Resurgence of Religion and the Transformation of International Relations*. Basingstoke: Palgrave Macmillan.

Toft, M. D., Philpott, D. and Shah, T. (eds) (2011). *God's Century: Resurgent Religion and Global Politics*. New York: Norton.

Towler, R. (1984). *Need for Certainty: Sociological Study of Conventional Religion*. London: Routledge.

Trzebiatowska, M. and Bruce, S. (2012). *Why Are Women More Religious Than Men?* Oxford: Oxford University Press.

Tschannen, O. (1991). 'The secularization paradigm: a systematization', *Journal for the Scientific Study of Religion*, 30: 395–416.

Tschannen, O. (1992). *Les Theories de la sécularisation*. Geneva: Librairie Droz.

Turner, B. (1991). *Religion and Social Theory: A Materialist Perspective*. London: Sage.

Turner, B. (ed.) (2010a). *The New Blackwell Companion to the Sociology of Religion*. Oxford: Wiley-Blackwell.

Turner, B. (ed.) (2010b). *Secularization, 4 volumes*. London: Sage.

Turner, B. (2011). *Religion and Modern Society: Citizenship, Secularisation and the State*. Cambridge: Cambridge University Press.

Uddin, Baroness Pola Manzila (2002). 'Multi-ethnicity and multi-culturalism', *House of Lords Hansard*, 20 March: 1423.

Voas, D. (2003a). 'Is Britain a Christian country?', in P. Avis (ed.), *Public Faith? The State of Religious Belief and Practice in Britain* (pp. 92–105). London: SPCK.

Voas, D. (2003b). 'Intermarriage and the demography of secularization', *British Journal of Sociology*, 54: 83–108.

Voas, D. and Bruce, S. (2004). 'Research note: the 2001 census and Christian identification in Britain', *Journal of Contemporary Religion*, 19: 23–8.

Voas, D. and Crockett, A. (2005). 'Religion in Britain: neither believing nor belonging', *Sociology*, 39: 11–28.

Voas, D., Olson, D. and Crockett, A. (2002). 'Religious pluralism and participation: why previous research is wrong', *American Sociological Review*, 67: 212–30.

Voyé, L. and Billiet, J. (eds) (1999). *Sociology and Religions: An Ambiguous Relationship/ Sociologie et religions: Des relations ambigues*. Leuven: Leuven University Press.

**281**

Wallerstein, I. (1979). *The Capitalist World-Economy*. Cambridge: Cambridge University Press.

Wallis, J. (2005). *God's Politics: Why the Right Gets It Wrong and the Left Doesn't Get It*. Grand Rapids, MI: Zondervan.

Walter, A. (1990). *Funerals and How to Improve Them*. London: Hodder & Stoughton.

Walter, T. (1994). *The Revival of Death*. London: Routledge.

Walter, T. (1995). *The Eclipse of Eternity*. Basingstoke: Palgrave Macmillan.

Walter, T. (ed.) (1999). *The Mourning for Diana*. London: Berg.

Walter, T. and Davie, G. (1998). 'The religiosity of women in the modern West', *British Journal of Sociology*, 49: 640–60.

Warner, M., Van Antwerpen. J. and Calhoun, C. (eds) (2010). *Varieties of Secularism in a Secular Age*. Cambridge, MA: Harvard University Press.

Warner, S. (1993). 'Work in progress towards a new paradigm for the sociological study of religion in the United States', *American Journal of Sociology*, 98: 1044–93.

Warner, S. (1997). 'A paradigm is not a theory; reply to Lechner', *American Journal of Sociology*, 103: 192–8.

Wasserstein, B. (1996). *Vanishing Diaspora: The Jews in Europe since* 1945. London: Hamish Hamilton.

Webber, J. (ed.) (1994). *Jewish Identities in the New Europe*. London and Washington, DC: Littman Library of Jewish Civilization.

Weber, M. (1927). *General Economic History*. New York: Greenberg.

Weber, M. (1963). *The Sociology of Religion*. London: Methuen (first published in German 1922).

Weber, M. (1965). *The Protestant Ethic and the Spirit of Capitalism*. London: Allen & Unwin (first published in German 1904–5 and in English 1930).

Weller, P. (2004). 'Identity politics and the future(s) of religion in the UK: the case of the religion questions in the 2001 decennial census', *Journal of Contemporary Religion*, 19: 3–21.

Weller. P. (2009). *A Mirror for Our Times: The Rushdie Affair and the Future of Multiculturalism*. London: Continuum.

Willaime, J.-P. (1995). *Sociologie des religions*. Paris: Presses Universitaires de France.

Willaime, J.-P. (1999). 'French language sociology of religion in Europe since the Second World War', *Swiss Journal of Sociology*, 25: 343–71.

Willaime, J.-P. (2004). 'The cultural turn in the sociology of religion in France', *Sociology of Religion*, 65: 373–90.

Williams, R. (1990). *A Protestant Legacy: Attitudes to Death among Older Aberdonians*. Oxford: Oxford University Press.

Wilson, B. (1961). *Sects and Society*. London: Heinemann.

Wilson, B. (ed.) (1967). *Patterns of Sectarianism: Organisation and Ideology in Social and Religious Movements*. London: Heinemann.

Wilson, B. (1969). *Religion in Secular Society: A Sociological Comment*. Harmondsworth: Penguin.

Wilson, B. (1976). *Contemporary Transformations of Religion*. Oxford: Clarendon Press.

Wilson, B. (1982). *Religion in Sociological Perspective*. Oxford: Oxford University Press.

Wilson, B. (ed.) (1992). *Religion and Contemporary Issues: The All Souls Seminar in the Sociology of Religion*. London: Bellew.

Wilson, B. (1998). 'The secularization thesis: criticisms and rebuttals', in R. Laermans, B. Wilson and J. Billiet (eds), *Secularization and Social Integration: Papers in Honour of Karel Dobbelaere* (pp. 45–66). Leuven: Leuven University Press.

Winsnes, O. (ed.) (2004). *Contemporary Religion and Church: A Nordic Perspective*. Trondheim: Tapir.

Wolfe, A. (2003). *The Transformation of American Religion: How We Actually Live our Faith*. New York: Free Press.

Woodhead, L. (2000). 'Feminism and the sociology of religion: from gender-blindness to gendered difference', in R. Fenn (ed.), *The Blackwell Companion to the Sociology of Religion* (pp. 67–84). Oxford: Blackwell.

Woodhead, L. (2001). 'Women and religion', in L. Woodhead, P. Fletcher, H. Kawanami and D. Smith (eds), *Religions in the Modern World* (pp. 332–56). London: Routledge.

Woodhead, L. (2004). 'Should churches look inward, not outward?', *Church Times*, 31 December: 6.

Woodhead, L. (2012), 'Introduction', in L. Woodhead and R. Catto (eds) (2012). *Religion and Change in Modern Britain* (pp. 1–33). London: Routledge.

Woodhead, L. and Catto, R. (eds) (2012). *Religion and Change in Modern Britain*. London: Routledge.

Woodhead, L. and Riis, O. (2010). *A Sociology of Religious Emotion*. Oxford: Oxford University Press.

Woodhead, L. with Heelas, P. and Martin, D. (eds) (2001). *Peter Berger and the Study of Religion*. London: Routledge.

Woodhead, L., Fletcher, P., Kawanami, H. and Smith, D. (eds) (2001). *Religions in the Modern World*. London: Routledge.

Woolever, C., Bruce, D., Wulff, K. and Smith-Williams, I. (2006). 'The gender ratio in the pews: consequences for religious vitality', *Journal of Beliefs and Values*, 2: 25–38.

Wuthnow, R. (1990). *The Restructuring of American Religion*. Princeton, NJ: Princeton University Press.

Wuthnow, R. (ed.) (1998). *Encyclopedia of Politics and Religion, 2 vols*. Washington, DC: CQ Press (a revised edition appeared in 2006).

Wuthnow, R. (1999). *After Heaven: Spirituality in America since the 1950s*. Princeton, NJ: Princeton University Press.

Wuthnow, R. (2005). *America and the Challenges of Religious Diversity*. Princeton, NJ: Princeton University Press.

Yang, F. (2005). 'Between secularist ideology and desecularizing reality: the birth and growth of religion research in communist China', in F. Yang and J. Tamney (eds), *State, Market and Religions in Chinese Societies* (pp. 19–40). Leiden: Brill.

*283*

Yang, F. (2011). *Religion in China: Survival and Revival under Communist Rule.* New York: Oxford University Press.

Yang, F. and Tamney, J. (eds) (2005). *State, Market and Religions in Chinese Societies.* Leiden: Brill.

York, M. (1995). *The Emerging Network: Sociology of the New Age and Neopagan Movements.* Lanham, MD: Rowman & Littlefield.

Young, L. (ed.) (1996). *Rational Choice Theory and Religion: Summary and Assessment.* London: Routledge.

# index

Note: the letter 'f' following a page number refers to a figure; the letter 't' refers to a table.